The Pentecostal Mission in Palestine

The Pentecostal Mission in Palestine

The Legacy of Pentecostal Zionism

ERIC NELSON NEWBERG

Foreword by Stanley Burgess

PICKWICK *Publications* · Eugene, Oregon

THE PENTECOSTAL MISSION IN PALESTINE
The Legacy of Pentecostal Zionism

Pickwick Publications
An Imprint of Wipf and Stock Publishers
199 W. 8th Ave., Suite 3
Eugene, OR 97401

www.wipfandstock.com

ISBN 13: 978-1-61097-553-7

Cataloging-in-Publication data:

Newberg, Eric Nelson.

The Pentecostal mission in Palestine : the legacy of Pentecostal Zionism / Eric Nelson Newberg ; foreword by Stanley Burgess.

xviii + 254 p. ; 23 cm. Includes bibliographical references and index.

isbn 13: 978-1-61097-553-7

1. Pentecostal churches—Missions—History. 2. Christian Zionism—History. 3. Arab-Israeli conflict. I. Title.

DS150.5 N265 2012

Manufactured in the U.S.A.

This book is dedicated to my wife, Carol Ann Lewis-Newberg.
We have been blessed to share a journey as soul mates with many wonderful
surprises along the way. One of these surprises was that our sabbatical at
the Tantur Ecumenical Institute of Jerusalem in 2002 led to my return to
graduate school and the writing of a doctoral dissertation on the Pentecostal
mission in Palestine. Carol has made many sacrifices to afford me the luxury of
doing what historians love to do: re-live the past. For her unwavering support
and faithfulness, I am inexpressibly grateful.

Contents

Foreword

NO OTHER COUNTRY PROVOKES such a range of reactions as does Israel. It is the enemy to most followers of Islam. It is the "Holy Land" to all three Abrahamic faiths—Judaism, Christianity, and Islam. In a world of intolerance, it is the object of scorn and hope; of shattered and unfulfilled dreams, present and past.

Into this land of religious diversity entered missionaries of all ilk, each convinced that theirs was the only truth, the only path to salvation. Of these, Pentecostal missionaries seemed at first to offer great promise of bringing successful evangelism. In the end, they brought philosemitism, the idealization of Jews and Judaism.

Most historians agree that the modern Pentecostal movement grew out of the famed Azusa Street Revival (1906–13). It should not be surprising that three out of the first five missionaries spawned at Azusa Street headed to the Holy Land. The story of these Pentecostal missionaries remained untold until now.

Based upon their apocalyptic predisposition, most scholar-writers recounting and evaluating Christian missionary activities in Israel/Palestine have tended towards triumphalism. Unrealistically, missionaries reasoned that because Israel had emerged as a state, the parousia must be at hand. What a great accomplishment! Missionaries had paved the way for the Second Coming!

Unrealistically, charismatic Christians also dreamed of a time when they might bridge the gap between Arab and Israeli, ending the long conflict between the two claimants to the land itself. After all, a significant percentage of Arabs in the Holy Land were Christians, and many of them were Charismatics.

Because of Dr. Eric Newberg's research, we now know that the efforts of Pentecostal missions in Palestine failed miserably, both in converting Jews and Arabs and then in their resorting to proselytizing Arab Christians. Sadly, in the long run the Pentecostals also "left a legacy that militates against peace in Israel/Palestine today." Perhaps the most significant part of that legacy was the development of Pentecostal Zionism. Unfortunately, Pentecostal missionaries also disregarded the civil rights of the Arabs—including Arab Christians. Newberg attempts to balance the account by telling the Arab side of the story.

To be sure, Pentecostal missionaries accomplished several things. Newberg credits them with keeping the American churches abreast of current events in Palestine. It also led the way in the "Love for Israel" movement.

In the end, Dr. Newberg's story is a realistic and truthful account of a sad story. Above all, from this story the Western church can learn "what *not* to do."

Stanley M. Burgess
Regent University, Virginia Beach

Preface

THIS BOOK IS ADAPTED from a doctoral dissertation completed in 2008 at Regent University in Virginia Beach. I was guided in the selection of the Pentecostal mission in Palestine as my dissertation topic by my advisor, Stan Burgess, as well as Ray Gannon, Gary McGee, and Vinson Synan. Yet, in retrospect, my interest in the topic at hand stemmed from a sabbatical spent at the Tantur Ecumenical Institute in Jerusalem in the fall of 2002. This sabbatical acquainted me with the Christian presence in Israel/Palestine and brought to my attention the problem of Pentecostal Zionism. In this preface, I will recount experiences of my sabbatical that constitute the backdrop of this book.

One of the highlights of the sabbatical at Tantur was the discovery of communities of charismatic Christians in Israel/Palestine.[1] I had the privilege of worshiping with indigenous Hebrew-speaking and Arabic-speaking charismatic congregations in Jerusalem and Bethlehem. My interest was piqued when I heard sermons on both sides of the Arab-Israeli fence expressing an earnest desire to pursue peace in the Holy Land. As a result, I was stirred with hope that the charismatic Christians of Israel/Palestine could possibly transcend the political impasse of the Arab-Israeli conflict. While Arab and Israeli believers have very different attitudes toward the State of Israel, they both affirm a commitment to Jesus' message of peace. Yet the chasm that must be crossed for peace to have a chance was forcibly impressed upon me during an auspicious afternoon spent at a pro-Israel parade in downtown Jerusalem.

As a bystander at a lavish "Love for Israel" parade in downtown Jerusalem, I was surprised to observe that the marchers in the parade were charismatic Christians who had come from across the globe for the celebration of the Feast of Tabernacles sponsored by the International Christian Embassy of Jerusalem (hereafter ICEJ). I saw delegations from Argentina, Australia, Brazil, England, Germany, Guatemala, India, Kenya, South Korea, New Zealand, Nigeria, the Philippines, South Africa, and Zimbabwe marching with banners inscribed with verses from the Hebrew Scriptures, carrying replicas of the Ark of the Covenant, singing praises to God with hands uplifted, and fervently acclaiming their love and support for the State of Israel. In talking with the participants, I was told that the parade is an annual event sponsored by the ICEJ during its Feast of Tabernacles convention. The ICEJ is one of the most visible Christian pro-Israel groups. To say the least, this first-hand exposure to Christian Zionism captured my attention.

1. Ateek, *Justice and Only Justice*, 60.

Afterward, I mulled over two questions: How did this diverse, multinational group of charismatic Christians get involved in the pro-Israel movement? And how extensive is the support for the State of Israel among charismatic Christians? In time, these questions gave rise to my research on Pentecostal Zionism.

In addressing the first question, concerning how charismatic Christians came to be involved with the pro-Israel movement, Raymond Gannon's 2003 Hebrew University dissertation, "The Shifting Romance with Israel: American Pentecostal Ideology of Zionism and the Jewish State," proved to be very thought-provoking. Gannon traces the development of the Pentecostal affinity to Zionism from the early Pentecostal Movement to recent times. He argues that early Pentecostals were avid Christian Zionists and that in recent decades Pentecostals have been notable supporters of the pro-Israel movement. Gannon characterizes the historic affinity between Pentecostals and Israel as a romance.[2] The romance metaphor is fitting, in that the attitude of Pentecostal and charismatic Christians toward Israel can be characterized as philosemitism.[3] I concur with Gannon's argument and will expand upon it in this book by showing that philosemitism was strongly avowed by the Pentecostal missionaries in Palestine.

As I investigated the second question, concerning the scope of support among charismatic Christians for the State of Israel, I discovered that the parade in Jerusalem was representative of an extensive phenomenon. David Aikman, former *Time* correspondent in the Middle East, observes that "the stronghold of pro-Israel sentiments among Christians is among the charismatics." In fact, the pro-Israel sentiments expressed by the 2002 parade in Jerusalem are widely held. Aikman states, "In my experience, looking at evangelical Christians in a lot of different countries over the years, charismatics seem to be intuitively pro-Jewish."[4] Aikman is not alone in his claim that charismatic Christians tend to support the State of Israel. For example, Pat Robertson states, "Ladies and Gentlemen, evangelical Christians support Israel because we believe that the words of Moses and the ancient prophets of Israel were inspired by God. We believe that the emergence of a Jewish state in the land promised by God to Abraham, Isaac, and Jacob was ordained by God." Touting optimistic statistical projections to assure his audience of the support for Israel among a large segment of the global Christian community, Robertson claims,

> It should be noted that today Christianity, with well over two billion adherents, is by far the fastest growing religion in the world. Within twenty years, that number will swell to three billion. Of these, at least six hundred million are Bible-believing evangelicals and charismatics who are ardent supporters of the nation of Israel. In twenty years, that number will reach one billion. Israel has

---

2. Gannon, "The Shifting Romance with Israel," 137.

3. Philosemitism is defined as "support or admiration for the Jewish people by non-Jews . . . the reverse of anti-Semitism, hostility to or dislike of Jews." Rubinstein and Rubinstein, *Philosemitism*, ix.

4. McDermott, "Evangelicals and Israel," 15–16.

millions of Christian friends in China, in India, in Indonesia, throughout Africa and South America, as well as in North America.[5]

Hence, it became apparent to me that the "Love for Israel" parade that I observed in Jerusalem in 2002 was far from an isolated phenomenon. It was indicative of a long-standing and extensive affinity to Zionism among evangelical Christians, including Pentecostals and charismatics.

The affinity of charismatic Christians to Zionism is corroborated by the results of a study conducted by the Pew Forum on Religion and Life, entitled "Spirit and Power: A 10-Country Survey of Pentecostals."[6] On October 6, 2006, at the Spirit in the World Conference at the University of Southern California, Timothy Shah, Pew senior fellow in religious and world affairs, presented a paper on "Pentecostal Zionism," based on the results of the Pew survey.[7] He reported that while it is well known that white evangelicals in the United States are more pro-Israel than any other American religious group except Jews, the data shows that among evangelicals, "renewalists," i.e., Pentecostals and charismatics, are the most likely to espouse pro-Israel attitudes. Further, the Pew study finds that renewalists in Asia, Africa, and Latin America display a greater pro-Israel tendency than other evangelical Christians.[8] The survey data presented by Shah comports well with my observations at the Jerusalem parade of 2002 and the subsequent findings of the research for this book.

My discovery of the extensive scope of support for the State of Israel among Pentecostal-charismatic Christians is one part of the backdrop of this book. The other part relates to my acquaintance with Palestinian Arab Christians, including Pentecostals. During the aforementioned sabbatical at the Tantur Ecumenical Institute, I was fortunate to study with a leading Palestinian theologian, Naim Ateek. As I listened to his lectures, I acquired an appreciation for the indigenous Christian presence in Israel/Palestine. As is the case with many Americans, I was not well informed concerning the "living stones" of the Holy Land. According to Munir Fasheh, a Palestinian educator and director of the Arab education forum of the Center for Middle Eastern Studies at Harvard University, Palestinian Christians are invisible to Christians in the United States.[9] In the course of visiting churches in the West Bank and hearing the stories of Arab Christians about life under Israeli occupation, I got a clear picture of the reality of the Palestinian situation and concluded that great injustices had been committed against the Palestinians. In conversing with Palestinian Christian leaders, I took note of recurring theological themes, such as a passion for peace and social justice, a way of reading the Bible in the situation of political oppression, identification

5. Robertson, "Why Evangelical Christians Support Israel," December 17, 2003, www.patrobertson.com/Speeches/IsraelLauder.asp..

6. "Spirit and Power: A 10-Country Survey of Pentecostals," Pew Forum on Religion and Public Life, 2006; hereafter referred to as "Spirit and Power." The ten countries surveyed are Brazil, Chile, Guatemala, India, Kenya, Nigeria, the Philippines, South Africa, South Korea, and the United States.

7. See the conference website at http://www.usc.edu/schools/college/crcc/pentecostalism.

8. "Spirit and Power," 56, 67.

9. Fasheh, "Reclaiming Our Identity and Redefining Ourselves," in *Faith and the Intifada*, 61–62.

with the redemptive suffering of Jesus, and a commitment to community development and ecumenical dialogue. Eventually I realized that Palestinian Christians—whether Orthodox, Catholic, Anglican, Evangelical, or Pentecostal—were giving voice to a contextual theology. The Danish biblical scholar Knud Jeppesen explains that "a theology is contextual, if it takes up and reflects upon the contemporary situation, in which the theologians in question live, and that is exactly what these Palestinians have done."[10] When I later pursued doctoral studies two years after the sabbatical, I specialized in the work of contemporary Palestinian theologians.

Since Palestinian contextual theology informs the interpretive stance of this book, a brief sketch of the perspectives of three representative Palestinian theologians—Mitri Raheb, Naim Ateek, and Elias Chacour—will be presented. Mitri Raheb,[11] pastor of the Christmas Lutheran Church in Bethlehem, acknowledges, "We have to confess that many of the tactics used by some of our people were devastating for us: the militarization of the Intifada, the use of guns in our otherwise nonviolent struggle, and the suicide bombings against civilians."[12] Raheb insists that he and the majority of Bethlehem's residents do not condone violence. Naim Ateek[13] writes, "I have always believed that the Church in Israel-Palestine can play a powerful role in promoting justice and peace through active nonviolent means."[14] The Palestinian theologians recognize that there is more to peace than the cessation of fighting. Ateek writes, "The word for peace in both Arabic (*salam*) and Hebrew (*shalom*) has the same etymological root and the same breadth of meaning: wholeness, health, safety, and security. It refers to a peace experienced and lived out in the everyday historical situation of life."[15] Elias Chacour[16] shares Ateek's holistic view of peace. In 1999 he established a Peace Center in the town of Ibillim. Chacour bemoans the cycle of violence:

> Violence begets violence. The cycle must be broken. I cannot react to violence with another bigger or smaller violence, and I must not encourage or enable others to do so either. In the face of violence, we must try to be genuine, creative, disarming. This is extremely difficult. We might be killed, but then we will know that we have chosen between a long, empty life and a short, full one. It is far better to get our hands dirty building a human society than to complacently keep our hands clean.[17]

10. Jeppeson, "Justice with Mercy: About a Contemporary Palestinian Theology," 201.

11. Mitri Raheb (1962–) is the pastor of the Evangelical Lutheran Christmas Church in Bethlehem and founder of the International Center of Bethlehem, the Ad Dar Cultural and Conference Center, and the Dar Al-Kalima Lutheran School and Academy.

12. Raheb, *Bethlehem Besieged*, 87.

13. Naim Ateek (1937–) is an Anglican priest. For thirteen years he served as canon of St. George's Cathedral in Jerusalem. At present he is the executive director of Sabeel Ecumenical Liberation Theology Center in Jerusalem.

14. Ateek, *Justice and Only Justice*, 135.

15. Ibid., 146.

16. Elias Chacour (1939–) is the first Israeli citizen to be selected as a Catholic bishop. He is president of Mar Elias Educational Institutions, chancellor of the diocese of Haifa, Archimandrite of the Melkite Church in Israel, and archbishop of Akko, Haifa, Nazareth, and Galilee.

17. Chacour, *We Belong to the Land*, 188.

In the 1970s Chacour worked closely with Joseph Raya, the Melkite bishop, about whom Chacour writes, "Although he was Lebanese, Bishop Raya had a keen sensitivity to the Palestinian justice issues. He had lived in the United States and worked closely with civil rights activist Martin Luther King, Jr."[18] In 1972 Chacour and Raya had an official audience with Prime Minister Golda Meir, during which they implored her to allow the Palestinians to return to the villages of Biram and Ikrit. She sternly refused, and in response they organized a peace march in Jerusalem on August 23, 1972 in which thousands of Jews, Christians, Muslims, and Druze participated. The march ended at the prime minister's office, where speeches were given. News of the march was carried in the international press. Chacour summed up the outcome: "I was grateful there had been no violence, no bloodshed. Palestinians inside Israel had been given the opportunity to speak out, and some Jewish people heard their cries for justice and were willing to support them publicly."[19]

A conception of peace as a quality of life is reflected in the priority that the Palestinian contextual theologians place on community development. Chacour could see that help could not be expected from Israel. He explains, "Palestinian villages in Galilee received little help or no government assistance, help readily available to neighboring Jewish towns and *kibbutzim*." He did a demographic study of Palestinian villages, finding that 75 percent were under twenty-eight years of age and 50 percent were under the age of fourteen, concluding, "I quickly saw that nothing was being done for this generation. The children and teenagers of the villages, some of whom were in school and others of whom did not continue after the eighth grade because of the absence of school facilities, idled away many empty hours every day, usually playing in the dusty streets. Their human rights, dignity, and future were being suppressed and even eliminated . . . I became determined to change the current situation for the Palestinian young people in Galilee."[20] As a result, Chacour devoted his life to building schools, libraries and community centers in the Palestinian communities of Israel. His dream, still not actualized, is to establish a Palestinian university in Israel. In a similar vein, Raheb saw that the educational resources available to the children of Bethlehem were very limited. To meet this need, he has led his congregation in upgrading the Lutheran school programs operated by his church and working with international organizations to obtain funding for Dar al-Kalima Academy, which specializes in music, art, and theology.[21]

In this preface, I have recounted formative experiences in 2002 and subsequent reflections that constitute the backdrop for my research on the Pentecostal mission in Palestine. A sabbatical at Tantur placed me on a trajectory that led me to focus my academic research on the situation in Israel/Palestine. Early in my doctoral program at Regent, when it was brought to my attention that there had been a Pentecostal mission in Palestine and that no academic research on it had yet been published, I

18. Ibid.
19. Ibid., 91–92.
20. Ibid., 61.
21. http://www.bethlehemmedia.net/ngo5.htm.

determined that this would be the topic of my dissertation. As I examined the primary sources, I found that not only the Pentecostal missionaries in Palestine but also early Pentecostals in general had jumped on the Christian Zionist bandwagon. It did not take long before a working hypothesis was formulated, making a connection between the Zionist sympathies of early Pentecostals and the significant contemporary involvement of Pentecostal and charismatic Christians in the pro-Israel movement.

As I turned the dissertation into a book, I once again pondered the conflicting claims of Christian Zionism and Palestinian nationalism. Frankly, I can see relative merit in both. On one hand, I resonate with the Pentecostal missionaries in their opposition to anti-Semitism and support for the Zionist vision of a restoration of the Jewish people to their ancient homeland. On the other hand, I am troubled that the missionaries, with few exceptions, did not advocate for the human rights of the Palestinian Arab population. There are those who deal with the clashing narratives of Arabs and Zionists by coming down decisively on one side or the other. Not being an ideologue, I prefer to accept the reality that there are two sides to this story, each of which brings something of value to the table. I don't want to give away my final appraisal of the Pentecostal mission just yet, so let's just say that the Pentecostal mission was a mixed blessing due to its espousal of Pentecostal Zionism. I have attempted to be balanced and fair in my interpretation of the history of the Pentecostal mission in Palestine. It is my conviction that the cause of peace in the Holy Land can be furthered by means of an empathetic hearing of both sides of the Arab-Zionist story. That is largely what this book attempts to do. I will leave it up to the reader to judge the extent to which I have succeeded in producing a balanced assessment of the legacy of Pentecostal Zionism.

Acknowledgments

A PROJECT OF THIS magnitude is a shared endeavor of a community of scholars. The contributions of special colleagues deserve to be acknowledged. My deepest thanks are extended to Stan Burgess, who encouraged me every step of the way from topic selection to publication. Ruth Burgess read the narrative chapters and offered sound and timely advice. Vinson Synan steered me toward the primary sources of Pentecostal Zionism. Gary McGee kindly supplied me with valuable archival material. Ray Gannon opened my eyes to the longstanding alliance between Pentecostals and Zionists and urged me to figure out what motivated the Pentecostal missionaries to go from the Azusa Street Revival to Palestine. Joseph Kickasola taught me to view Islam with respect and fairness. Wolfgang Vondey instilled in me an appreciation for the ecumenical promise of Pentecostal theology. Amos Yong encouraged my use of Edward Said's *Orientalism* as a methodological tool for a postcolonial assessment of Pentecostal Zionism. Finally, the Lilly Endowment for Religion funded the sabbatical without which this project would not be as enriched as it was by an extended period of study, field experience, and reflection in Israel/Palestine.

While I am indebted to many, I bear sole responsibility for any errors in fact and interpretation that are present in my work.

1 | Introduction

T HE EXPANSION OF Pentecostalism between 1906 and today constitutes one of
the most significant developments in recent religious history. Pentecostalism
has grown from an anomalous coterie of religious and social discontents to a
massive global renewal movement, estimated at about 27 percent of all Christians.[1]
The Pentecostal mission in Palestine is a virtually unknown episode in the history of
Pentecostalism. The story of this mission starts out modestly, as did Pentecostalism, on
the wrong side of the tracks in Los Angeles in an abandoned building requisitioned for
the Azusa Street Revival (1906–10). Palestine was the destination of three of the first
five missionaries sent out from the Azusa Street Revival. The purpose of this study is
to construct a historical narrative of the Pentecostal mission in Palestine. The scene of
the narrative swiftly shifts from Los Angeles to Jerusalem. From 1908 on, Jerusalem
served as the home base of the Pentecostal mission in Palestine and its satellite outposts in Syria, Transjordan, and Persia. Much of the story of the Pentecostal mission in
Palestine is taken up with events in the Middle East, yet the vantage point from which
the missionaries viewed the realities on the ground in Palestine was that of North
American Pentecostalism.

DEFINITION OF THE PROBLEM

The problem addressed in this book was defined in the author's mind when the reports of the Pentecostal missionaries in Palestine in American and British Pentecostal
periodicals came to his attention. A careful reading of these reports, published from
1906 on, reveals a distinctly pro-Zionist sympathy, hereafter referred to as "Pentecostal
Zionism." The primary problem addressed below can be stated in a question: What
were the historical and theological connections between the Pentecostal mission in
Palestine and the diffusion of Pentecostal Zionism? This book will attempt to ferret out
these connections and their repercussions. The author will argue that the history of
the Pentecostal mission in Palestine represents a window through which the historical
and theological development of Pentecostal Zionism and its checkered legacy can be
closely observed.

The crimson thread that connects the Pentecostal mission in Palestine with
the development of Pentecostal Zionism is the network of diffusion provided by the

---

1. Barrett and Johnson, "Global Statistics," *The New International Dictionary of Pentecostal and
Charismatic Movements*, 284; hereafter NIDPCM.

Pentecostal periodicals. The reports of the missionaries in Palestine were published in the periodicals, providing the wider Pentecostal constituency with on the scene observations of and commentary on events in Palestine. These reports were embedded with an ideological perspective known as Christian Zionism,[2] the driving force of which is a preferential option for a Jewish national home in Palestine. A case can be made that the pro-Zionist stance of the Pentecostal missionaries shaped Pentecostal attitudes toward the Arab-Zionist conflict in Israel/Palestine. The evidence upon which this case rests consists of two layers of discourse. The first layer is the reports of the missionaries. The second is the numerous articles in Pentecostal periodicals dealing with current events in Palestine and the Zionist movement. By connecting the dots, one finds inter-textual strands of ideas that make up Pentecostal Zionism. As this book traces the connections between the Pentecostal missionaries in Palestine and Pentecostal Zionism, painstaking proof will be extracted from the Pentecostal periodicals to argue for the contribution of the missionaries in Palestine to the diffusion of Pentecostal Zionism and its legacy.

Scope of the Historical Narrative

The story of the Pentecostal mission in Palestine begins in 1906 at the Azusa Street Revival in Los Angeles. Some of the very first missionaries sent out from Azusa Street went to Palestine. In its first ten years the Pentecostal mission in Palestine gained a foothold in Jerusalem, due primarily to the efforts of three major pioneering missionaries, Lucy Leatherman, Charles Leonard, and Anna Elizabeth Brown. In the interwar period the Pentecostal missionaries established a mission station in Jerusalem and expanded their territory into Transjordan, Syria, and Persia. The mission was severely tested and lost traction during the Arab Revolt of 1936–39, World War II, and the Partition Crisis of 1947. With the War of 1948 the Pentecostal missionaries fled from the field of battle and their predominately Arab clients were swept away in the Palestinian Diaspora. After 1948 a valiant attempt was made to sustain the Assemblies of God mission in Jerusalem but it eventually lost its vitality and met its demise in the 1970s. In contrast, the Church of God (Cleveland, Tenn.) established an active mission with stations in Bethlehem, the Mount of Olives, and the village of Aboud. Led by the indomitable Margaret Gaines from 1964 to 1999, the Church of God succeeded in developing an indigenous leadership that continues to sustain a vital Pentecostal presence in the West Bank.[3] Recent attempts have been made to put new Pentecostal missionary ventures in Israel on an indigenous footing.

Thesis and Argument

The thesis of this book is that the Pentecostal missionaries in Palestine functioned as brokers of Pentecostal Zionism. A *broker* is one who arranges transactions, a dealer

2. Saddington, "Prophecy and Politics," 9.
3. Gaines, *Of Like Passions: Missionary to the Arabs*, 133–221.

in secondhand goods. The missionaries were ideally situated to play the role of brokers because as eye-witnesses they observed and reported on the unfolding of events on the ground in Palestine. Although the Pentecostal missionaries failed to achieve their primary objective of converting Jews and Muslims, and resorted to proselytizing Arab Christians, they can be credited with advocating philosemitism (love for the Jewish people) and promoting the restoration of a Jewish national home in Palestine. However, in jumping on the Christian Zionist bandwagon, they disregarded the civil rights of the Arabs, provoked cultural antipathy toward Muslims, and left a legacy that continues to militate against peace in Israel/Palestine today.

It is hardly coincidental that today Pentecostals are numbered among the major players in the pro-Israel movement. This is a development to which the Pentecostal missionaries in Palestine made a marked contribution. A notable figure in this regard is Peter Derek Vaughan Prince (1915–2003), who married one of the Pentecostal missionaries in Palestine, Lydia Christensen (1890–1975). Prince went on to become a prominent leader of both the global charismatic movement as well as the pro-Israel movement. He played a significant role in transmitting the legacy of Pentecostal Zionism among charismatic Christians. As stated above in the Preface, the pro-Israel stance of contemporary Pentecostals and charismatics has been substantiated by the Pew Charitable Trust survey, "Spirit and Power." The Pew survey found that sympathy toward Israel among Pentecostals and charismatics is common even in countries with no direct political stake in the conflict in the Middle East, indicating that the motivating factor is probably religious rather than nationalistic. It is significant that the countries shown by the Pew study to have a stronger sympathy with Israel among Pentecostals and charismatics—Brazil, Kenya, Nigeria, India, and South Korea—were represented in the parade described in the Preface.[4]

The legacy of the Pentecostal mission in Palestine is related to the role that the missionaries played as the brokers of Pentecostal Zionism. Pentecostal Zionism had positive and negative repercussions. On the positive side, Pentecostal Zionism fostered philosemitism. On the downside, Pentecostal Zionism was imbued with cultural prejudices against Arab Christians and Muslims, which subverted the contextualization of the Pentecostal mission in Palestine. Unfortunately, the Pentecostal missionaries in Palestine failed to develop an effective missionary strategy in Palestine. Worse yet, as Pentecostals afforded theological legitimacy to the Zionist project, they turned a blind eye to the injustices suffered by the indigenous Arab population in Palestine.

METHODOLOGY EXPLAINED

The methodology of this book can be described as a postcolonial assessment. It is shaped by Allan Anderson's penetrating critique of Pentecostal missions and Edward Said's seminal study of Orientalism. Each of these influences has made an imprint on the methodology of this book.

---

4. "Spirit and Power: A 10-Country Survey of Pentecostals," 67.

Allan Anderson's Postcolonial Critique

Allan Anderson (1949–) is Professor of Global Pentecostal studies and Director of the Graduate Institute for Theology and Religions at the University of Birmingham in England. Anderson worked as a pastor in Southern Africa in classical Pentecostal, charismatic Baptist, and independent charismatic churches. He earned a doctorate at the University of South Africa with a dissertation on "African Pentecostalism in South Africa," which explores the intermixture of shamanistic ritual practices and Pentecostal spirituality.[5] Anderson disputes the allegation of syncretism leveled at African initiated Christian movements, retorting that Western Christians are blatantly syncretistic in regards to cultural imperialism, civil religion, and consumerism.[6]

Anderson contends that historians of Pentecostalism must hear the voices from the margins.[7] He is speaking of a chorus of voices that he thinks have been ignored for decades in the historiography of Pentecostalism. First of all, these are the voices of people in the Majority World, i.e., Africa, Asia, Latin America, and the Pacific Islands. Second, these are the voices of peoples who were oppressed throughout the long, violent history of colonialism and continue to be exploited by the capitalist economies of the West. Third, these are the voices of indigenous workers in the Christian missionary enterprise, Pentecostal and otherwise, whose contributions are overlooked in the Pentecostal periodicals. And fourthly, these are the voices of Christians in the independent church movements who unabashedly blend folk religious traditions with Christian theology.

Anderson begins a chapter on the writing of Pentecostal history in his *An Introduction to Global Pentecostalism* by asserting that Pentecostal historiography is flawed by cultural bias. Most of the historians of classical Pentecostalism have tended to be white males from the so-called "first world." Their version of the story of the expansion of Pentecostalism depicts the Pentecostal Revival as beginning in North America and fanning out across the world as the "full gospel" was brought to the heathen in remote locations. Anderson regards this telling of the story as a myth that is slanted by ethnocentrism. According to Anderson, the Azusa Street mission was important, and should be credited as a catalyst of tremendous missionary zeal, yet it was not the center of operations from which the Pentecostal missionary movement originated and was diffused around the world. In actuality, Anderson says, the Pentecostal Movement was global from the start. Anderson points to John Christian Aroolappen's revivals in India in the nineteenth century, the Korean Revival of 1903, the Mukti Revival led by Pandita Ramabai in 1905 as three countervailing episodes that do not sustain the prevailing narrative of Western Pentecostal historians. Anderson is pained that early Pentecostal reports of the Mukti revival failed to give the name of the Indian leader, Pandita Ramabai. This omission is indicative of a larger problem. In the reports of Western missionaries to Pentecostal periodicals "back home," the names of

5. "Biosketch: Allan Heaton Anderson," http://artsweb.bham.ac.uk/aandeson/Main/personal.htm.

6. Anderson, "Signs and Blunders."

7. Anderson, *Spreading Fires*, 290.

4

the indigenous workers were often misspelled or simply not given. Anderson bemoans the loss of historical documentation of the indigenous Christians who spread the full gospel in their languages of origin, prayed with their families and neighbors to receive the baptism of the Holy Spirit accompanied by speaking in tongues, healing, and exorcism. Sadly their names were omitted from most missionary reports. Anderson fears that the contributions of indigenous Pentecostals may be irretrievable. Nonetheless, Anderson is committed to listening for the voices from the margins in any way he can, as he guides students in selecting dissertation topics and doing research on the forgotten heroes and heroines of Pentecostal missions in Majority World contexts.[8]

As stated above, Anderson's approach to Pentecostal history is a form of "postcolonial critique."[9] One of the aims of postcolonial critique is to expose the evils and injustices of the history of Western imperialism. Robert Young defines postcolonial critique as "the reconsideration of this history, particularly from the perspectives of those who suffered its effects, together with the defining of its contemporary and cultural impact."[10] The methodology of this study is attuned to the issues raised by Anderson's postcolonial critique. The author shares Anderson's chagrin over the notion of "global spiritual conquest" embraced by many Pentecostal missionaries. Anderson sees this notion as rooted in "an expansionist conviction influenced by their premillennial eschatological expectations that the nations of the world had to be conquered for Christ before his imminent coming to rule the earth."[11] The Pentecostals were not the only ones whose concept of missions and eschatology was tainted by the imprint of imperialism. Almost unconsciously, Western Christians assumed that it was their mandate to bring both the gospel message and the supposedly superior culture of the West to the non-Western world. This was not all bad, some have argued, because missionaries were often compassionate.[12] They engaged in community development and fought for social justice. For instance, in Africa and the Pacific Islands missionaries struggled against the illicit slave trade. However, Western missionaries also disseminated the metanarrative of Christendom. This can be seen in their intolerant attitude toward folk religious traditions and their implicit support of colonialism.[13] Missionaries often looked down upon their "clients" as inferiors. They were socially exclusive, tucking themselves away in mission stations. In some cases they were plainly racist. And when the education received in mission schools empowered nationalist movements and struggles for liberation, missionaries objected strenuously and in some cases ended up on the wrong end of the barrel of a rifle.[14]

Given the preponderance of non-Western peoples in the make-up of global Pentecostalism, it follows that historians of Pentecostalism should be wary of what

8. Anderson, *An Introduction to Pentecostalism*, 166–83.

9. Walia, *Edward Said and the Writing of History*, 79.

10. Young, *Postcolonialism*, 4.

11. Anderson, *Spreading Fires*, 256.

12. Stanley, "Conversion to Christianity"; Walls, *The Cross-Cultural Process in Christian History*.

13. Neill, *A History of Christian Missions*, 314–16; Shenk, "The 'Great Century' Reconsidered."

14. Beaver, *Envoys of Peace*, 83–98.

Stan Burgess calls "Americocentric historiographical assumptions," which are grounded in the view that America is the home base of the global renewal movement.[15] Burgess urges us to question the traditional claim that global Pentecostalism stems from a central point of origin in Topeka or Los Angeles. In a similar vein, David Bundy argues, "Certainly no theory that makes the American experience paradigmatic can explain the global realities of Pentecostalism."[16] Bundy is saying that the paradigm of American centrism ought to be put on the shelf as we read and write the history of Pentecostalism. The author intends to heed the advice of Burgess, Bundy, and Anderson in his recounting of the story of the Pentecostal mission in Palestine.

Edward Said's Orientalism

The methodology of this book is also based on the postcolonial literary analysis of Edward Said (1935–2003), as articulated in his seminal work, *Orientalism* (1978), which is a critique of Western conceptions of the Orient. Below Said's conception of Orientalism is described and its relation to the methodology of this study is explained. Said grew up in Palestine and Egypt, attending Anglican schools in Jerusalem and Cairo. He came to the U.S. for further schooling at Mount Hermon Academy, Princeton University, and Harvard University. For many years he was Parr Professor of English Literature at Columbia University. Said was a leading figure in the emergence of post-colonial literary analysis. He made a turning point in his scholarly path after the Israelis soundly defeated the Arabs in the Six Day War in 1967. From that time, Said wrote extensively on the question of Palestine. In 1977 he joined the Palestine National Council, which was the Palestinian parliament in exile. His political affiliations and his scholarship were of one piece.[17] As he put it, he "tried in a certain sense, to combine [his] own literary, philosophical and cultural interests with contemporary political interests."[18] His writings clearly reflect an acute alienation from the pro-Israeli bias of American culture and politics. Said laments that "the life of an Arab Palestinian in the West, particularly in America, is disheartening."[19] He was particularly vexed by what he perceived as "a web of racism, cultural stereotypes, political imperialism, dehumanizing ideology holding the Arab . . ." Hence, his writings took on an oppositional stance from which it was his avowed intention "to speak the truth to power."[20]

Said's scholarly project was by design critical. He was deeply influenced by the works of Joseph Conrad (1857–1924), in whom he found one who was, like himself, "out of place." Said saw his own life as a story of the "the displaced form of departures,

15. Burgess, "Pentecostalism in India," 86.

16. Bundy, "Bibliography and Historiography of Pentecostalism Outside North America," *NIDPCM*, 417.

17. Said, *Orientalism*, 25–26.

18. Said, "Reflections of an Exile," 13.

19. Said, *Orientalism*, 27.

20. Said, "Representations of the Intellectual," 24.

arrivals, farewells, exile, nostalgia, homesickness, belonging, and travel itself."[21] He found a kindred spirit in Conrad, whose homelessness seemed to parallel his own existence as a perennial expatriate. As with Conrad, Said used his writing as a means of preventing personal disintegration.[22] His awareness of being out of place served as the inspiration for his critique of literature and politics. The contours of Said's project were shaped by two other thinkers, Michel Foucault (1926–84) and Antonio Gramsci (1891–1937).[23] From Foucault's notion of the "relation between power and knowledge, and his view that representations are always influenced by the systems of power in which they are located," Said developed a method of "reading against the grain."[24] From Gramsci's notion of "hegemony," which explicated the Western myth of power and dominance, Said came to see his task as that of a "contrapuntal critic" who takes a stance of ideological resistance.[25] Borrowing from Conrad, Foucault, and Gramsci, Said engaged in a critical analysis of texts imbued with the Enlightenment ideals of rea-son and progress. His expressed intent was to oppose the legitimization of European colonialism. Such was the agenda that lay behind Said's classic work, *Orientalism*, and his other prodigious and controversial works of scholarship.[26]

The term "Orientalism" customarily denotes a domain of scholarship occupied with the study of the ancient texts, literature, philology, and anthropology of the Orient, or the East, which is commonly counterpoised to the West. Said starts out by saying that by "Orientalism" he means three things. First, in a conventional sense Orientalism is the academic study of the Orient by Western scholars. Secondly, Orientalism is "a style of thought based upon an ontological and epistemological distinction made be-tween 'the Orient' and (most of the time) 'the Occident.'" He claims that a large mass of writers in the West have embraced this distinction as a starting point for their depic-tions of the Orient. Thirdly, Orientalism is "a Western style for dominating, restructur-ing, and having authority over the Orient." Far from being disinterested, the Western image of the Orient is a mythical construct invented by Europeans on the basis of an historic fear of the Arabs and Islam. A view of the "other" is constructed, and indeed fabricated, in the interest of bolstering the political, cultural, military, ideological, and scientific dominance of Europe over the Orient. Said piles through a wealth of liter-ary material in which Western writers depict the Orient as an "exotic other," with an essence made of strangeness, cruelty, sensuality and decadence, constituting a mirror image of opposite qualities ascribed to the West. Said denounces the Western repre-

21. Said, *Out of Place*, xiv.

22. Walia, *Edward Said and the Writing of History*, 5.

23. Said, *Orientalism*, 3, 6–7.

24. Olson, "Politics, Power, Discourse and Representation," 320–21; Kennedy, *Edward Said*, 25.

25. Said, *Representations of the Intellectual*, 11–13.

26. Said's other major works include *Covering Islam* (1981); *Culture and Imperialism* (1993); *Peace and Its Discontents* (1995); *The Politics of Dispossession* (1994); *The Question of Palestine* (1980); and *The World, the Text, and the Critic* (1984).

sentation of the Orient as false and impugns it as a tool of Western colonialism and imperialism.[27]

Further, Said links Protestant missions in the Middle East to European colonial expansion in the region. He points out that Britain safeguarded its interests in Islamic territories by protecting a "complex apparatus" of missionary organizations that included the Society for Promoting Christian Knowledge, the Society for Propagation of the Gospel in Foreign Parts, the Baptist Missionary Society, the Church Missionary Society, the British and Foreign Bible Society, and the London Society for Promoting Christianity Among the Jews. Said asserts, "These missions openly joined the expansion of Europe."[28] Said also perceives a connection between traditional missionary discourse and Orientalism. He describes this connection as a latent religious impulse. Said says that Orientalism has "retained, as an undislodged current in its discourse, a reconstructed religious impulse, a naturalized supernaturalism."[29] He states,

> My thesis is that the essential aspects of modern Orientalist theory and praxis (from which present-day Orientalism derives) can be understood, not as a sudden access of objective knowledge about the Orient, but as a set of structures inherited from the past, secularized, redisposed, and re-formed by such disciplines as philology, which in turn were naturalized, modernized, and laicized substitutes for (or versions of) Christian supernaturalism. In the form of new texts and ideas, the East was accommodated to these structures.[30]

Hence, Said sees the origins of Orientalism in the discursive structures of Christian religious discourse. Foremost among these structures is what Said calls "dualism." Said defines dualism as "the absolute and systematic difference between the West, which is rational, developed, humane, superior, and the Orient, which is aberrant, undeveloped, inferior." It is precisely this us-and-them view of the other in Orientalism and Christianity that grates at Said. He identifies its source as the Bible and the rise of imperial Christianity.

According to Said, Western writers have imposed "secondhand abstractions" of Orientalist imagery, drawn from Christian traditions, upon the people of the Near East. In this connection, Michael Martin points out that, interestingly, Said uses the language of conversion in *Orientalism*.[31] For example, Said writes,

> All cultures impose corrections upon raw reality, changing it from free-floating objects into units of knowledge. The problem is not that conversion takes place ... To the Westerner, however, the Oriental was always *like* some aspect of the West ... The Orientalist makes it his work to be always converting the Orient

27. Said, *Orientalism*, 2–3.

28. Ibid., 100.

29. Ibid., 121.

30. Ibid., 122.

31. Marten, *Attempting to Bring the Gospel Home*, 17.

from something into something else: he does this for himself, for the sake of his culture, in some cases for what he believes for the sake of the Oriental.[32]

In reading Christian missionary discourse against the grain, Said construes it to be a part of the grand narrative of imperialism. He depicts the conversion of the Orient to Christianity as a two-step process. First, any identity which Orientals might wish to define for themselves had to be restructured, converted, and replaced by Western fabrications. Second, the missionaries could then "convert" Orientals to Christianity. But, for Said, the stark reality is that conversion performed the function of confirming the Western missionaries' understanding of their place in the divine economy. What Marten says of the Scottish missionaries in Palestine is also true of the Pentecostal missionaries. In their own minds they saw themselves as fulfilling what they understood to be biblical imperatives. They thought they were being altruistic in their desire to share the gospel. But they could not see their own ethnocentrism. "Their complicity in the imperialistic framework, intellectual, theological, and practical, was not something they considered, indeed, it is doubtful their worldview accommodated such a position."[33] Nonetheless, the missionaries rode the coattails of British imperial rule in Palestine and benefited from the British victory over the Ottoman regime and subjection of the Muslim social order.

Edward Said and the Study of Christian Missions

Said's proposals raise searching questions for scholars of the history of Christian missions. This study takes a relevant cue from Herb Swanson's article on "Said's Orientalism and the Study of Christian Missions."[34] Swanson observes that the voluminous scholarly debate over Said's *Orientalism* is "largely absent from missiological literature."[35] To make up for the neglect of Said by missiologists, Swanson aims "to point out a variety of ways in which the scholarly debate concerning Orientalism can contribute to the study of historical and contemporary international missions." Swanson "looks upon that debate as a tool for critical analysis and for cross-cultural reflection, a tool of potential value to the field of missiology."[36] We will build upon Swanson's article by applying the salient concepts of Said's *Orientalism* to a postcolonial assessment of the attitudes of the Pentecostal missionaries in Palestine. The concepts in question are discourses of power, dualism, the Other, textual attitudes, and intimate estrangement. These concepts will be briefly explained.

The dark side of Orientalism inhered in the vested political interest that it surreptitiously promoted. Said believed that, as a *discourse of power*, Orientalism misrepresented the East in the interest of legitimating the colonial domination of the

32. Said, *Orientalism*, 67.

33. Marten, *Attempting To Bring the Gospel Home*, 18.

34. Swanson, "Said's Orientalism and the Study of Christian Missions," 107–12.

35. Ibid., 107.

36. Ibid.

West over the East. As noted above, Said uses the term *dualism* to refer to the polar distinction made between the West and the East in oppositional terms, as "us" and "them." As Said sees it, Western Orientalists concocted an image of the *Other* that was an opposite reflection of their self image. This image is oppositional in the sense that it counterpoises the progressive qualities of the West against the static qualities of the East. Said contends that dualism can be detected in *textual attitudes*, that is, the ideology which is imbedded in discourse. According to Said, the ideology of Orientalism entails an oppressive strategy of caricaturing the "essence" of the Orient in pejorative terms as a means of justifying the Western domination of the Arab and Muslim East.[37] Said characterizes the relationship between Orientalists and the Orient as one of *intimate estrangement*. Although intimately acquainted with the cultures of the Orient, the Orientalists were estranged from Orientals by their presumption of Western superiority.

In applying the above concepts to the study of Christian missions, Swanson offers four proposals. First, Swanson thinks that missiologists should utilize Said's emphasis on the relationship of knowledge and discourses of power. He thinks that it behooves missiologists to take an honest look at how missionary discourses in both words and deeds have embodied and used power. Swanson writes, "Said helps to expose the missionary relationship to the convert church as a power relationship, one that does not always benefit the churches."[38] Second, Swanson sees relevance in Said's critique of the oppositional dualism of Orientalism. Working from Said's notion that Western Orientalists stored negative stereotypes in a bin that encapsulated their distorted view of the essence of the Orient, Swanson raises a searching question for missiologists. How have missionary prejudices influenced missionary relationships not only with people of other cultures and faiths, but also with the churches they founded?[39] Third, Swanson points to Said's indictment of the textual attitudes of Orientalism. Swanson suggests that Said's argument raises the issue of the role of the Bible in Protestant missions and asks, "Is it fair to say that missionaries in the past misused Scripture, turning it into an ideological textbook?"[40] Fourth, Swanson sees promise in Said's notion of intimate estrangement. He thinks that the letters and reports of nineteenth-century missionaries may reflect attitudes toward local cultures that are hauntingly similar to Said's notion of intimate estrangement. The missionaries knew the people, spoke their languages, ate their food, visited their homes and villages, and spent much of their daily lives in close proximity to the natives. But they seemed never quite to forget that those natives were representatives of a less advanced and heathen nation.

Following Swanson, one might wonder if the Pentecostal missionaries in Palestine lived in intimate isolation, and, if so, how that might have influenced the reception of the Christian faith by local peoples.[41] The issues raised by Swanson have been incorporated into the author's analysis of the historical narrative that follows.

37. Said, *Orientalism*, 12, 35, 37, 86, 92–96, 100–101, 122–23, 229–40, 328.

38. Swanson, "Said's Orientalism and the Study of Christian Missions," 110.

39. Ibid.

40. Ibid.

41. Ibid., 111.

ORGANIZATION OF THE TASK

Chapter 1 has introduced the topic at hand by defining the research problem, proposing a thesis statement, and explaining the influences that have shaped the author's methodology. The main body of the book is a historical narrative of the Pentecostal mission in Palestine. The narrative chapters will be followed by two chapters of critical analysis in which Pentecostal Zionism and its legacy are evaluated.

Chapter 2 will create a backdrop for the history of the Pentecostal mission in Palestine by following the trek of the "Palestine missionary band" from the Azusa Street Revival in Los Angeles to Jerusalem. Chapter 3 will describe the political, cultural, religious, and historical realities of Jerusalem at the turn of the twentieth century, and then address the question of whether an intercultural connection between the American Pentecostal missionaries and the people of Ottoman Jerusalem was a realistic possibility.

Chapter 4 will describe the work of the pioneer missionaries, Lucy Leatherman, Charles Leonard, and A. Elizabeth Brown, who planted the Pentecostal mission in Jerusalem. Chapter 5 will narrate the advancement of the mission station in Jerusalem and the expansion of the Pentecostal mission into Syria, Transjordan, and Persia. Chapter 6 will portray the vicissitudes of the mission against the backdrop of the Arab Revolt of 1936–39 and World War II, during which the mission held the fort in the face of trying circumstances and a negative assessment by denominational officials of the Assemblies of God. Chapter 7 will narrate the final period in the history of the mission, covering the retreat of the missionaries during the War of 1948, the establishment of a new mission station in the West Bank by the Church of God, the demise of the Assemblies of God mission station in Jerusalem, and a recent attempt to regroup the Assemblies of God mission in Israel. Chapter 7 will close with a summative assessment of the accomplishments of the mission from the perspective of one of the missionaries.

Chapter 8 will investigate the ideology of Pentecostal Zionism, exploring its sources, the views of its leading proponents, its dissemination in Pentecostal periodicals, and the contribution of the missionaries in Palestine to its diffusion. Chapter 9 will assess the legacy of the Pentecostal mission in Palestine from a postcolonial perspective. In short, it will be shown that this legacy is intertwined with the legacy of Pentecostal Zionism, specifically in regards to its correlate aspects of philosemitism on the one hand and antipathy toward Arabs and Muslims on the other hand. Chapter 9 will conclude with an assessment of the contribution of the Pentecostal missionaries to the prospect for peace in Israel/Palestine.

In chapter 10, the conclusion, the findings of this study will be summarized, the missiological implications of the findings will be educed, and the contribution of this project to the study of Pentecostalism will be suggested.

2 | Palestine Missionary Band from Azusa

IN THIS CHAPTER, a portrait of the Azusa Street Revival will be sketched with the aim of representing the religious milieu in which the Pentecostal mission in Palestine originated. Eyewitness accounts of the prodigious spirituality of the revival will be presented. The place of Palestine in the missionary vision of early Pentecostalism will be discussed. Finally, the trek of the Pentecostal missionaries sent out from Azusa to Jerusalem will be narrated. In the next chapter a portrayal of the distant cultural world of Jerusalem into which the missionaries bravely ventured will be constructed.

AZUSA STREET REVIVAL

The spark that ignited the Azusa Street Revival did not come suddenly from heaven. Rather it came from Kansas by way of Texas.

William Seymour and Charles Parham

The leader of the revival, William J. Seymour (1870–1922), was a protégé of Charles F. Parham (1873–1928). The two met in 1905 in Houston, Texas when Parham admitted Seymour as a student to his Apostolic Faith Bible Training School. Parham went on to establish himself as the "projector" of the Apostolic Faith movement, holding significant revival campaigns in Kansas and Texas. In the estimation of James R. Goff, "On the eve of the great revival at Azusa Street, Parham stood as the Pentecostal movement's greatest preacher and teacher, and clearly ranking as its most recognized personality."[1] When Seymour received an invitation to go from Houston to Los Angeles in 1906, Parham loaned him money for the train fare and sent Seymour off with his blessing. Despite some early squabbles in Los Angeles, Seymour soon collected a following, preaching the full gospel, including speaking in tongues. By April, 1906 the Azusa Street Revival had caught fire and was burning brightly. Seymour had it in his mind to ask his mentor, Charles Parham, for guidance and assistance. In October, 1906 Seymour drummed up interest in Parham in preparation for a much anticipated visit to the mission. He writes, "This man has preached in different languages over the United States, and men and women of that nationality have come to the altar and sought God. He was surely raised up of God to be an apostle of the doctrine of Pentecost."[2] During Parham's much anticipated visit to Azusa, Seymour's hopes for fatherly encourage-

1. Goff, "Charles F. Parham and His Role in the Development of the Pentecostal Movement," 232.

2. "The Pentecostal Baptism Restored: The Promised Latter Rain Now Being Poured Out on God's Humble People," *Apostolic Faith* 1.2 (October 1906)," 1.

ment were dashed when Parham castigated Seymour and his leadership team for their unseemly interracial familiarities. From this point on Parham's influence on Seymour and Azusa ceased. Nonetheless, the fact remains that Parham and Seymour both made significant contributions to the early phase of the Pentecostal movement. Parham bequeathed to Seymour the doctrine of speaking in tongues as the Bible evidence of the baptism of the Holy Spirit.[3] Seymour bequeathed to the Pentecostal movement what he had received from Parham, plus his own contribution, a prodigious ecstatic spirituality with leveling tendencies that Parham could not abide.[4]

Eyewitness Accounts of the Azusa Street Revival

Several eye-witness accounts of the prodigious spirituality of Azusa were published, a few of which will be offered below. In what follows, participant observers will be allowed to speak for themselves as to what they experienced and how they understood it. An article on the front page of the *Apostolic Faith* boldly proclaims, "The Pentecostal Baptism Restored." The unidentified author declares that God is bringing back the fullness of the gospel as found in the second chapter of the book of Acts. The author traces this breakthrough to the ministry of Charles Parham and his missionary training school in Topeka, Kansas. The article goes on to recount the story of how Agnes Ozman "was filled with the Holy Ghost and spake with other tongues as the Spirit gave utterance." Then it reports that this same phenomenon, which had accompanied Parham's revival meetings throughout the United States, has now "burst out in great power on the Pacific coast and is being carried from here over the world."[5] To illustrate the phenomenon in question, the editor of the *Apostolic Faith* describes a number of cases. When a missionary from Africa, "Brother Mead," went forward in response to an altar call, someone laid hands on him and prayed that he might receive the baptism of the Holy Spirit. Mead testifies that upon assuming an attitude of "complete abnegation of self" his "soul was flooded with Divine love; and I commenced to speak as I would sing a new song." The testimony of his wife, "Sister Mead," follows. She went to the altar and was prayed for by Seymour, Florence Crawford, and "another sister." Three weeks later she came "under the power from early morning till about five at night, prophesying in the Scriptures, and then began to speak in tongues, as the Spirit gave me utterance. I spoke most of the afternoon, having some very sweet revelations concerning the precious blood of Christ."[6]

Another eye-witness account of Spirit-baptism is provided by Lucy M. Leatherman (circa 1870–1925), who went from Azusa to Palestine as a Pentecostal missionary. Leatherman, a former student at Nyack Bible College, testifies,

---

3. Goff, "Parham: A Reevaluation," 236.

4. Irvin, "Pentecostal Historiography and Global Christianity," 40–41.

5. "The Pentecostal Baptism Restored: The Promised Latter Rain Now Being Poured Out on God's Humble People," *Apostolic Faith* 1.2 (October 1906) 1.

6. "New-Tongued Missionaries for Africa," *Apostolic Faith* 1.3 (November 1906) 3.

While seeking for the Baptism of the Holy Ghost in Los Angeles, after Sister Ferrell [sic] laid hands on me, I praised God and saw my Savior in the heavens. And as I praised, I came closer and closer and I was so small. By and by I swept into the wound in His side, and He was not only in me but I in Him, and there I found that rest that passeth all understanding, and He said to me, you are in the bosom of the Father. He said I was clothed upon and in the secret place of the Most High. But I said, Father, I want the gift of the Holy Ghost, and the heavens opened and went through me. He said, Praise Me, and when I did, angels came and ministered unto me. I was passive in His hands working on my vocal chords, and I realized they were loosing me. I began to praise Him in an unknown language.[7]

Mel Robeck observes that Leatherman used a type of decentering language that was common in testimonies of Pentecostal Spirit-baptism. "Her focus was not upon herself—it was upon her Savior."[8]

From the very beginning, belief in xenolalic tongues[9] was a centerpiece of the spirituality of the Azusa Street Revival. This was due to the influence of Charles Parham who long before Azusa had come up with the novel idea that the purpose of speaking in tongues was world evangelization. He insisted that Jesus had put the Great Commission on hold until the outpouring of the Holy Spirit in the Pentecostal Revival, which set the stage for the resumption of world evangelization. He writes, "I am looking for a people that will come up with the languages and go to the ends of the earth, speaking the language of the nations. This accompanied the Baptism of the Spirit among the early Christians for five hundred years. If God ever did that, He can do it again. God gave Pentecost for a purpose."[10] Hence, speaking in tongues was not only the incontrovertible proof of the baptism of the Holy Spirit, but also the power source of the missionary impulse of early Pentecostalism. According to Parham's biographer, James Goff, "As the sign of the baptism, tongues served a crucial role as evidence and also as a utilitarian missions tool."[11] With the gift of tongues, recipients became instant missionaries.

In the first issue of the *Apostolic Faith*, the official organ of the Azusa Street Revival, the editor draws a correlation between speaking in tongues and the missionary commission: "The gift of languages is given with the commission: 'Go ye into all the world and preach the Gospel to every creature.' The Lord has given languages to the unlearned." The author lists a number of different languages, including the "deaf mute language," and asserts that "the Holy Spirit speaks all the languages of the world through His children."[12] A plethora of testimonies is advanced to make the case for missionary tongues. Sister Hutchins "received the baptism with the Holy Ghost and

7. "Pentecostal Experience," *Apostolic Faith* 1.3 (November 1906) 4.

8. Robeck, *The Azusa Street Mission and Revival*, 182.

9. The terms "xenolalia" and "xenolalic tongues" denote speech in an unlearned human language that can be understood by a person for whom it is a known tongue.

10. Parham, "The Baptism of the Holy Spirit," 71.

11. Goff, "Charles Parham's Endtime Revival," 105.

12. *Apostolic Faith* 1.1 (September 1906) 1.

the gift of the Uganda language, the language of the people to whom she is sent."[13] Lillian Keyes "speaks and sings in tongues as the Spirit gives utterance. She also interprets . . ." Mrs. Mead, the visiting missionary cited above, was said to have corroborated the language Keyes spoke as an African dialect that was difficult to pronounce, "but the Holy Ghost, through the young lady, had given the perfect accent."[14] Lucy Leatherman, cited above, claimed to have received the Turkish language and tells that on her way to church she met a lady who was talking to her children in a language that sounded to her like the "words God had given me. I spoke a sentence to her, and she said, 'What you say means God has given Himself to you.' She is from Beyroute, Syria, and speaks Arabic."[15]

By the end of 1906 the Pentecostal movement had been propelled outward from Azusa. The editor of *Apostolic Faith* proudly exclaims, "We can truly say that Pentecost has come, for all the signs are following. God is pouring out His Spirit upon His sons and daughters and giving dreams and visions, speaking in tongues. A woman who had been an invalid for 18 years is walking and shouting and praising God. The blind have received their sight. Missionaries are going out without purse or scrip. Everything points toward the coming of the Lord."[16] Reports from elsewhere soon demonstrated that the Pentecostal full gospel was gaining adherents in far flung places. As at Azusa, people attested to being baptized in the Spirit and presented the same sort of pneumatic manifestations.

In New England, Samuel (1842–1926) and Addie Otis (circa 1850–1927), proprietors of the holiness periodical, *Word and Work,* joined the Pentecostal movement. They reported the case of one who would later serve as a Pentecostal missionary in Palestine. "Bro. Charles S. Leonard (a Baptist minister) was prostrated under 'the power of God' and laid for three hours on the floor; and again for two hours near evening; he then arose saying, 'Glory!'" This pneumatic manifestation of being slain in the Spirit was common among Pentecostals and gained them the opprobrium of being called "holy rollers."[17] The report goes on to say that, "Charles S. Leonard was bubbling over with joy, his mouth was filled with laughter, and his tongue with singing. He seemed a child again, in giving expression to his happiness." From Chicago the *Latter Rain Evangel* reported the case of a girl who was overheard speaking in tongues by a Jewish man, who remarked, "My God, I can understand what she is talking about." The girl sang a psalm and told of the coming of the Messiah, warning him that unless he accepted Jesus he would be lost. Reportedly, this Jewish man "said she spoke in the Slavonic language."[18] Writing from Baltimore, Philip Sidersky, the "Yiddish Evangelist,"

---

13. "Testimonies of Outgoing Missionaries," *Apostolic Faith* 1.2 (October 1906) 1.

14. "A Message Concerning His Coming," *Apostolic Faith* 1.2 (October 1906) 3.

15. Leatherman, "Pentecostal Experience," *Apostolic Faith* 1.3 (November 1906) 4.

16. *Apostolic Faith* 1.4 (December 1906) 1.

17. "Pentecostal Work in Boston," *Word and Work* (May 1907) 147–48.

18. *Latter Rain Evangel* (November 1908) 14.

reported that in 1907 he "received his Pentecost" and subsequently gathered a church of about fifty who had also "received Pentecost," i.e., speaking in tongues.[19]

In short order, the spread of the Pentecostal movement was widely attested.[20] Reports radiated from distant places. One such hot spot was the Anglican parish of the Rev. Alexander A. Boddy (1854–1930) in Sunderland, England. The first one in the Boddy family to speak in tongues was the vicar's daughter, Jane, who testified that "the Holy Ghost fell on me in great power, causing me to shake very much and praise His Holy Name. This went on for some time, until a wonderful power seized my tongue and jaws, and I spoke in 'an unknown tongue,' . . . Several messages were given, but, it was not me at all, but Christ in me. I was powerless."[21] As for himself, in 1906 Rev. Boddy shared with his prayer group "the first paper telling of what seemed to be an apostolic outpouring of the Holy Spirit in the West." Thomas B. Barratt (1862–1940), a Norwegian Methodist, was at Sunderland for a special meeting on March 5, 1907 when the "inflow of the blessed Holy Spirit occurred," but it was not until nine months later that Boddy experienced the "sign of the tongues." Boddy describes what transpired on December 2, 1907: "So on that Monday night He took my tongue as I yielded and obeyed. First speaking quickly but quietly and then more powerfully. The whole meeting at this point was adoring and praising God with great joy . . . My voice in tongues rose with theirs as a torrent of words poured out . . . Hallelujah to the Lamb!"[22] In another report Boddy rejoiced that during an international Pentecostal congress at Sunderland, "many seekers were baptized in the Holy Spirit." Boddy was beaming, "Pentecost has girdled the world. There were over 300 delegates, and they came from the east and from the west, from the north and from the south. The fire has touched every land. Germany, Holland, France, Italy, Russia, Norway, Sweden, U.S.A., Canada, Ceylon, India, and the four sister states of Britain, were all represented."[23]

The global reach of the Pentecostal movement was truly astounding. A writer in *Trust* states, "Never in the history of the world has a movement attracted so much attention in so short a space of time as this 'latter rain' of the Holy Spirit, which commenced about nineteen months ago amongst a few humble people in Los Angeles, California, in Pentecostal power, accompanied with 'signs and wonders.'"[24] It seemed

---

19. Sidersky, "Leaksville, N.C." *The Evening Light and Church of God Evangel* 1.19 (December 1, 1910) 6.

20. "Assemblies of God Missionary Policy," *Redemption Tidings* 2.2 (February 1926) 9.

21. J. Boddy, "Testimony of a Vicar's Daughter," *Confidence* (May 1908) 6–7.

22. A. Boddy, "Pentecost in Sunderland," *Latter Rain Evangel* (February 1909) 9–10.

23. "Sunderland International Pentecostal Congress," *Confidence* (June 1909) 127. Boddy organized and chaired the Sunderland Conventions during the Season of Pentecost from 1908 to 1914. Each convention lasted six days. These conventions were attended by many who would become prominent leaders of the Pentecostal Movement. For example, Smith Wigglesworth was baptized in the Spirit at the 1909 convention and Thomas Myerscough at the 1909 convention. Stanley Frodsham, later editor of the *Pentecostal Evangel*, attended in 1912 and 1913. Kay, *Inside Story*, 25, 30.

24. W. L. L., "The End at Hand," *Trust* (February 1909) 17.

that the Pentecostal movement was "fast penetrating to the remote regions of the world's great empires. God is roaring out of Zion."[25]

GLOBAL MISSIONARY MOVEMENT

The Pentecostal Revival gave rise to a global missionary movement. This was widely recognized by the first generation of Pentecostals. Years afterward Azusa, D. W. Kerr could declare, "We cannot be filled with the Holy Ghost and fail to be filled with a burden for missions . . . When we are filled with the Holy Spirit we will be missionaries, either at home or abroad."[26] Indeed, Pentecostalism was from its beginnings and continued to be driven by an intense impulse for world evangelization.[27] The magnitude of Azusa's prolific missionary impulse can be measured, numerically, by the worldwide growth of Pentecostalism, continuing until today. Gary B. McGee asserts that this fact has been "largely overlooked by most historians of the expansion of Christianity."[28]

There is no denying the missionary productivity of the early Pentecostals. Frank Bartleman asserts, "The greater work will be accomplished in foreign fields."[29] Addie Otis reports, "Reports continue to come to us of the spread of this wonderful work of God. We only wish we had space to tell of the glorious work in India, China, Holland, Norway, Australia, Japan, Scandinavia, Switzerland, Scotland, England, Ireland, Africa, Jerusalem, Central America, South America, Canada, and the states of our Union."[30] William Piper recalls, "The Latter Rain began to fall in a small way in California nine years ago; it fell in greater abundance in California, and now encircles the globe. Hundreds of people baptized in the Holy Spirit have gone to various parts of the world, carrying the Gospel of Jesus Christ, all brought about through intercession."[31] *Confidence* flatly affirms, "The Pentecostal Movement is truly a Missionary Movement."[32] The editor of *Trust* comments on the global scope of Pentecostal missionary activity, "Truly the world is being girdled with Pentecostal showers. We regret that we have not space to quote from the many letters from all parts of the earth, telling of the hunger that is being created everywhere. Recent letters have been received from missionaries and Christian workers in Africa, Australia, Turkey, Syria, Scotland, Wales, India, China, Japan, England, and elsewhere."[33] The significance of Pentecostalism for world missions was not lost upon John M. Pike, editor

---

25. Ibid., 18.

26. Mrs. D. W. Kerr, "A World Wide Appeal," *Latter Rain Evangel* (November 1922) 22.

27. McClung, *Azusa Street and Beyond*, 8; McGee, "*This Gospel . . . Shall Be Preached*," 44.

28. McGee, "The Azusa Street Revival and Twentieth-Century Missions," 58.

29. Bartleman, "The Pentecostal Work," *Word and Work* (January 1908) 19–20.

30. Otis, "Jesus Is Coming," *Word and Work* (June 1908) 176.

31. Piper, *Latter Rain Evangel* (March 1909) 7.

32. "The Pentecostal Movement," *Confidence* (June 1909) 9. The Pentecostal Missionary Union was formed at a meeting chaired by Alexander Boddy in Sunderland. Cecil Polhill served as president until 1925 when the PMU was merged into the Assemblies of God. Kay, *Inside Story*, 43.

33. "Girdling the World," *Trust* (July-August 1909) 16.

of the influential *Way of Faith* periodical. He writes, "The Pentecostal movement has stirred the hearts of myriads of Christian people throughout the world, and prompted to earnest prayer for deeper consecration on the part of the church of God, and has awakened missionary zeal for the evangelization of the world beyond all precedent."[34]

Despite the iconic stature of Azusa in the history of the Pentecostal Revival, some have questioned whether it was actually the central point of origin of the Pentecostal missionary movement.[35] But this was not in doubt among the participant observers of Azusa, who widely regarded Azusa as the place from which the Pentecostal missionary impulse originated. As Boddy put it during his 1912 visit to Azusa, "Thence it spread and was carried all over the world, including Europe and Great Britain, where at Sunderland, in the North, the outpouring began afresh under different conditions, and some hundred received the Baptism of the Holy Ghost, the Sign of the Heavenly Tongue."[36] That was then, but as things stood in 1912, he reports, "Though regular meetings are not what they were, yet 'Azusa Street' is a sort of 'Mecca' still to Pentecostal travelers. They like to kneel in the place 'where the Fire fell.'"[37] Borrowing a phrase from Bartleman, B. F. Lawrence trumpets, "*Azusa became the center.*" Then he goes on to report, "Missionaries carried the Pentecostal message and power with them. Almost every country on the globe has been visited by them. The work is almost stronger in some other countries than it is even in America. It has been my privilege to 'see the mighty works of God' in Pentecostal power in England, Scotland, Wales, France, Holland, Switzerland, Germany, Norway, Sweden, Finland, Russia, Egypt, Palestine, Ceylon, India, China, and in the Islands of the Sea, outside of the United States and Canada."[38] Although Lawrence and Bartleman may have been reading into the story of Azusa more than was there, it is still an established fact that Azusa played a formative role in the Pentecostal missionary movement. What is less well known, however, is the place of Palestine in the world view and missionary vision of early Pentecostalism.

THE METANARRATIVE OF EARLY PENTECOSTALISM

Early Pentecostals were motivated by a particular view of the world. It is the author's contention that the Pentecostal world view can be construed as a "metanarrative." In *Telling the Truth about History*, Appleby, Hunt, and Jacob define a metanarrative as "a grand scheme for organizing the interpretation and writing of history."[39] A metanarrative is not an individual narrative, consciously or unconsciously perceived by an author, but rather a "model" or "paradigm" that structures ways of thinking within a society or group. Appleby, Hunt, and Jacob argue that metanarratives should not be

34. Pike, "The Wheat and the Tares," *Pentecostal Evangel* (November 27, 1920) 7.

35. Creech, "Visions of Glory," 405–24.

36. Boddy, "At Los Angeles, California," *Confidence* (October 1912) 233–34.

37. Boddy, "A Meeting at the Azusa Street Mission, Los Angeles," *Confidence* (November 1912) 244.

38. Lawrence, "The Pentecostal or 'Latter Rain' Outpouring in Los Angeles," *Weekly Evangel* (March 11, 1916) 5, 8. This first history of Azusa was printed in installments in the *Weekly Evangel*.

39. Appleby, Hunt, and Jacob, *Telling the Truth about History*, 232.

eschewed by historians. Granting the critique of grand narratives, they take the position that there is still room for master narratives which do not make claims to universal validity. They think that metanarratives are necessary for both for individuals and groups, because they serve three sociological functions. A metanarrative structures normative ways of thinking, builds and upholds identity, and affords coherence and meaning to history.[40]

The approach to construing the grand narrative of early Pentecostalism taken here is selective, in that a particular theme, the role of Palestine, will be highlighted. Below the role of Palestine in the missionary vision and eschatology of early Pentecostalism will be appraised. My view is that the theme of Palestine served the interest of structuring normative ways of thinking about the world view of early Pentecostals.

Palestine in the Missionary Vision of Early Pentecostalism

The worldview of early Pentecostalism was largely synonymous with its so-called missionary vision. According to McGee, "The history of Pentecostalism cannot be properly understood apart from its missionary vision."[41] The missionary vision of early Pentecostalism was composed of a conglomerate of core Pentecostal values, such as the baptism of the Holy Spirit, the restoration of the apostolic sign of speaking in tongues, pre-millennial eschatology, and the imperative for world evangelization.[42] In addition, one finds a clear and persistent emphasis on Palestine. In the first history of the Pentecostal Revival, B. F. Lawrence observes, "Even old Jerusalem has heard again the sound of 'speaking in other tongues as the Spirit gives utterance.'"[43] Among the early Pentecostals, there was a widely held belief that, at the time of the outbreak of the Pentecostal Revival, God was effecting a double restoration of ultimate significance. First, the apostolic power of the Holy Spirit was being restored through the Pentecostal Revival. Second, the Jewish homeland in Palestine was being restored through the Zionist Movement.[44] And Pentecostal missionaries, it was fervently hoped, would have an important role to play in the unfolding of both of these dramatic restorations.

As early as 1899, Charles F. Parham made a connection between missionary tongues and Palestine. Parham tells of how he read a report in a holiness journal about Jennie Glassey, a missionary in Palestine, who reported having received a foreign language as a gift to aid her missionary work:

> Glassy [sic] now in Jerusalem, received the African dialect in one night . . . She received the gift while in the Spirit in 1895, but could read and write, translate and sing the language while out of the trance or in a normal condition, and can until now. Hundreds of people can testify to the fact, both saint and sinner, who

40. Ibid., 387.

41. McGee, "Early Pentecostal Missionaries," 6.

42. Blumhofer, *The Assemblies of God: Volume 1—To 1941*, 285–86.

43. Lawrence, "The Pentecostal or 'Latter Rain' Outpouring in Los Angeles," *Weekly Evangel* (March 11, 1916) 8.

44. Gannon, "The Shifting Romance with Israel," 111–12, 116–17, 121–22.

heard her use the language. She was also tested in Liverpool and Jerusalem. Her Christian experience is that of a holy, consecrated woman, filled with the Holy Ghost. Glory to God for the return of the apostolic faith.[45]

From this Parham supposed that there would be a divinely orchestrated confluence of events involving Pentecostal missionaries and the Jews. According to his scheme, Spirit-filled Pentecostal missionaries would be sent to Jerusalem, where they would convert the Jews to Christ as they returned to the Holy Land, hence quickening the Second Coming of Christ.[46] The outpouring of the Spirit and the Jewish restoration to Zion were corresponding signs of the pending Second Coming. Some even went beyond Parham and predicted that the Jews would join the cause of the Pentecostal missionaries. For example, Alexander A. Boddy boldly declares, "The Jews will become a nation of Spirit-filled missionaries."[47]

It is probably due to Parham's influence that the *Apostolic Faith* attributed special eschatological significance to current events in Palestine. In commenting on Jesus' prophecy of the budding the fig tree, an unnamed author argues that this stands for the Jews and emphatically states, "We see the signs of new life in them, in their gathering back to Palestine, where they are now going by thousands, and may soon become a nation again. They have the means to purchase Palestine and are making all preparations to rebuild the temple in Jerusalem." In corroboration of these bold predictions, the author offers two pieces of evidence, first, that "God is making their land which was cursed, to blossom as the rose and bring forth fruits abundantly," and second, that "the rainfall has been restored to that country and it has become very productive."[48] Clearly, this shows that the leadership of Azusa had embraced Parham's Pentecostal Zionism and incorporated it into their eschatological scheme.

Palestine in Pentecostal Eschatology

Parham was the first of many to cast the Pentecostal missionary vision in eschatological terms. As Pentecostal theology developed, it continued to manifest a central eschatological element which acted as a motivational impulse for world evangelization and missions.[49] According to Grant McClung, "Eschatological urgency is at the heart of understanding the missionary fervor of early Pentecostalism"[50] McClung argues that the central motivational element in Pentecostal missiology "has been an intense premillennial eschatology. Premilliennialism, dispensationalism, and the belief in the imminency of Christ's return forged the evangelistic fervor of the movement in its infancy."

---

45. *Apostolic Faith* (Kansas) 1.1 (May 3, 1899) 5.

46. Goff, *Fields White Unto Harvest*, 78–79.

47. *Confidence* 13.3 (October-December, 1920) 55.

48. "Signs of His Coming," *Apostolic Faith* 1.6 (March 1907) 5.

49. McGee, "Early Pentecostal Missionaries," 6.

50. McClung, *Azusa Street and Beyond*, 8, 51.

However, another aspect of the early Pentecostal eschatology has not been fully appreciated. This is the special place reserved for Palestine as a sign of prophetic fulfillment. According to Ray Gannon, "Pentecostals viewed the restoration of Zion as the fulfillment of prophecy."[51] They almost universally included the return of the Jews to Palestine in their lists of the signs of the Second Coming of Christ.[52] In fact, some Pentecostals felt that events in Palestine were of exceptional eschatological importance. Albert Weaver writes, "If one wishes to understand the signs of the times they need only to look eastward to the land so dear to the Lord, Palestine."[53] As was the case with all dispensationalists, early Pentecostals reserved an important role for the Jews in their scenario of the end times. In fact, they viewed the return of the Jews to Palestine as the hinge which would open the door for the final redemption of the kingdom age. According to Parham,

> Redemption takes place in the time of trouble, and in that time of trouble the Jews will go back to Palestine and establish their seat of government in Jerusalem. For fifteen years their Congress (i.e., the Zionist Congress) has met as a legislative body in Bern, Switzerland, or London, and has exercised all the functions pertaining to legislative bodies. They have already carried the flag to Jerusalem, and every Congress has met and adjourned sine die,—"next year we meet in Jerusalem," but they never have, and they never will until the appointed time shall come. We are now living in the dawn of that time.[54]

Early Pentecostals regarded the Jew as "God's timepiece" and closely watched the current events for happenings with the Jewish people that might be construed as a sign that the Second Coming of Christ was imminent. They interpreted the increasing immigration of Jews to Palestine and the establishment of agricultural colonies in Eretz Israel as proof that the remnant was coming back, just as promised by the Old Testament prophets. This was a popular theme in Pentecostal preaching and received prominent coverage in Pentecostal publications. In a lecture delivered at the Stone Church in Chicago, William H. Cossum declared that the Zionist Movement was a sure sign of the nearness of the Second Coming. He says, "It thrills our hearts not merely

51. Gannon, "The Shifting Romance with Israel," 164. See Jones, "Further Facts about Palestine," *The Elim Evangel and Foursquare Revivalist* 10.22 (September 29, 1929) 339–41.

52. Boddy, "Seven Signs of His Coming," *Confidence* (December 1910) 291–93; Cook, "God's Prophetic Timepiece," *Church of God Evangel* (October 28, 1957) 4–5, 13; Jamieson, "The Second Coming of Christ," *Weekly Evangel* (February 26, 1916) 6–7; Pocock, "Present-Day Signs of the End," *Trust* (January-February 1926) 16, 20; Stuernagel, "Signs of the Approaching End of the Age," *Latter Rain Evangel* (May 1927) 4–8; King, "Signs of the Coming of Our Lord," *Trust* (October 1915) 12–20; Booth-Clibborn, "The Goal of Prophetic Scripture," *Trust* (December 1918) 11–14; A. Frodsham, "The Return of the Lord: The Signs of the Times," *Pentecostal Evangel* (February 18, 1922) 6–7; Parker, "Christ is Coming Soon! An Outstanding Sign," *The Elim Evangel and Foursquare Revivalist* 9.19 (December 1, 1928) 313–15.

53. Weaver, "Palestine," *Word and Work* 31.9 (September 1909) 198.

54. Parham, "Redemption," *Apostolic Faith* (Kansas), 3.2 (February 1914) 5.

on account of the Jews, but because the quicker the Jews get together the quicker Jesus will come. The dry bones are twitching and it thrills us with expectation."[55]

In the minds of early Pentecostals, events in Palestine were viewed as sure attestations of the imminence of the Second Coming of Christ. David Wesley Myland felt that the precipitation reports from Jerusalem provided proof of the hand of divine providence in the Pentecostal Revival. He purports to present evidence, in the form of a precipitation chart from Palestine, courtesy of the American Colony, demonstrating that rainfall had been increasing in Palestine between 1890 and 1900. He surmises that this increase was a sign of "God's last work for this dispensation, to bring about the unity of the body, the consummation of the age, and the catching away of spiritual Israel, the Bride of Christ."[56] Myland points to a divinely orchestrated confluence of events, stating, "We have literal Israel returning to their land at the same time that the literal latter rain is coming to its normal fall upon that land. This together with the spiritual latter rain falling upon God's spiritual Israel today, betokens in a remarkable way that the closing days of the Dispensation are upon us."[57] The special place afforded to the restoration of the Jewish people to Palestine in the worldview of early Pentecostalism gave special significance to the missionaries who were sent out from Azusa to Jerusalem.

TREK OF THE PALESTINE MISSION BAND
FROM AZUSA TO JERUSALEM

The missionary impulse unleashed during the Azusa Street Revival produced immediate and far-reaching results, as missionaries answered the call and streamed across the globe disseminating the Pentecostal message. It is noteworthy that three of the first five missionaries sent out from the Azusa Street Revival went to Palestine. In fact, as Larry Martin points out, the very first missionary sent out from the Azusa mission went to Jerusalem.[58] On July 12, 1906 William Seymour wrote to W. F. Carothers, "We have workers to India. God paid their way since they got the Baptism with the Holy Ghost. Some going to Jerusalem—about 4 workers; some are going to Africa, some to China."[59] In the first issue of *Apostolic Faith*, the three missionaries sent out to Jerusalem are highlighted. The report reads, "A band of three missionaries, Bro. Andrew Johnson and Sisters Louise Condit and Lucy M. Leatherman, who have been baptized with the Holy Ghost and received the gift of languages, have left for Jerusalem."[60] At this early juncture in the Pentecostal movement, Parham's view, that

---

55. Cossum, "Mountain Peaks of Prophecy and Sacred History," *Latter Rain Evangel* 2.8 (May 1910) 6.

56. Myland, "The Latter Rain Covenant," 95.

57. Ibid., 129.

58. Martin, *The Life and Ministry of William J. Seymour*, 233.

59. Letter from W. J. Seymour to Brother Carothers, July 12, 1906, Parham Papers.

60. *Apostolic Faith* 1.1 (September 1906) 4.

when people spoke in tongues they were speaking actual languages, was widely held.[61] Hence, the article went on, "Bro. Johnson has received seven different languages, one which is the Arabic. Sister Leatherman speaks the Turkish language . . ."[62] Dispensing with the normal time demanded for language training, these trailblazing Pentecostal missionaries directly headed off in the direction of Palestine.

Letters from the outgoing missionaries and reports of their progress were published in the *Apostolic Faith*, from which a rough itinerary of their trek can be reconstructed. We know that the "Palestine missionary band" first went to Oakland, California, accompanied by G. W. Evans, his wife, and Florence Crawford. They stayed there, ministering in the mission of a Brother Manley for six weeks, until August 10, 1906. According to Evans, during these meetings "hundreds have been at the altar, many converted, sanctified, healed, and thirty have received their Pentecost and are speaking in tongues. Praise God! The saints in Los Angeles rejoice to hear the good report." While in Oakland Leatherman was walking down the street, speaking in tongues, "just as a man wearing the Turkish fez came by. He listened in wonder and asked what college she had attended, saying she spoke the most perfect Turkish tongue he had heard spoken by a foreigner." As the story goes, this "educated man from Constantinople . . . was the first person that had interpreted for her."[63] Such stories were amassed by the early Pentecostals to justify their belief in xenolalic tongues.

The missionaries then traveled to Colorado Springs, Denver, Chicago, Greenwich, Connecticut, and New York City. The report came back to Azusa that, as a result of the ministry of the Palestine mission band, "four souls received the Pentecost in Colorado Springs and three in Denver." The *Apostolic Faith* was proud to report that, "Sister Lizzie Fraser of Colorado Springs, Colorado, was one of those who received the gift of tongues when the Palestine Missionary Band passed through there."[64] Leatherman evidently traveled through Chicago because *Word and Work* carried a story of her ministry there. Mrs. D. E. Whitnal writes, "In Jan., 1906, I began seeking the Holy Ghost baptism and sought it till July, when Sister Leatherman came to Chicago. She prayed for me and it seemed the Lord told her I was ready."[65] It is conceivable that Leatherman could have stopped by her hometown of Greencastle, Indiana on her way to the east coast, but no mention is made of this in the periodicals. From Chicago, Leatherman moved on to Greenwich, Connecticut. Estrelda Alexander notes that while in Connecticut Leatherman collaborated with Orphelia Wiley and Adolpho de Rosa in evangelistic campaign that drew the ire of neighbors for excessive noise. According to a newspaper report, angry citizens destroyed the tent used by the Pentecostal evangelists, alleging that Leatherman and company were practicing witchcraft and hypnotism, prompting Leatherman to move on, conceding, "We will no longer work further in this locality."[66]

61. Frodsham, *With Signs Following*, 38, 57, 243.

62. *Apostolic Faith* 1.1 (September 1906) 4.

63. "Missionaries To Jerusalem," *Apostolic Faith* 1.1 (September 1906), 4.

64. *Apostolic Faith* 1.2 (October 1906) 1.

65. Whitnal, "Pentecostal Experience," *Word and Work* (October 1908) 303.

66. Cited in Alexander, *The Women of Azusa Street*, 73.

The final stop before sailing for Palestine was New York City. One evening Leatherman happened to be at a prayer meeting led by Maud Williams, at which the Norwegian Methodist minister, Thomas B. Barratt, was also present. Leatherman laid her hands on Barratt as he sought the baptism of the Holy Spirit. According to Barratt, "At about twelve I asked another brother there and Sister Leatherman to lay their hands on my head again. Just then she says she saw a crown of fire and cloven tongues over my head. The brother saw a supernatural light. Immediately I was filled with such a power that I began to shout as loud as I could in a foreign language."[67]

The members of the Palestine Missionary Band rendezvoused in New York City and pondered what the future might hold. Brother Johnson writes, "I am, God willing, going to leave New York in a few days for Palestine and Jerusalem . . . Please pray for me. I would like for God to send me a brother to help me in Palestine . . . The Lord has been giving me more freedom and power than I ever had before. I now speak eleven or twelve languages . . . My heart goes out for the Jews and every lost soul in this world."[68] Louisa Condit writes, "Mrs. Bushnell, an old friend about sixty years old, is with me, and is going to Jerusalem with me. We shall sail, God willing, September 15. I praise God we can meet every day at the throne of grace. Pray for the peace of Jerusalem. Pray for the dear Jews, and ask all of the dear saints there to pray also."[69] Leatherman too was mulling over her expectations. She writes, "Eight years ago, in A. B. Simpson's missionary school in Nyack, New York, I heard the Macedonian cry to go to Jerusalem, but it is to the Arabs. I am told that there are more Arabs than Jews there, and God has been speaking to me and asks me if I would be willing to go with Him to the wild Arab of the desert."[70] Given the greater success that Pentecostal missionaries in Palestine would enjoy with Arabs, this was perhaps a prescient insight on Leatherman's part.

Finally, *Word and Work* announced that Lucy Leatherman was all set to sail from New York in October of 1907 with a Mrs. Bishop Newman. The editor then comments, "A glance at present conditions in Palestine shows God is preparing for scenes in the closing drama of this age."[71] There was clearly a sense of eschatological expectation over the upcoming Pentecostal mission in Palestine. As is often the case, great expectations are not fully realized. After sailing the Atlantic, the missionaries came ashore at Gibraltar, where Johnson had a change of heart and returned to his home in Sweden. He later explained that he had misunderstood his divine calling. When the Spirit was prompting him to go to Jerusalem, Johnson only later understood that he was actually being called to his native "Jerusalem," i.e., Sweden.[72] Cecil M. Robeck states that

---

67. *Apostolic Faith* 1.2 (October 1906) 3.

68. Ibid.

69. Ibid., 4.

70. *Apostolic Faith* 1.3 (November 1906) 4.

71. "Extracts from Exchanges," *Word and Work* 29.9 (September 1907) 247.

72. *Confidence* (January 1909) 8. Johnson recounts the development of the Pentecostal Assemblies of Sweden and his experiences as a missionary in Estonia in "The Pentecostal Work in Sweden: Sacrifice and Hardship for the Gospel's Sake," *The Elim Evangel and Foursquare Revivalist* 6.5 (March 2, 1925) 49–50; 6.6 (March 16, 1925) 65.

Condit arrived in Jerusalem and served there, but he does not identify the source of this information.[73] In contrast, it is well documented that Leatherman arrived at her destination in late 1907 and succeeded in planting the Pentecostal flag in Jerusalem.

Prior to tracing Leatherman's pioneering missionary exploits, in the next chapter we will construct a portrayal of Jerusalem as it was at the outset of the Pentecostal mission in Palestine.

73. Robeck, *The Azusa Street Mission and Revival*, 215.

3 | Azusa-Jerusalem Connection

T HE GEOGRAPHIC DISTANCE between the Azusa Street Revival in Los Angeles, California, and the city of Jerusalem in Palestine was considerable, not to mention the immense cultural differences. One can hardly imagine more incommensurable cultural realities than a Pentecostal revival and Ottoman Jerusalem. The Pentecostal missionaries from Azusa arrived on the scene in Jerusalem with preconceptions based largely on their reading of the Bible. Most of what they had to go on was derived from the discourse of Western geo-piety inherited from the popular religious literature of Christian Zionism. The purpose of this chapter is to depict what was at stake in the formation of an intercultural connection between the Pentecostal missionaries from Azusa and the people of Jerusalem in 1906. The bulk of the chapter is taken up with a detailed description of the political, cultural, religious, and historical realities of Jerusalem at the turn of the twentieth century. Based on that portrayal, the realistic possibility that an intercultural connection could be forged between the American Pentecostal missionaries and the people of Ottoman Jerusalem will be critically analyzed.

JERUSALEM AS IT WAS IN 1906

We now turn to a description of the world of Jerusalem as it was in 1906 when the missionaries from Azusa headed out to plant the Pentecostal flag in Palestine, figuratively speaking.

Political Context

Jerusalem was a Muslim municipality. When the first Pentecostal missionaries arrived in Jerusalem, they entered a city under the political jurisdiction of the Ottoman Empire. Since its surrender to Caliph Umar in 637 CE, Jerusalem had been under Muslim governance, aside from a hiatus during the Crusader period (1095–1187). During the Mamluk period (1250–1517), Jerusalem was a sub-district of the province of Syria, which was divided into seven areas, or *maklaka*, comprised of Damascus, Aleppo, Tripoli, Hamat, Safed, Gaza, and Kerak.[1] The Ottoman Empire, which came to power in 1517, adopted the Mamluk territorial scheme with Palestine in the province, or *eyalet*, of Syria.[2] In about 1800 Syria was divided into four administrative provinces,

1. Drory, "Jerusalem during the Mamluk Period (1250–1517)," 193.
2. Europeans referred to Ottoman Syria as "Greater Syria." The Arabic word for Syria is *Sham*. The

which were Aleppo, Damascus, Tripoli, and Sidon. Each province was governed by a *pasha* (governor) who was appointed by and was answerable to the sultan in Istanbul. Eventually the Ottomans divided Palestine into three districts, known as *sanjaks*, which were Acre, Nablus and Gaza. From the 1780s Jerusalem was an independent *pashalik* governed by its own *pasha*. It did not attain district status until the nineteenth century.[3] Because of the religious importance of Jerusalem, tactful politicians were appointed to the position of *pasha* in Palestine. The Ottomans enforced their occupation of Jerusalem with a small military detachment which was garrisoned in the citadel of David.[4]

With the decline of the Ottoman Empire, the power of the Sultan was severely curtailed in outlying regions such as Palestine. The result was a weakening of the centralized administration. Increasingly, the provincial governors ruled their domains as kingdoms unto themselves, disregarding edicts from Istanbul. To counteract the autonomy of the pashas, the sultan replaced them on a yearly basis, a practice which disturbed the continuity of governance in the provinces. To make up for a brief tenure, pashas often aggrandized their power. If a pasha was so inclined, he could make quick money from his district by means of excessive taxation, onerous fines, bribery, patronage, and confiscation of land. The result was the disaffection of the local population. Out of expediency the sultans resorted to the practice of appointing local Arab notables as pashas in Jerusalem. This provided for a more effective working relationship with the Arab elites, safer travel conditions vouchsafing the flow of revenue from pilgrims and tax collectors, and the defusing of strife among vying Arab factions. Arab pashas were in a position to appoint their relatives and friends to a good number of Ottoman administrative posts and key positions in the Muslim *shari'ah* court. Under these conditions, the leading Husaini, Khalidi, and Nababishi clans of Palestine acquired large landholdings.[5]

In the nineteenth century a municipal council (*baladiyya al-quds*) was established in Jerusalem. It was made up of ten members, the mayor and six Muslims, two Christians, and one Jew, who served four-year terms. In 1908 the number of Jews was increased to two. Councilors were elected by vote of the male Ottoman citizens who were over twenty-five years old and paid an annual property tax of at least fifty Turkish pounds. The pasha appointed the mayor of Jerusalem from among the members of the council. This post was usually held by a notable from the above-mentioned clans. The council played a significant role in the development of modern Jerusalem, improving the streets, sewage system, lighting, and sanitation. In the 1890s the council arranged for garbage collection, tree planting, and the creation of a public park on Jaffa Road. At the turn of the century, shortly before the arrival of the Pentecostal missionaries, the council introduced a police force, a municipal hospital, a museum of antiquities, and

Ottoman province of Syria included the present nations of Israel, Palestine (West Bank and Gaza), Jordan, Lebanon, and Syria.

3. Tibawi, *A Modern History of Syria Including Lebanon and Palestine*, 23.

4. Armstrong, *Jerusalem: One City, Three Faiths*, 323.

5. Ibid., 341–43.

a theatre featuring dramatic presentations in Arabic, French, and Turkish. According to Karen Armstrong, among Ottoman cities Jerusalem was exceeded only by Istanbul in the steps its council had taken toward modernization.[6]

Cultural Context

The culture of Jerusalem in the late Ottoman period was steeped in tradition. Its city plan, population composition, languages, educational institutions, and general way of life were the product of centuries of development. Life in Jerusalem had an Arabic flavor common to its Jewish, Christian, and Muslim inhabitants. One might say, with all due respect to Edward Said, that the culture of Jerusalem was "oriental" in its food, dress, dwellings, and behavior patterns at home and in the streets, bargaining in the markets, the use of animals for transporting goods, and means of collecting water. The tell-tale signs of the oriental culture were the aromas of distinctive spices, the veiling of women in public, the flowing robes, decorative daggers, head scarves and Turkish fez hats worn by men, and the ubiquitous blue "evil eye" talismans. These visible signs of the folk culture gave Jerusalem an exotic appearance in the eyes of Westerners, such as the Pentecostal missionaries from Azusa.

Jerusalem was demarcated by its imposing walls, with the Old City inside and the New City outside. Some historians see Jerusalem as a typical Muslim city of the Middle East. Others argue that Jerusalem never became a Muslim city.[7] The city plan of a Muslim city would normally have a large central mosque, a religious school adjacent to the mosque, sometimes a center of higher learning, a central government building, a palace or citadel, the governor's official residence, a Turkish bath, an inn, and a central market with other markets in outlying areas. Normally, the neighborhoods of Muslim cities were segregated according to religious and ethnic identity, each with its own mosque, church or synagogue, bath house, and market place. Yehoshua Ben-Arieh states that only some of the above features of a typical Muslim city can be found in Jerusalem.[8] There are Muslim markets and public bath houses, and the Old City is divided into religiously defined quarters. However, there is no central mosque. The main al-Aqsa Mosque is located on the eastern periphery near the Dome of the Rock. The city plan follows the outlines of the Roman city built by Hadrian with Jerusalem's government buildings located on sites established in the Second Temple period. The main thoroughfares and major intersecting streets were also established before the Muslim period. Under Muslim administration the city plan of Jerusalem was not altered, largely because the layout of Jerusalem is oriented around its holy sites, giving the city its distinctive geographic features. The Jews had the Wailing Wall; the Christians the Church of the Holy Sepulcher; and the Muslims the Dome of the Rock and al-Aqsa mosque.

6. Ibid., 359.
7. Goitein, "Jerusalem in the Arab Period (638–1099)," 168.
8. Ben-Arieh, *Jerusalem in the 19th Century*, 391.

During the late Ottoman period, the population of Jerusalem increased steadily. In 1850 the total population was 15,000 with 5,350 Muslims, 3,650 Christians, and 6,000 Jews. By 1900 there were 55,000 people living in Jerusalem, with 10,000 Muslims, 10,000 Christians, and 35,000 Jews. Ten years later the population had climbed to 70,000 with 13,500 Muslims, 14,700 Christians, and 45,000 Jews. The biggest demographic shift was the increase in the Jewish population.[9] The same trend prevailed throughout Palestine. According to Sami Hadawi, by 1917 there were 56,000 Jews in Palestine and 644,000 Arabs. By 1922 there were 83,794 Jews and 663,000 Arabs. And by 1931 there were 174,616 Jews and 750,000 Arabs.[10] Of the Arab population of Palestine, less than 15 percent were Christians, most of whom were Greek Orthodox.

The population of Arab Palestine was made up of three types of people: the town dweller (*madani*), the villager (*quarawi*), and the nomad (*badawi*). Most Arabs lived in rural areas where the structure of society was semi-feudal. Elementary education was theoretically compulsory, but the Ottoman regime never provided universal public education for boys and much less so for girls. As a result the literacy rate was quite low. Higher education was available only to the rich. Since there was no college in Palestine, students had to go to Cairo or Beirut for the nearest higher education. The economy of Palestine remained in a comparatively primitive stage of development, largely because of the inadequacy of the schools. The average Arab was at a disadvantage compared with the Jewish immigrant whose settlement had superior educational institutions and a more advanced level of economic development. This economic and educational disadvantage had serious social and political repercussions, leading to seething resentments and intermittent outbreaks of violence.[11]

The official language of the Ottoman regime was Turkish, which was spoken in the government offices, courts, and public schools of Palestine. Nevertheless, the language of the people was Arabic, which was accorded special respect since it was the language of the holy book of Muslims, the Qur'an. Jews felt likewise about the Hebrew language, which had undergone a more or less recent renascence. It is widely held by both Israeli and Arab historians that Turkish never gained a fulsome acceptance among the populace of Palestine, thus remaining the language of an occupying force.[12]

Religious Context

It is well known that Jerusalem was and is the meeting place of the three Abrahamic faiths—Judaism, Christianity, and Islam—each of which venerates Jerusalem as a holy city. Jews venerate Jerusalem as the historic seat of power of the Davidic monarchy; Christians as the place of Christ's crucifixion and resurrection, as well as the Christian Pentecost; and Muslims as the third holy place of Islam from which Muhammad is thought to have ascended to heaven. Each of the Abrahamic faiths has a prominent

9. Ben-Arieh, "The Growth of Jerusalem in the Nineteenth Century," 262.

10. Hadawi, *Bitter Harvest*, 43–44.

11. Tibawi, *Arab Education in Mandatory Palestine*, 15–16.

12. Ibid., 136.

holy place of supreme symbolic importance in Jerusalem. According to Anthony O'Mahony, "for Muslims, the Haram al-Sharif is a symbol of victory; for Jews the Wailing Wall is a symbol of loss; and for Christians, the Holy Sepulchre a symbol of victory through loss."[13] The Jews, Christians, and Muslims of Jerusalem zealously guard the status quo of their shrines, so that their pilgrims can come from far and wide for the celebration of holy days and seasons, commemorating the sacred events and personages associated with the Holy City.

Each of the Abrahamic faiths also had its own residential enclave in Jerusalem. Under Muslim governance, occupied cities were divided into religiously defined neighborhoods, as dictated by the Qur'an and traditions of Islam. In the *millet* system of the Ottoman Empire, one's religion defined one's political status. By definition Jews and Christians belonged to the general category of *dhimmi*, people who were protected by a pact of protection. By an edict of the sultan, *dhimma* groups could be afforded the rights of the *millet*, authorizing them to regulate and perform the civil functions of marriage, education, and inheritance in their own communities. The first Christian *millet* was the Greek Orthodox Church. The Roman Catholic Church was not given *millet* status, but was allowed to perform the functions of the *millet*. Protestants were granted *millet* status in 1850.[14] Muslim scholars commend this arrangement as tolerant and humane.[15] Although obligated to live in self-contained neighborhoods, Jews and Christians governed themselves according to their own religious beliefs, laws, leaders, and courts. As long as they remained within their *millet*, abided by restrictions placed upon outward expressions of their faith, and paid a poll tax to the Muslim authorities, Jews and Christians were largely left to themselves.[16]

In Jerusalem, as in other Muslim-dominated settings, crossing over from one faith to another was quite uncommon. Most religious crossovers occurred through interfaith marriage, which is really a misnomer, since such unions required conversion as a condition of solemnization.[17] The penalty for converting to another faith was social ostracism in the case of Jews and Christians, and death in the case of Muslims. Coming from a democratic culture that cherished the value of religious freedom, the American Pentecostal missionaries did not fully appreciate the sacrifice they were asking of their potential Jewish and Muslim converts. What Lawrence Davidson says of American missionaries in general surely pertains to the missionaries from Azusa: "Coming from a culture that separated church and state, and made religion a personal choice, the first generation of missionaries were ignorant of, and unprepared to work in, a culture that divided itself into 'millets,' or religiously defined communities."[18]

13. O'Mahony, "Palestine Christians: Religion, Politics and Society," 9.

14. Ibid., 19–22.

15. Samir, "The Christian Communities, Active Members of Arab Society throughout History," 70–72.

16. Tibawi, *A Modern History of Syria*, 21–22.

17. Fargues, "The Arab Christians of the Middle East: A Demographic Perspective."

18. Davidson, *America's Palestine*, 5.

By the nineteenth century, Jerusalem was divided into four quarters: the Jewish Quarter, the Christian Quarter, the Muslim Quarter and the Armenian Quarter. Each quarter had its own cluster of buildings and neighborhoods oriented to a focal point.

During the time of the Pentecostal mission in Palestine, the *Jewish Quarter* was located where it had been since the thirteenth century CE, on a slope in the center of the city with a view of the Mount of Olives. Its main avenues were Meidan Street and the Street of the Jews, which ran eastward toward the Wailing Wall. No Christian or Muslim holy sites were located in this area. The Jewish Quarter increased in size as the swelling Jewish population acquired property, renovated old houses, and built new homes.

There were two varieties of Jews in Palestine. These were the Sephardim and the Ashkenazim. Since the sixteenth century the Sephardim dominated the Jewish community in Palestine. They traced their origins to the expulsion of the Jews from Spain during the Inquisition in the late fifteenth and early sixteenth century. Some found their way back to Palestine. Others settled in North Africa and other locations in the Middle East. The Sephardim adopted Arabic culture and accepted Ottoman citizenship. The Sephardi Chief Rabbi enjoyed considerable prestige in Ottoman society, holding the title of "the first in Zion" and the privilege of a detachment of Turkish guards.

During the nineteenth century a new group of Jewish people appeared on the scene in Jerusalem. These were the Ashkenazim. In Hebrew the term "Ashkenaz" literally means Germany. It refers to the Jews who settled in Central and Eastern Europe in the medieval period. In current usage, "Ashkenazim" denotes the Jewish people who are from Western, Central, and Eastern Europe. Until 1872 the Sephardim were in the majority, but by 1877 the Ashkenazim constituted about 60 percent of the total Jewish population. The Ashkenazim differed from the Sephardic Jews significantly. They followed different religious customs. They did not care to learn the Arabic language. They did not accept the authority of the Sephardic Chief Rabbi. And they did not wish to subject themselves to Ottoman rule. They preferred to remain under the consular protection of their country of origin.[19]

The Jewish community in Palestine was known as the *yishuv*.[20] Jewish source materials from the nineteenth century on employ the categories of "old yishuv" and the "new yishuv," drawing a distinction on the basis of the aim of settlement. The aim of the old yishuv was religious. It was founded upon a philanthropic base and relied on outside contributions of *halukka* money for its livelihood.[21] It originated with a

19. Friedman, "The System of Capitulations and its Effects," 280–81.

20. The Hebrew word *yishuv* literally means "settlement." This term refers to the Jewish residents of Palestine prior to the establishment of the state of Israel in 1948. The Jewish residents and settlers of Palestine were first identified as the *yishuv* in the 1880s.

21. The Hebrew word *halukkah* literally means "distribution." When a Jew living in the Diaspora could not make a pilgrimage to Palestine in person, he or she often gave financial help to those who could or to the Jewish settlers in Palestine. Such contributions were *halukkah* funds. This money was seen as a substitute for the donor's own personal pilgrimage. By contributing *halukkah* money, the Jews of the Diaspora were linking themselves with the *yishuv* in Palestine.

nucleus of Eastern European *hasidim*[22] who immigrated to Palestine at the end of the eighteenth century. Most of its members lived in close proximity in the Old City of Jerusalem, as well as in Safed and Tiberias, and devoted themselves to the study of Torah and worship.[23] While the aim of the old yishuv was religious, the aim of the new yishuv was political. The new yishuv consisted of settlers who established agricultural communities which were intended to be self supporting, and were dedicated to a renewal of Jewish nationalism and the end of the Diaspora and all it stood for.[24] For example, the Bilu Society intended "to raise the national banner and arouse toward it the sentiments of all those who go by the name of Jew."[25]

Not everyone concurs with the above terminology. Israel Bartal objects to a preoccupation with the terms "old yishuv" and "new yishuv." He argues that because these categories overlook the Sephardic Jewish population in Jerusalem, they misrepresent the Jewish presence in Jerusalem as it really was. The truth of the matter is that the Sephardic Jews had been well integrated into the socio-economic fabric of Ottoman Palestine for centuries before the arrival of the Ashkenazi Jews of the new yishuv.[26]

In the nineteenth century the *Christian Quarter* of Jerusalem was located in the northwestern part of the Old City. Its residents were mostly Greek Orthodox and Latin (Roman) Catholic, along with other Eastern Christians, such as the Assyrians, Syrians, Melkites, Maronites, Copts, and Ethiopians. Christians were concentrated in this sector of Jerusalem due to its proximity to the Church of the Holy Sepulchre. It is believed that the Church of the Holy Sepulchre was established by Helena, the mother of Emperor Constantine the Great, and completed in 335 CE. This magnificent church was composed of many parts and built in the shape of a cross. In 1808 it was destroyed by fire. There was a constant battle among the different Christians groups for control over the sanctuaries, chapels, and shrines of the Holy Sepulchre, which were largely controlled by the Greek Orthodox and the Latin Catholics. The Greeks and Latins blamed the Armenians for the fire, for whom they felt an intense animosity. However, others attributed the fire to a group of inebriated Greek Orthodox priests who lit a fire for warmth and attempted to extinguish it with brandy which they mistook for water.[27] This accusation was most likely a reflection of Arab resentment of Greek control over senior ecclesiastical appointments, barring local priests from high office in the Church.

22. The Hebrew word *hasidim* literally means "the pious," and refers to those Jews who maintained the highest standard of religious observance and moral purity. The *hasidim* should be distinguished from *hasidism*, as the latter applies to the movement, founded by Baal-Shem-Tov in Poland in the eighteenth century, which stressed the mercy of God and encouraged joyous religious expression through music and dance. Because it prized the value of ecstatic worship over Talmudic learning, *Hasidism* was condemned as a heresy in 1774.

23. Kaniel, "The Terms 'Old Yishuv' and 'New Yishuv': Problems of Definition," in *Jerusalem Cathedra*, I, 232.

24. Ibid., 233.

25. Bartal, "'Old Yishuv' and 'New Yishuv' Image and Reality," in *Jerusalem Cathedra*, I, 216.

26. Ibid.

27. Ben-Arieh, *Jerusalem in the Nineteenth Century*, 202–3.

There were three subdivisions of Christians in Jerusalem—Eastern Christians, Latin Catholics, and Protestants. The varieties of Eastern Christians were baffling to the Pentecostal missionaries who bunched them together as "Greeks" or "Greek Christians." While the majority of Christians in Palestine belonged to the Greek Orthodox Church, the proportion was decreasing with "defections" to the Catholic and Protestant churches. Other than the Greek Orthodox, the Eastern Christian family of churches included the Uniate Catholics (Armenian Catholics, Chaldean Catholics, Syrian Catholics, Melkites and Maronites) and the Monophysites (Armenian Orthodox, Syrian "Jacobite" Orthodox, Coptic Orthodox, and Ethiopian Orthodox). The Latin (or Roman) Catholics were viewed as newcomers by the Eastern Christians, since they had only returned to Jerusalem in 1847 after an absence of over 500 years since the Crusades. The Protestant Churches in Jerusalem were mainly the Church of England and the Lutheran Church of Germany which had joined in common cause to establish a Jerusalem bishopric in 1841. The joint Anglican-Lutheran venture continued until 1886. After a parting of the ways, the Anglican work was led by Bishop George Francis Blyth (1887–1914) and the Lutheran work was led by Pastor Carl Schlicht (1885–95). The missionary arms of the Anglican Church were the London Jews Society and the Church Missionary Society. The Lutheran Church managed the Syrian Orphanage and the Kaiserswerth Deaconesses' Homes.[28] At the turn of the twentieth century various missionary organizations and independent missionaries were active in Jerusalem. Between 1888 and 1894 the Keswick Conference in England sent thirty female missionaries to Palestine. Several of them later affiliated with the Church Missionary Society, but thirteen of them worked independently, starting day schools, visiting homes, and ministering to women and children.[29] A number of Protestant denominations established a visible presence in Jerusalem, including the Church of Scotland (1839), the Moravian Church (1853), the Adventists (1866), the Society of Friends (1869), and the Christian and Missionary Alliance (1890). In 1908 the Pentecostals arrived on the scene in Jerusalem.[30]

The focal point of the *Muslim Quarter* was the *Harem Sharif*, on which the Al-Aksa mosque and the Dome of the Rock are located. Muslims lived as close to the *Harem Sharif* (known as the temple mount by Jews and Christians) as they could, clustering near its eastern and northern perimeters. A large Muslim population resided near the Wailing Wall, which was sacred to the Jews. The Muslim enclave there, known as the Magharibah (North African) neighborhood, was near the Magharibah mosque, located above on the temple mount. This mosque commemorates one of the most sacred events of Islamic tradition, the night journey of the Prophet.

28. Richter, *A History of Protestant Missions*, 243–70.

29. Ibid., 243, 250; Thompson, *A Century of Jewish Missions*, 176–80.

30. *Souvenir of the Twentieth Commencement of the Missionary Institute, May 1st, 1902*, 8, Christian and Missionary Alliance Archives, Colorado Springs, Colorado; *"What Hath God Wrought?" 1907 to 1908, Eleventh Annual Report*, The Christian and Missionary Alliance, Adopted at the Annual Meeting of the Society, May 27, 1908, Nyack, NY, 24, Christian and Missionary Alliance Archives, Colorado Springs, Colorado; Colbi, *A History of the Christian Presence in the Holy Land*, 110–41; Tibawi, *British Interests in Palestine, 1800–1901*, 160–65; Vogel, *To See a Promised Land*, 96–123.

For Muslims, Jerusalem is the third most holy place of Islam because it was sanctified by the Prophet's Night Visit and Ascension. This sacred tradition is alluded to in Surah 17:1 of the Qur'an: "Limitless is His glory is he who transported His servant by night from the Inviolable House of Worship [at Mecca] to the Remote House of Worship [at Jerusalem]—the environs of which We had blessed—so that We might show him some of Our symbols: for, verily, He alone is all-hearing, all seeing."[31] The traditions surrounding this verse are expostulated in commentaries on the Qur'an and in the *hadith*, traditions attributed to the companions of the prophet Muhammad. Commenting on Surah 17:1, Muhammad Asad points out that the night journey of Muhammad and his Ascension are two stages of one mystical experience, dating to one year before Muhammad's flight to Medina in 621 CE. Asad states, "The Apostle of God, accompanied by the Angel Gabriel, found himself transported by night to the site of Solomon's Temple at Jerusalem, where he led a congregation of many of the earlier, long since deceased prophets in prayer; some of them he afterwards encountered again in heaven."[32] It is believed by Muslims that when the Prophet's conveyance, a winged steed named *Buraq,* set him down near the precincts of the long since razed Jewish temple, it was at this moment that Surah 43:45 was revealed: "Yet ask any of Our apostles whom We sent forth before thy time whether We have ever allowed that deities other than the Most Gracious be worshipped!"[33] This Qur'anic verse is thought by Muslims to teach that "no Religion really teaches the worship of other than Allah."[34] Muhammad then ascended to heaven by means of a celestial ladder placed down on the rock of Mount Moriah, now enclosed in the Dome of the Rock. When Muhammad arrived in the seventh heaven, he experienced the beatific vision, and before the night was over he was transported back to Mecca.[35]

Furthermore, it is held by Muslims that when the when Caliph 'Umar conquered Jerusalem in 637, he located the places hallowed by the Prophet's Night Vision. Guided by the Christian Patriarch Sophronius, 'Umar also discovered the site of the destroyed Jewish temple at the base of Mount Moriah, concealed under a dunghill, and unearthed it. 'Umar strictly ordered that no prayers be offered on or near it until the place was washed by rain three times. This place was commemorated by the Magharibah Mosque and the waqf property immediately adjacent to the Wailing Wall. In 691, the Umayyad Caliph, Abd al-Malik ibn Marwan, built the Dome of the Rock, which is falsely called the Mosque of Omar in popular parlance. When his son al-Walid built a large mosque at the southern end of the Haram, it was called *al-Aksa,* the Remote Mosque, to identify it with the "Remote Mosque" of the Surah 17:1.[36] After the recovery of Jerusalem from the Crusaders in the twelfth century, the son of the renowned Muslim commander Saladin, al-Malik al-Afdal Nurud-Din 'Ali, dedicated the

31. Asad, *The Message of the Qur'an,* 465.

32. Ibid., 1137.

33. Ibid., 854.

34. 'Abdullah Yusuf 'Ali, trans., *The Meaning of The Holy Qur'an,* 1273.

35. Tibawi, *Jerusalem: Its Place in Islam and Arab History,* 7.

36. Werblowsky, "The Meaning of Jerusalem to Jews, Christians, and Muslims," 9–10.

area outside the western wall of the *Harem Sharif* as *waqf*[37] property for the benefit of Moroccan residents and pilgrims. From that time the property adjacent to the Wailing Wall was the inalienable property of Moroccan Muslims.[38]

An appreciation of Muslim devotion to the sacred sites on the *Harem Sharif* is absolutely essential for a fair and unbiased understanding of the sanctity of Jerusalem as the third holy place in Islam and of its significance in the history of Palestine. In subsequent chapters the response of the Pentecostal missionaries to the Arab riots of 1929, provoked by the attempt of Zionists to purchase the *waqf* property near the Wailing Wall, will be discussed. It will become apparent that the Pentecostal missionaries failed to respect the Muslim veneration of the holy sites of Islam in Jerusalem.

The Armenians have maintained a presence in Jerusalem since the fourth century CE. The *Armenian Quarter* was situated on Mount Zion in the southwest corner of the Old City where they had acquired a church from the Georgians, which they dedicated to St. James, or "Surp Hagop," as he was called in Armenian. This was the James who was beheaded in Jerusalem in about 42 CE. Through the centuries the Armenians increased their property holdings to the point that they had a sizable complex consisting of churches, a convent, schools, and many houses. The Armenian Quarter stretched along the western wall from the Citadel of David on the north to the southern wall, and eastward to the Jewish Quarter. The Armenian population was rather modest, largely because the Armenian Christians did not receive converts and remained ethnically separate. The Armenians belonged to the Monophysite branch of Eastern Christianity.[39]

The Armenian Quarter was the most clearly defined and homogenous neighborhood in the Old City. The center of its life was the Convent and Church of St. James, surrounded by an inner wall, sealing it off from the rest of the city. For practical purposes, the Armenian Quarter was an independent unit, having its own network of public services. The Armenian Convent was the richest and largest in Jerusalem, with 350 rooms that could accommodate up to 3,000 pilgrims during the peak Easter season. The Armenians were adept and successful business people, known for their craftsmanship in tile, ceramics, silver lamps, elaborate carpets, and costly paintings.[40]

At the beginning of the twentieth century the Armenian population increased substantially as refugees from the massacres in Turkey flooded into Jerusalem. In reaction to its declining power, the Ottoman state embarked on an official policy of "deporting" the Armenian population in retaliation for alleged subversive activities. There was an added consideration. The Protestant missions in Turkey had opted for

37. The Arabic term *waqf* means literally "prevention" or "restraint." In Islamic law *waqf* property is a pious foundation that is free from being alienated and is safeguarded in perpetuity for purposes pleasing to God, i.e., mosques, schools, hospitals, the maintenance of scholars and pilgrims, and assistance to the poor.

38. Tibawi, *The Islamic Pious Foundations in Jerusalem*, 13.

39. Ben-Arieh, *Jerusalem in the 19th Century*, 243–46; Burgess, *The Holy Spirit: Eastern Christian Traditions*, 111–18.

40. Armstrong, *Jerusalem*, 264–66.

a strategy of proselytizing the Armenian Christians. The Muslim Turks knew that if the Armenians were gone, so would the Christian missionaries whom they regarded as intruders in *dar al-Islam*.[41] Although Palestine was Ottoman territory, the refugees were safe in the Armenian Quarter from the molestation of the Turkish authorities. They found shelter in the Convent of St. James with the monks, a privilege usually only afforded to the religious orders alone.[42]

Historical Context

Due to geopolitical developments at the turn of the 20th century, the prospects of Christian missions in Palestine were markedly improved. The history of missions in the region is inexorably related to Western colonialism.[43] Whether missionaries understood it or not, the interests of the Western powers directly influenced the ability of Christian missionaries to penetrate Jerusalem and Palestine, within *dar al-Islam*, with the Christian message.[44] To explain how this propitious opportunity came about, we must look back into the previous century.

Napoleon's campaign in Palestine in 1799–1800 had a long-term effect on Palestine, opening the door for the establishment of a Protestant presence in Jerusalem. In 1826 John Nicolayson had attempted to establish a Protestant Christian mission in Jerusalem but failed. In 1830 Muhammad 'Ali successfully wrested Palestine from Ottoman control and temporarily installed Egyptian rule under his son, Ibrahim Pasha. In the interest of placating the Great Powers, Ibrahim Pasha adopted an overtly liberal policy toward the expatriate non-Muslim population in Palestine. Nicolayson later remarked, "Only when the Egyptian forces headed by Ibrahim Pasha first entered Palestine could I really settle down in Jerusalem . . . and therefore the permanent Protestant mission proper could first be founded only in 1833."[45] With successive Egyptian victories in Syria and Asia Minor it appeared that the Ottoman Empire was on the verge of collapse. In order to prevent destabilization in the region, England, Russia, Austria, and Prussia intervened, pushed the Egyptians out of Asia Minor, Syria, and Palestine, and restored these territories to the sultan. Hence, Palestine was returned to the Ottomans in whose hands it remained for another eighty years.

Not since the Crusades had the Western powers found themselves with such an opportunity to regain control over the lands of the Bible. Prussia's Protestant king, Friedrich Wilhelm IV (1795–1861), seized the opportunity to propose a joint English-Prussian Anglican bishopric in Jerusalem. In spite of fears of a violently adverse Muslim reaction, the Ottomans reluctantly agreed and Michael Solomon Alexander

41. Pikkert, "Protestant Missionaries to the Middle East: Ambassadors of Christ or Culture," 91–96.

42. Armstrong, *Jerusalem*, 369–70.

43. Jongeneel, *Philosophy, Science, and Theology of Mission in the 19th and 20th Centuries*, 228; Neill, *Christian Missions*, 207–8, 215.

44. Murre-van den Berg, ed., *New Faith in Ancient Lands*, 4, 10, 17.

45. Cited in Carmel, "A Note on the Christian Contribution to Palestine's Development in the 19th Century," 303.

(1799–1845), a Jewish Christian, was installed as the first Anglican bishop in 1843. Alexander was followed by others. The conditions that allowed for the appearance of an Anglican bishop in Jerusalem also opened the door for an expanded Christian presence, including the first Latin patriarch since the Crusades, who was sent with the express purpose of neutralizing the Protestant influence. The competition among rival Christian bodies led to a struggle among European governments for political influence. Soon a plethora of foreign consular officials were ensconced in Jerusalem.[46]

The consuls served as advocates for their national citizens living in Palestine. This system was known as the "capitulations," a term taken from the chapters, *capitula,* in the treaties between the Ottomans and the European governments. The capitulations were based on the concept of extraterritoriality. At this time sovereignty was related to persons rather than territory. A ruler or state was thought to have the right to exercise jurisdiction over his or its nationals and not over aliens, who were subject to the jurisdiction of their country of origin, from which they had to seek protection. This system had particular value in a state in which juridical equality was not extended to nonbelievers in the dominant religion. In Muslim countries, such as Palestine, the jurisdiction of the Islamic courts did not apply to non-Muslims and aliens. According to the dhimma system, legal rights were only extended to those Christians and Jews who were Ottoman subjects. To resolve this inequity faced by extraterritorial nationals living in Palestine, a number of European governments made treaties with the Sublime Porte, securing the right to protect the interests of their subjects who were visiting or living in the Ottoman Empire.[47]

At first it appeared that the Capitulation system would benefit both sides. The Ottoman government did not have to administer the legal affairs of foreign visitors whose presence stimulated trade and increased security. However, with the decline of the Ottoman Empire, the system worked to its disadvantage, allowing for the flouting of local regulations. Foreign banks, post offices, and commercial houses outstripped local services and businesses. The consuls consolidated their power to the point of defiance of Ottoman authority, claiming immunity from Ottoman laws and local taxation. Finally, the Ottomans came to the realization that the Capitulations were working greatly to their detriment, redounding to their further humiliation by the West.[48]

The original intention of the Protestant bishopric was to seek converts among the Jews. Two significant mission organizations pursued this work, the Church Mission Society and the London Society for Promoting Christianity amongst the Jews. Despite considerable efforts, positive results were not forthcoming. The option of targeting Muslims never received serious consideration out of fears of arousing a violent response among the local population and stubborn resistance on the part of Ottoman officials. Hence, most Protestant missions chose the path of least resistance and proselytized the Arab Christian communities. The number of Arab Christians in

---

46. Shepherd, *The Zealous Intruders,* 107–21.

47. Friedman, "System of Capitulations," 281.

48. Gaudeul, "Encounters and Clashes," 252.

Palestine had increased steadily during the nineteenth century due to favorable political conditions in the late Ottoman Empire as a result of the political and economic influence of European nations. By 1914 the ratio of Christians to the general population of Palestine had risen to 25 percent, the highest proportion since the Crusades.[49] Christians attained higher levels of education and economic success than Muslims. Due to the social equilibrium caused by political changes in the Ottoman Empire, the Arab Christians were more receptive to the Western missionaries and benefited from the education provided by the missionary schools. As the Christians of Palestine emerged from the millet world and embraced the values of the Western missionaries, they were enabled to exercise a progressive influence in Palestinian society, for which the Western missionaries should be credited. The missionaries accomplished much good and made a significant contribution to the development of Palestine.[50] In the estimation of Alex Carmel, "nowhere else in the world were so many missionary institutions built in such a short time over such a small area as in Jerusalem in the second half of the 19th century."[51] These institutions included the Gobat School for Boys, the Syrian Orphanage, the Augusta Victoria Hospice, and several medical facilities throughout Palestine. Nevertheless, the "Christian mission among Christians" caused considerable tension among the Christian communities in Palestine and in the Christian world at large.

When the Pentecostal missionaries arrived in Jerusalem, increasing numbers of Jewish immigrants were arriving in Palestine. The Jewish immigrants came in two waves, known as the First and Second Aliyahs. The First Aliyah occurred from 1881 to 1904, the Second Aliyah from 1908 to 1912. The first Pentecostal missionaries arrived on the heels of the First Aliyah and at the beginning of the Second Aliyah. The First Aliyah differed from previous Jewish immigration in that it led to the establishment of about twenty agricultural settlements, adding about thirty-thousand to the Jewish population of Palestine. The founders of these settlements wanted to raise up a new generation of Jews who would support themselves by manual labor. Economically the settlements of the First Aliyah were largely unsuccessful. Without massive infusions of capital provided by Baron de Rothschild (1845–1934), they would have failed. Just the same, in asserting the historical ties of the Jewish people to the land of Israel and raising the banner of Jewish nationalism, the First Aliyah prepared the ground for the Zionist Movement, which inspired the Second Aliyah.[52]

To conclude, with Jewish immigration to Palestine on the rise, the stage was set for a clash of monumental proportions. The Ottoman regime in Palestine would soon be dismantled and replaced by the British Mandate. The ensuing battle between Arab nationalists and Zionist militants for supremacy over the Holy Land would not only

49. Mitri, "Christians in the Arab East," 853.

50. Kark, "The Impact of Early Missionary Enterprises on Landscape and Identity Formation in Palestine."

51. Carmel, "A Note on the Christian Contribution to Palestine's Development in the 19th Century," 306.

52. Ettiner and Bartal, "The First Aliyah: Ideological Roots and Practical Accomplishments," 198–99.

result in the downfall of British rule but also would demonstrate that the name of the holy city was a misnomer, for Jerusalem ("city of peace") has been the site of more violence, warfare, conquests, and inter-religious strife than perhaps any other city.

INTERCULTURAL CONNECTION?

One might rightly wonder what kind of connection could possibly be forged between Azusa and Jerusalem. Geographically, Azusa and Jerusalem were distant locations. The Azusa Street Mission, where the Pentecostal Revival originated, was located in Los Angeles, California; whereas Jerusalem, the place of the first Christian Pentecost, was located in Palestine, a remote region of the Ottoman Empire. The two cultures could not be more dissimilar. The host culture of Azusa was North American, English-speaking, literate, urban, mobile, industrial, and individualistic, with a social structure comprised of nuclear family units; whereas that of Palestine was Middle Eastern, Arabic-speaking, largely illiterate, rural, traditional, pre-industrial, and collectivistic, with a social structure made up of tribal and extended family units. Nonetheless, a connection of sorts was made between Azusa and Jerusalem when a company of brave souls at the Azusa Street Revival heard God calling them to go as missionaries to Palestine and without much hesitation headed off for Jerusalem. They went without the benefit of even the most rudimentary schooling in biblical studies, missiology, and comparative religion. The missionaries from Azusa neither recognized how woefully ignorant they were of the incommensurability between their image of Jerusalem and the realities on the ground, nor could they have comprehended that their world view was a reflection of the world from which they had come.

The Pentecostal missionaries went to Palestine as exemplars of the religious culture of the emerging Pentecostal Movement. In 1902 A. J. Tomlinson (1865–1943), soon to become a leading figure in the Pentecostal Movement, raised the idea of launching a "foreign mission work" in Jerusalem. He writes, "While we have had the love of Jerusalem in our heart for several years and been much interested to have it restored to God's chosen people, yet we feel now to begin to show our interest by taking some active part in the mission work there."[53] In Tomlinson's mind there was a connection between mission work in Jerusalem and the restoration of God's chosen people. Tomlinson's point of view was typical of the early Pentecostal rationale for missionary activity in Jerusalem. For Pentecostals, the logic of sending missionaries to Jerusalem was based on their fascination with Palestine as the ancestral home of the Jews and the birthplace of the Christian church. Further, Pentecostals seemed to think of their mission in Palestine as an act of solidarity with the Zionist project of restoring Jerusalem to the Jewish people. The outgoing missionaries did not seriously consider the possibility that solidarity with the Zionists might antagonize Jerusalem's Arab population. From the Arab point of view, the presence of pro-Zionist missionaries from the West would be seen in a decidedly negative light. That the Pentecostal missionaries could have possibly appreciated why Arabs resented their presence is unlikely.

---

53. Tomlinson, "Jerusalem," *Samson's Foxes* 2.1 (January 1902) 2.

The Pentecostal missionaries arrived in Jerusalem with little knowledge of the culture, languages, peoples, history, politics, and religions of Palestine. Their image of Jerusalem was constructed from mental pictures derived from their reading of the English Bible, anti-Arab stereotypes in popular Christian literature, slanted Western newspaper reports of current events in the Near East, and travel journals of Christian pilgrims and tourists extolling geo-piety.[54] The significance of missionary activity in Jerusalem was heightened for Pentecostals by its location, being the exact place of the outpouring of the Holy Spirit on the Day of Pentecost, recorded in Acts 2. Frank Bartleman likened the Azusa Street Revival itself to the original Pentecost in Jerusalem:

> Next to old Jerusalem there is nothing like it in the world. (It is on the opposite side, near half way around, with natural conditions very similar also.) All nations are represented, as at Jerusalem. Thousands are here from all over the Union, and from many parts of the world, sent of God for "Pentecost." These will scatter the fire to the ends of the earth. Missionary zeal is at white heat. The "gifts" of the Spirit are being given, the church's panoply restored. Surely we are in the days of restoration, the "last days," wonderful days, glorious days.[55]

Needless to say, Bartleman's mental image of Jerusalem was an inaccurate representation of Jerusalem as it was. This he discovered years later when he visited Jerusalem and remarked that "the 'Holy Land' of our closet visions and the Palestine of today are for the most part very different propositions."[56] Consequently, the world of Jerusalem proved to be as strange to the Pentecostal missionaries as the missionaries were to the indigenous population. The resulting estrangement on both sides was aggravated by mistrust exacerbated by painful memories of the Crusades and Western intrusions in the region.

Pentecostals possessed an image of Jerusalem that was slanted by their ideological interests. The eschatology of Pentecostals was embedded with an ideological perspective on Jerusalem. Jerusalem figured largely in the eschatological discourse of early Pentecostalism. Pentecostals understood certain select biblical passages to predict a fixed sequence of historical events that would culminate during the last days in the city of Jerusalem with the Jewish people converting to Jesus as their Messiah. This eschatological vision colored the Pentecostals' interpretation of current events happening in Palestine in the first part of the twentieth century. By and large, Pentecostals believed that the immigration of Jewish people to Palestine was a sign of the imminence of the second coming of Christ and a signal that very soon a chain reaction would be activated leading to the War of Armageddon and the establishment of Christ's Millennial Kingdom in Palestine. In retrospect, it is evident that image and reality parted company in Pentecostal eschatology. To begin, what the Pentecostals predicted did not happen. But, more than that, the Pentecostals were prejudiced in favor of Zionism.

---

54. Vogel defines geo-piety as "the expression of dutiful devotion and habitual reverence for a territory, land or space." Vogel, *To See a Promised Land*, 8.

55. Bartleman, *Azusa Street*, 63–64.

56. Bartleman, "Around the World By Faith: With Six Weeks in the Holy Land," 31.

By elevating the role of the Jews in their eschatological scenario, Pentecostals blocked from their field of vision the rights of other peoples, Arab Muslims and Christians, who made up the overwhelming majority of the population of Palestine.[57] As a result, the Pentecostal image of Jerusalem amounted to a representation of Jerusalem as seen through the eyes of geo-piety rather than an accurate picture of Jerusalem as it was.

Based on the above portrayal of Jerusalem as it was in 1906, it is evident that the Pentecostal missionaries from the Azusa Street Revival faced a steep challenge in adapting the Pentecostal message to the political, cultural, religious, and historical context of Palestine. How well they met that challenge and forged bridges of intercultural connection would in large part determine the success or failure of their mission. In the next four chapters, the history of the Pentecostal mission in Palestine from 1908 to 2007 will be narrated.

57. Aburish, *The Forgotten Faithful: The Christians of the Holy Land*, 3.

4 | Planting the Pentecostal Flag, 1908–1918

T HE NEXT FOUR chapters will narrate the history of the Pentecostal mission in Palestine from the arrival of the first missionaries in Jerusalem in 1908 to the current state of Pentecostal mission work in Israel and Palestine as of 2007. These narrative chapters are arranged in four historical periods of the mission: 1908–18, 1919–35, 1936–44, and 1945–2007. This chapter begins by reconstructing the objectives of the mission in Palestine and then tells the story of the planting of the Pentecostal flag in Palestine from 1908 to 1918. The historical narrative in the following chapters is reconstructed mostly from the reports of the missionaries themselves. The salient events of each period will be recounted and the accomplishments of the mission will be traced in terms of facilities, personnel, and outreach. Attention will also be given to pertinent articles in Pentecostal periodicals.

MISSION OBJECTIVES

A reconstruction of the objectives of the Pentecostal mission in Palestine is problematic, because the Pentecostal missionaries never attempted anything like strategic planning. One must rely on intermittent progress reports in missionary correspondence and the occasional pronouncements on mission policy in Pentecostal periodicals. From these primary sources, one can reconstruct a relatively coherent picture of how missionaries and denominational officials probably viewed the objectives of the mission in Palestine.

Based on the extant evidence, it can be surmised that the objectives of the Pentecostal mission in Palestine were three-fold.

Conversion of the Heathen

The first and foremost objective of the Pentecostal mission was "world evangelization."[1] In the terminology of the day, this objective called for the conversion of the "heathen."[2] By definition, the heathen were those who did not believe in the God of the Bible. Technically speaking, Jews and Muslims, who were adherents of monotheistic

---

1. Perkin, "Call to Advance," 9.

2. Aside from connotations of being uncivilized and irreligious, the term "heathen" by definition denotes a person who does not acknowledge the God of the Bible. Nowadays the use of this term is frowned upon.

Abrahamic faith, should be exempted from the category of heathen.[3] However, since Pentecostals rarely entertained such fine distinctions, their missionaries in Palestine conceived of the heathen as all who were not converted believers in Jesus Christ. Hence, the target population of their mission included the Muslims, Jews, Druses, and Bedouins, as well as Roman Catholics and Eastern Christians. All of the above were candidates for conversion as far as Pentecostal missionaries were concerned. The Pentecostal missionaries took it as axiomatic that only the evangelical Christian formulation of the Christian message offered the hope of eternal salvation; and further, that the Pentecostal full gospel formulation was supremely true.

The objective of conversion was not unique to Pentecostals. Other evangelical Christian missionaries in Palestine shared this objective, at least in theory. However, there was a tendency among longstanding Protestant missions in Palestine to eschew confrontational evangelism among Jews and Muslims and adopt an indirect approach that featured charity, education, and medical care.[4] For instance, the Jerusalem and East Mission of the Anglican Church eschewed confrontational evangelism and opted for inculcating the values of Western civilization through schools such as the Jerusalem Girls College. The same was true of the Christ Church School, St. George's School, the Bishop Gobat Boy's School in Jerusalem and the English High Schools for Girls in Jaffa and Haifa, as well as other schools founded by the Palestine Native Church Council.[5] The Pentecostals launched no such educational mission endeavors and in fact some of their missionaries were emphatically opposed to doing so.[6]

Baptism in the Holy Spirit with Tongues

The second objective was unique to Pentecostalism. Like the other Protestant missions in Palestine, the Pentecostals offered a doctrinal package made up of truths common to other evangelical Christians along with their own distinctive emphases. Unlike the other missions, the Pentecostals urged their converts to seek and receive the baptism of the Holy Spirit with speaking in tongues. For Pentecostals, this was their unique trademark. They viewed Spirit baptism with tongues as the essential means of empowering Christians for effectual missionary activity. Concerning the link between Spirit-baptism and missions, Allan Anderson writes, "It is very important to understand the significance of this, because just as Spirit baptism is Pentecostalism's central, most distinctive doctrine, so mission is Pentecostalism's central, most important activity."[7] In fact, Pentecostals were so adamant about making this connection that they strived to

---

3. At present Roman Catholic and mainline Protestant denominations generally look with disfavor upon the proselytizing of Jewish people. This is not true of conservative evangelicals and renewalists. The problem of Christian attempts to convert Jewish people is treated in Braybrooke, *Jewish-Christian Dialogue*, 96–108 and Saperstein, *Moments of Crisis in Jewish-Christian Dialogue*, 61–63.

4. Cleveland, *A History of the Modern Middle East*, 115–16.

5. Murre-van den Berg, ed., *New Faith in Ancient Lands*, 14–16; Colbi, *A History of the Christian Presence in the Holy Land*, 147.

6. Weaver, "The World Gone Mad," *Word and Work* 33.6 (May 1911) 167.

7. Anderson, *Spreading Fires*, 65.

convince other Christians that the Pentecostal way ought to be normative for Christian missionary praxis.[8] In a sense, one might say that the Pentecostal missionary strategy entailed a two-step order of salvation; first, a conversion of the heathen to the Christ; second, baptism in the Spirit with the sign of speaking in other tongues.

Planting of Self-Supporting Churches

The third objective of the Pentecostal mission was to establish self-supporting native churches.[9] The Pentecostal missionaries in Palestine intended to plant indigenous churches that would be self supporting, self governing, and self-propagating. Early Pentecostals embraced the three-self strategy which was adumbrated in the prior century by Rufus Anderson and Henry Venn and mediated to them through the writings of Roland Allen.[10] The following statement in a report from a conference of mission boards in South China is indicative of the prevalence of the three-self objective in Pentecostal missions: "Let us keep in mind that our goal is the establishment of a self-supporting, self-governing, and self-propagating Church in China."[11] Noel Perkin (1893–1979), missions director of the American Assemblies of God, and Donald Gee (1891–1966), chairman of the British Assemblies of God, were among the notable Pentecostal leaders who espoused the three-self strategy.[12] According to this strategy, the key to missionary success was the establishment of an indigenous church as soon as possible. This necessitated that missionaries identify, recruit, and train indigenous leaders. A close reading of the letters of the missionaries in Palestine shows they consciously monitored their progress toward the development of an indigenous church. In chapter 6, we will see how the three-self strategy came into play as a standard of evaluation when a delegation of American Assemblies of God leaders, including Perkin, paid a visit to the mission in Palestine in 1937.

PIONEER MISSIONARIES IN PALESTINE

In its first ten years the Pentecostal mission in Palestine gained a foothold in Jerusalem primarily due to the efforts of three pioneering missionaries, Lucy Leatherman, Charles Leonard, and A. Elizabeth Brown.

---

8. Bays, "The Protestant Missionary Establishment and the Pentecostal Movement," in *Pentecostal Currents in American Protestantism*, 50–67.

9. "Missionary Secretary's Report, 1925," Combined Minutes of the General Council of the Assemblies of God in the United States of America and Foreign Lands, 1914–1925, 47.

10. McGee, "Overseas (North American Pentecostal) Missions," 896–97; Shenk, "The 'Great Century' Reconsidered," 137–38.

11. "Modern Missionary Methods Examined: The Present Crisis in China," *Redemption Tidings* 2.8 (August 1926) 9.

12. Bundy, "Gee, Donald," *NIDPCM*, 662–63; McGee, "Perkin, Noel," *NIDPCM*, 982.

Lucy Leatherman

The distinction of being the missionary who planted the Pentecostal flag in Palestine belongs to Lucy Leatherman. As noted in chapter 2, Leatherman had experienced the Pentecostal baptism of the Spirit with speaking in tongues in 1906 at the Azusa Street Mission in Los Angeles. Years later she staked her claim for primacy among the Pentecostal missionaries in Palestine, declaring, "I was the first Pentecostal Missionary in Jerusalem and Egypt, where the Lord started the work soon after my arrival."[13] Leatherman arrived in Jerusalem in late 1907. We know little about her first months on the field. But we do know that the significance of missionary activity in Jerusalem was heightened for Leatherman by its location, being the exact place of the outpouring of the Holy Spirit on the Day of Pentecost, recorded in Acts 2. In her first letter, Leatherman exclaims, "Praise God! God started this movement in A.D. 33 in this dear old city, and the 'latter rain' is falling in 1908."[14]

From the outset, Leatherman met with many rebuffs. For starters, she was unable to afford an interpreter. "So far God has not provided the money for . . . someone to interpret." Those who could converse with her without an interpreter, the English-speaking Protestant missionaries, refused to endorse Leatherman's Pentecostal message. To make matters worse, the local Arab population took umbrage at her practice of glossolalia, describing it with an Arabic word denoting the tangling up of one's tongue. Leatherman attempted to correct them: "I tell them our tongues are not tangled up, they are loosened up." In the face of resistance from the locals, Letterman assured herself that God is "jealous for this land, and we will not be discouraged." She took comfort in the publication of a multi-lingual Pentecostal paper in Arabic, English, and Hebrew, about which she writes, "The message has been fought very bitterly by the Christians here, but the natives and Jews are the ones who appreciated the little paper we published, part in Arabic and part in English. If God wills, we will get out another issue, all in Arabic and Hebrew."[15] There is no evidence that a second issue ever appeared.

Perhaps one of the most important early developments in the Pentecostal mission in Palestine was the winning over of Anna Elizabeth Brown (1866–1940) to the Pentecostal cause. Brown had served as a Christian and Missionary Alliance missionary in Jerusalem since 1895. She was well known for her evangelistic work in and around Jerusalem and was regarded in Alliance circles as "one of the most effective missionaries in the country."[16] Reporting on Brown's baptism in the Spirit, Leatherman writes,

> Glory to God! Miss Elizabeth Brown . . . received her baptism more than two weeks ago. She had the real old-fashioned manifestations like many had at Azusa Street. The secret of the matter was she was so given up to God. Praise His name!

13. Leatherman, "Returned from S. America," *Word and Work,* 43.6 (June 4, 1921) 9.

14. *Apostolic Faith* 2.13 (May 1908) 1.

15. Leatherman, "Letter From Jerusalem," *Word and Work* 30.11 (November 1908) 347.

16. Smalley, *Alliance Missions in Palestine, Arab Lands, Israel,* 14–15.

> She came to my room and requested me to lay hands on her for her baptism. She felt waves of fire passing through her head and face and then began to speak in tongues. She sings the heavenly chant. It is precious to hear her.[17]

Apparently Brown's departure from the Christian and Missionary Alliance was amicable. An Alliance missionary writes, "She left our work in 1909 at the time of the disturbances caused by the Pentecostal divisions in the Alliance but remained a faithful friend during the following years."[18] From this time on, reports from Elizabeth Brown appeared regularly in Pentecostal periodicals. Her ministry included evangelistic visitation, a training home for Bible Women (indigenous parish workers) and weekly prayer and evangelistic meetings.[19] Brown later affiliated with the Assemblies of God and was appointed as one of the fledgling denomination's official missionaries in 1917.[20]

In the United States, Elizabeth A. Sexton, editor of the *Bridegroom's Messenger*, pondered a letter from Leatherman, dated May 26, 1908, and pictured in her mind the stirring events reported by the pioneering missionary, imagining the scene to be "not far from the very spot where the very first Pentecost fell on the 120 souls in the upper room." Sexton could hardly contain herself: "Praises burst forth as we see the prophetic vision, the dear old city of Jerusalem being shaken again by the power of God as on the day of Pentecost."[21] The stimulus for Sexton's response was the good news that "five have had the baptism of the Holy Ghost and speak in tongues as the Spirit gives utterance." This was just the beginning. Knowing that financial resources were required to sustain a Pentecostal mission in Palestine, Leatherman solicited funds for this purpose, asking, "Will you pray God to send means to open a full gospel mission, and a press to publish the upper room truths that the saints may gather together in one accord?"[22] Judging from ensuing reports in *Confidence*, a British Pentecostal periodical, Leatherman's prayer request must have gained a good return.

In 1908 the editor of *Confidence* reports, "Miss Leatherman forwards us a copy of the first Pentecostal Jerusalem paper (in English, with some columns in Arabic). It is called 'Promise of the Father.' Though very few have spoken in Tongues at Jerusalem, we believe that the Lord is specially interested in the Holy Land and will soon bless abundantly."[23] The editor, Anglican rector Alexander A. Boddy, had served as a short-term chaplain with the Church Missionary Society in Palestine and Egypt in previous years. Boddy warmed to Letterman's report of a convention in Ramallah, about six

---

17. *Apostolic Faith*, 2.13 (May 1908) 1.

18. Smalley, *Alliance Missions in Palestine,* 15.

19. "Pentecostal Items," *Confidence*, 5.1 (January 1912) 18. A. Elizabeth Brown's "retirement" from the CMA mission in Palestine is duly recorded in *The Annual Report of the Christian and Missionary Alliance,* 9.

20. "A. Elizabeth Brown, Application For Ordination Certificate," Flower Pentecostal Heritage Center, Springfield, Missouri.

21. Sexton, "Pentecost in Jerusalem, Palestine," *Bridegroom's Messenger*, 1.16 (June 15, 1908) 1.

22. "Letter from Lucy Leatherman," ibid.

23. Boddy, "Jerusalem," *Confidence,* 5 (August 15, 1908) 15.

miles north of Jerusalem, interjecting, "The Writer slept at Ramallah on his first visit to the Holy Land, when He was writing the book, 'Christ in His Holy Land.'"[24]

The celebrated Norwegian Methodist, Thomas B. Barratt, shared Boddy's interest in the Holy Land. In September 1908 he made a trip to Jerusalem and visited Lucy Leatherman. Barratt reported that the non-Pentecostal missionaries in Jerusalem and Palestine were working faithfully, but they "did not seem to understand as yet the importance of the '*Pentecostal Revival*' and what an impetus for good it would give the mission." Despite a cold reception from the other missionaries, Barratt reported that "Mrs. Featherman [sic] says she is sure of victory in the long run. A young man has lately been in Jerusalem from *Egypt* and returned about a fortnight ago filled with the Holy Ghost and speaking in tongues."[25] The young man in question was Ghali Hanna, an Egyptian evangelist. According to Leatherman's account, spiced with biblical allusions, Hanna received the baptism of the Holy Spirit in a hotel lobby located "inside the city wall, not far from where is David's tomb and the upper room, where the Holy Ghost fell on the disciples Jesus loved. Our brother was like Cornelius, he was prayed up and in about ten minutes after hands were laid on, he says his jaw fell down and he began to speak as the Spirit gave utterance."[26]

Lucy Leatherman's aspirations for a "full gospel mission" in Palestine were buoyed by a chain of events, beginning in September, 1908, when she laid hands on a visiting Syrian evangelist named Zarub and prayed for him to receive the Pentecostal baptism of the Holy Spirit with speaking in tongues. Her prayer was met with the desired effect. Upon returning to Syria, Zarub crossed paths with a Danish missionary couple, a Brother and Sister Mygind, who shared his Pentecostal experience. Together they organized a revival that would make a lasting impression on the Pentecostal mission in the region. Led by native workers, the revival immediately caught fire and was in full swing when Thomas B. Barratt arrived in Jerusalem. At first Leatherman was stymied because she had "no hall for him to hold meetings."[27] Seizing an opportunity farther afield, she arranged for Barratt to accompany her to the village of Shweifat.[28]

In a letter dated October 18, 1908, Barratt vividly describes the dramatic pneumatic manifestations that occurred during an afternoon courtyard meeting. After presenting a Bible study on the "latter rain" and "tongues," Barratt says that he sat down on the floor, waiting upon God. "Suddenly the Spirit fell on a Bible-woman close by . . . The trembling sounds that came over her lips rose at times with tremendous force, mixed with praises and shouts . . . The Bible woman laughed outright for

---

24. Ibid. Leatherman's paper and the convention in Ramallah are also mentioned in Sister Lydia, "Jerusalem," *Word and Work* (October 1908) 311: "That reminds me that Mrs. Lucy Leatherman has published a paper, 'The Promise of the Father.' She is now at the Ramallah convention, where we hear they are having a very good time. About 300 are there, I hear, and the speakers are much liked."

25. "Letter from Pastor Barratt," *Confidence* 7 (October 15, 1908) 19.

26. Letterman, "An Egyptian Missionary Receives His Baptism," *Bridegroom's Messenger* 2.23 (October 1, 1908) 1.

27. Leatherman, "Letter From Jerusalem," *Word and Work* 30.11 (November 1908) 346–47.

28. Leatherman, "Sound of Abundance of Rain," *Bridegroom's Messenger* 2.25 (November 1, 1908) 1.

very joy at times. But it was no wild, hysterical laugh, it had the real ring of 'Holy Laughter.'" Attracted by the strange sounds, a crowd of onlookers came to the gate of the courtyard and peered in to see what was happening. Just then the Bible woman's daughter began, as Barratt tells it, "to speak plainly in a very beautiful language. So when the neighbors came (the children and some young people had already come) she was speaking clearly with a loud voice in tongues." After some time she interpreted the meaning of her words in Arabic and English, sentence by sentence, accompanied by joyous shouts of praise. For about two hours, Barratt says, this young girl also sang in tongues. "I have never seen a stronger influence of the 'tongues' than this case. The people seemed convinced that God had spoken to them through this child."[29] Apparently the pneumatic manifestations at Shweifat also made a positive impression on the faculty of the nearby Protestant Syrian College, or, at least that is the gist of the story as related by the American Pentecostal Albert Weaver, who in a letter of June 5, 1909 reports, "Bro Barratt tells me that the Prof. of Beirut stood up in a meeting over which he was presiding and said if this is not of God nothing is of God."[30]

The effect of the revival in Shweifat was long lasting. Among those gathered in the courtyard that September afternoon was a young woman named Yumna Malick, who wrote a letter to Barratt, dated October 18, 1908, in which she apprised him of events that had transpired since he left. On the upside, Malick reported that two detractors who had publicly opposed the revival had since admitted the error of their ways. A professor from the Syrian Protestant College in Beirut had testified on behalf of the revival. But, on the downside, the girl who had spoken in tongues had been beaten by her father and forbidden to come to the meetings again. Furthermore, a schoolmistress in Shweifat, Sister Amelia, lost many students from her school, as "their parents would not send them any more to her because she has the Holy Spirit," as they put it. As for herself, Malick relates that she recently had a vision of the accusing devil falling from heaven under the power of the "precious Blood of Jesus," which filled her with laughter and joy. The impression that the revival had exercised on Malick was life-changing. Not many years later, with the encouragement and support of Pentecostal friends, Malick traveled to the United States to attend the Elim Missionary Training School in Rochester, New York. Following the First World War, she would return to the village of her birth to serve for many years as a Pentecostal missionary, collaborating with Elizabeth Brown and other Pentecostal missionaries in Palestine on many evangelistic tours and other endeavors.

In the wake of the Shweifat revival, Leatherman ventured out on a solo outreach trip in Syria. Beginning in Shweifat, she went to Beirut where she held meetings in an Adventist Church until she was barred on account of excessive noise. Moving on to Brumana she attempted to gain entrance to two Quaker schools but was turned away, about which she remarks, "We fully realize that this message of full salvation is only for

---

29. Barratt, "In Syria," *Confidence* 7 (October 15, 1908) 20.

30. Albert Weaver to Bro. Otis, "Sunderland, England," *Word and Work* 31.6 (June 1909) 124. Weaver was an American Pentecostal who shortly thereafter served as a short-term missionary in Palestine. The professor of whom he speaks was from the Syrian Protestant College of Beirut, then Syria.

'whosoever will.'"[31] Looking for a receptive audience, the intrepid Leatherman trudged on to Balbee, Damascus and Ryshia, sometimes walking, sometimes riding a mule. She writes, "I had many opportunities to witness in Ryshia on and I believe seed was sown that Jesus will bring forth fruit for eternity."[32] Then, retracing her steps, she made her way back to Palestine, stopping off in Nazareth and Tiberias, before returning to Jerusalem.

Lucy Leatherman had Pentecostal co-laborers in Jerusalem. In July of 1908 Elizabeth Sexton reports that T. J. McIntosh and his wife had "joined the other workers here and have very probably opened a Pentecostal mission in the city where Pentecost fell on waiting hearts." Gladdened by the arrival of the McIntoshes, Sexton declares, "The fire is burning and spreading and leaping from place to pace."[33] The McIntoshes were bumptious Pentecostal missionaries on a world tour of sorts.[34] According to a report in the *Apostolic Faith,* McIntosh was under the impression that the Lord told him to go to Palestine.[35] Now in Palestine, he borrowed from past experience in Hong Kong, where McIntosh and Mok Lai Chi produced a Pentecostal paper named "Pentecostal Truths."[36] He suggested the idea of setting up a printing press in Jerusalem. He also proposed to convene a Pentecostal convention, a practice employed in many places for promotion of Pentecostal spirituality. But McIntosh did not stay long enough to implement his ideas, as he returned to the United States for the winter with plans to return the following summer and conduct tent meetings in Jerusalem, Joppa, Beirut, Port Said, and Aden.[37]

It was not long before Leatherman herself was on the move. In the late fall of 1908 she accepted Ghali Hanna's invitation to go to Assiout, Egypt and hold revival meetings. By December 1, 1908 Leatherman was reporting on the results of her ministry in Egypt. With some overstatement she exclaims that "God is baptizing souls with the Holy Ghost in this city." One man, a "great lion of a fellow has been saved and sanctified, and baptized with the Holy Ghost and fire." She claims that this man had "spoken in an Italian tongue, that it has been translated that he speaks of a great Pentecost." We get a more realistic picture from Leatherman's admission that she had only been out of the yard four times in seventeen days, supposedly because she had "been given up to praying, altogether."[38] As the revival picked up momentum, Leatherman reported, "Some are singing the song of the redeemed, or the 'heavenly choir' we have in Assiout."[39]

31. Leatherman, "A Missionary Trip Through Syria and Palestine," *The Pentecost* 1.4 (December 1908) 5.

32. Ibid.

33. Sexton, "Pentecost in Jerusalem," *Bridegroom's Messenger* 1.17 (July 1, 1908) 1.

34. Woods, "Failure and Success in the Ministry of T. J. McIntosh, the First Pentecostal Missionary to China."

35. *Apostolic Faith* (May 1908) 4; Bays, "The Protestant Missionary Establishment and the Pentecostal Movement," 54.

36. The masthead of McIntosh's paper is reproduced in *Confidence* 5 (August 15, 1908) 21.

37. "From Brother T. J. McIntosh," *Bridegroom's Messenger* 2.38 (May 15, 1909) 2.

38. Leatherman, "From Assiout," *Bridegroom's Messenger* 2.29 (January 1, 1909) 1.

39. Leatherman, "From Egypt," *Bridegroom's Messenger* 2.30 (January 19, 1909) 3.

By January 1909 Ghali Hanna was ecstatic over the progress of the revival. Exuding gratitude to Leatherman, he wrote to Alexander Boddy, "God in His love has sent us our dear sister, Lucy M. Leatherman, who was used in God's hands to lead us to this precious truth of Holy Fire. Five of us here in Assiout have already received the Baptism, and speak in tongues as the Spirit gives utterance."[40] He wrote similarly to the *Bridegroom's Messenger*: "Sister Lucy M. Leatherman came here to Assiout about six weeks ago, and God is using her mightily in saving, sanctifying and baptizing souls."[41] According to Leatherman's count, one hundred had been "saved" in ten weeks as the revival outgrew the meeting place to the point that "many have to go to the fields to hold meetings." To top it off, "many have received 'Roral Goodness,' the Arabic word for the Holy Ghost."[42] Just the same, the rigors of the revival had taken a toll on Leatherman's health. Later she recalled how she was suffering from a "congested lung" in Egypt yet toiled on out of a sense of "deep consecration to Him" even though she knew her condition was serious.[43] Nonetheless, Leatherman's ministry in Assiout was not in vain. When A. H. Post arrived on the scene in 1910, he observed, "We have a small beginning of a real Pentecostal work here in Egypt, very largely at Assiout."[44] It would be fair to construe the work done by Lucy Leatherman in Egypt as a foundation on which other missionaries, most notably the incomparable Lillian Trasher, would later erect a major Pentecostal mission complex.

Leatherman returned to Jerusalem long enough to pack her bags and head off on a tour through China, Japan, and the Philippines, arriving back in the United States in 1911. In her correspondence from the Far East she often spoke as if they had left her heart in Jerusalem.[45] She often expressed a longing to return to Jerusalem, which she did in 1912.[46] While Leatherman was in distant lands, A. Elizabeth Brown was in the process of severing her official ties with the Christian and Missionary Alliance and establishing a network of support in Pentecostal circles, mainly in America. In a letter, dated May 7, 1909, she tells her readers of her new commission as an evangelist in the villages of Palestine and then asks for their support: "As I enter this service, it is laid upon my heart to ask from God, some who will be 'helpers together by prayer'—prayer partners, who will commit themselves definitely with us to the salvation of souls in these Palestinian villages—they to prevail in prayer in the power of the baptism of the Holy Ghost and fire."[47] She was forthright about her financial needs, estimating the cost of supporting her missionary work, including a modest salary for a Bible woman, to be between $100 and $150 per month. Brown proved to be a consummate fundraiser, which will be evident as the historical narrative continues. She undoubtedly

40. Hanna, "Egypt," *Confidence* 2.1 (January 1909) 22.

41. Hanna, "Pentecost in Egypt," *Bridegroom's Messenger* 2.32 (February 15, 1909) 1.

42. Leatherman, "Apostolic Revival in Egypt," *The Pentecost* 1.5 (January–February, 1909) 5.

43. Leatherman, "From Sister Lucy Leatherman," *Bridegroom's Messenger* 3.48 (October 15, 1909) 2.

44. Post, "Egypt," *Confidence* 3.7 (July 1910) 165.

45. Leatherman, *Bridegroom's Messenger* (November 15, 1909) 1; (December 1, 1909) 4.

46. Leatherman, "Coming Home," *The Pentecost* 1.10 (September 15, 1909) 4

47. Brown, "Requesting Prayer for Palestine," *Bridegroom's Messenger* 2.41 (July 1, 1909) 1.

recognized that the development of an ample support network necessitated itineration back home, the cultivation of major contributors, and the solicitation of new "prayer partners."

With the need for expanding her support base in mind, in 1910 Brown left for a furlough in the U.S. While on furlough she found an answer to prayer in the person of Mary Smithson, a teacher at Holmes Bible and Missionary Institute in Altamont, South Carolina, who had sensed a call to Jerusalem and inquired of Brown if she might join her in Palestine. Brown was overjoyed and in her letters to the *Bridegroom's Messenger* immediately made known her need for funds to cover the tickets and a year's rent in Jerusalem which had to be paid in advance. With the help of Smithson, Brown hoped to open a Pentecostal Training Home in Jerusalem. Her eagerness to return to Jerusalem was palpable: "My heart is longing to get back to the people among whom I have lived and labored for nearly sixteen years."[48] Upon receiving word that the tickets were in hand, Elizabeth Sexton made an editorial comment in the *Bridegroom's Messenger* that was indicative of the attitude of the Pentecostal constituency toward the mission in Palestine. She writes, "We are interested in dear Jerusalem and in those workers whom God has called to represent Pentecost in the city where the Spirit first fell among waiting saints. Our prayers shall ascend for these, asking God to go before them, and prepare the way for the opening of the Pentecostal Home and Bible School of which He has been speaking to them."[49] These prayers were answered, as the *Bridegroom's Messenger* published letters from Brown and Smithson, telling of their journey to and arrival in Jerusalem.[50]

Charles Leonard

In the meantime, Charles Leonard of Springfield, Massachusetts, had sensed a call to Jerusalem. Leonard was an independent evangelist and a close associate of Samuel and Addie Otis, leaders of the Pentecostal Movement in New England and proprietors of the Holiness-Pentecostal periodical, *Word and Work*. An article entitled, "Missionary to Jerusalem," provides a glimpse of the function of Pentecostal periodicals in raising funds on behalf of "faith" missionaries. After mentioning Leonard's financial needs, the editor, Abbie Morrow Brown, notifies her readers that "any funds sent here would reach him at an early date."[51] The money must have come in because the next issue reports that "Brother Leonard sailed on the 7th (of November) as he expected and that he was in the best of spirits. Praise God from whom all blessings flow."[52]

Apparently Leonard only went as far as England because the next issue has a letter from his wife, Linda M. Leonard, dated May 31, 1909, telling of their attendance at the International Conference at Sunderland, the parish of Alexander Boddy. It

48. Brown, "Two Missionaries for Jerusalem," *Bridegroom's Messenger* 4.73 (November 1, 1910) 2.

49. Sexton, "Going with a Message," *Bridegroom's Messenger* 4.76 (December 15, 1910) 1.

50. "From Our Missionaries in Jerusalem," *Bridegroom's Messenger* (April 15, 1911) 4.

51. "Missionary to Jerusalem," *Word and Work* 30.10 (October 1908) 306.

52. "Missionary to Jerusalem," *Word and Work* 30.11 (November 1908) 337.

would appear that Leonard had garnered support from the newly founded Pentecostal Missionary Union. Its stated purpose was "to co-operate with those Pentecostal workers who felt called to the foreign field and to assist them in every way possible." As Linda Leonard puts it, it was "very helpful to meet with such a gathering of persons from various parts of the world who were of one mind and Spirit being drawn together by the one bond of union in Christ."[53] One can surmise that the purpose of the Leonard's extended stopover in England was to expand their support base.

It was not until the fall of 1909 that the Leonards made the journey to Jerusalem, arriving on September 25, 1909.[54] They took up temporary residence with a Miss Lovell, an independent missionary who operated a group home for blind orphan girls. In exchange for two rooms for their family of seven, the Leonards agreed to help Miss Lovell in her ministry. On their first missionary excursion the Leonards ventured out to Bethlehem with an Arabic-speaking Bible Woman and were gratified "to see how her words were received when she spoke to any about Jesus." They visited a Muslim home in which the family asked that the Bible be read to them. Nonetheless, the Leonard's overall impression was not very positive. They write, "Such things encourage us, but things seem dry and shut up spiritually in Jerusalem."[55] One month later Brother Leonard was singing a different tune. It seems that he had confirmation of God's call to Jerusalem and his family now felt like it was their home. Leonard reported that a promising field of service had opened up to him, as he was teaching English to young Jewish men whom he hoped to evangelize. He hinted to the folks back home that he could make use of Scripture portions and tracts in Yiddish if he had them.

Leonard soon developed a network of close associates that included E. O. Jago, Archibald Forder, and a Brother Camp. According to William Smalley, in his manuscript on the mission work of the Christian and Missionary Alliance (hereafter CMA) in Palestine, Jago was characterized as loud, flamboyant, sociable, friendly, undignified, unscholarly, and much loved wherever he went. Jago was stationed in Hebron with the CMA.[56] Although his original intent was to evangelize Jews, he was assigned to work with Arabs, whom he referred to as "the dark-skinned, dark-souled sons of Ishmael." Jago found the Muslim population of Hebron to be "as fanatical a people as you will find on the face of the earth." He observed that those few who converted to Christianity tended to be children, and after doing so their lives were threatened if they admitted that they believed in Christ. One such young girl, Jago reports, was chained to a wall and beaten, but was undaunted and said to her family, "You may beat me but I love the Lord Jesus Christ." Her courage and that of other young converts proved to Jago that "Mohammedans can be saved."[57] Eventually Jago established an

53. Leonard, "Letter From England," *Word and Work* 31.6 (June 1909) 124.

54. Brown, "Personal," *Word and Work* 31.10 (October 1909) 227; Brown, "From Our Missionaries in Jerusalem," *Bridegroom's Messenger* 4.84 (April 15, 1911) 4, states that "Brother Leonard came to Jerusalem about a year and a half ago."

55. Leonard, "From Jerusalem," *Word and Work* 31.11 (November 1909) 265.

56. Smalley, *Alliance Missions in Palestine,* 25.

57. Jago, "A Great Crisis! The Mohammedan's Slogan, a Call to the Church to Awake," *Latter Rain Evangel* (October 1913) 2–7.

underground railroad of sorts for secreting converts away from Hebron to the protection of the CMA community in Jerusalem.

Forder originally came to Palestine in 1891 with an independent mission in Kerak, east of the Dead Sea. After the Church Missionary Society took over the work in Kerak, Forder could not continue because he was not an Anglican.[58] In 1897 he then affiliated with the CMA; and later served as a Pentecostal missionary.[59] Prior to the arrival of the Pentecostal missionaries, Forder had served valiantly in the region of Moab. A turning point occurred during his time of service in Kerak when his wife died and Arab Muslims took pity on Forder and assisted with her burial. A mystical bond was formed out of shared grief. As the local chiefs expressed it, "Now you have buried your dead in our midst you have become a son of the land, one of ourselves, and you must not think of leaving us." From this point on, Forder observes, "we were better friends than ever, and the work went well."[60] Eventually his Muslim friends began to show interest in Forder's Christian teachings and he seized the opportunity to evangelize them. By 1909 Jerusalem was Forder's home base, and his ministry consisted of itineration among Bedouin encampments in the region of eastern Palestine and Sinai.[61]

Brother Camp was a tent-making missionary who taught in the Friends School in Ramallah and spent weekends as a voluntary missionary in Jerusalem. Although he was an independent missionary, he was regarded by the CMA as "in full fellowship with the Alliance."[62] According to Leonard, Camp "loved the Jews especially, and whilst in Jerusalem he lost no opportunity of presenting the Gospel to them, notwithstanding the persecution he received at their hands." Leonard recalls a time when Camp came home "with his clothes torn and muddy, and with marks where the stones had struck him. But he went out the next day just the same to preach to them."[63] On behalf of these friends, Leonard pleads, "These brethren with the other missionaries throughout the Turkish domain all need our sympathies, prayers, and help, as this is a very hard field, being under Mohammedan rule."[64]

At this time many missionaries, including Leonard and his friends, viewed the prospects for the evangelization of Jews and Muslims as quite promising. Jago saw the time as ripe for Jewish and Muslim evangelism because of a "decided change as to the reception of the gospel by Mohammedan and Jew." As evidence of this change, he observed that "whereas once and that until recently they bitterly opposed the missionaries, and foreigners, now some of the chief officials and Jews are sending their

58. Forder, *With the Arabs in Tent and Town*, 76–79.

59. Ibid., 81; Smalley, *Alliance Missions in Palestine*, 16; Schmidgall, "American Holiness Churches in the Holy Land, 1880–1990," 72; Eddy, "Islam in Syria and Palestine," 71.

60. Forder, *With the Arabs and Tent and Town*, 50.

61. Ibid., 45–50, 57, 76–79, 81; Forder, "And Ishmael Will Be a Wild Man," *Latter Rain Evangel* 1.11 (August 1909) 2–7.

62. *Twelfth Annual Report of the Christian and Missionary Alliance*, 15.

63. "Death of Brother Camp," *Word and Work* 32.7 (July 1910) 219.

64. Weaver, "News from Palestine," *Word and Work* 31.12 (December 1909) 301.

children to the Alliance school." Muslims were showing an interest in having the Bible read to them. According to Leonard, all of this was cause "for rejoicing and thankfulness to God, and should call forth earnest prayer for still greater conviction on the people."[65] Forder was likewise bullish on the prospects of Muslim evangelization. His sympathies with Muslims were to some extent countervailing among Pentecostals. He writes, "Much is heard about the return of the Jews to their own land, and the re-peopling of Palestine, but nothing has been written or told about the re-peopling of the land across the Jordan, the old country of Moab, that was written about and famous long before the Jews possessed their land." Forder was quick to share success stories of evangelizing Muslims. Once he gained their trust, he found that Muslims were open to hearing the Christian message. Some even became secret converts. Forder was indebted to the Muslims for protecting him from danger during a clash between Arab rebels and Ottoman Turks in the city of Kerak.[66] In a talk at a Pentecostal church in Chicago in 1911, he concludes, "It will be a lasting disgrace to the world of missions if the Moabites are not evangelized."[67]

The Pentecostal missionaries in Palestine were in a strategic position to report on events on the ground in Jerusalem. That their reports were slanted, one can see from Leonard's observations concerning the Jewish community in early 1910. He writes, "Many of the Jews admit that there must be the supernatural as it was in the days of Moses to bring about a restoration."[68] Leonard is alluding to the restoration of a Jewish homeland in Jerusalem. As with virtually all of the Pentecostals missionaries, Leonard was sympathetic to the Zionist project, for reasons that will be elucidated in chapter 8. He was especially interested in the increased activity at the Jewish Wailing Wall. He observes in 1910 that whereas the Jews used to go to the wall adjacent to the temple mount on Fridays, now they are going there every day "to write prayers and put in the crevices of the rocks, burn candles, weep, moan, read and sway their bodies and kiss the stones."[69] To Leonard this development appeared to be an indication of "an increase in soul travail." He offers a telling commentary: "Now what these, the seed of Abraham, are praying for in their blindness and superstition is what the Spiritual Israel is praying for and expecting—*The Messiah*."[70] We might miss a significant nuance if we pass over Leonard's comment too quickly. Leonard points to the common ground between Judaism and Christianity, i.e., a shared messianic expectation, yet he swiftly dismisses it. With his own perspective as a criterion of validity, he judges Jewish messianic expectation as the product of "blindness and superstition." Leonard's anti-Judaism surely must have been a formidable impediment to his relationship with the Jewish community in Jerusalem.

65. Leonard, "News from Palestine," *Word and Work* 31.12 (December 1909) 301.

66. "Syria—Safety of Brother A. Forder," *Confidence* (January 1911) 15.

67. Forder, "The Re-peopling of Moab," *Latter Rain Evangel* 3.6 (March 1911) 7–8.

68. Leonard, "Some Impressions about Jerusalem and Palestine," *Word and Work* 32.1 (January 1910) 28.

69. Ibid.

70. Ibid.

It is ironic that while most of the Pentecostal missionaries sympathized with the Zionist movement, they shared Leonard's pejorative view of Judaism. Their attitudes toward Arab Muslims were also were generally scornful. Archibald Forder stands out as a notable exception to this generalization. In some ways his views were consistent with his fellow missionaries, but in other ways they were countervailing. For example, on the one hand, he agreed with his colleagues when he averred, "What Jerusalem really needs is a revival of real religion on Pentecostal lines, and nothing short of this will avail for the final redemption of the Land and City"[71] On the other hand, he espoused a positive view of the virtues of the Arabs. Forder had a deep affection for Arab peoples, especially the Bedouin tribes among whom he itinerated widely. Using St. Catherine's Monastery as a home base, Forder made many evangelistic forays among the Bedouins encamped in secluded locations of the Sinai. With fondness he remembers, "While drinking our after-supper coffee, I told these people the Old, Old Story, and have reason to believe that some, at least, realized that they were sinners and their only hope was in the Saviour Jesus Christ."[72]

The Leonards continued to enjoy a close association with the Christian and Missionary Alliance in Palestine. They moved into the rented house of a CMA missionary, Lucy Dunn,[73] while she was off on an extended evangelistic mission in Arabia. This house was located near the newly built CMA tabernacle, later known as the American Church. With a seating capacity of 200, this building was often utilized by the Pentecostal missionaries for conventions and other special meetings. At this juncture the Pentecostals had no mission buildings other than rented houses.

Leonard's letters are sprinkled with tales of evangelistic forays. On one occasion, Leonard went with a CMA native evangelist named Hannush to Emmaus, "distributing religious literature and reading the Bible to the natives with blessed results." Leonard writes,

> We found twenty Moslems sitting out in the sun, going through one of their hourly devotions, which they do five times a day. We read the Scriptures and talked to them about Jesus and they listened attentively. Their Sheikh was sitting by and several of them turned to him and said, "Why have you not told us these things?" Then he got a little stirred up and said that we should not come around to lead the people from the good way; but with it all he was very nice, accepted a gospel and promised to read it.[74]

In reflecting on the above incident through his Pentecostal lens, Leonard employed the metaphor of spiritual warfare in sizing up the challenge of evangelizing Muslims. He insisted that this was a battle that could be won only through supernatural spiritual empowerment. He reasoned that since Jerusalem was the center of

71. Forder, "Some Facts about Modern Jerusalem," *Latter Rain Evangel* (December 1910) 9.

72. Forder, "Hunting Arabs at Sinai," *Latter Rain Evangel* (January 1913) 13–14.

73. Lucy Dunn attended A. B. Simpson's Missionary Training Institute in Nyack, New York and went to Palestine as a missionary in 1890. She affiliated with the Christian and Missionary Alliance in 1893. Thompson, *A Century of Jewish Missions*, 179.

74. Weaver, "Letter From C. S. Leonard," *Word and Work* 32.3 (March 1910) 88.

the world, it was also the "devil's stronghold and where he yet, we believe, will put up the strongest fight of his existence."[75] This was Leonard's way of making sense out of the resistance of Muslims to Christian evangelism. Another explanation might be that unlike his friend, Archibald Forder, he was caught in the grip of Islamophobia.

Nothing encouraged the Pentecostal missionaries in Palestine more than re-inforcements in the form of incoming missionaries. Leonard mentions the arrival of two new missionaries on the scene in Jerusalem, James Roughhead and Nathan Sapirstein.[76] The former was an Englishman, sent out by the Pentecostal Missionary Union in the spring of 1910. At the time of his commissioning he said, "It is now over two years since I received my Baptism, and over 1 ½ years since He called me to Jerusalem, and we expect some hard work there, and God has given me a message, 'Jesus must reign,' and if He has set His throne up in us then He will reign and bring others to Himself."[77] Leonard confirmed Roughhead's arrival in a letter dated April 7, 1910, in which he also told of the arrival of Saperstein, a Russian Jew who had, in Pentecostal jargon, "received his Pentecost" in Mrs. Moss' mission. Sapirstein's min-istry was targeted at the numerous Russian pilgrims in the Holy Land. Leonard was also buoyed over a Church Missionary Society (hereafter CMS) missionary who was seeking "her Pentecost." He also mentions a visitor from Wisconsin, interjecting that "the Lord is stirring her up along the lines of healing and Pentecost." Most exciting of all, though, Leonard proudly announced the birth of a daughter, Miriam Esther.[78]

Soon after Roughhead's arrival, he and Leonard coincidentally traveled to Shweifat, Syria, near Beirut without each other's knowledge. Leonard arrived just one day earlier. In their reports both Roughhead and Leonard refer to Barratt's momentous visit. Roughhead remarks, "This is the place where Pastor Barratt was made a great blessing two years ago."[79] Leonard points out that this was "the place where the fire fell when Bro. Barratt visited Syria and found several real hungry hearts."[80] The min-istry of Leonard and Roughhead went well enough in Sheifat for Leonard to "safely say that the Lord met and saved all who were old enough to believe." Even though he may have been somewhat disappointed that "the Lord did not come in mighty outward manifestations, but in stillness, filling hearts with joy and peace," Leonard still came away with an assurance that "God is working mightily in Old Palestine and Syria." He told of a CMS missionary "receiving her baptism" in the village of Kafr Josef, which opened the door for many "Greeks" to attend meetings in a good sized hall. Roughhead beamed, "Since coming here I have had a previous impression confirmed that God is working more in other lands than at home."[81] Not to detract from the satisfaction that Roughhead and Leonard derived from their work at Kafr Yosef, in

75. Ibid.

76. Leonard, "Jerusalem, Palestine," *Word and Work* 32.5 (May 1910) 149.

77. "Off To Jerusalem," *Confidence* 3.4 (April 1910) 89.

78. Ibid.

79. "Latest News from our Jerusalem Missionary," *Confidence* 3.7 (July 1910) 172.

80. Leonard, "Jerusalem, Palestine," *Word and Work* 32.7 (July 1910) 218.

81. "Latest News from our Jerusalem Missionary," *Confidence* 3.7 (July 1910) 172.

their reports one can discern indications of what Alex Carmel calls the "Christian mission to Christians." For the term "Greeks" denoted Eastern Christians. As with most Protestant missions in Palestine, when the Pentecostals found that Eastern Christians were receptive to their message, they gravitated towards proselytizing them rather than evangelizing Jews and Muslims, who were far less receptive.

By the end of the summer of 1910, Leonard was ebullient over what he perceived as an increased response to the full gospel message. He writes, "The people eagerly hear the truth as presented thru interpretation . . . Some of these poor ignorant ones are entering in before those who have had enlightenment for years." For instance, he approvingly tells of a woman who showed him her corn barrel, claiming that the miller has verified that her corn turns out better than other people's because she prays over it. Leonard reports that he had the opportunity to preach in four different schools, reaching an audience of about 400 pupils. At one school, which he dubs as "Jesus' school," he thought that "all have believed who are capable of believing."[82] After being in Jerusalem for one year, Leonard was optimistic. Looking back over a "year of blessing," he and his wife could see that their work was not done there yet.[83] With the fields white for harvest and new doors opening, Leonard received word from his friends, the Weaver's, that they were in Switzerland on their way to "help our dear Bro. Leonard in the work in Palestine and Syria."[84] On top of that, Frank Bartleman, who had crossed paths with the Weaver's in Amsterdam, sent word that the next stop on his world tour of Pentecostal mission stations would be Jerusalem.[85]

Bartleman arrived on September 11, 1910. Leonard reports that he was in good health and Lord was making him a blessing to many.[86] According to Bartleman, he was cordially received by the Leonard family. Bartleman's impressions provide us with an example of how a North American Pentecostal perceived the people, places, and religions of Palestine. He writes, "At last I stood at the centre of the world. The most sacred and historical spot of all ages."[87] He noted that the population of Jerusalem was Jewish, yet with an international complexion, which evoked in Bartleman an image of "what it will be in the 'last days,' when all nations will gather for the final 'Armageddon.'" He takes comfort in the thought that "God has given it to the Jews, and will give them Palestine also."[88] Reporting on a trip to Bethlehem and Hebron with Leonard, Bartleman observes that Bethlehem is largely Christian but of a kind that he thought was "without Christ." At Hebron he observed Jewish people wailing as they prayed, just as they did at the Wailing Wall in Jerusalem. "They wept for their desolate state as a nation."[89] He also visited the CMA station in Hebron. However, his

82. Leonard, "Jerusalem," *Word and Work* 32.8 (August 1910) 251.

83. Leonard, "Jerusalem, Palestine," *Word and Work* 32.10 (October 1910) 311.

84. Weaver, "Regions Beyond," *Word and Work* 32.9 (September 1910) 281.

85. Bartleman, "Work Abroad," *Word and Work* 32.9 (September 1910) 284–85.

86. Leonard, "Jerusalem, Palestine," *Word and Work* 32.10 (October 1910) 311.

87. Bartleman, "Around the World By Faith: With Six Weeks in the Holy Land," 30.

88. Ibid., 41.

89. Ibid., 48.

most memorable side-trip in Palestine was in the Galilee region, after which he states, "My Bible was fast becoming a new Book to me. I had a Fifth Gospel now, the sight of the things and places themselves."

Bartleman says very little about the Pentecostal missionaries in Palestine, giving one the impression that they were merely accessories to his excursions in geo-piety. He mentions that he stopped over one night in Haifa to visit the mission of a Hebrew Christian, Brother Joseph, and he recalls that he "had preached a number of times in Jerusalem, in the Christian Alliance Church, with much blessing from the Lord." He justifies his preoccupation with tourism on two grounds. First, the lack of an interpreter made it impossible for him to preach in the villages. Second, he says that he needed "a time of recuperation and spiritual profit principally for my own soul." It is just as well, Bartleman seems to say, because "God was preaching to me. I had now a new Bible. The places and events were now so real."[90]

The Weaver's arrived in Jerusalem on October 18, 1910 and found that Bartleman was still there but scheduled to leave for India the next Saturday. After attending the CMA prayer meeting, led by Jago, Weaver grants that he was much impressed with Leonard's CMA friend, commenting, "He is in for all that God has," by which he presumably meant the full gospel, including speaking in tongues.[91] Weaver took part in the weekly Jewish meeting and was impressed yet sobered, remarking, "I feel I must have what the 120 had on the day of Pentecost. The battle is intense and demons numerous, but God is more than they all. Hallelujah!"[92] Weaver did not exactly jump at the invitation extended by Leonard and Jago to accompany them on an extended preaching trip to Beersheba in the Negev and Safed and Beth Shan in the Galilee region. He writes, in an ambivalent tone, "If I remain here, I shall probably go with them." Later he was glad he did go. The evangelistic troupe was made up of Leonard, Jago, a professor and two students from an American university, and Weaver. The itinerary of their nine-day trip included stops in Beersheba, Gaza, and the ancient Philistine city of Ashdod. Like true Bedouins, they pitched a tent at the outskirts of town and received visitors. This strategy seems to have worked well, judging from Weaver's glowing account: "The Moslems and Greeks flocked to hear the Gospel. God was with us from start to finish. We talked for hours, specially to the Moslems, and they listened attentively without a dissenting voice, and invited us back again. In Ashdod we preached to crowds in the streets, and one Moslem invited us to his home, where he had a sick son. We went and prayed for him in the name of Jesus, and he was healed."[93] Weaver's summation of the trip was an indication of how the Pentecostal missionaries were feeling at this juncture of their mission in Palestine: "We are all well and happy in the Lord."

Emboldened by their recent success, the trio headed out for another evangelistic foray, this one in the area of Jericho, with the purpose in mind of "distributing religious literature and holding gospel services." This time they were not entirely success-

90. Ibid., 59.

91. Weaver, "Extracts from Letters," *Word and Work* 32.10 (October 1910) 342.

92. Weaver, "Extracts from Letters," *Word and Work* 32.12 (December 1910) 378.

93. Weaver, "Letters from Palestine," *Word and Work* 33.1 (January 1911) 23.

ful. Even though they were free to do as they wished with the Jews and Greeks, they were prevented from preaching to Moslems by the Governor, "a very strict Moslem" who objected "to anyone preaching the gospel to the Mohammedans." Well aware that discretion is the better part of valor, Weaver states, "we did not do it." But they did mingle with the large crowd of Russian Orthodox pilgrims gathered along the shores of the Jordan River for an Epiphany service of the renewal of baptismal vows.[94] Weaver provides an exceptionally vivid description of this service and then affirms, "This is a sight long to be remembered, and from the intense earnestness of these dear, simple-hearted people, many lessons can be learned."[95] He goes on to explain that many of the participants from Russia, Bulgaria, and Greece had made great sacrifices for a pilgrimage to the Holy Land, sparing no expense to procure expensive baptismal robes which would be treasured afterwards and preserved for burial shrouds. Weaver's account stands out because it displays a degree of respect toward an Eastern Christian rite that was uncommon among the Pentecostal missionaries in Palestine.

On January 31, 1911, the Weavers left Jerusalem on their way to visit the Pentecostal mission stations in India, China and Japan. Leonard reports that although he was sad to bid the Weavers' adieu, he was cheered by the return of A. Elizabeth Brown with Mary Smithson in February. As they were getting settled, Leonard was seeing positive results in his work with the CMA boy's school.[96] He reports that at a recent meeting "the Spirit put most of them on their faces, some crying for salvation and some for the Holy Spirit. The Spirit manifested His presence in shaking some of them mightily and we trust that He will shake everything that is shakable from them."[97] Leonard was pleased with what he called the "Spiritual gymnastics," but was desirous of further "refreshing" according to the second chapter of Acts, by which he meant speaking in tongues, the *sine qua non* of Pentecostal spirituality. In the meantime, Leonard and Jago were making plans for another evangelistic tour.

By this time, Abbie Morrow Brown, former editor of *Word and Work*, had arrived on the scene in Jerusalem. Morrow Brown felt compelled by the Spirit to go to Jerusalem, attesting to inner promptings that were "quite unmistakable."[98] The current editor, probably Addie Otis, explains that "God began to talk to our dear sister, Abbie Morrow Brown, about Jerusalem and His message was given her in tongues . . ."[99] The next day God said, "Go to Jerusalem." So she did. Now there, she exclaims, "I suppose there is no place in the world that is of more universal interest than Jerusalem."[100]

94. See Graham, *With the Russian Pilgrims to Jerusalem.*

95. Weaver, "Experiences Around Jericho," *Word and Work* 33.3 (March 1911) 87.

96. In 1911 the CMA operated schools in Jerusalem, Hebron, Jaffa, Ain Karim, Beersheba, and Aboud. In Jerusalem the CMA had three schools: a boy's preparatory school, a girl's preparatory school, and a day school. Schools were integral to the CMA mission strategy in Palestine. According to Schmidgall, "The chief way the CMA made inroads into the local Arab communities was by establishing churches and schools together." Schmidgall, "American Holiness Churches in the Holy Land," 91, 101.

97. Leonard, "Letter From Jerusalem," *Word and Work* 33.3 (March 1911) 90.

98. Brown, "God's Best," *Word and Work* 33.2 (February 1911) 41.

99. Brown, "Back to Jerusalem," *Word and Work* 33.2 (February 1911) 55.

100. Brown, "A Plea for Jerusalem," *Word and Work* 33.4 (April 1911) 124.

Morrow Brown's practical interest in being in Jerusalem was "to send out free litera-ture, thus giving to the world the word of the Lord from Jerusalem (Isa. 2:3), and en-abling recent Jewish converts to the Christian faith to obtain a living . . . Four of the Jews in the society where our printing is done were converted in Brother Leonard's home. God is using him much."[101] Here we get a glimpse of the implications of after care for Jewish converts. Given that Jews who converted to Christianity were usually disowned by their families and denied a means of employment, it was simply a matter of necessity, not to mention Christian compassion, to provide them with job training.

Abbie Morrow Brown reports a harrowing experience she had in Hebron during a jaunt to see the brook of Eschol. She was particularly enthused about seeing the spring that commemorated the place where the Hebrew spies had gathered a bunch of grapes so large that it took two men to carry it (Num 13:23), but she was sorely disappointed. She writes, "A lad escorted me to the spring of Escol. On the way a Moslem woman struck me a sharp blow on the back of the head and some boys and girls stoned me." With her ankle injured, she hurried to the spring and took refuge in a grove of mulberry trees. She gathered up her courage to face her "young persecu-tors" whom she could see waiting for her back down the trail. She admits of no fear as she prayed, "Father, I welcome the stones." Fortunately, her attackers turned and fled. Shortly afterward Morrow Brown had another unpleasant run-in with Muslims, which she recounts: "After that one day a Moslem woman lifted her veil and stuck out her tongue at me and another edged up to me as if friendly and drew my pin out of my hat and walked away with it." These experiences took the wind out of Morrow Brown's sails. Crestfallen, she states, "So the roof was my refuge in the early morning and dur-ing the rest of my two week's stay, though I did not hesitate to walk in the street when it was necessary."[102]

By the summer of 1911 the Pentecostal mission in Palestine numbered seven missionaries—A. Elizabeth Brown, two "native girls" under her care, Mary Smithson, Charles Leonard and his wife, and Paul Joyner. Joyner, an American dentist from Union City, Tennessee, had cashed out his practice and come to Jerusalem as a mis-sionary affiliated with the Church of God (Cleveland, Tennessee). Elizabeth Brown outlines the meeting schedule for the mission: Sunday School on Sunday afternoons; a tarrying meeting on Monday afternoons, followed by an evangelistic meeting in the evening; a children's meeting on Thursday afternoons; and an evangelistic meeting on Friday evenings. Brown observes in measured tones that "quite a little interest is being shown, and some curiosity is being excited by the speaking in tongues and other manifestations of the Spirit's presence. Best of all, Brown gleefully tells the readers of the *Bridegroom's Messenger* that both of her girls had "received the baptism of the Holy Spirit, and their changed lives are proving that 'this is that' which was spoken of by the prophet Joel and showing forth the power of the Holy One who has taken up His

101. Brown, "Letter from Jerusalem," *Word and Work* 33.4 (April 1911) 125.
102. Brown, "A Visit to Hebron," *Bridegroom's Messenger* 5.96 (October 15, 1911) 4.

abode within." This was Pentecostal jargon for saying that the girls were speaking in tongues.[103]

About this time T. J. McIntosh and his wife returned to Jerusalem from China and were warmly welcomed by the missionaries and the "natives." McIntosh describes the impression made on him by the Jewish poor in the Old City: "As we went down the street to the Jew's Wailing place, we saw great crowds of Jewish beggars. I looked at them as they sat there in their rags, holding out their hands for money to buy something to eat, and my heart went out to them." He thereupon felt a compulsion "that I should open a home for these poor beggar Jews, and feed and clothe them and preach Jesus to them."[104] Although McIntosh probably had good intentions, nothing materialized in terms of a Pentecostal home for the Jewish poor. This could have been an effectual bridge into the Jewish community. Other Protestant missions had used such methods of gaining a hearing for the gospel message among the Jewish people.[105]

Anna Elizabeth Brown

By the end of 1911 both the McIntoshs and the Leonards had departed Jerusalem, the former returning to the United States and the latter relocating in Egypt, leaving Brown and Smithson to carry on the mission in Palestine.[106] While Smithson plodded along in her Arabic language studies, Brown was feeling the crunch of inadequate facilities and asked her readership to pray for space to accommodate a Bible Training Home, a Sunday School, and tarrying and evangelistic meetings.[107]

On Christmas Day, 1911, a special visitor from the U.S. arrived in Jerusalem. Joseph H. King, later the General Overseer of the Pentecostal Holiness Church, was on a world tour of Pentecostal mission stations.[108] Years later he published a travelogue of his world tour in the *Pentecostal Holiness Advocate.* Subsequent to his death, his wife collected his articles and incorporated them into his memoirs, *Yet Speaketh,* containing a lengthy account of his experiences in Palestine in 1911–12. Although King was more actively involved in the work of the Pentecostal mission than Bartleman, he still does not say a great deal about the Pentecostal missionaries. He mentions Miss Brown's house, in which he stayed, complaining about the cold and damp conditions. He tells of two occasions upon which he assisted Paul Joyner in his missionary work. First, at Joyner's Thursday morning "feast for the poor," King gave a message and handed out food. Likening this ministry to the feeding of the five thousand, King writes, "I experienced joy and delight such as was never known in connection with any other service that I ever rendered. Whether the multitude received the words that I spoke in preaching the gospel I know not, but I do know that they received the food that I de-

103. "From Sister A. E. Brown, Jerusalem," *Bridegroom's Messenger* 4.91 (August 1, 1911) 3.
104. "From Bro. T. J. McIntosh," *Bridegroom's Messenger* 4.92 (August 15, 1911) 2.
105. Murre-van den Berg, *New Faith in Ancient Land*, 12–15.
106. Brown, "From Jerusalem," *Confidence* 5.2 (January-February, 1912) 18.
107. Ibid.
108. *Bridegroom's Messenger* 5.102 (January 15, 1912) 1.

livered with all readiness and delight."[109] The second occasion was one of King's lighter moments in Palestine. King, Joyner, and two Arab workers attempted to hold an open air meeting in a village near Bethlehem. They made a crude platform and mounted it as a crowd gathered. King then said, "Why do you not begin, Dr. Joyner?" But Joyner couldn't figure out what to say and King knew no Arabic. So the crowd could only laugh at the silly missionaries. "Finally," King says, "we descended amid the laughter and fun-making in our audience. I became very much amused over our ridiculous show-off, and laughed heartily over it, especially after I returned to my place of abode in Jerusalem." But perhaps he might have gone too far in making sport of his colleague, for King acknowledges that "Dr. Joyner never asked me to go with him any more to an Arab village and assist in open-air meetings."[110]

Out of the blue, Lucy Leatherman re-appeared in Jerusalem in March of 1912, picking up where she left off. Elizabeth Brown writes that Leatherman was "a real help and blessing. We praise God for sending her."[111] Brown asks for prayer over two who were on the verge of experiencing the Pentecostal baptism of the Holy Spirit. From a letter from Leatherman published in *Confidence*, it appears that these prayers were nearly answered: "I praise God that he is doing a quick work. One Armenian girl received heart cleansing last night, and one also received three days ago. A young dentist last Tuesday came very near receiving the Baptism into the Spirit. We are praying that His fame may go throughout Syria once more."[112] As it turned out, Letterman settled in the town of Kafashema, Syria (now Lebanon), reporting that she had ecstatically spoken in many languages. Her spiritual joy was nonetheless overshadowed by the clouds of approaching warfare. Because of concerns among the population that French and Italian troops were approaching, she asks for prayer for the Turks, Armenians, Syrians, and Jews.[113] Leatherman was referring to events that were re-writing the map of the Ottoman Empire. In 1911 the Italians occupied Tripoli in North Africa and in 1912 almost all Ottoman territory in Europe was lost to the Balkan League. Concerning the impact of these events in Syria, Abdul-Latif Tibawi writes, "To the average Syrian Muslim it was the power and prestige of Islam that was thus diminished."[114] While some Syrians were eager to rush to the defense of the Turks, others saw the moment as opportune for an Arab revolt against Ottoman rule. Faced with the prospect of destabilization, the French were poised to intervene. Hence, Leatherman had good cause for her sense of alarm.

---

109. King, *Yet Speaketh: Memoirs of the Late Bishop Joseph H. King*, 253.

110. Ibid., 255–56.

111. Brown, "Jerusalem, Palestine," *Bridegroom's Messenger* 5.107 (April 1, 1912) 2.

112. Leatherman, "Jerusalem," *Confidence* 5.3 (March 1912) 59.

113. "Elizabeth Brown Letter," *Bridegroom's Messenger* (April 1, 1912) 2. Lucy Leatherman settled in Lebanon, *Bridegroom's Messenger* (June 1, 1912) 3; "Letter from Sister Leatherman," *Bridegroom's Messenger* (September 15, 1912) 4; (December 1, 1912) 1. "News from Mrs. Lucy Leatherman," *Confidence* (July 1912) 184.

114. Tibawi, *A Modern History of Syria*, 204.

News was received from the Leonards of their hopes for an imminent return to the United States. It appears that Linda Leonard sensed that the Lord had said to her, "When He putteth forth His sheep He goeth before them."[115] As it turned out, the Leonards were not allowed to sail for Naples as they hoped. In the meantime, Jago and Joyner were sending good news of positive outcomes in their missionary work. Jago reports that "twenty-five Jews held up their hands for prayers," which he interprets as "a token for good."[116] Joyner tells of how the services of an interpreter enabled him to "preach in the streets to hundreds, anointed and prayed with the sick, and have seen them take off rags, bandages and chains, and go away rejoicing, healed and saved." On a trip to Beersheba he had visited Arab and Bedouin tents and was received gladly. The people "would bring their sick children, daughters and wives, to have us anoint and pray for them." Joyner's account is a prime example of what Gary McGee calls the "radical missions strategy" of Pentecostals, which holds that the primal spirituality of Pentecostalism is culturally transferable. Joyner goes on to assert, "There is no greater need in all the East we believe than for men to do this kind of work. The dusky Arab and Bedouin, though a Mohammedan, knows a child of God when he sees one, and the power of God when manifested, and I believe he is more ready to accept deliverance from sin and sickness than the average westerner." Joyner should be credited for his positive attitude toward Muslim people, whom he found to be "really easy of approach and willing to listen, and accept the *Truth*."[117] Joyner was far ahead of other Pentecostal missionaries who tended to denigrate Islam out of fear.

A. Elizabeth Brown was also in a mood for rejoicing. She relates a testimony from one of the girls under her care, Esgooree, who saw a vision of Jesus as she was baptized in the Spirit and exclaimed, "Only this I can say, I praised Him in other tongues and I *will* praise the Lord, for He hath done so much for me. Please shout with me, hallelujah!"[118] Brown was also "greatly helped and cheered" by a fascinating episode in the history of the Pentecostal mission in Palestine. Early in 1913 Dr. Florence Murcutt came from Los Angeles "hoping to distribute about 5,000 Gospels among the Jews, she herself being a converted Jewess."[119] Murcutt, a Pentecostal and a trained physician, had sensed a divine call to go to Palestine and "scatter the precious Word broadcast and that His Word would not return to Him void."[120] In transit while in Port Said, Egypt she chanced upon a Bible Society outlet and purchased a trunk load of Gospels and New Testaments. Upon arriving in Jerusalem she went to see Brown, who was more than willing to help her. Her first attempt at distributing the Scriptures did not go well. As Murcutt tells it, the Jews "simply snatched them from me, tore them up, burnt them and shook their fists in my face."[121] Brown suggested that they spend time

115. "Coming Home," *Word and Work* 34.3 (March 1912) 91.

116. "Reports from the Field," *Word and Work* 34.5 (May 1912) 123.

117. Ibid., 123–24.

118. Brown, "From Jerusalem," *Trust* 11.4–5 (June–July 1912) 26.

119. Brown, "Jerusalem: Distributing the Gospels," *Confidence* 6.2 (February 1913) 39.

120. Murcutt, "Gospel Seed Sowing in Palestine," *Weekly Evangel* (November 11, 1916) 4.

121. Ibid.

in concerted prayer, in which Joyner and other missionaries participated. This seemed to make a big difference. In time Murcutt could say, "It is really wonderful to see the people sitting around coffee shops, men and women in carriages, on horseback, and all over the place, reading the Word. They say such a sight was never seen in Jerusalem before." As she was traveling by carriage to Jericho, she observed a group of Bedouins and stopped to distribute portions to them. Later, Archibald Forder wrote to Murcutt informing her that he had seen a Bedouin at Ramoth Gilead reading to the whole encampment from the Scripture portions she had distributed.[122]

Despite such success stories, the work in Palestine was an uphill battle. In the same letter in which she chronicled the Murcutt episode, Brown also spoke of the "opposition of many here, especially among the missionaries because we stand uncompromisingly for the Baptism of the Holy Spirit with the speaking in other tongues as the Spirit gives utterance." Brown asks her readers to realize the magnitude of "mighty power of the combined forces of Judaism, Islamism, and apostate Christianity (worse yet than heathen idolatry) against King Jesus here, and against His ambassadors!" She then throws down the gauntlet, declaring that only the "mighty, persistent, prevailing prayer and faith can enable us to stand and win souls to Jesus from their darkness and death." It was a battle for sure, but one that was helped by arrival of new recruits, Anna and Florence Bush, to join the band of Pentecostal missionaries in Jerusalem.[123]

Fresh eyes sometimes see glaring shortfalls that long-timers have accepted with equanimity. As Sarah Smith, another new missionary, sized up the situation upon arriving in Jerusalem in 1913, she writes, "There are 9 or 10 Pentecostal missionaries here from America, but most of us have not been here long enough yet to learn the language . . . I find no Pentecostal mission here, but Pentecost has fallen in the German colony here and they are speaking in tongues as in Acts 2:4."[124] Florence Bush also saw the lack, observing, "At present there is no mission here."[125] Lucy Leatherman too laments that "we have no mission" in Palestine and prays for one to open near the Jaffa Gate.[126] There was good reason for concern over the lack of adequate facilities for the Pentecostal mission in Palestine. But that was not the only reason for alarm.

THE GATHERING STORM OF THE FIRST WORLD WAR

The First World War was around the corner and the situation of the missionaries was getting more difficult by the day. Word came that the Leonards were unable to find a way home and were returning to Jerusalem.[127] Given the evolving situation, Mary

---

122. "Dr. Florence Murcutt," *Weekly Evangel* (October 21, 1916) 13.

123. Brown, "Jerusalem: Distributing the Gospels," *Confidence* 6.2 (February 1913) 40.

124. Smith, "Jerusalem, Palestine," *Word and Witness* (August 20, 1913) 1.

125. Bush, *Word and Witness* (November 20, 1913) 3.

126. Leatherman, "Letter From Egypt," *Word and Work* (November 1913) 350.

127. Leonard, "From Egypt to Jerusalem," *Word and Work* (April 1914) 122; Lucy Leatherman, *Bridegroom's Messenger* (December 1, 1912) 1. A Miss Robertson in Egypt reports that, "Brother Leonard is going to Jerusalem in April." *Word and Witness* (April 20, 1914) 4.

Smithson requested prayer.[128] Then in 1914 the Great War broke out and escalated out of control. In these difficult times the Pentecostal missionaries attempted to go on with their ministry. Florence Bush wrote to assure the readers of the *Christian Evangel* that the Pentecostal missionaries in Palestine who had been "independent of one another" were now "coming together as a body." With no indication of a particular location or building, she reports, "The Pentecostal Mission is open every night and we do praise God for the way that He is working. We feel the mighty power of God in the meetings and souls are under conviction; several have been saved."[129]

American Pentecostal leaders imagined the worst based on the reports they were receiving in the press. Commenting on a New York newspaper report issued by a Presbyterian missions agency on the severe conditions in Syria, E. N. Bell extrapolated, "Now if these sad conditions exist among well organized churches whose missionaries before the war were regularly supplied with good salaries, how much greater is the need of all faith missionaries who do not have regular salaries, but only such occasional offerings as good and faithful souls are prompted now and then to send them."[130] In the same issue of the *Christian Evangel*, an unidentified source in Jerusalem reports that people were short of water due to a dry winter, but God heard the cries of the righteous and sent the much needed "latter rain," plus droppings of "spiritual Latter Rain." The author continues, "A man of God, who is baptized with the Holy Ghost, has just come to Jerusalem with his family, he says, 'to stay.' He expects to learn the language, and as the Lord leads, open up a mission near the Jaffa gate where the crowds pass, and hold evangelistic services." At a recent Jewish meeting six men from Es Salt had come forward for prayer. Ministry to a nearby leper colony met with an enthusiastic response, cheering the author because "they do not know Jesus, the divine comforter, for most of them are Mohammedans."[131] The arrival of a new missionary would be unlikely, unless it is Leonard, now back in Jerusalem, who reported that many of the missionaries are leaving Jerusalem which is under martial law, imposed by the Turkish soldiers who are confiscating what they can get away with. Indeed, troubles were abounding. The London Jew Society and the Church Missionary Society had closed their schools. Pentecostal missionaries Frank and Alberta Boothby write, "About the last of January, 1914, we came out of Jerusalem when I was just recovering from Typhus or typhoid fever." According to Alberta Boothby, they had served nine years in Jerusalem and played a role in the conversion of a rabbi.[132]

As for Leonard, at this juncture he asserts, "We have no desire nor leading to leave as yet."[133] In one of his next letters Leonard paints a picture of woe. Carriages, mules, and horses have been appropriated by the Turks without compensation. There are no

128. Smithson, "Jerusalem, Palestine," *Christian Evangel* (July 11, 1914) 4.

129. Bush, "Tidings from Jerusalem," *Christian Evangel* (September 12, 1914) 4.

130. Bell, "War Paralyzed Us, Missionaries Write," *Christian Evangel* (October 10, 1914) 4.

131. "Jerusalem, Palestine," *Christian Evangel* (October 10, 1914) 4.

132. Boothby, "An Interesting Letter from Egypt," *Weekly Evangel* (February 19, 1916) 12; "Missionaries Back From Jerusalem," *Weekly Evangel* (March 3, 1917) 3.

133. Leonard, "News from Jerusalem," *Word and Work* (October 1914) 314–15.

more potatoes, rice and sugar, but water and bread are in good supply. The services in our hall are meeting every night. Amazingly, Jews and Mohammedans are agreeing that Jesus is coming soon. The missionaries desire to be a "Gideon band." From the vantage point of Elizabeth Brown, there was "much suffering among the poor, English missionaries have left, schools closed, food stuffs getting dearer." But there was a bright side. "We know all this spells the coming of Jesus." To her it seemed propitious that "there is greater willingness to hear the Gospel than ever before." Brown was also cheered by those nearest to her, a precious German helper, a Bible woman recently married, and a young Jewess who is "not far from the Kingdom."[134]

From his vantage point in North America, J. Roswell Flower supposed that once Turkey entered the war on the side of Austria and Germany, the eschatological ante had been upped. Hence, he saw silver linings in the clouds of war storming over Palestine and predicted the demise of the Ottoman Empire and the resurgence of Israel as a nation. "We are confident that the outcome will be the overthrow and annihilation of Turkey, the wresting of Palestine from her slimy grasp, and the return of Israel in triumph to once more take her place among the nations of the earth . . ."[135] Yet, for the time being life in Palestine was just plain hard for the missionaries. Florence Bush could see no silver lining in the wartime conditions. All she could see was confiscation, conscription, and martial law. She writes, "Famine is in Jerusalem, and sooner or later, the people will have to rob the shops and houses in order to live." It is a time of anxiety and trial, yet, as Bush plods on with her study of Arabic, she notices an upturn in spiritual interest, observing, "Since the war trouble began, we have found the women in the homes very open to the Gospel . . . The mission is open every night, and many come in to hear the messages from the Word, and we believe that the Lord is working in their hearts."[136]

On route from Egypt, Pentecostal missionary Frank Moll stayed five weeks in Jerusalem and attested to the valor of the Pentecostal missionaries in Palestine. He lauds Leonard for serving faithfully for two years before seeing his first convert and commends Joyner for leaving his dental practice to go to Jerusalem. Moll's assessment of Joyner agrees with King's: "He has such love for the people that he loves them into the kingdom . . . He is not gifted to preach but he loves them and he and his interpreter go from place to place and many are being saved and 'loved' into the kingdom."[137]

The missionaries were well aware of the dangers posed to them. In an emergency phone call to Albert Weaver in the United States, Jago communicated his fear that "the Leonards and all missionaries in Jerusalem are in danger of being slaughtered at any moment."[138] Some, such as Lucy Leatherman, were fortunate to extricate themselves from danger. She had left Egypt and arrived in France just as war was declared. Paris was in a panic, but she says she was not fazed, "for I had been reading my Bible

134. "Jerusalem," *Christian Evangel* (October 31, 1914) 1.

135. Flower, "The Kings of the East," *Christian Evangel* (November 7, 1914), 1.

136. Bush, "Trouble in Palestine," *Christian Evangel* (November 7, 1914) 1.

137. Moll, "The Work in Africa and Egypt," *Christian Evangel* (November 14, 1914) 1.

138. "Missionaries in Danger," *Word and Work* 36.11 (November 1914) 341.

much."[139] While Leatherman was on a steamer bound for home, other missionaries were stuck in Egypt and Palestine for the time being. According to Jago, a lack of funds was preventing Leonard from returning home. By the next month the Leonard family and Mary Smithson had relocated in Egypt and planned to spend the winter in Minia, even though the American Consul there regarded the situation serious enough to advise all missionaries to leave. Elizabeth Brown, Paul Joyner, a Brother Randall, and others were staying on in Jerusalem.[140] The *Latter Rain Evangel* reported the alarming news that Archibald Forder had been detained by the Turkish army and was placed under house arrest in Damascus, stating that had it not been for the American consul in Damascus, Forder might have been shot.[141] From what Alexander Boddy could tell, "Most of the Missionaries have left."[142] A few months later Boddy published the story of the forced evacuation of 5,000 Jews from Jaffa to Alexandria. Among them was the Pentecostal Jewish evangelist, D. C. Joseph.[143]

In 1915 Florence Bush and her mother fled Palestine, seeking refuge in Egypt where they started up a promising ministry. Bush explains, "Two years ago, we went to Jerusalem, Palestine and remained there in the work until we were forced to leave that city on account of the war, two months ago."[144] As it stands in Jerusalem, "Bro. Randall remained and is keeping the mission open every day, no one being allowed on the streets at night, and he is continuing the work there."[145] At the Bush's new location in Ben Suef, Egypt, conditions were far from ideal. Bush writes, "It has been a very long time since we could receive mail, and could only write Arabic, Turkish, French or German. Every letter was read by the authorities and we were not permitted to tell anything that happened in Jerusalem." Bush explains that the situation required that "we have a soldier in all of our meetings as the Moslems stone us and try to break the windows while the services are being held and also through the day."[146] Bush was feeling increasingly insecure, as "now day by day the conditions are becoming more grave here . . . We are loath to leave Egypt and the dear native brethren, but God knows best."[147] Finally, Florence Bush and her mother were evacuated from Egypt and returned to the U.S.[148]

---

139. Leatherman, "Back From Jerusalem," in Ibid., 342.

140. A. H. Post & Wife, "Missionaries Leave Egypt," and "Charles S. Leonard, Egypt," *Christian Evangel* 72 (December 26, 1914) 4; Leonard, "Letter from Egypt, Dated 11–22–14," *Word and Work* 37.1 (January 1915) 26–27.

141. "Rites Marking Holy Edict," *Latter Rain Evangel* (January 1915) 13.

142. "The War," *Confidence* (February 1915) 27.

143. "A Jewish Missionary Escapes from Haifa," *Confidence* (May 1915) 94–95.

144. "Florence I. Bush and Mother, Letter from Tanta, Egypt," *Trust* (May 1915) 19.

145. "Florence I. Bush and Mother, Egypt," *Christian Evangel* (January 9, 1915) 4.

146. "Florence I. Bush and Mother, Egypt," *Weekly Evangel* (April 24, 1915) 4.

147. "Florence Bush and Mother," *Weekly Evangel* (May 22, 1915) 4; Bush, "God's Guidance and Blessing in Difficult Fields," *Latter Rain Evangel* (December 1915) 9–11.

148. *Word and Witness* (June 1916) 6.

In Palestine conditions were worsening. Elizabeth Brown describes an awful state of affairs in Jerusalem. Starvation, disease, and moral degradation were widespread. Most able-bodied men had fled from the dreaded prospect of military conscription, leaving their wives and children to fend for themselves. "Starving Turkish soldiers have carried away the livestock, raided the shops, etc."[149] The missionaries were bracing for whatever might come, faced with ominous developments in Palestine and the region. Turkish troops were amassed near Nazareth for the defense of Palestine and were reportedly being trained by German advisors. This development elicited a sardonic comment from the editor of *Word and Witness,* charging that the collaboration of Turkish troops and German officers was producing a new breed of crusaders.[150] The Pentecostal periodicals provided good coverage of the Armenian genocide with reports from Pentecostal missionary Maria Gerber, who was caring for orphaned Armenian children in Turkey. Gerber calculated the casualties, estimating, "It is said that 500,000 Armenians had been massacred by the Turks."[151] In spite of the carnage, she assures her readers that the children in her orphanage were alive and well.[152]

As the situation worsened, Brown attempted to exert a calming influence, writing, "Whatever reports you may have heard I have confidence that all can be done, is being done . . . There are so many who need our ministry. Many hearts are open as they see the signs of the near coming of Jesus." Brown was confident in God's provision, attesting that when her funds were depleted, "that very day, the money which had been sent to Mrs. Beck for me was telegraphed to the Consul here, who gave it to me two or three days later. We have a God who *cares* and a God who *can.* Hallelujah."[153] The best the missionaries could do in these dire straits was to ease the suffering of others. Charles Leonard describes the shortage of food as verging on the real possibility of widespread starvation. He stresses the need for relief and appeals for money.[154] Elizabeth Brown waxed eschatological in her appeal for help. She believed that God would come through with provision for the hungry under these difficult circumstances, which were surely a sign that Jesus "is coming soon to take us to Himself, that where He is (above all the storms and convulsions that shake the earth and rend it asunder) we may be also."[155] Word arrived that Paul Joyner had also fled to Egypt, leaving an ever dwindling crew of missionaries in Jerusalem, made up of Brown, Forder's wife, Miss Lovell, and three other "C.M.A Sisters" to tend for the natives who were "facing starvation in Jerusalem and all lower Palestine, and awful massacres are occurring in Armenia."[156] Now back in the United States, Charles Leonard reported that he had received a letter from Miss Lovell, still running her school for blind girls, reporting that the fighting between the

---

149. Brown, "Jerusalem," *Confidence* (May 1915) 91.

150. "Nazareth," *Word and Witness* (August 1915) 1.

151. *Confidence* (November 1915) 213.

152. Gerber, "Orphanage in Turkey," *Word and Work* (November 1915) 314.

153. Brown, "Jerusalem, Palestine," *Trust* (July 1915) 27–28.

154. Leonard, "Suffering in Jerusalem," *Word and Work* (November 1915) 311.

155. Brown, "Jerusalem in War-Time," *Confidence* (December 1915) 227.

156. "Arrives in Egypt, Paul M. Joyner," *Weekly Evangel* (January 1, 1916) 13.

British and Turkish armies was within seventy miles of Jerusalem and it looked like the British would come out ahead. As the war advanced to the area of Gaza, it appeared that there would be a fierce battle for Jerusalem. Famine was widespread. According to Brown's assessment, conditions could hardly be more atrocious: "Many houses have been opened where women sell themselves to sin in order to keep from starving. Whole villages depopulated . . . [and] the dead have been gathered up by night in wagons. All missionary work of all belligerent powers is necessarily stopped."[157]

In early May of 1917 the American Consul in Palestine directed all Americans to evacuate Jerusalem. Brown complied and made preparations for her departure, finding homes for the two girls under her care. She left Jerusalem on May 15, 1917, traveling with a party of sixty people, led by Dr. Ward of the Syrian Protestant College of Beirut. This group made a circuitous overland journey to Damascus and then on to Istanbul. Brown was able to visit with Forder and even do some sightseeing in Damascus. From that point on, though, her escape from the war zone was filled with many privations, which she describes graphically in her reports.[158] She arrived back in the United States in November of 1917 and promptly attended to itinerating among her support network. She let it be known that she would be traveling cross country to visit her sister on the West Coast and would be available to speak in churches on the way and tell the story of her remarkable journey and conditions in Jerusalem and the Holy Land.[159]

By the end the first phase of its history (1908–18), the Pentecostal mission in Palestine had gained a foothold in Jerusalem. The efforts of pioneering missionaries, namely Lucy Leatherman, Charles Leonard, and A. Elizabeth Brown, were bearing fruit. The missionaries could take comfort in knowing that converts had been made and a few had spoken in tongues, even though little progress had been made in building a self-supporting indigenous church. In the next phase of its history (1919–35), the Pentecostal mission would make significant advancements under the leadership of A. Elizabeth Brown. Less than a year after she had left Jerusalem in dire straits, Brown was eager to return and resume her missionary service, resolutely declaring, "I feel it is in preparation to serve Him there in ministry to His needy ones in Jerusalem and my heart longs to return."[160] To that story, we will turn in the next chapter.

---

157. Brown, "Back from Jerusalem," *Weekly Evangel* (October 6, 1917) 12.

158. Brown, "Safe Return from Jerusalem of a Veteran Missionary: Ninety Days Thro' the War Zone Amid Peril and Hardship," *Latter Day Evangel* (October 1917) 20–24.

159. "Miss A. E. Brown," *Weekly Evangel* (January 15, 1918) 10.

160. Brown, "Returning to Jerusalem," *Weekly Evangel* (March 9, 1918) 11.

5 | Expanding the Territory, 1919–1935

T HE DOMINANT THEME of the mission in the period between the world wars was the expansion of territory. Prior to recommencement of the narrative, the post-war realities facing the missionaries as they resumed their mission work in Palestine are described. Then the story picks up with the return of the Pentecostal missionaries to Jerusalem at the close of the war. Led by A. Elizabeth Brown, the Pentecostal mission made advancements in facilities, personnel, and outreach. Among the important developments in this period are the return of Yumna Malick to her home village of Shweifat (near Beirut), the arrival of Laura Radford, the establishment of the "Shemariah" mission station in Jerusalem, the flowering of the outstation in Es Salt, Transjordan, and the launching of a satellite outpost in Persia. Reports of the missionaries and commentary in Pentecostal periodicals on the watershed event of the Wailing Wall Riots of 1929 are also discussed.

POST-WAR REALITIES

The aftershocks of the "Great War" rocked the world. With the myth of Europe as the epitome of high civilization shattered beyond repair, the post-war period was a time of soul searching. President Wilson's idealistic hope that this war would make the world safe for democracy had been shattered. As the leaders of the Great Powers and their allies met in Paris for peace talks in 1919, they were faced with the monumental task of reconstructing a new world order. Along with the terms of peace, the issues on the agenda included the creation of an international peacekeeping body, the League of Nations, re-configuration of national boundaries, establishment of Mandatory powers in disputed territories, and disarmament. The mood among Pentecostals concerning the prospect for peace was skeptical. In 1919 the *Latter Rain Evangel* printed an excerpt from an address by the missionary statesman John R. Mott on the impact of the war on Christian missions, in which Mott declared, "We are not yet through with the war." This alarming comment was made in reference to the prediction of Henry Morgenthau, former American ambassador to Turkey, that the U.S. would be involved in another war within fifteen or twenty years."[1] It did not take that long for conflict to break out in Palestine.

---

1. "Not Through with the War," *Latter Rain Evangel* (August 1919) 23.

Easter Riots of 1920

The early 1920s were an auspicious time in Palestine. The British Government was pursuing a tenuous policy in Palestine, based on the Balfour Declaration. Having made promises of self-determination to both the Zionists and Arabs during the First World War, the British Government was chasing the impossible dream of favoring the establishment of a Jewish National Home while at the same time claiming to uphold the civil and religious rights of the Arab population. Neither side was satisfied that enough was done to advance their side of the bargain. The Zionists pushed for unlimited immigration of Jewish settlers and the Arabs demanded the curtailment of immigration, threatening to resist with force if necessary. The Arabs made good on their threats when an anti-Jewish riot broke out in Jerusalem during Easter of 1920.[2]

In 1920 the religious holidays of the three Abrahamic faiths happened to fall on the same weekend of April 2–4. Jews were observing Passover, Christians were celebrating Easter, and Muslims were commemorating the Nebi Musa festival. Hence, Jerusalem was packed with pilgrims. As Jewish pilgrims from Hebron entered the Jaffa Gate, they were met by an Arab crowd. An altercation ensued escalating into a pitched battle, resulting in casualties on both sides. At the end of the day five Jews and four Arabs were dead. A total of over two hundred Jews and twenty Arabs were injured. In the aftermath the British organized a commission of inquiry, which prepared a report that was never published. The commission's findings were sympathetic to the Arabs, characterizing the Zionist attitude as "arrogant, insolent, and provocative." The report concluded, "If not carefully checked they (Zionists) may easily precipitate a catastrophe, the end of which it is difficult to forecast."[3] The next year the British convened a conference of Arab leaders in Cairo for the purpose of mollifying Arab fears. At this conference Winston Churchill emphatically defended the British policy, further solidifying the Arab desire for self-determination and unity.[4] The British failed at Cairo partly because they underestimated the extent of the awakening of Arab nationalism, but mostly because the goal of their policy, an Arab-Zionist bi-national state in Palestine, was not feasible.[5]

The response of the *Pentecostal Evangel* to these events was laced with dreadful imprecations of God's judgment. It carried an article by the British pastor and editor of *Dawn*, D. M. Panton, who comments on the Easter riots and Arab protests in Palestine. He writes, "A mere trifle may precipitate at any moment a massacre of Jews in the Holy Land." With Russian Jews fleeing from persecution and heading for Palestine, on foot if necessary, the stage was being set for an epic confrontation. It is now the "eleventh hour of missionary opportunity."[6] Several articles appeared in the

---

2. Antonius, *The Arab Awakening*, 386–412.

3. "Report of Commission of Inquiry on Jerusalem Riot," July 1, 1920, in McTague, *British Policy in Palestine, 1917–1922*, 102.

4. Gilbert, *Churchill and the Jews*, 50–51.

5. Klieman, *Foundations of British Policy in the Arab World*, 246.

6. Panton, "Israel's Peril," *Pentecostal Evangel* (August 7, 1920) 2–3.

Pentecostal Evangel under the heading, "The Budding Fig Tree," leaving no doubt as to the editor's Zionist sympathies. One such article stated that, as it was with Haman, whom God brought down, so it will be with Russia. "The Bolshevik commissars have proclaimed 'There is no God.' He can overthrow them in His own time and He will."[7] A second article in this series parroted the question posed to Jesus by his disciples in Acts 1:6: "Wilt Thou at this time restore the kingdom to Israel?" The answer: He will, in His own time. In the meantime, Israel is trying to restore herself. The blessing is coming. It will be "life from the dead." As God blessed Abraham, He will bless Israel. God's plans and purposes are to restore it.[8] A third article states, "You are seeing the fig tree budding. You are seeing the drying up of the Euphrates. You are seeing increasing life coming to the Jews, to Israel. At the same time, decreasing life, the dying of the Turk." This, the writer asserts, is opening the way for Russia to invade Israel and be defeated, as was Sennacherib's army.[9] A fourth article observes that the Arabs have filled themselves with vindictive wrath and threatened the British Government that they will make Palestine worse than Ireland.[10] A fifth triumphantly proclaims, "True in Disraeli's day, truer today, Jews, Arabs, Turks, British, French, Italian, all realize that Palestine is the coming center . . . The land is getting ready for the people, the city is getting ready for the King."[11]

The Pentecostal missionaries in Palestine saw what was transpiring in Palestine from the privileged position of first-hand observers. Hence, they were regarded as expert witnesses who were qualified to assess the implications of events on the ground. As most of the Pentecostal missionaries, A. Elizabeth Brown was a Zionist sympathizer. It was therefore fitting that she would exude enthusiasm over Jewish immigration to Palestine: "It thrills our hearts as we think of the actual returning of the Jews to the land promised to Abraham and his seed."[12] Paul Joyner, a Church of God missionary who returned to Palestine after World War I and opened a mission station at Beit Jala, was of the same mind.[13] He writes, "Many are watching the Jews and know from the Scriptures that they must return and they are returning but not in great numbers." He implores his readers, "Dear ones, especially preachers and Christian workers, read Romans eleven and see how much we owe to the Jews and pray much for them."[14] Joyner and Brown were witnesses to the violent Arab reaction prompted by Jewish immigration to Palestine, which was a matter of concern for missionaries in Palestine, who, according to Brown, were in danger of their lives during the Easter

7. "The Budding Fig Tree," *Pentecostal Evangel* (October 1, 1921) 4.

8. "The Budding Fig Tree," *Pentecostal Evangel* (April 15, 1922) 1, 7.

9. "Ezekiel's Prediction of Impending Judgment," *Pentecostal Evangel* (May 13, 1922) 1, 9.

10. Watson, "The Time of Jacob's Trouble: Copy of a Letter to a Jewish Rabbi," *Pentecostal Evangel* (September 30, 1922) 3.

11. "Keep Your Eye on Palestine," *Pentecostal Evangel* (November 25, 1922) 4.

12. "The Land of Palestine," *Pentecostal Evangel* (December 25, 1920) 13.

13. Joyner, "News from Jerusalem," *Church of God Evangel* (December 24, 1921) 4.

14. Joyner, "News From Jerusalem," *The Evening Light and Church of God Evangel* 12.51 (December 24, 1921) 4.

riots. Searching for an explanation of why people were killed, she simply states, "There is strong feeling against the Jews in Palestine. The natives do not want them to return to their own land."[15] Commenting on the implications for missionaries, Joyner reports that his work of village evangelism with the Arabs was made much more difficult "on account of hatred of returning Jews."[16] He points out that it was not only Muslims who held the Jews in disrepute, but also the indigenous Christians, including "the Catholics who have their holy places of worship are against them and oppose the Jew coming back." In fact, Joyner avers, the Catholics "would slay all if they could or were not afraid of the English government who protects the poor, despised and hated Jew."[17]

Missionary Challenges

The First World War had disrupted the missionary enterprise on a global scale. Many missionaries had left their stations due to endangerment and the stoppage of mail delivery, drying up the flow of funds in war zones. As they prepared to resume full scale missionary activity after the war, Pentecostal missionaries took stock of the opportunities and challenges before them at a missionary conference held by the Assemblies of God in St. Louis in 1919.[18] Pentecostals understood their approach to missions in contradistinction to mainstream missionary methods. This attitude was not a new development. In the pre-war period, Elizabeth Sexton had written of her deep reservations over the Edinburgh Missionary Conference of 1910.[19] In the post-war period Pentecostals were, if anything, more skeptical. In an article entitled, "Advancing Backwards," the *Pentecostal Evangel* criticized the Student Volunteer Movement for its business savvy and emphasis on "the better things of modern civilization. The 'better things of modern civilization' are the present-day substitute for the signs which Jesus promised should follow them that believe."[20] Max W. Moorhead expressed suspicions that the Young Men's Christian Association and the Student Volunteer Movement are "responsible for anti-Christian doctrines which are rapidly spreading in the churches, like leaven everywhere."[21]

The challenges facing the Pentecostal mission in Palestine are best understood when seen against the backdrop of the dire situation in Jerusalem. During the war all of the Pentecostal missionaries in Palestine had been evacuated. With the end of the war, they longed to return to their stations and pick up where they left off. As Elizabeth Brown looked back at the conditions in Jerusalem during the war, she remembered well the horrors of famine made worse by a visitation of locusts. She also

15. "Elizabeth Brown," *The Pentecostal Evangel* (May 29, 1920) 13.

16. Joyner, "Jerusalem, Palestine," *Word and Work* (August 27, 1921) 3.

17. Joyner, "News From Jerusalem," 4.

18. "The Fourth Missionary Conference," *Pentecostal Evangel* (October 18, 1919) 1, 4.

19. Sexton, *Bridegroom's Messenger* 3.69 (September 1, 1910) 1.

20. "Advancing Backwards," *Pentecostal Evangel* (January 10, 1920) 4.

21. Moorhead, "The Perils of Bolshevism at Home and Abroad," *Pentecostal Evangel* (February 7, 1920) 2–3.

remembered that, in spite of the starvation of many, she and the other Pentecostal missionaries did not go hungry. Turning her thoughts to the future, Brown made it clear that the mission in Palestine ought to reach both Jews and Muslims. She writes, "People think that the work in Jerusalem is exclusively Jewish, and I would like to correct that impression." As she saw it, "The Mohammedans are much more open to the Gospel than the Jews, but for both family and governmental reasons it is almost as much as a Mohammedan's life is worth to confess Christ in any public way." Brown admits that most Muslim converts to Christianity "have met with the poisoned cup or in some way sealed their testimony with their blood." As a countermeasure, the missionaries in Palestine would usually "get a Mohammedan convert out of the country just as quickly as possible after he has given his life to Jesus."[22] If Brown was hopeful, she was also realistic.

As the time drew near for Brown to return to Palestine, she rejoiced, "I am glad that the way seems to be opening for me to go back again to Jerusalem . . . This is the third time I go back to Jerusalem." Brown reveals her leaning towards the Arabs, surmising, "We may not be able to do much among the Jewish people, because when they get there they are satisfied, and the usual reception they give us is, 'Go on. We do not want either you or your Book.'" Brown stresses, "But I believe that these will be golden days among the Mohammedans."[23] In the same vein, she relays a good report to the *Christian Evangel*: "Religious liberty has been proclaimed in Palestine, and the teaching is being circulated among Mohammedans by their own leaders that Jesus is coming back very soon, and when He comes, being then the last of the prophets, He will be the greatest; therefore they must accept Him and prepare to meet Him. The Jews will soon be coming back as a nation . . . The prospect brightens."[24]

With Jerusalem still in shambles, one might legitimately ask what accounts for Brown's prognostication of a brightened prospect in Palestine. There are two reasons for her optimism. First, epochal events had altered the political situation. In November 1917, in the final stages of the war, the Balfour Declaration affirmed that the British Government looked with favor towards the establishment of a Jewish national home in Palestine. A month later the British General Allenby captured Jerusalem from the Turks without a shot being fired. Soon thereafter the Ottoman Empire crumbled and the Treaty of Versailles laid the groundwork for a British Mandate in Palestine. Pentecostals interpreted these events as a turning point in history of momentous eschatological significance.[25] As Brown put it, "Events, God's sign posts seem to whirl by us, while many do not understand that it is because we are hastening to the end of our journey." She names the events she has in mind: "Delegates are at the Peace table. 'Kingdoms at their base are crumbling.' A League of Nations is about to be formed

22. Brown, "Recent Conditions in Jerusalem," *Latter Rain Evangel* (April 1918), 5.

23. Brown, "A New Regime Among the Moslems," *Latter Rain Evangel* (January 1919) 4.

24. Brown, "Back to Jerusalem," *Christian Evangel* (February 22, 1919) 13.

25. Employing the apocalyptic imagery of Armageddon theology, E. N. Bell held that the League of Nations would serve first and foremost to prepare the way for the coming of the Beast of the Book of Revelation. Bell, "The League of Nations," *Christian Evangel* (March 8, 1919) 2.

which will change the map of all Europe and much of Asia, both geographically and politically." Then Brown offers an eschatological aside, alluding to the apocalyptic event that she, along with most Pentecostals, believed was near, the second coming of Christ. "Time is short, it hasteneth greatly. 'At such an hour as ye think not, the Son of Man cometh!'"[26]

A second reason for Brown's optimism was her affiliation with the Assemblies of God (hereafter AG). In 1917 she had been authorized to serve in Palestine by the General Council of the AG. She proudly announces the fact in correspondence with two Pentecostal periodicals. In a letter, dated January 7, 1919, to the readers of the *Latter Rain Evangel*, she writes, "I am going out, not as a relief worker but as a Pentecostal missionary under the General Council of The Assemblies of God to carry the glad tidings to whomever I can reach. I ask a very great interest in your prayers."[27] A month later, she conveyed the same message to the *Christian Evangel*, coyly averring, "I go out, a little Pentecostal missionary, under the General Council of the Assemblies of God to carry the glad tidings to whomsoever I can reach—not a relief worker, under the Relief Committee."[28] Brown would have abundant missionary opportunities as she did relief work among the distressed people of Jerusalem. With the AG as her support system, Brown was cheered by the thought that that she was not going alone. She continues, "God has called and fitted a dear young sister for the work, and she will accompany me if she can get ready to go by the time the ship sails." More than this one volunteer, whom she does not identify, Brown was hoping that "God is calling and sending others soon for He needs some Pentecostal workers in that corner of His vineyard, which is so dear to Him. Pray that He will thrust them out very soon."[29]

On March 22, 1919 Brown wrote from Port Said, Egypt, estimating that she would arrive in Jerusalem in early April.[30] By June of 1919 word was received of Brown's arrival in Jerusalem. She now held the position of senior missionary and leader of the Pentecostal mission in Palestine. In her first report she observed that Jerusalem was vastly improved since she left two years beforehand, attributing the better conditions to the work of the American Red Cross and the presence of British soldiers everywhere.[31] Stephen Trowbridge, the British official who headed up the relief and recovery effort

26. Brown, "Behold, He Cometh," *Christian Evangel* (April 19, 1919) 3.

27. Brown, "A New Regime Among the Moslems," *Latter Rain Evangel* (January 1919) 5. The British military administration in Palestine obliged Protestant missionaries to participate in post-war relief projects of the Red Cross as a condition for residing in Jerusalem.

28. Brown, "Back to Jerusalem," *Christian Evangel* (February 22, 1919) 13.

29. Ibid.

30. Brown, "Port Said, Egypt," *Christian Evangel* (May 17, 1919) 2.

31. Brown, "Jerusalem, Palestine," *Christian Evangel* (June 28, 1919) 11. A group of fifty-eight persons were sent out by the American Red Cross Commission to Palestine on a mission of relief and recovery. This group included doctors, nurses, social workers, engineers, secretaries, and missionaries. Brown participated in the work of the Red Cross upon her return to Palestine. Full scale missionary work was not permitted until the work of the Red Cross was completed. On June 3, 1919 the resumption of missionary activities was officially authorized by British Major General A. W. Money. Smidgall, "American Holiness Churches in the Holy Land," 103.

in Palestine, corroborates Brown's account in reporting on conditions in Jerusalem and the work of the Red Cross expedition. He tells of companies of Armenian refugees who had escaped from Kerak arriving in Jerusalem stripped of their clothes. The farmlands were largely unsown owing to a shortage of oxen. The Red Cross was feeding 7,000 unemployed in soup kitchens, providing rations for hundreds of stranded pilgrims. The tattered clothes of the families of Jerusalem were being mended and free medical care was being administered by Zionist medical units and graduates of the Syrian Protestant College in Beirut. The funds for this aid had come from the United States. In gratitude the Muslim sheikhs of Jerusalem addressed a letter of thanks to the American public.[32]

ADVANCEMENT OF THE MISSION

Despite the lack of adequate facilities for meetings, within a few months Brown began to see results. She reports a baptism and issues an appeal for volunteers, ideally a pastor and wife. As one might imagine, the extent of human need was overwhelming due to the degree of suffering and poverty.[33] Yet in the midst of it Brown gladly observes, "There is a spirit of inquiry and a readiness to hear the gospel in both the Jewish and Moslem population that is far beyond what I expected to find."[34]

As Brown celebrated her 25th anniversary as a missionary in Palestine, she was virtually alone in the management of the mission. With opportunities for expanding the territory of the mission staring her in the face, Brown appeals, "I need helpers and need them badly, but they must be of the right sort." Brown reported that she had abundant opportunities knocking at her door. "The land of Palestine offers peculiar possibilities for missionary work at the present time. It is a land of many peoples. Besides the Arabs who claim the land as their own, there are the Mohammedans, the Greek and Roman Catholics and Jews. Missionary work must be done among all these people."[35] If the potential for missionary work was great in Palestine, so were the difficult conditions for missionaries. The swelling Jewish population in Jerusalem caused a housing shortage that proved detrimental to Brown's search for a suitable home to rent. She estimated that "the Jews are coming at a rate of 1,000 a month."[36] As a result, "Jerusalem is so crowded that there are from thirty to forty families in one house, three and four families being crowded into one room. The house problem for the next year promises to be even more serious than it was last year." When she found a house, she had to pay two years rent in advance at an exorbitant price.[37] Nevertheless, the Pentecostal missionaries welcomed the increase in Jewish immigration. Indeed,

---

32. "Latest News from Jerusalem," *Pentecostal Holiness Advocate* 2.18 (August 29, 1918) 12.

33. "Sister A. E. Brown writes from Jerusalem," *Christian Evangel* (August 9, 1919) 10.

34. "Miss A. E. Brown writes from Jerusalem Palestine," *Christian Evangel* (September 20, 1919) 10.

35. "The Land of Palestine," *Pentecostal Evangel* (December 25, 1920) 13.

36. *Latter Rain Evangel* (April 1921) 14.

37. Brown, "A Haven Found in Jerusalem," *Pentecostal Evangel* (January 22, 1921) 13; "Palestine and the Jew," *Latter Rain Evangel* (February 1921) 22.

S. B. Rohold, a Pentecostal Hebrew Christian missionary, was rejoicing over recent baptisms. He was enjoying success among the Jewish population in Haifa. "We have an increasing number of Hebrew Christians here in the Holy Land, and their burdens and trials are by no means light."[38] Joyner was also upbeat, reporting that although only a few Jews had accepted Jesus, "many are buying the New Testament and reading, some secretly for fear of other Jews. Pray for them!" He also saw signs of progress in the Arabs with whom he was working in Beit Jala, averring, "God is working, many are having dreams and visions of the Holy Spirit being poured out and I am expecting greater blessings and a Pentecostal revival."[39]

According to her correspondence, Brown's missionary work was yielding unprecedented fruit. She reported a steady flow of converts, including Muslims and Jews. She writes, "There was never a time in my 26 years on the field when Jews and Moslems were so open to the Gospel as they are now."[40] In the summer of 1921, Harold K. Needham, the overseas representative for the General Council of the American AG, arrived in Jerusalem on a missions tour and organized Brown's converts into a church with a native worker, Brother Samuel, as pastor. Special meetings were planned for the fall.[41] To assist with these meetings, Brown called upon her missionary colleagues in the region, Yumna Malick from Shweifat, Syria (now Lebanon) and Sister Salyer from Cairo, Egypt. The meetings were successful. According to Brown's count, out of the 80–100 in attendance, "20 or so confessed faith in Jesus. One sister was saved and waited on the Lord for healing and anointing."[42]

Yumna Malick Returns to Shweifat, Syria

Yumna Malick, who had been a participant in the 1908 revival led by Thomas B. Barratt, was longing for the day when she could return from schooling in America to serve as a Pentecostal missionary in her home village of Shweifat (near Beirut, Lebanon). That day had come. From 1921 on, Brown and Malick worked together closely.

After graduating from the Elim Bible Institute in Rochester, New York, Malick did parish work in Pentecostal churches connected with the Elim movement in the United States. In 1918, she supplied a progress report to the Elim periodical, *Trust*, as was customary for former students of the Elim Institute. After relating that she had left her home "in the Lebanon of Palestine and Syria to come to Elim Bible School," she speculated on her future plans: "I do not know anything yet about the time, or the plan God has for me in regard to going back to my country. I have not heard from my people for fifteen months and have tried different ways of reaching them by correspondence, all in vain. I am resigned to the will of my Father for I know whom I

---

38. Rohold, "Baptisms at Haifa," *Trust* (May 1923) 12.

39. Joyner, "News from Jerusalem," *Church of God Evangel* (March 18, 1922) 4.

40. Brown, *Word and Work* (October 8, 1921) 14.

41. "Miss A. Eliz. Brown," *Pentecostal Evangel* (July 23, 1921) 13.

42. Brown, "Special Services in Jerusalem," *Pentecostal Evangel* (October 15, 1921) 12.

have believed . . . I also know He doeth all things well."[43] By 1921, Malick was back in Shweifat, telling of a stirring response to her first prayer meeting.[44] Early the next year she told of the testimony of a Muslim converted at the watch-night service, and states, "I am sure that the Lord has many souls in this place, and am looking for the time when 'Lebanon shall be turned into a fruitful field.'"[45]

Apparently Elizabeth Brown took a special interest in Yumna Malick, who writes, "God has been good to me in sending along Miss Brown from Jerusalem with her God given automobile which was a great help to me in reaching several villages with the gospel message."[46] At this point Malick was weighing the opportunities that were presented to her. "In many places people have begged me to open schools for them, and they are willing to help toward expenses."[47] She was seeing mixed results. A young man was converted but hesitated to make public his conversion out of fear of the repercussions, which was reasonable, given the practice of ostracism in such cases. Malick worked with children, visited in homes, and conducted cottage meetings, i.e., home Bible studies. Her strategy can be ascertained from a comment she makes concerning her village ministry: "I usually take along with me some of the young converts to train for the work. They are also a help in their testimonies and singing."[48] In one village a woman was "led by the Spirit" to appeal urgently for a missionary like Malick to be sent to her village, pleading, "My people do not know God, and our children are running wild like heathen. What Roman Catholic schools we have are not able to change them. I will offer my house for prayer-meetings and a school-room if you will come." The Pentecostal audience imbibed deeply of such reports, as can be seen from the editorial comment immediately following: "When a Mohammedan woman will come pleading for a meeting in her village and offering her home for this purpose, is it not a marked sign that God is visiting these dark places?"[49]

Throughout the 1920s Yumna Malick reported promising developments in her ministry in Syria. An American with "a burdened heart for perishing souls" joined her mission in 1925 and was going out into distant villages preaching and distributing literature. "The only thing needed now," Malick points out, "is his support. Will you pray with me that God may soon supply this great need, especially that our Lord's coming draweth nigh?"[50] Malick's school and orphanage continued to thrive. In 1927 she reports, "The school and orphanage is doing well and increasing in number of children. Anything in the way of clothing, shoes or foodstuff such as cereals and other

43. Malick, "Letters from Students: From Miss Yuma G. Malick," *Trust* (April 1918) 2, 10.

44. Malick, "Lebanon, Beyrout, Syria," *Pentecostal Evangel* (April 16, 1921) 13.

45. Malick, "The New Year in Syria," *Pentecostal Evangel* (March 18, 1922) 20.

46. Malick, "Syria," *Trust* (February 1923) 15.

47. Ibid.

48. Malick, "Work in Syria," *Pentecostal Evangel* (July 28, 1923) 12.

49. Malick, "The Gospel in Syria," *Latter Rain Evangel* (September 1923) 23.

50. Malick, "Sweifat-Lebanon-Syria," *Trust* (March 1925) 23.

things I can get out of the customs in Beyrout without paying duty on it. Have secured a permit to do so for the sake of my poor children."[51]

Establishment of the Mission Station in Jerusalem

As Malick's mission in Shweifat was now up and running, Brown's was exploding. Most significantly, the doors of the prisons of Palestine were swinging open for Brown to enter freely with the Pentecostal message. As early as Christmas of 1920 she remarks that "God is blessing in the Prison work."[52] The next year Brown's prison ministry expanded when she was invited to teach a Sunday School class in the boy's reformatory of Jerusalem.[53] With her work load increasing, Brown took a spill and sprained her knee. Hobbled and in a splint, she received much appreciated help from a Norwegian Brother and Sister Biorness, whom she spoke of as "God's answer to our prayers for a man and wife to help us."[54]

From this time on, interlaced in Brown's accounts of one breakthrough after another in her prison ministry, one finds emphatic pleas for help in meeting two pressing needs. First and foremost was the need for securing a Pentecostal mission hall in Jerusalem. In one report Brown tells of the conversion of a thirteen year-old Muslim boy and states that her prison work is being blessed with 200 attending a midweek meeting. Then, as if to ask for more contributions, she interjects a word of thanks for money donated for a meeting place.[55] In her very next letter to the *Pentecostal Evangel* she stresses that there is a great need for a permanent mission home. Then she turns her attention to the prison ministry, relating a story about a Muslim prisoner who trusted in Christ just prior to his execution. Brown had prime opportunities for making an impact on the prison population, as "Jews, Moslems and nominal Christians come into the meetings freely and we have many requests for Bibles."[56] In one case, a prisoner was granted a short-term leave to help Brown with her ministry and "was very preciously baptized before he had to return to the prison." As if to seize the opportunity for an appeal, Brown quickly adds, "We have been waiting upon the Lord especially about the Mission Hall. His word to me this a.m. is 'Arise and build.'"[57]

Motivated by this inner prompting, Brown felt constrained to expand the scope of her missionary activity. She fully expected that she would have a mission hall and a mission home too. In 1922 she explained to potential donors that we "could have had two more baptisms if we had a place." At this time Brown received permission from the British authorities to expand her jail ministry to the prison in Jaffa, and intended

51. Malick, "Sweifat-Lebanon, Syria," *Trust* (September–October 1927) 21.

52. "The Land of Palestine," *Christian Evangel* (December 25, 1920) 13.

53. Brown, "Jerusalem, Palestine," *Pentecostal Evangel* (April 16, 1921) 13.

54. "Epistle from Jerusalem," *Pentecostal Evangel* (November 12, 1921) 12.

55. "Miss A. Eliz. Brown," *Pentecostal Evangel* (April 1, 1922) 13.

56. Brown, "A Lighthouse in Jerusalem," *Pentecostal Evangel* (May 27, 1922) 12.

57. Brown, "A Prisoner Taken Captive," *Pentecostal Evangel* (August 5, 1922) 12.

to ask for a permit to work in the Haifa prison.[58] Perhaps she was pressing too hard, because a month later she writes from the Lebanon Mountains, where she was on a retreat with Yumna Malick and other missionary friends from Egypt, Brother and Sister Doney, Sister Salyer, and Jennie McConnell: "As I am very weary and have come to rest I must not write long letters. The Lord has provided a helper to remain in the home with the girls, and to look after the work in Jerusalem during my absence."[59] Very soon she returned to the fray, announcing that God has opened the doors of four more prisons and telling of her intense travel schedule, village work, and, of course, the increased need for a mission hall in Jerusalem.[60] It is noteworthy that Brown was privileged to have access to all the prisons in Palestine.[61] And she had results to show for her labors. In the fall of 1923 she reports that a Muslim man and his wife were asking for baptism and a young Jewish boy had accepted Jesus as his Messiah and Savior.[62] In 1924 she circulated an intriguing story of a prisoner's dramatic conversion. After openly admitting his guilt and freely making restitution for his wrongdoing, the prison authorities permitted an early release. When the man returned home, his house was bombed, but he stood firm in his faith.[63]

Brown was doing all she could to stir up support for a mission hall in Jerusalem. She took every opportunity to pull on the purse strings of Pentecostal tourists. One such person was the evangelist Mae Frey, who submitted an article to the *Pentecostal Evangel* with observations of her tour of Palestine. She writes, "In Palestine, and in Egypt the doors are wide open for the Gospel; but Jerusalem, the place where Jesus suffered and died to bring us to God, is without a Gospel Mission, and almost destitute of missionaries."[64] Brown also practiced the golden rule of giving: give unto others as you would have them give unto you. In her Sunday School class, she took up a special offering for the Central Bible Institute of the AG in Springfield, Missouri, about which she says that "our offering was the equivalent of the dollar which I enclose with this. As our people are all poor and we are not very many, I think they did pretty well, and the dollar will help to even build a Bible School, and the love of our people and the willingness of their offering and their prayers, will help a little too."[65]

Besides the facilities she ardently desired, Brown identified a second pressing need of the mission in Palestine, namely, recruits who were well suited for the particular demands of Jerusalem. She explained that only those who are endorsed by the General Council and are willing to work under the District Council can come.[66]

58. "Miss A. Elizabeth Brown," *Pentecostal Evangel* (September 30, 1922) 13.

59. Brown, "A Vacation in Syria," *Pentecostal Evangel* (October 28, 1922) 12.

60. "Miss A. Elizabeth Brown," *Pentecostal Evangel* (January 20, 1923) 13.

61. "Glory out of Shame," *Latter Rain Evangel* (August 1923) 13–14.

62. "Miss A. Elizabeth Brown," *Pentecostal Evangel* (September 8, 1923) 12.

63. Brown, "Good News From Jerusalem," *Pentecostal Evangel* (January 26, 1924) 10–11.

64. Frey, "Things as They Are in Society Today: Conditions That Call for Prayer and our Utmost Endeavor," *Pentecostal Evangel* (May 24, 1924) 2–3.

65. "Helping to the Build the Bible School," *Pentecostal Evangel* (November 17, 1923) 8.

66. "Missionaries for Jerusalem," *Pentecostal Evangel* (September 4, 1920) 12.

Presumably, some who had come were not a good fit. One of these may have been C. M. Grace, who appeared on the scene and said, "I am looking to hear directly from heaven."[67] Brother Grace was probably too ethereal to be of much earthly utility. However, the two new recruits who arrived in 1923, Laura Radford and Vida Baer, were just the kind of missionaries for whom Brown was looking. According to the *Latter Rain Evangel,* "Miss Laura Radford who spent seventeen years in India, and has since done aggressive work in the homeland largely among the soldiers, is sailing Nov. 12th for Palestine, with Mrs. V. Baer of Pasadena, Calif., both of whom are expecting to labor in that field."[68] In Radford, the Pentecostal mission in Palestine had gained an accomplished organizer and Bible teacher. Obviously pleased, Brown writes, "God has graciously sent Sister Radford."[69] Vida Baer was also a valuable asset. She was a gifted writer with a broad network of contacts in North American Pentecostal circles. In her first letter she describes Elizabeth Brown's prison ministry with overtones of geo-piety that played well with the Pentecostal audience. She also reports that Laura Radford is starting Bible classes.[70]

As Radford surveyed the mission work in Jerusalem, she observed that "a few are seeking the Baptism in the Holy Spirit." For Radford this was a promising sign that "surely the time has come for the latter rain to be poured out upon Jerusalem."[71] Despite the addition of gifted personnel, Brown was not satisfied with things as they were. Still there was no mission hall in Jerusalem. Then a breakthrough came. When Brown was forced to vacate the house she had been renting, she found a house for sale on a piece of property with room to build a mission hall. The house was large enough to accommodate a Sunday School, an assembly hall, and a reading room on the lower level, with living rooms above. Stepping out in faith, Brown immediately submitted an offer to the owner and then challenged her constituency, declaring, "God has therefore put before the Pentecostal people this door of large opportunity to go forward."[72] While awaiting the funds for the purchase of this property, located at the corners of King George V and Mamillah Streets, Brown rented it, named it "Shemariah" (kept by God), and occupied it in faith.[73]

All things considered, the 1920s were a period of advancement for the mission work in Jerusalem. As seen through the eyes of both the missionaries and the Pentecostal periodicals, a spirit of relative tranquility was now prevailing in Palestine. From New England, Albert Weaver surmised that "at present peace and quiet seem to reign." Weaver gave three reasons for saying so. First, "Miss Brown is doing a splendid work, especially in the prisons." Second, the Pentecostal Hebrew Christian evangelist, S. B. Rohold, claimed to be making inroads into the Jewish community of Haifa. Third,

67. Grace, "Jerusalem, Palestine," from a letter dated 9/29/23, *Word and Work* (October 1923) 14.

68. "Outgoing Missionaries," *Latter Rain Evangel* (October 1923) 10.

69. Brown, "Our Work in Jerusalem," *Pentecostal Evangel* (March 29, 1924) 9.

70. Baer, "A Letter from Palestine," *Pentecostal Evangel* (March 15, 1924) 7.

71. Radford, "In a Dry and Thirsty Land," *Pentecostal Evangel* (February 16, 1924) 4.

72. Brown, "A Plea for the Work in Jerusalem," *Pentecostal Evangel* (March 29, 1924) 9.

73. Perkins, "Israel and Missions," 15.

Archibald Forder was reporting a positive response to the Arabic Scriptures he was distributing among the Muslim population.[74] Vida Baer also thought that events were moving in a favorable direction. "A great change is coming gradually over this land, old things are passing away. The Jews are coming back to their own land and are more open to the New Testament than ever before."[75]

Radford was also upbeat. She concurred with Brown concerning the necessity of enlarged facilities for the mission to advance further. She sized up Brown's new property, concluding that it will "give us a room seating about 100, and an office, prayer-room and Bible depot." She continues, "Upstairs we will have our missionary quarters, with a spare room for any fellow-missionary who may be needing a quiet place to wait upon God . . . Miss Brown will continue her home for girls in a suitable house out in a quiet part of the city, and is praying that God will send a suitable worker to take over the care of the Training Home, so she may be free to give all of her time to her Prison work, to which the Lord has so definitely called her."[76] Baer describes the division of the territory worked out between Brown and Radford: "Miss Brown will keep on with her prison work and keep her girls with her. She will have the evangelistic work, and the public meetings, and Miss Radford will have the Bible classes."[77] Indeed, the future looked promising.

In the fall of 1924, Brown, Baer, and a Miss Easton made a mission trip to Syria to check in with Yumna Malick in Shweifat, observe her school, and do evangelistic visitation in nearby villages. Malick had started the school three years earlier with fifty-four children of different faiths and nationalities. She was proud of an eight year-old Muslim girl who "will tell you, if asked, how Jesus came into her heart; others will too, while others are getting interested in learning to pray in the name of Jesus."[78] Baer was impressed with what she saw, commenting that "of the children we have seen in Syria, surely the brightest and most intelligent looking were in her school. The little girls wear black dresses with white embroidered collars which they worked themselves." From Shweifat they went on to Tyre where they stayed with a native pastor, Matta Abboud, and his family. Baer describes the accommodations as "a nice, large parlor with two divans, tile floors covered with Persian rugs. The meals are served on a little table less than one foot high. We sit on cushions and drink tea and eat native bread served on a tray on the floor—sheets of bread, perhaps a foot and a half in diameter and folded up, thin as a shaving, honey and cheese and cusa, cucumbers and eggs." After "an unusually long night" spent in cramped sleeping conditions foreign to Westerners, the missionaries were on their way early to the coast where they did prison ministry in Tyre and Acre, and then enjoyed tourist stops in Shechem and Tel Aviv. Baer takes note that Palestine "is changing, the Jews are coming back to their land." She describes the modern features of Tel Aviv—wide streets, modern houses,

74. Weaver, "Jerusalem, Palestine," letter dated February 25, 1924, *Word and Work* (April 1924) 10.

75. Baer, "Bible Evangelistic Mission Jerusalem," *Pentecostal Evangel* (October 25, 1924) 10.

76. "Miss Laura Radford," *Latter Rain Evangel* (August 1924) 14.

77. Baer, "The Work in Jerusalem," *Pentecostal Evangel* (August 9, 1924) 10.

78. Malick, "Pentecost in Syria," *Pentecostal Evangel* (October 4, 1924) 10.

electric lights, even ice cream signs on the streets, and good substantial houses. Then she remarks, "Three years ago it was all a barren wilderness of sand; now a thriving, progressive, modern city of some thousands of well dressed, well fed, happy Jewish people in their own land. Israel is being gathered again."[79] One detects a contrast in tone in Baer's depiction of the native pastor's home and diet, as opposed to her glowing tribute to the modern amenities of Tel Aviv. In any event, Brown must have worn out her car because soon after returning from Syria she writes, "My Ford has made its last trip, I fear." She then asks her supporters to "trust with me that in a month's time I may have the price of a new car."[80]

In the fall of 1924 an unforeseen opportunity for the expansion of the mission in Palestine presented itself when the Christian and Missionary Alliance mission in Jerusalem asked Brown to take over its day school and Sunday School in the German Colony.[81] In response, she says, "It seems that God is planning to enlarge the work even more than we have thought." However, Brown was already overworked. Given her responsibilities as senior missionary, plus the prison work which she would not relinquish, Brown insists that it is "imperative that someone come out to help me." Wistfully she remarks, "I would like to know how to divide myself up to do the work of three." She asks for two Spirit-filled and equipped young women to be sent out to run the school, village work, and training home work while they study Arabic. Turning to Radford's role in the mission, Brown says that she has "excellent plans for prosecuting and enlarging the general work, the nucleus of which has been going on for several years, Sunday School and meetings and her Bible classes, a reading room and a book room. Also she plans an English meeting which would be a great blessing to the community."[82] As there was only so much the two of them could do, the need for additional personnel weighed heavily upon Brown, leading her to pray earnestly "that a young man and wife will offer themselves for the work and will come and begin the study of the language soon."[83]

Of all the accomplishments of the mission in the inter-war period, the most significant was the establishment of a mission station in Jerusalem. This was made possible when a sizable gift, designated for the renovation of the home purchased by Elizabeth Brown and construction of a chapel, was received from an AG church in Pasadena, California. The missionaries extended their hearty thanks to the pastor, J. S. Norvell, and the congregation. More contributions would be forthcoming from this church for the funding of the chapel building adjacent to the renovated home. Finally,

79. Baer, "Evangelizing in Bible Lands," *Pentecostal Evangel* (September 13, 1924) 7.

80. Brown, "Progress in Jerusalem," *Pentecostal Evangel* (October 4, 1924) 8.

81. In the early 1920s the missions strategy of the CMA changed abruptly with the transition in leadership following the death of A. B. Simpson. The new leaders of the CMA, Paul Rader, successor to A. B. Simpson, and William Turnbull, dean of the Nyack Missionary Training Institute, depreciated the role of educational institutions in evangelization on the mission field. When funding for the CMA schools in Palestine was slashed, the CMA missionaries were forced to relinquish the day school in the German Colony in Jerusalem. Schmidgall, "American Holiness Churches in the Holy Land," 108–12.

82. Ibid.

83. "The Missionaries in Jerusalem," *Pentecostal Evangel* (October 18, 1924) 10.

the Pentecostals had a mission station, which would serve them well as a home base in Jerusalem. Baer describes the schedule for utilization of the new facility: "We have a Saturday evening meeting to which all, including Jews, are invited. In connection with the Gospel Hall, we have a Reading Room and a Prayer Room, in which are provided both Arabic and Hebrew Bibles, and Gospels are always available." The money had not yet come in for furnishings, but trusting that it would materialize soon, the missionaries planned to commence special evangelistic meetings within a month with hopes and prayers "that the Latter Rain may fall again in Jerusalem."[84]

The home base provided a site for expanded ministries. Radford was clearly overwhelmed with "the thought of the open doors before us here. God is blessing the Word as it is given out every night in our evangelistic services. There are many non-Christians coming in to listen and to ask questions as the opportunity is given. Miss Brown so much needs someone to help her in the work. Is there not someone to come? Surely there must be!"[85] There was no doubt that Brown and Radford had a vision for expanded outreach. About that Baer writes, "There is no end to Miss Radford's vision of great things for God, and I know He will meet her faith. Miss Brown does prison and relief work. We are now entirely separate from her, and ours is the public work in the city."[86] Baer even went so far as to claim that the older missionary societies were sitting up and taking notice of the evangelistic effectiveness of the Pentecostals. In reporting on recent special evangelistic meetings at the new Pentecostal mission station, Radford mentions that Rev. Habeeb Bushara of the Christian Holiness Mission in Cairo spoke on September 29 and Kamil Effendi Mansour, a convert from Islam, on October 12, both with good effect. "One Sheikh (a Moslem teacher and leader) who had come in often last winter for Bible study, we invited for a personal interview with Kamil Eff., who himself had been a Sheikh, and a full surrender was made to Christ."[87] Baptized converts included one from the Latin Church, two from the Church Missionary Society, three from the Christian and Missionary Alliance, and the others from the Pentecostal mission.

Initially Radford had joined forces with Brown at the Shemariah Mission Station, but they later divided the mission work. This came about when a number or men were converted through the ministry of Radford. This presented a cultural dilemma, because by 1927 Brown was caring for a large number of orphaned girls at the Shemariah facility. Brown and Radford thought it wise to segregate the men from the girls. Hence, Radford rented a large building at the Mandelbaum Gate and registered her ministry as the Bible Evangelistic Mission with the British Consulate in St. Louis, Missouri on February 2, 1927.[88]

---

84. Baer, "Bible Evangelistic Mission Jerusalem," *Pentecostal Evangel* (October 25, 1924) 10.

85. Radford, "Help Needed in Palestine," *Pentecostal Evangel* (December 13, 1924) 10.

86. "Here and There," *Pentecostal Evangel* (January 3, 1925) 6.

87. Radford, "A Sheikh Becomes a Christian," *Latter Rain Evangel* (January 1926) 15.

88. Perkins, "Israel and Missions," 16.

Expansion into Transjordan

The second most significant accomplishment of the mission in Palestine was the expansion of its territory into Transjordan. A new outstation was established in the town of Es Salt in 1927. Its beginning, as Radford put it, "reads like the story of the wise men seeking Jesus." A group of dissident Arab Greek Orthodox Christians from Es Salt came to Jerusalem looking for an American missionary. Providentially, they came into contact with Radford and told her that "the head of the Greek Church is wholly corrupt; that for six years they had no one to give them the Holy Communion or bury their dead, and that all the heads of his family (clan) had vowed a sacred oath to be Protestant in faith and not to return to the Greek Church." The native Pentecostal pastor interjected, "But we do not administer Holy Communion to the unsaved nor do we baptize children." Taken aback, one of the men from Es Salt said, "Oh, will you not just dip two fingers in a bowl of water and make the sign of the cross on the forehead?" Radford emphatically replied, "No, we cannot do that." The delegation then departed, leaving Radford to suppose that was the end of that. But the delegation returned the next day saying they would accept the teaching of the Pentecostal mission. Upon arriving in Es Salt, Radford was welcomed by a throng of 1,000 people, including the local leader of the Muslim residents. She met with a group of over eighty Arab Christians who had broken away from the Greek Orthodox Church and wanted an American mission church and school. The editor of the *Latter Rain Evangel* exclaims, "What an opportunity! It was one that comes rarely in the life of a missionary." On the spot Radford concluded, "There must be a Bible School to teach these young men, teachers for the women, an assembly formed. There are over a thousand people entailed in this landslide. Who is sufficient for these things?" The editor interjects, "Only our God!" The Stone Church in Chicago sent out Charles Peters to assist Radford in getting the mission in Es Salt up and running. An Egyptian evangelist was hired to do the preaching. Within a year the congregation had grown to 365 people, led by a native pastor, a Bible woman, and three teachers in two schools.[89]

The mission in Es Salt continued to prosper. In March of 1928 the *Latter Rain Evangel* reports that "Miss Laura Radford, writing from Es Salt, in Trans-Jordania, says that 'a few weeks ago there was a real break and a number of the girls in the school were saved. They have since been praying for others, and in the Women's Meeting there was a deep spirit of prayer.'"[90] Radford suggests that Es Salt may be the Ramoth Gilead of the Old Testament, a city of refuge. It would appear that she was attempting to make a case for the Es Salt outstation that would be appealing to the Christian Zionists in her reading audience. She traces the route from Jerusalem to Es Salt, then describes its people as "rugged, hospitable, fiery, with large ambitions, but often moved by childish whims and fancies; we love them and thank God for the

---

89. "The Earthquake That Shook Palestine: When Tribes Begged for the Gospel," *Latter Rain Evangel* (September 1927) 10–11.

90. *Latter Rain Evangel* (March 1928) 16.

confidence they have in us, and their willingness to gather several times each week to be taught the Word of God."[91]

Lamenting that the potential for Christian missions was untapped in Es Salt, Amman, and the adjoining Muslim lands, Radford issued an "urgent appeal for two young men, with the ability and willingness to learn Arabic, to hold a splendid opening recently secured in Trans-Jordania."[92] Two young aspiring Pentecostal missionaries responded to Radford's appeal, the first of whom was a woman. Vera Swarztrauber of Zion, Illinois went to Palestine as a first-time missionary to work with Radford in 1929.[93] The second was Roy Whitman, who was fluent in Arabic, and served in Es Salt with great success. In July of 1929 Whitman reported that an "awakening has come not only to our own congregation, but the Greeks, Latins and Catholics have come into the meetings and some have been gloriously saved."[94] Radford rejoices over the testimonies of the converts, who "describe their present changed condition by saying, 'Since we received the Light,' and the men who have been born of the Spirit say, 'Now that I am free.'" One man said, "We were in darkness, but now we are moving out from under the shadow that has been so long upon all of us in Transjordania."[95] Once the word spread about what was happening in Es Salt, several villages in Transjordan were expressing interest in the services of a Pentecostal missionary.

Satellite Outpost in Persia

During the 1920s the Pentecostal territory in the region expanded even beyond Transjordan. In 1924 John Warton, an American of Iranian origin, came through Jerusalem on his way to serve as a Pentecostal missionary in Persia (now Iran).[96] Warton had attended the Nyack Missionary Training Institute (Christian and Missionary Alliance) and the Elim Bible Institute (Pentecostal) in Rochester, New York.[97] He settled in the town of Hamadan, the city of Queen Esther of the Bible. He was glad to find "a deep desire in the hearts of the people for the real truth and we feel the Lord has brought us here in due time."[98] The next year Warton reported good attendance and "some have already given their hearts to the Lord." At this point he thought it "not

91. Radford, "Trans Jordan and the Borders of Arabia," *Latter Rain Evangel* (June 1928) 10.

92. "Missionary Briefs," Supplement, *Redemption Tidings* 3.3 (March 1927) iv. Donald Gee made known Radford's appeal while itinerating in Australia, informing audiences of the Pentecostal mission in Jerusalem. "Our sister, Laura Radford, has a splendid healthy work going on there. One thing she is always writing to me about: 'Brother Gee, can't you send me young men?' Young men, there is a magnificent place for you in the very place where John the Baptist used to preach." Gee, "The Romance of Pentecostal Missions," *Australian Evangel* 3.1 (July 1, 1928) 10.

93. *Latter Rain Evangel* (March 1929) 15.

94. Radford, "A Forty Days Revival," *Latter Rain Evangel* (July 1929) 19.

95. Radford, "Transjordania and the Borders of Arabia," *The Elim Evangel and Foursquare Revivalist* 11.33 (September 18, 1931) 604.

96. Wharton, "Persia's Open Door," *Pentecostal Evangel* (January 12, 1924) 6–7.

97. McGee, *This Gospel . . . Shall be Preached*, 63.

98. "Brother John G. Wharton Arrives in Persia," *Pentecostal Evangel* (November 22, 1924) 10.

so difficult to deal with the Mohammedans as formerly, for they are crying, 'Who will bring us the light?' and there is a real hunger in their hearts for the truth."[99] Without the convenience of modern conveyances of transportation, Warton traveled on horseback to reach the towns and cities that were receptive to his preaching.

Trouble on the Horizon

Just when the prospects for success looked as if they were being actualized, trouble was appearing just over the horizon. The sun was beginning to set on the period of expansion and a dark night of unimaginable suffering was close at hand. A number of articles published in Pentecostal periodicals in the 1920s were representative of the ignorance among Pentecostals concerning the mounting crisis in the Middle East in the interwar period. In "Signs of the Times," E. L. Langston states that since 1917 a spiritual awakening has been underway among the dry bones of Israel, made possible by Great Britain's conquest of the Promised Land under General Allenby. Why has Britain had this privilege? For an answer to his own question Langston turns to Old Testament prophecy, which, he believes, predicts the restoration of the Jews in Palestine. For Langston this is proof positive that Christ will soon be enthroned in the Promised Land. To be prepared, it is incumbent upon us to "Save others!"[100] In "Prophecy Fulfilling in Jerusalem," the *Pentecostal Evangel* reports that Chief Rabbi Kook of Palestine has announced a new "Yeshibah" (seminary), which is an urgent necessity for the rebuilding of the temple. The editor then comments, "How wonderful are the signs accumulating which indicate the imminent coming of the Lord Jesus Christ."[101] In an editorial collage, "Here and There," the *Pentecostal Evangel* is bullish on Muslim evangelization. Drawing from an article, "Disciples in Moslem Lands," by Mary Holmes in *The Moslem World*, the editor relates stories of many "Mohammedans" turning to Christ, including a Pasha, i.e., a Muslim government official. The editor also includes a piece on "Seven Thousand Converts," telling of a prominent *sheikh* in Abyssinia whose reading of the Bible led him to renounce the Qur'an and then convince his 7,000 followers to convert from Islam to Christianity.[102] In "Turkey's Women Unveiled," the *Latter Rain Evangel* reports that the women of Turkey "are removing their veils. They are not only going about with their faces uncovered, but they are also taking part in politics and business." This trend started with the Turkish women who did relief work during the World War and were allowed to remove their veils. Now they do not want to put them on again. "Since the war unveiled women work in stores, operate typewriters and switchboards, and there are many women clerks." There is even talk of doing away with the harem. From this the editor concludes, "There is no doubt that within a few years the women of other heathen lands will be set free from the superstition and cursed customs that have bound them for centuries. Wherever

99. *Latter Rain Evangel* (February 1925) 23.

100. Langston, "Signs of the Times," *Pentecostal Evangel* (March 3, 1923) 2–3, 8.

101. "Prophecy Fulfilling in Jerusalem," *Pentecostal Evangel* (November 3, 1923) 9.

102. "Here and There," *Pentecostal Evangel* (August 16, 1924) 6–7.

Gospel light shines it drives away the darkness."[103] Exactly what the "gospel" has to do with Muslim women shedding their veils is not explained.

The above forecasts in the Pentecostal periodicals proved to be unfounded. Colored by a pro-Zionist bias, the Pentecostal press painted a rosy picture of current events in Palestine. In short, the Pentecostal view of Palestine was not an accurate representation of the events on the ground because the editors of the Pentecostal periodicals left out the Arab side of the story. Nevertheless, now and then a glimmer of reality was seen, such as when the *Latter Rain Evangel* observed in 1925, "Today the deepening shadows are settling down on Palestinian Syria. The fear and dread of men, of war, racial hatred and petty strife are abroad in that land."[104]

WAILING WALL RIOTS

In 1929 the peoples of Palestine were tottering on the edge of a turbulent period of unrest and violence. The Wailing Wall Riots of 1929 came as a great shock to the Pentecostal missionaries and the reading audience of the Pentecostal periodicals, yet the rage that gave rise to the riots had been building up for years. Previous clashes between Arabs and Zionists in 1920 and 1921 had resulted in significant loss of life. For instance, in the riots of May 1921 the casualties were forty-seven Jews dead and 146 wounded; and forty-eight Arabs dead and seventy-three wounded. The casualties in 1929 were far worse. According to the Shaw Commission, the toll at the end of the week-long riots stood at 133 Jewish dead and 339 injured, while the Arabs sustained 116 dead and 232 injured.[105] The hatred leading up to the Wailing Wall Riots crested when a strident Zionist attempt to purchase *waqf* land in the Magharibah neighborhood adjacent to the Wall went awry, was publicized, and incensed the Muslim population as a flagrant affront to their religious convictions. As explained in chapter 3, Muslim tradition and law did not allow the sale or transfer of *waqf* property. This led to demonstrations on both sides which escalated existing tensions. On August 15 a large contingent of Haganah and other paramilitary Zionist youth organizations marched in military formation to the government office at the Damascus Gate and then to the Wailing Wall, where "they hoisted the Zionist flag, sang the Jewish national anthem, listened to a political speech and raised the cry 'the Wall is ours!'"[106] The following Friday, which was the birthday of the prophet Muhammad, a counter-demonstration was organized at the al-Aqsa mosque just above the Wailing Wall. The riots broke out a week later on August 23 when an Arab mob rampaged through the Old City, brutally attacking Jewish people at random. The violence spread from Jerusalem to Hebron and Safed, and continued for one week.[107] Based on a comparison with the available statistics for the riots of 1920 and 1921, Avraham Sela states, "The riots of 1929 were

103. "Turkey's Women Unveiled," *Latter Rain Evangel* (December 1924) 20–21.

104. *Latter Rain Evangel* (December 1925) 13.

105. Sela, "The 'Wailing Wall' Riots," 60.

106. Tibawi, *The Islamic Pious Foundation in Jerusalem: Origins*, 26.

107. Porath, *The Emergence of the Palestinian-Arab National Movement, 1918–1929*, 265–69.

unprecedented in the history of the Arab-Jewish conflict in Palestine, in duration, geographical scope and direct damage to life and property."[108]

Causes of Unrest

The riots were fueled by socio-political factors. The impact of Jewish agricultural colonies on the rural Arab population was deleterious. Jewish land ownership in the rural areas of Palestine rose from 300,000 dunums (67,000 acres) in 1919 to 1,250,000 dunums (280,000 acres) in 1930. With one-third of the arable land of Palestine passing into Jewish hands, Arab peasants and Bedouins were adversely affected. It is estimated that 20,000 peasant families were evicted by the Zionists. According to Ghassan Kanafani, a partisan of the Palestinian nationalist movement, "the transfer of land ownership created an expanding class of dispossessed peasants who turned to seasonal salaried labor. The majority eventually made their way to the cities and sought unskilled labor." As a result, the unemployment rate among the Arab working class rose to astronomical levels, creating the conditions ripe for social and political unrest.[109]

Missionary Reports and Pentecostal Commentary

The Pentecostal missionaries were close at hand during the Wailing Wall Riots. Their reports provided the readership of the Pentecostal periodicals with on the scene accounts of the mayhem. In a letter dated August 31, 1929, Elizabeth Brown reports, "Battles have raged fiercely, lives and property have been wantonly destroyed; but the Lord has kept us above fear or terror. Airplanes by day and machine guns by night seem to be the outward accompaniment of life just now, but we thank God for them and rejoice, knowing that they are ordained of Him for our protection." In an attempt to convey the theological significance of what had ensued, Brown muses, "This is surely an index finger pointing to the speedy return of our Lord and King, Christ Jesus."[110]

Laura Radford provides a graphic report of the carnage. From her perspective, the riots of August 23, 1912, were instigated by the Muslim religious leaders of Jerusalem, who sent out "a raging mob of several hundred men, armed with knives, daggers, 'lathis,' and stones, intent upon killing every Jew in Jerusalem." A group of 2,000 streamed out from the Damascus Gate, "stoning or killing every Jew they met, and breaking into many houses, killing men, women, and children alike." Radford describes how the massacre spread to outlying areas, giving lurid details of the rampage in Hebron. She writes,

> But it was in Hebron where hate and lust raged uncontrolled for many hours. The Rabbinical school was attacked and most the young men killed, some in a most horrible manner. One woman, afterwards brought to the hospital in Jerusalem, told of how a ruffian grabbed her baby from her arms and with relentless hands

108. Sela, "The 'Wailing Wall' Riots," 60.

109. Kanafani, *The 1936–1939 Revolt of Palestine*, 8–9.

110. Brown, "News From Palestine," *Pentecostal Evangel* (October 19, 1929) 10.

rent the mouth asunder and then tore the body limb from limb. Another woman in the hospital told of how the ruffians flung her husband across her knees and there cut him to pieces; then they seized her twenty-year-old daughter and abused her and then cut her in pieces, then they began cutting the woman's arms and body and left her for dead. She has perhaps twenty separate deep cuts on her arms and body.[111]

Radford inflates the casualties as 600 dead, including eight American citizens, two British government officials, and eight rabbis. She places blame for the riots on the Grand Mufti of Jerusalem, Haj Amin al-Husseini, who brazenly denied any complicity in the uprising. The above reports of Brown and Radford painted a very dark picture of the outlook for peace in Palestine and reinforced a negative view of Muslims in the minds of the Pentecostal constituency.

In the aftermath of the Wailing Wall Riots, missionary S. B. Rohold writes "The recent catastrophe that has befallen the land of our Redeemer is far greater than people can imagine. The past few weeks have wrought much havoc. Not only innocent lives have been lost and much property destroyed, but worse than all is the awful hatred in the hearts of men." Rohold saw ominous evidence of this hatred in a parade he observed in Haifa on the anniversary of the Balfour Declaration. He describes a procession carrying a black flag inscribed, "The Moslem-Christian Unity." Rohold interjects, "Such a union is absolutely impossible." He says that the procession visited the Christian churches, again interjecting that "by Christian I mean the so-called Christian Catholic, Maronite and Greek churches." Rohold was deeply troubled that at each church the Muslims and Christians exchanged vows of solidarity. From there the procession went to foreign consulates, protesting against the Balfour Declaration, and ended up at the Governor's headquarters, where a mob formed and had to be dispersed by the British police.[112]

It is well to underscore the ideology that was imbedded in the response of the missionaries to the unraveling political situation in Palestine. For the most part the missionaries assumed a biased point of view on the Arab-Zionist strife. Their reports were interspersed with pro-Zionist political commentary, offered up with the usual eschatological ruminations. The missionary reports were interconnected to the discourse of the wider Pentecostal movement. The missionaries saw the political situation in Palestine through the lens of Pentecostal Zionism and its attendant eschatological stigmatism. A brief glance at the interpretation of current events in Palestine in the Pentecostal periodicals will show that Pentecostals understood events in Palestine as signs of the fulfillment of their eschatological scenario.

Commentaries in the Pentecostal press will be treated further in chapter 8. For now two examples will suffice to show the tenor of the Pentecostal response. George F. Taylor, editor of the *Pentecostal Holiness Advocate* comments on the Wailing Wall

111. Radford, "Days of Terror in Palestine: Jerusalem the Scene of Bloody Massacre. Hebron and Safed filled with Indescribable Atrocities," *Pentecostal Evangel* (October 26, 1929) 15.

112. Kratz, "A Place Called Armageddon," *The Elim Evangel and Foursquare Revivalist* 12.2 (January 9, 1931) 30.

Riots. In an article in his series, "I Saw It in Palestine," he gives a brief sketch of the location, history, and liturgy of the Wailing Wall. He then discusses the controversy that led to the riots, describing the offending chairs and partition which sparked the conflict. Taylor explains both sides of the conflict. On one side, "The Arabs say that for the last ten years the Jews have been progressively encroaching on their property." On the other side, "The Jews are determined to maintain their rights to wail at the wall, and they have recently appealed officially to all nations urging that the Mohammedan desecration of the place be stopped and that it be returned to the Jews through government action." He says that the riots broke out after some Jews kicked a soccer ball into an Arab yard, and a fight ensued, leading the Arabs to demand that the British Government revoke the Balfour declaration." According to Taylor, "this started the present trouble in Palestine," resulting in a hundred or more deaths on each side. Taylor thinks that "it is possible the whole Mohammedan world would rise in the defense of the Arabs in Palestine, and so a world-wide war could come out of this present trouble."[113] While Taylor is fair to the opposing viewpoints and grasps the scope of the danger, he seems to underplay the Zionist provocation of the Arabs by chalking it up to an errant soccer ball.

Another article on the Wailing Wall Riots, also in the *Pentecostal Holiness Advocate*, is entitled "Unrest in Palestine." The author points out that the cause of dispute and contention was the Balfour Declaration, which promised the Jews "their national ambition to enjoy Palestine as their ancestral home." In spite of the fact that "all religions and nationalities have been enjoying equal rights under the British Mandate," the Arabs were not satisfied and "assaults upon the Jews have resulted." According to the Rev. Malcolm M. Maxwell of Jerusalem, "Jews living in the Holy City are painting up large crosses over their houses, in order to shelter under the sign of the Cross." The author states that this forcibly reminds us of "the sprinkling of blood on the door-posts of the Jewish families in Egypt at the time of the Passover to protect them against the angel of death." The Jews were driven to this measure out of fear, not because of a change of heart in regards to Jesus. During the riots an anonymous proclamation was circulated, calling for a holy war of the Arabs to drive out the Jews. The author summarizes the opposing demands of the Arabs and Jews: "The Arabs claim that their country has been divided and that the Jews have been unduly favored in political appointments and other privileges. The Jews make ten demands on the government including a commission of inquiry, security for Jews in all the cities and colonies, the restoration of property, fines on Arab villages, establishment of an armed Jewish police force to protect Jewish communities." The author argues that harmony between Muslims, Jews, and Christians will not be achieved by "the domination of any one class or race or in the physical development of the country," but only by "the recognition of Him who is the Prince of Peace and in loyal submission to Jesus Christ whose right it is to reign."[114] It is striking that in the articles in the Pentecostal periodicals on the

113. Taylor, "I Saw It in Palestine: Wailing Wall," *Pentecostal Holiness Advocate* 13.27 (October 31, 1929) 9–10.

114. "Unrest in Palestine," *Pentecostal Holiness Advocate* 43.22 (December 12, 1929) 7, 10.

Wailing Wall Riots in particular, and the Arab-Zionist conflict in general, no attempt is made to adjudicate the relative civil rights of each side or to propose remedies that are informed by Christian social ethics.

CONTINUED ADVANCEMENT OF THE MISSION

In the midst of political turmoil, the missionaries pressed on with the work of the mission. Steady progress continued to be made on all fronts of the mission in Palestine.

Haifa

R. H. Rohold also had encouraging news concerning his ministry among the Jewish people of Haifa and surrounding settlements. He reports in the *Elim Evangel* that everywhere he went people were "anxious to hear about Jesus, what His relationship is to the Father, what His relationship is to Israel, and what His relationship is to mankind and the world." Aside from the publications from Christian sources, Rohold says that 1929 was a banner year for publications written in Palestine in the Hebrew language, dealing in a sympathetic way with Jesus and his claims. Furthermore, Rohold writes, "Attendance at services, Bible classes, and missions, and seeking privately for information and instruction were so prevalent that we were expecting a mass awakening, for always movements among the individuals spread through the community, and from the communities to the nation."[115]

Jerusalem

In April of 1930 Laura Radford rented a sizable house in the new city north of the Damascus Gate, seeing its potential as a "real life-saving station." She affixed a sign reading "Victory" and listing the Sunday meeting schedule; prayer service at 9 a.m., preaching service at 3:45 p.m. Fortuitously the first Sunday in the new building, May 13, happened to be the day of the Jewish feast of Simon the Righteous, and by Radford's count "more than six thousand Jews, besides the usual number of Arab pedestrians, passed down our street on their pilgrimage to his tomb, and nearly all turned to read our sign which is printed in the three official languages of Palestine, English, Arabic, and Hebrew." Her deepest desire was that Jews, Muslims, and "nominal" (i.e., Eastern) Christians would find common ground in her mission, "seeking forgiveness of sins and a clean heart. Racial hatred and national ambitions are lost sight of as Jesus Christ and Him crucified is revealed to them through the study of the Word and the preaching of the gospel."[116] Or at least one might hope so.

Elizabeth Brown continued to struggle with housing issues. In early 1931 she was asking for prayer concerning the urgent need of adding to her building, writing,

115. Rohold, "Concise Comments and Interesting Items," *The Elim Evangel and Foursquare Revivalist* 11.12 (March 21, 1930) 181.

116. Radford, "Victory," *Pentecostal Evangel* (August 2, 1930) 11.

"The present condition makes it unsafe for the girls under her care since it is easy for thieves to gain entrance."[117] Security was evidently a concern. Serena Hodges, having recently arrived in Jerusalem, was lodging with Brown. She explains, "The top floor of the house, here at Miss Brown's, is still unfinished and we are more or less upset until it is complete." Hodges was in the throes of adjustment. Hence, she continues,

> As I look forward to the tasks that are confronting me I see so many things to pray about. Our two native helpers, one an elderly man, and one a young man, are not yet baptized in the Spirit. Pray that God will give them a hunger and thirst for the infilling. The women's meetings are in need of readjustment, and that seems to be my task . . . Then the prayer meetings and the two Sunday services are a real burden . . . Then the need for a pastor from home is still unmet . . . Our Sunday school has grown nicely in numbers. We do rejoice in this. But very few of the children are saved . . . And once more I would like to remind you that the door to Arabia proper still needs to be opened to the gospel.[118]

Vera Swarztrauber found an open door, much closer than Arabia, when she tagged along with Im Raja, a Bible woman, to a Druze village. "We visited a girls' school and Im Raja asked me to sing an Arabic chorus to the children. I did and then wanted to teach it to them but Im Raja told me that it was forbidden, because the Druse women and girls are not allowed to sing." As they continued on, Im Raja "suddenly dived through a low doorway," pulling Swarztrauber with her into a room shared by a donkey, a couple of cows, a calf, and a baby donkey. The Druze family heartily welcomed the missionaries and sat them down on a straw mat on the floor. They "listened most attentively despite the many interruptions, children coming and going, chickens straying in and having to be shooed out." Swarztrauber was amazed at the aplomb with which Im Raba "gave out the Way of Salvation to about eleven persons, men and women." Afterwards she exclaimed, "We do praise the Lord for the opportunities of this day."[119]

Radford's love for Jerusalem is evident in her reflections on the Easter season of 1932 in Jerusalem. Noting "the absence of the normal amount of pilgrims and tourists from far-away places," she writes,

> Yet as one moves through the crowded streets one sees in the midst of the mixed crowd representatives from many of the near-by countries, men and women who have come to worship at the place where Christ arose on that wonderful Easter morning. The hunger in the hearts of these people is seen on their faces, and one prays that in Jerusalem it may again come to pass that men can say, 'How hear we every man in our own tongue, wherein we were born?' It is only as the gospel of the living Christ is given to these people that their great hunger will be satisfied.[120]

117. "A Request for Prayer," *Pentecostal Evangel* (February 14, 1931) 10.
118. Hodges, "Back in Jerusalem," *Pentecostal Evangel* (May 2, 1931) 11.
119. Swarztrauber, "An Afternoon in a Palestine Village," *Pentecostal Evangel* (May 30, 1931) 7.
120. Radford, "Easter in Jerusalem," *Pentecostal Evangel* (March 26, 1932) 7.

Radford goes on to observe a changing attitude on the part of many seekers. Jews are showing appreciation for Christ as "the greatest Jew the world has ever known." Roman Catholics and Greek Catholics are asking for information about the Holy Spirit and the second coming of Christ.[121] This particular Easter was memorable because of a much needed rainfall, which came after Christians, Moslems, and Jews united in prayer for rain. Then "showers began as the resurrection of Christ was commemorated." For Radford it was certainly no coincidence that "at this time a Pentecostal Convention is being held in Jerusalem, the speakers at which are Donald Gee and Milton Fish (the writer of our Adult and Young Peoples' Teachers' Quarterly notes). Bro. Fish writes: 'Pray for the *latter rain* to fall in Palestine.'"[122]

In Jerusalem the Pentecostal mission continued to be stirred with its usual mix of pressing needs and brimming hopes. Serena Hodges stresses the need for a pastor for the Jerusalem church along with a list of prayer requests, such as increased attendance at the Young Women's English Bible Class, healing of a young woman, and "real" growth in grace in the young people.[123] Anna Adams requests prayer for "God's blessing upon the Sunday School and the women's meetings."[124] Radford asks for donations of Sunday School cards for use in the Sunday Schools of Palestine, but the need most on her mind was a suitable hall for the meetings in Haifa, which was "a new open door and it is important that a good room or building be secured soon."[125] Radford also raises a need of greater import to the mission objectives. She points to a hopeful development. As she sees it, many Jews believe that Jesus Christ is the Messiah to the point that "those who now believe this are usually willing to talk about Him as their Messiah. But our great concern is that they do not know Him as Saviour, and this revelation cannot come to them apart from the conviction of sin." She remonstrates with her readers that united prayer for these splendid Jewish young people would bring about the desired result and urges all who "love His appearing" to pray daily "for the Holy Spirit to be poured out upon this land, so that true repentance may be given and Jesus Christ will be revealed as Saviour to these hungry hearts." Expanding her purview, she inquires, "May I ask for united prayer for Palestine and Transjordania during the coming three months. Among the Arabs there is a real hunger for God in the hearts of most who are not in close touch with fanatical leaders. They want God and many are willing to listen eagerly to the preached Word."[126]

Anna Adams also had reason for hope. She writes, "I find the response to the gospel much better than previously, but still hope to see increased conviction." She describes a recent meeting in which a woman who was unacquainted with evangelical theology was deeply moved by a Pentecostal gospel presentation and said through her tears, "So we really have a door of hope for our sins being forgiven and a life free from

---

121. Ibid.

122. "Rain in Palestine," *Pentecostal Evangel* (April 16, 1932) 3.

123. "Jerusalem, Palestine," *Pentecostal Evangel* (January 6, 1934) 10.

124. Ibid.

125. "Need of Cards in Palestine," *Pentecostal Evangel* (January 26, 1935) 11.

126. Radford, "A Request from Palestine," *Pentecostal Evangel* (March 16, 1935) 5.

sin through Jesus Christ!"[127] In a similar way Elizabeth Brown rejoices, "We want to give praise for the salvation of a young man who was very happily saved in the prison Bible class, and ask prayer that he may be kept by the power of God through faith unto salvation."[128] Similarly, Adams writes, "I am happy to state that there is an increasing hunger for the Word of God manifested among the prisoners, and also among the people in their homes. We have seen several homes transformed in recent weeks."[129] The positive reports continued to flood in. Brown relates a testimony from a member of her prison Bible class who came to her after class with his face lit up and sparkling with joy and said, "Since you have been coming to us I have been saved by the Lord Jesus and I know my sins are all forgiven."[130]

In 1935 Brown celebrated her 40th anniversary as a missionary in Jerusalem and on that occasion she remembered well that "there have been years of peace and years of war; years of plenty and years of famine and pestilence but He has kept me through them all and given me His own joy and peace within. He has most wonderfully provided for all personal needs as well as the needs of the work He has committed to my care."[131] In this same report Brown also cites biblical texts and demographic statistics showing a steady increase in the Jewish population of Jerusalem, from which she deduces that "the 'fig tree' certainly is budding; Israel is gathering back according to the Word of God (Isa. 49:19–23), but in blind unbelief for the time of purification (Mal. 3:3) and her final glorious destiny. Rom. 11:26; Rev. 21:9–27."[132] The "glorious destiny" Brown has in mind is the conversion of the Jewish people to Jesus as Messiah as a last moment escape from the apocalyptic doom of the War of Armageddon. This view was widely held among Pentecostals at that time.

During the spring of 1935 George Jeffreys, leader of the Foursquare Alliance of England and Ireland and a notable Pentecostal revivalist, made an unannounced visit to Palestine. Catching Radford unawares, Brother Correy, pastor of the Jerusalem assembly, notified her that Jeffreys and his revival team had arrived and planned to visit the mission that afternoon. Radford scrambled to drum up interest in a hastily convened communion service, which turned out to be "very precious" though not well attended. The next meeting went exceptionally better. Radford says that "as the Principal presented Christ in all His beauty, hearts began to melt and yield. Many who had been Christians in name only found the joy of receiving Christ as an indwelling Saviour. What a change has been made in their lives!" Jeffreys stayed long enough for Radford to schedule evangelistic meetings in Jerusalem, Amman, Es Salt, and Haifa. Radford reports that at Amman "many were gloriously saved and there were several marked healings." Jeffreys held two meetings in Es Salt. In the first he gave a message of "tremendous force," which compelled many to pray for salvation. In the second, people

127. Adams, "Jerusalem, Palestine," *Pentecostal Evangel* (March 30, 1935) 11.

128. Brown, "Jerusalem, Palestine," ibid.

129. Adams, "Jerusalem, Palestine," *Pentecostal Evangel* (May 25, 1935) 11.

130. Brown, "Jerusalem," *Pentecostal Evangel* (June 29, 1935) 9.

131. Brown, "Forty Years as a Missionary," *Pentecostal Evangel* (April 6, 1935) 11.

132. Ibid.

came forward in groups for prayer with the result that "the burden of sin was gone; the sick babies were well; the ache in the heart had given way to peace and praise!" During the meeting in Haifa it seemed to Radford that the Lord was "saving, blessing and healing, and lifting depressed, sin-sick lives out from the depth of their bondage into the glorious liberty of the sons of God." In summation, Radford exclaims, "How we praise the Lord for sending Principal George Jeffreys and his revival party into our midst. The uplift given to leaders and congregations alike has helped us greatly."[133]

Syria

As Malick reflected on her missionary service, she recalled, "Ten years ago the Lord sent me back to Syria, the land of my birth. After the great World War the people were in great distress and misery."[134] In 1930 she was sad to say, "We are the only Pentecostal work in Syria." Yet she was glad that "some have received the Baptism of the Holy Spirit." Nonetheless, she clearly wished that other native Christian Arabs would be like her. "We would like every one to become a missionary in his own land."[135] In 1932 Malick was joined by Pearl Lovesy, an AG missionary who later married Saul Benjamin, at this time serving in Transjordan. Lovesy and Malick joined a comrade from Jerusalem, Anna Adams, on an evangelistic tour of the Hauran and *Jebel-ed Druse,* the "Bashan" of the Bible. The three of them were guided by Jadoon, a Bedouin convert, of whom Malick writes, "Through our brother Jadoon, the young soldier who spent over a year in Shweifat for military training, we were invited to hold meetings at the Bedouin camp in Beirut." Malick describes the receptivity of the people they visited: "The story of the love of Jesus gripped their hearts and it was almost midnight before we could induce them to go away . . . We were invited into many homes to pray for the sick."[136] As another indication of the collaboration between the Pentecostal missionaries in Syria and Palestine, Lovesy and Vera Swarztrauber took a trip to Elhusen where they held outreach meetings and "five made professions of faith."[137]

Malick's ministry was multi-ethnic. In 1932 the religious backgrounds of her students and orphans included Druses, Moslems, Jews, Protestants, Roman and Greek Catholics.[138] Like the varied missionary work of Elizabeth Brown, Malick's ministry was multi-faceted. Along with prison ministry, she also carried on an extensive ministry among Bedouins, of whom she writes,

> They are very interesting people, and I am sure you would enjoy a prayer meeting with them. God is blessing in their midst, and we are blessed with a very good native worker for them. The rent of the hall is only $5.00 per month, while the worker needs only $20.00 for his support. At the institute we have 180 poor and

133. Radford, "Days of Blessing in Palestine," *Pentecostal Evangel* (April 27, 1935) 10–11.

134. Malick, "Results of Gospel Preached in Syria," *Latter Rain Evangel* (April 1930) 17.

135. Ibid., 18.

136. Malick, "Among the Bedouins," *Pentecostal Evangel* (January 9, 1932) 13.

137. Lovesy, "A Word from the Land of Palestine," *Pentecostal Evangel* (January 7, 1933) 11.

138. Malick, "Syria," *Trust* (January–February 1932) 22–23.

orphan children, all studying the Bible daily. Many lives are being transformed here through the agency of the living Word and the tender care and influence of godly workers.[139]

In addition, Malick trained the children in her school and orphanage to assist her in ministering to villages near Shweifat. However, money was an ongoing concern, especially when the worldwide depression cut into missionary contributions. As Malick put it, "Now the financial question is the great problem. Offerings have dropped almost to half what they were in the past, and the value of the dollar has gone the same way, but prices have not gone down accordingly in this part of the country. In fact the government has raised taxes enormously so the people are groaning under the burden."[140]

Apparently a missionary romance had been brewing between Saul Benjamin of Es Salt and Pearl Lovesy of Shweifat. The closeness of the Pentecostal missionary community had the advantage of giving single missionaries opportunities to enjoy each other's company. A wedding announcement was published in the *Pentecostal Evangel*: "We are pleased to announce the marriage of Miss Pearl Lovesy to Mr. Saul Benjamin, both missionaries under Council appointment in Palestine. The wedding ceremony took place in the Mission Hall in Jerusalem on December 14 (1933). The happy couple are planning to work for God in Es Salt, Transjordan, where a very blessed work has been started."[141] Lovesy's marriage was undoubtedly Malick's loss, as once again she was the solo missionary in Shweifat. Nevertheless, Malick continued on. Her love for the orphans under her care shows in her reports. She tells of "one of our poor orphans," a 14 year-old girl, who came to her with a book in her hands and tears in her eyes and said, "Look here. His pierced hands and wounded side! This is Jesus. He suffered all this for me. Oh, my heart is trembling." Sobbing and looking up through her tears, she said, "I am very glad he saved me; I must tell others about Him." Malick goes on to say, "Since then she has been the means of leading one little lamb to the fold. This dear girl has nobody supporting her. Others as worthy as she is are without support too."[142] Malick was known to support many native workers out of her own finances.

The harvest of Malick's missionary work was not numerically abundant. At a baptismal service on the shores of the Mediterranean Sea in 1935, only three were baptized, a Bedouin husband and wife from the mission in Beirut and a man from the Shweifat assembly. Malick was always hopeful. She perceives a new interest among the kindergarten children and a new spiritual awakening among the older girls. Her strategy, as with other missions, was to reach the children, and through them to reach their parents, who highly valued the education provided by mission schools.[143] The ministry of healing was also of strategic importance in Malick's missionary work. She relates

139. Malick, "Missionary Activities in Syria," *Pentecostal Evangel* (May 12, 1934) 10.
140. Ibid.
141. "Wedding in Jerusalem," *Pentecostal Evangel* (January 14, 1933) 11.
142. Malick, "Missionary Activities in Syria," *Pentecostal Evangel* (May 12, 1934) 10.
143. "New Converts in Syria," *Pentecostal Evangel* (January 26, 1935) 11.

the case of a Bedouin woman in Beirut, who was suffering from tuberculosis and was headed for a sanitarium. Her husband asked Malick to pray and she describes what happened as she did so. "That night as I prayed in my room I felt the power of God for healing our sick sister. Her family were also praying and fasting. God answered prayer in a mighty way and healed the woman. Two days later I received a letter from the husband telling me of the miraculous healing of his wife."[144]

Transjordan

A revival broke out in 1930 in the Arab work in Es Salt, Transjordan. Laura Radford had received a plea for help from Roy Whitman, the missionary in charge, who was rejoicing that "truly the power of God is in our midst, and never in my life have I felt Him working so, and His Presence is so near; and soon we trust the waters will be waters to swim in and Pentecost fullness will be ours."[145] Radford immediately went to Es Salt to assist Whitman and stayed for several months. She describes what she observed: "Frequently both men and women who have not been in any of the meetings are suddenly brought under deep conviction in their own home and begin to confess their sins and to cry out to God for mercy, and beg someone to bring them to the meetings where they can be saved. Those saved during the early part of the revival are now praying faithfully for the new seekers." Radford was most impressed with the impact of the revival upon the women. She writes,

> Many have been completely overcome by the awful conviction for sin that has come upon them; but relief usually comes when they have made a full confession and restoration of what they may have stolen. The fact of God's holiness seems to be burned into their very souls. Very few of them can read, and to many of these God has granted a vision or revelation of Jesus more accurate and complete than could have been received through many years of careful study of the written Word. Changed hearts, changed faces, changed lives, changed homes—oh! it is all so wonderful and beyond description.[146]

Radford was overjoyed that significant progress was being made toward the accomplishment of two out of three of the objectives of the Pentecostal mission. As she put it, "The Holy Spirit has indeed fallen upon Salt, and many have been gloriously saved, and some are now seeking earnestly the Baptism in the Holy Spirit."[147] The next step was to cultivate a self-sufficient indigenous church.

Radford carefully monitored the situation in Transjordan, about which she writes, "We thank God that Trans-Jordan has been kept quiet on the whole, notwithstanding the efforts of the agitators in Palestine. Both Mr. Whitman and Mr. Benjamin write most encouragingly of the meetings in Salt." Saul Benjamin, an American of Assyrian

144. Malick, "Syria," *Pentecostal Evangel* (March 9, 1935) 11.

145. Radford, "Revival in Trans-Jordania: Spiritual 'Latter Rain' Falling," *Redemption Tidings* 6.8 (August 1930) 15.

146. Ibid.

147. Ibid.

extraction and a recent graduate of Southern California Bible School, was a first-time missionary. Whitman was a veteran. And both were fluent in Arabic. Radford continues, "We are now getting in shape for a mission house and Gospel Hall (in Amman). Mr. Whitman will be stationed there for the present and Mr. Benjamin will continue in the work at Salt . . . This is our day of opportunity for Transjordan."[148] The addition of two missionaries who were fluent in Arabic was a boon to the Pentecostal mission in the region. Other Pentecostal missionaries were also proficient in Arabic. Brown was known for her mastery of Arabic and Malick in Syria had the advantage of speaking Arabic as her native tongue.

By 1931 Laura Radford had broadened her theological horizon to encompass the mission to the Arabs. She formulated a biblical case for evangelization of all of the sons of Abraham. In an article in the *Elim Evangel*, she states, "Therefore, it is evident from the Scriptures that 'the seed of Abraham' is more than just an earthly Hebrew nation, and that the territory outlined in that Covenant has been set apart for more than just a national home for the Jewish people."[149] Her point is that the Abrahamic covenant extends to the Arab peoples living in Syria, Transjordan, and Arabia. She poses the question, "Is there no hope expressed in the Word of God for these peoples?" Radford responds that all of the descendents of Abraham are "included in what was wrought by the blood shed in Gethsemane and on the Cross, and though through the centuries they have been neglected by the Church, yet the printed Word is now being distributed in some parts of the land, and there is hope that soon every closed door will be opened." She concludes that, because the blessing of salvation is for Arabia also, "we stand full assured that we are in the centre of His will in sending forth His Word into the regions beyond . . . These lands have been redeemed. It is our commission to make known to them their inheritance in Christ."[150]

The work of the mission among the Arabs was going strong in the mid-1930s. The reports of Saul and Pearl Benjamin give evidence of spiritual vitality in the Es Salt assembly. In 1933 Pearl Benjamin writes, "Pray for four young men who are desirous of serving the Lord that they may be filled with the Holy Spirit and be taught what it really means to seek out the lost." She makes mention of the village of Rumaineen, requesting prayer that "conviction may be upon the people, and that souls be saved."[151] In 1935 the Benjamins reported that their day school had an enrollment of 175 children, whom they "instructed in the Word of God." Three girls earned certificates, qualifying them to continue in higher education. At the graduation ceremony, "there were people present who do not agree with us either in doctrine or practice, yet they gave appreciative addresses." In the same report, Saul Benjamin tells an endearing story of his reunification with a younger brother with whom he had lost touch during a massacre in Persia. Benjamin writes, "He was only three years old when we had to flee from

148. "News from the Mission Fields," *Latter Rain Evangel* (February 1930) 18.

149. Radford, "Transjordania and the Borders of Arabia," *The Elim Evangelist and Foursquare Revivalist* 11.33 (September 18, 1931) 604.

150. Ibid., 605.

151. Benjamin, "Salt, Trans Jordan," *Pentecostal Evangel* (March 4, 1933) 10.

Persia for our lives. He was with my father in an ox cart when they were captured by the Turks and my father was slain. This little boy was spared and was taken in by a kind lady together with some other children and a few older people who escaped the awful massacre. There he has been kept until I was able to help him out of Persia. Pray that he may now grow to love the Lord."[152] The Benjamins announced another cause for joy. In June of 1931 their "first native evangelist was married and it was a grand occasion."

Roy Whitman also made a significant contribution to the Pentecostal mission among Arabs. With his assembly growing in Amman, he submitted a deftly nuanced article to the *Pentecostal Evangel*. Whitman's thesis is that a scriptural case can be made for the Arab mission. Yet he was caught in a bind, as were all Pentecostal missionaries working with Arab people groups in this period. His article reflects a logical disjunction between his Zionist sympathies and the vested interests of his Arab clients who were diametrically opposed to the Zionist project in Palestine. Hence, Whitman straddles the fence, lauding Jewish immigration to Palestine as the fulfillment of Old Testament prophecies of the restoration of Israel. He argues that anti-Semitic persecution is driving the Jews back to Palestine: "The hatred of the Jews will spread, enforcing a return to their own land. Thus we find that every tide of persecution is just fulfilling God's purposes. It accelerates the promises."[153] He points out that in Jerusalem there are approximately 53,000 Jews and 38,000 Gentiles. He then tries to reconcile Zionism and Arabism, stressing that there are other peoples in Bible lands, not just Jews, about whom we can read in the Scriptures. He strongly promotes mission work among Arabs, asserting that "these naturally unlovable people will respond to the gospel of grace." In closing, he emphasizes that the last people mentioned in "that Pentecostal chapter, Acts 2," are the Arabs and he ends with a provocative question: "May not this indicate that the last to be gathered into the Church will be the sons of Ishmael, or the Arab-Moslem race?"[154] This is probably as far as Whitman could go, in view of the Zionist proclivities of his Pentecostal constituency.

Persia

It is evident from the missionary reports published in the Pentecostal periodicals that an alliance was formed between the Pentecostal missionaries of Palestine and those serving in the wider Middle East region. One of those was Philip Shabaz, who passed through Palestine on his way to Persia. He writes, "While in Jerusalem we had the privilege of staying with Miss Brown for a few days and also with Miss Radford, both Council missionaries. The Lord made our time useful while there, and we were enabled to preach through an interpreter. God blessed the Word as it went forth and souls were saved by His mighty power . . . Yet in this city there is so much unbelief that it saddens one's heart. Let us pray for the peace of Jerusalem."[155] Moving on to Persia,

152. Benjamin, "Blessings in Transjordan," *Pentecostal Evangel* (August 31, 1935) 9.

153. Whitman, "Fulfilled Prophecy in Bible Lands," *Pentecostal Evangel* (February 16, 1935) 8.

154. Ibid., 9.

155. Shabaz, "Arrived in Persia," *Pentecostal Evangel* (June 20, 1931) 11.

Shabaz temporarily stopped in Kermanshah and ministered to a small group gathered sometime ago by John Warton. He reached his final destination of Hamadan. Although initial indications confirmed Shabaz' belief that he was in the will of God, he requested prayer, explaining, "As far as the government is concerned, religious freedom has been granted, although there is considerable opposition from the public."[156] Christian missions in Muslim lands were always an upward climb but the Pentecostal mission in Persia made progress. By 1935 S. J. Kamber, another Pentecostal missionary, could report that "many Moslems, mostly young men, are coming regularly to the meetings now. Some of them have raised their hands, requesting prayer for salvation. We hope to do more when we have our own chapel finished, because there will be no fear of interference from the government."[157] Shabaz also reported favorable results in his work with school children, saying that "a number of them have been saved and filled with the Holy Spirit. It was a blessed scene to see them under the power of God, then come through speaking in tongues and magnifying God."[158] There was persecution but three promising native pastors, Adrashes Monosarian, Warda Malham, and Youel Neesan, were poised to assume leadership roles if their support could be raised.[159]

Laura Radford may not have had to deal with persecution like that endured by her colleagues in Persia, but she knew her share of heartaches and disappointments. In a conversation with Lydia Christensen, a Danish friend and later the wife of Derek Prince, Radford confides, "Ten years ago I, too, came to Jerusalem without knowing what I would find waiting for me . . . They have been ten difficult years with many heartaches and disappointments." Christensen asks, "Are you sorry, then that you came?" "No, Miss Christensen, I'm not sorry. In spite of everything, Jerusalem is its own reward. She demands that you love her so completely that no suffering or discouragement or danger can ever change your love for her."[160]

In 1935, to Pentecostals all appeared quiet on the Eastern front. The editor of the *Pentecostal Evangel* writes, "Though world upheavals may interrupt at any time, quiet reigns in the Holy Land." He then relays the observations of a recent visitor to Palestine which are laced with a Zionist bias: "There is about the country an atmosphere of calmness and tranquility that gives character to the whole effort to rebuild the Jewish National Home. Everywhere is peace and serenity, a spirit which for Jews probably cannot be found anywhere else."[161] There was a measure of truth to this statement, given the rushing torrent of Nazi anti-Semitism in Europe. Yet, what was true for the Jews was not true for the Arabs of Palestine, who took a wholly different view of the burgeoning Jewish population in Palestine. For them, a bad moon was on the rise. For Pentecostals, the future looked bright. At year's end there was happiness in the

---

156. Ibid.

157. Kamber, "Persia," *Pentecostal Evangel* (February 9, 1935) 11, 14.

158. Ibid., 14; Shabaz, "Spirit Falls on Children in Persia," *Pentecostal Evangel* (June 15, 1935) 9.

159. Shabaz, "Our Persian Workers," *Pentecostal Evangel* (November 23, 1935) 5.

160. Prince, *Appointment in Jerusalem*, 101.

161. "The Peace of Jerusalem," *Pentecostal Evangel* (April 13, 1935) 6.

Pentecostal community over the news from Es Salt that "Mr. and Mrs. Saul Benjamin are the happy parents of little Ruth Elizabeth, born in Transjordan, December 29."[162]

To sum up, in the second phase of its history (1919–35), the Pentecostal mission in Palestine made significant progress in Jerusalem and beyond. This progress was made possible during the British Mandate by the removal of the impediments to Christian missions imposed by the Ottoman regime. Specifically, because of the abrogation of the Muslim restriction on the building of new churches, Elizabeth Brown was able to pursue her longtime dream of constructing a Pentecostal Missionary Home and Chapel in Jerusalem. With the development of the "Shemariah" mission station in Jerusalem, the missionaries had the facilities necessary to accommodate growth. They also had a solid home base from which to expand their reach into outlying areas. At the very time when it seemed that the mission was on the verge of success, the Wailing Wall Riots broke out, foreshadowing the troubles that were to come. The Pentecostal response to the Wailing Wall riots accentuated the pro-Zionist stance of the missionaries in Palestine and the Pentecostal periodicals. This stance proved to be a critical factor in the long term viability of the mission, as we shall see in the next chapter.

162. "News Items," *Pentecostal Evangel* (February 22, 1936) 6.

6 | Holding the Fort, 1936–1945

THIS CHAPTER WILL carry the historical narrative of the Pentecostal mission in Palestine up to 1945. This turbulent period in the history of the mission will be set in the broader context of the events leading up to World War II. The causes of the Arab Revolts of 1936–39 and their effect on the mission will be recounted. The visit of a team of Assemblies of God (hereafter AG) officials to Syria, Palestine, and Transjordan in 1937 and the subsequent assessment of the Pentecostal mission in Jerusalem will be scrutinized. The difficulties imposed on the mission during World War II and the departure of longstanding missionaries and the arrival of new personnel will be described.

ARAB REVOLTS OF 1936–1939

This period of the Pentecostal mission should be seen in the context of interconnected events in Palestine and Europe leading up to the Second World War. In 1924 Adolf Hitler published *Mein Kampf*, an autobiographical and propagandistic tract in which he unveiled his scheme for the extermination of the Jews. Hitler's anti-Semitism was inflamed by his reading of the spurious *Protocols of the Elders of Zion*, which he incorporated into the Nazi polemic of a Jewish conspiracy.[1] In 1933 Hitler became Chancellor of Germany and unleashed a campaign of terror against the Jews, leading inexorably to the Holocaust and a huge increase in Jewish immigration to Palestine. During Hitler's first year in power the concentration camp at Dachau was established. The Pentecostal periodicals reported on developments related to the Nazi persecution of the Jews and the consequent flood of European Jewish immigrants to Palestine. Many Pentecostal authors attributed eschatological significance to the restoration of a Jewish homeland in Palestine and viewed with dismay the apparent hardness of heart of Arabs who wanted to close the doors of immigration to Jews seeking a safe haven in Palestine.[2]

From the Arab point of view, the increasing Jewish population was seen as a trend that would eventuate in a Zionist takeover of Palestine, the establishment of a Jewish state, and the complete loss of the Arab right of national self-determination

---

1. Saddington, "Prophecy and Politics," 247.

2. "Who's the Landlord of Palestine?" *Pentecostal Evangel* (February 4, 1933) 5; "Exodus of Jews from Germany," *Pentecostal Evangel* (March 11, 1933) 5; "Back to the Land," *Pentecostal Evangel* (January 18, 1936) 10; "Mass Movement to Palestine," *Pentecostal Evangel* (February 1, 1936) 11.

in Palestine. The transfer of vast stretches of Palestinian land into Jewish possession sparked the Arab Revolt of 1936–39. In desperation the Arab nationalists organized a resistance movement, beginning with an economic boycott. On May 7, 1936, at a conference of Palestinian Arabs, it was decided that the payment of taxes would be withheld from the British Mandatory Government. Arab peasants volunteered to be trained for armed struggle, left their villages, and went to secret training camps.

The British responded by imposing harsh measures. On June 18, 1936, the British made a corridor through Jaffa by dynamiting many buildings, destroying the homes of 6,000 people. On July 30, 1936, the British declared martial law. Those suspected of organizing the economic boycott or taking part in a fighting unit were detained in prison camps. The houses of those who sympathized with the Revolt were demolished. In spite of 20,000 reinforcements, by 1938 the British troops were unable to contain the Revolt and turned to the Zionists for help. Jewish fighters entered the fray on the British side in three units, numbering 2,863 recruits for the Colony Police; 12,000 for the *Haganah* led by a British officer, Orde Wingate; and 3,000 for Vladimir Jabotinsky's National Military Organization, the *Irgun*. By 1939 the Zionist military units included 14,411 fighters. The advantage enjoyed by the Zionist units was that they were consti-tuted of local militia that could strike more quickly when hot spots of Arab insurgency flared up.[3]

In typical British fashion, in the aftermath of the Revolts, a Royal Commission was established in 1937 under the chairmanship of Lord Peel. The "Peel Commission" was charged with the task of investigating the causes of the Revolt. It concluded that the two main causes were the disappointment of Arab aspirations for self-determina-tion and the burgeoning increase in Jewish population and land holdings. The Peel Commission identified three central Arab demands: (1) An immediate stop to Jewish immigration; (2) Prohibition of the transfer of Arab lands to Zionist colonists; (3) Establishment of a democratic government in which Arabs would have a dominant position.[4] In response the British agreed to clamp down on Jewish immigration. This pleased the Arabs but it enraged the Zionists, for whom the restriction of immigration could not have been more ill-timed. The Zionists were pained that as the Holocaust was intensifying during the Second World War, the British were taking steps to ame-liorate the Arabs by imposing severe quotas on Jewish immigration.[5]

Looking ahead to future political developments, at the end of the Second World War thousands of Jewish refugees set their eyes toward Palestine but were barred from reaching their destination and were confined to cramped relocation centers in Cyprus. The militant Zionists in Palestine reacted with armed insurgency, launching terror-ist attacks against both the Arabs and the British. Seeing no other viable solution, the United Nations approved the partition of Palestine into two states, one Arab and the other Jewish. As soon as the UN partition was announced in November of 1947,

---

3. Kanafani, *The 1936–1939 Revolt in Palestine*, 39, 96.

4. Ibid., 31.

5. Bauer, *From Diplomacy to Resistance*, 5–15.

clashes between Arabs and Zionists erupted and outright warfare broke out in early December. The British then announced the termination of their Mandate in Palestine, to take effect on May 15, 1948, which in turn intensified the fighting between Zionists and Arab nationalists, as both sides jockeyed for territory.[6] The Pentecostal missionaries were caught in the crossfire.

Mission in the Cross Fire

The first half of 1936 was the lull before the storm. The Pentecostal missionaries in Palestine and the surrounding regions went about their business as normal. The missionary reports from Jerusalem were encouraging. The sale of books and Bibles was up, which was significant in a land with a relatively low literacy rate. As Laura Radford explained, "In this land very few men spend money on books, so these Scriptures sold make us to know that at least 2,000 more men are reading the Scriptures today than there were a year ago."[7] Anna Adams was also upbeat due to her perception that "God is answering prayer and we feel greatly encouraged by the eager response of many to hear and study God's Word. Some of the converts are giving themselves to prayer and sometimes arise in the night to pray."[8] Another reason for gladness was that two new missionary recruits were on their way, Ida Beck and Joyce Jones.[9]

By this time John Warton had relocated from Persia and established his headquarters in Jerusalem, assuming a new role as regional director of the network of AG missions in Palestine, Syria, Transjordan, and Persia. The *Pentecostal Evangel* announced that "Brother Warton plans to make Jerusalem his headquarters, from which point he will be able to supervise the work in several fields."[10] Uncanny as it may seem, given that Warton was of Middle Eastern descent, he too was a Zionist sympathizer. He writes, "Time and space will not permit me to write about the amazing developments taking place in Palestine according to the prophecies, but it is wonderful to see these things coming to pass. Nations are preparing for the great conflict, the Jews are gathering in and Jerusalem is preparing to receive her King from glory."[11]

In Syria, Yumna Malick was counting her blessings. She writes, "You will be glad to know that the Lord is answering prayer for revival here." Apparently she had organized a Pentecostal convention at which "some were seeking the baptism of the Spirit." She expresses concern over the absence of a Pentecostal work in Damascus and suggests that a mission station should also be opened up in Beirut." Of course, this would cost "a good bit of money" for which she appeals to those who were holding her up in prayer and financial support, whom she duly thanks and implores, "Your loving cooperation is much needed and appreciated." She then offers an eschatological incentive

6. Pappe, *A History of Modern Palestine*, 123–31.

7. Radford, "Scripture Sales in Palestine," *Pentecostal Evangel* (February 22, 1936) 6.

8. Adams, "Palestine," *Pentecostal Evangel* (June 6, 1936) 9.

9. "New Workers for Palestine," *Pentecostal Evangel* (January 4, 1936) 4.

10. "Missionary News," *Pentecostal Evangel* (January 4, 1936).

11. Warton, "Survey of the Far East," *Pentecostal Evangel* (April 25, 1936) 6.

for financial investment in her ministry: "Such privileges of service here on earth may not be of long duration, for 'in such an hour as we think not, the Son of Man cometh' and at the sound of the trumpet the scene will be changed."[12] For the time being, Malick went on with her work, reporting that one of her young charges in Beirut, who had been the means of "bringing another trophy to the Lord Jesus quite recently," was suffering persecution in his own home.[13] This was to be expected for most converts in Palestine and the surrounding region. Malick itinerated among the Bedouins of Hauran, of whom she speaks affectionately, "The Bedouins sing heartily unto the Lord, though often entirely out of tune, and they gladly testify to the love and goodness of Jesus their Saviour." The affection was mutual. On one occasion when Malick indicated she might not come the following Sunday, the Bedouin leaders quickly retorted, "Do come. We feel like orphans when you don't; we are refreshed when you are with us." She quickly adds, "Traveling in extension work takes a good bit of money as it is usually done by hired car. Please pray that God may supply this need. We hope to open a mission in Damascus and request your prayers that sufficient funds may come in regularly."[14] Malick rarely missed an opportunity to appeal for financial contributions.

Saul Benjamin was also reporting positive results in Transjordan. During the feast of Ramadan, the Muslim governor and town officials of Es Salt attended his meetings. He writes, "While it is true that they did not accept Christ as their Saviour, yet for almost an hour they sat silent, listening carefully to the message of the gospel." Benjamin also reports, "The Sunday School is doing splendidly and our day school is a beehive of activity where the Word is being taught daily. We are greatly desiring to open such schools in the surrounding villages where there is great need."[15]

In the summer of 1936 the mood of the missionary reports abruptly changed tune with the onset of the Arab Revolt. Saul Benjamin offers a pungent analysis of the turmoil. He writes, "The political unrest in the world has reached this part too. Palestine is following in the footsteps of Syria, striking in order to get what they want from the British." As Benjamin saw it, the Arabs were "demanding the stopping of Jewish immigration and the sale of land to them and national independence." As a consequence, he laments that commerce and transportation are paralyzed, there has been bloodshed on both sides, and attention has been diverted from the gospel. Yet, he is relieved to say, "In Trans-Jordan we have had comparative peace and so far no movement is started such as is in Jerusalem." With a sense of urgency Benjamin speaks of the great need for missionary penetration of northern Transjordan, where "the people are in spiritual darkness and ignorance with only a shadow of the real thing and they are asking for light."[16] But it was not to be, for the days of the expansion of the Pentecostal mission were no more.

---

12. Malick, "Blessings in Far-Away Syria," *Pentecostal Evangel* (March 21, 1936) 9.

13. Malick, "Missionary Notes—Syria," *Pentecostal Evangel* (March 28, 1936) 7.

14. "Visiting the Bedouins," *Pentecostal Evangel* (September 5, 1936) 7.

15. Benjamin, "Officials Inquire about Gospel," *Pentecostal Evangel* (June 20, 1936) 8.

16. Benjamin, "Pray for the Peace of Jerusalem," *Pentecostal Evangel* (July 11, 1936) 7.

Pentecostal Response to the Arab Revolts

American Pentecostals responded to the news of the Arab Revolt with great alarm. Writing in the *Pentecostal Evangel*, Harry J. Steil describes the "bitter internal conflict now going on in Palestine, between the Moslems or Arabs, and the Jews. A virtual state of war exists, Britain is sending 8,000 new troops into Palestine, also sending several warships into the Mediterranean." Steil was particular vexed over what he perceived as the complicity of the Italian fascist leader Mussolini in the Arab revolt. Rumors had spread that Mussolini was offering fifteen dollars a day to anyone who incites the Arab rebellion against the British. Worse yet, Steil sees the Arab revolt as an "open volcano" which could be used by Satan as the spark to start the War of Armageddon. He writes, "There is wide spread unrest, threatening to burst into open warfare, against Britain through most of the Arabian Moslem territory."[17]

A month later the *Pentecostal Evangel* published a report from Jerusalem confirming that conditions were growing steadily worse.

> Nearly 12,000 British troops are now in the land besides the large police force but it seems that the thirst for blood in most of the Moslem Arabs now knows no bounds. About 30 Jews have been killed. Every wheat field which had not been harvested was burned and it seems to be the purpose of the vandals to destroy every tree and garden in all the land. Probably 40,000 fruit trees have been destroyed and also many of the forests which have been planted during the last seven years.[18]

In the face of such carnage, the report continues, "The Jews have shown remarkable restraint and are doing their best to carry on, even though to do so means loss of life in many instances. Most towns are now under curfew. A penal camp has been opened in the desert where about 100 of the Arab leaders have been sent and another larger camp is now under construction. This segregation of these crazed leaders of the rioters is the only way of getting the common people again into control."[19] The strategy of the Zionist Agency up to this point had been to strike against the Arabs in self defense and to refrain from random reprisals. But the "revisionist" strategy of Vladimir Jabotinsky became more appealing as the atrocities of the Arab Revolt piled up. Briefly stated, Jabotinsky advocated guerilla warfare.[20]

A first-hand report on the Arab Revolt was offered by Pentecostal evangelist William Nagel, living in Jerusalem at the time. In "Palestine—Why the Disturbances?" Nagel explains to readers of the *Pentecostal Evangel* that the cause of the disturbances was Jewish immigration.[21] He points out that Arabs were alarmed over the increase in the Jewish population of Palestine from 83,000 in 1917 to 375,000 in 1936. When

17. Steil, "The Trend Toward Armageddon," *Pentecostal Evangel* (July 18, 1936) 2.

18. "Uprising in Palestine," *Pentecostal Evangel* (August 29, 1936) 9.

19. Ibid.

20. See Caplan, "Zionist Visions of Palestine, 1917–1936."; Shavit, "Fire and Water: Ze'ev Jabotinsky and the Revisionist Movement."

21. Nagel, "Palestine—Why the Disturbances?" *Pentecostal Evangel* (September 5, 1936) 8.

the British High Commissioner, Sir Arthur Grenfell Wauchope, announced that the immigration quota for the next six months was 12,000 Jews, nationalist Arabs took up arms against the English. The violence started when two dead Arabs were found near Tel Aviv. Believing them to have been murdered by the Jews in revenge for two Jews killed by Arab bandits a few weeks earlier, Arab riots broke out in Jaffa on April 17 and spread throughout Palestine. Nagel states, "Now Palestinian Arabs are demanding that they also rule themselves. Great Britain consequently finds herself in much the same position as that in which Abraham found himself when domestic difficulties arose between Sarah and Hagar." Whereas in the biblical story Sarah cast out Hagar, presently it is the sons of Hagar who are crying, "Throw out the Jews. We need a Hitler here." It appears that Nagel may be alluding to Nazi Germany's recognition of Arab aspirations to independence and support for the contravention of the Jewish national home in Palestine. Nagel leaves no doubt as to his sympathies, averring, "The Arabs must either be reconciled to the Jews or deposed."[22]

From Es Salt Saul Benjamin reported that peace was prevailing in Trans-Jordan, much unlike Palestine. "In Palestine there seems to be no letting up of trouble, rather the Arabs are determining to hold out to the bitter end." He heard through the Arab grapevine that "other Arab countries are sending help to aid their brethren." This piece of intelligence may refer to the Muslim Brothers of Egypt, who were actively involved in organizing the Arab insurgency.[23] Benjamin laments, "We are well up into the fifth month of this intercity conflict. The people are tired of the whole affair, but their heads are persistent in their demands. There has been much blood-shed in the land of Palestine." In the midst of the rumblings of armed conflict, the good news was that "the Lord was seemingly going out of His way to help the people of Ar Runaineen," a nearby village. "This is a real encouragement to us," Benjamin continues, "enabling us to dare to believe our God for another poor benighted soul in darkness suffering from demon possession."[24]

In "A Word from Jerusalem," Elizabeth Brown tells how the Pentecostal mission-aries responded to the Arab Revolt. They scheduled three days of concerted prayer and John Warton delineated a two-point agenda for prayer and fasting: "1. A restoration of peace to this troubled land, that the gospel may no longer be hindered in the going forth. 2. For a spiritual awakening in our midst." It is evident that the crisis at hand was conducive to a certain degree of ecumenicity, which is indicated by Brown's report that "the Alliance and Baptist missions co-operated with us and we had three precious days of drawing near the Lord and fellowship with Him and with one another. Many have testified of great blessing received, and we almost wished, like Peter, to build us a tabernacle that we might remain on the mountain top."[25] But, alas, they had to come down from the mountain and carry on the mission in the crossfire between the Arabs, Zionists, and British. In the meantime, Serena Hodges channeled her energy into

22. Ibid., 9.

23. El-Awaisi, *The Muslim Brothers and the Palestine Question, 1928–1947*, 34–45.

24. "Good News from Trans-Jordan," *Pentecostal Evangel* (October 3, 1936) 6.

25. Brown, "A Word from Jerusalem," *Pentecostal Evangel* (October 17, 1936) 11.

collecting Christmas presents for sixty to seventy children in the Jerusalem Sunday school. She asked for gifts for the women too, who, she reminded her American donors, "do not wear the same style of clothes as in America, so that we have to buy the materials for them, hence, just send money."[26] In need of rest, Laura Radford departed for the United States on furlough.[27]

By December the fighting had temporarily relented and John Warton put the situation in historical perspective. He reflects on the emergence of the Zionist movement and asserts that the "greatest miracle" of recent history had to be the "gathering of the Jews from different parts of the world into Palestine and the way they are building and developing this country." Of course, the Arabs decried this development not as a miracle, but as an impending disaster. Wharton supposed that the Arabs "think that if the Jews continue coming into Palestine, it may crowd the Arabs out. Therefore, the Arabs arose with fear and violence against the Jews." In Warton's eyes, the marvel was that "the Jews refused to be discouraged," inferring that their resiliency was "supernaturally inspired." Nevertheless, he states, "We are very grateful that after nearly six months of unrest at last the strike and troubles are over. The conditions are almost normal again." He is overjoyed that, despite the fighting, things are going well at the new outstation in Ramallah where "a good number of souls are hungry for the Baptism with the Holy Spirit." He also mentions that in Reseah, Persia "our faithful native workers are proclaiming the word of Life and the Lord is blessing the work by saving and baptizing precious souls."[28]

VISIT OF ASSEMBLIES OF GOD OFFICIALS

With the dawning of 1937, a delegation of officials from the AG in America made a tour of the mission stations in the region. E. S. Williams and his wife came to Beirut, where they were met by Yumna Malick and taken to her home in Shweifat. They stayed for a week, observing the work of Malick's Full Gospel Mission and Training School. The training school for girls was housed in the homestead of Malick's parents, a large home with many rooms and a large hall which could seat the entire student body of 186. Concerning the faculty, Williams writes, "We were well impressed with the bright faces and friendliness of spirit that we found among these helpers, most of whom received their own education in the training school." The delegation was intrigued by the diversity of religious backgrounds. "Some had come from homes of the Greek Orthodox Church, and others had been born in homes of Druses, a branch of Mohammedans that have secret rights [sic] which none seem clearly to know except the initiated. Our visit with these young women showed us the possibilities in all of mankind if opportunity is afforded." Williams was equally impressed with the student body. "Children come from homes where Christ is unknown and it is a cause for thankfulness that these children, sent to learn to read and write, are given instruction

26. Hodges, "Suggestions for Christmas Giving," *Pentecostal Evangel* (October 24, 1936) 18.

27. *Pentecostal Evangel* (November 21, 1936) 6.

28. Warton, "God's Ways with the Jews," *Pentecostal Evangel* (December 12, 1936) 7.

in the Word of God." Williams recognized the value of Malick's training school to her students, in that there are no free schools in Syria and most of the people are deprived of education. The cost is nominal so that parents of modest means can afford to send their children. In fact, about half of the students are not required to pay anything because of the poverty of their parents.[29]

Williams had several opportunities to preach in the chapel, which was crowded at every meeting so that extra chairs had to be brought in. "God blessed the Word and several came forward to seek the Lord and some testified to definite blessings." Williams also toured Malick's prison ministry at the Basida and Beirut Prisons, and Williams addressed the prisoners in the former. The Williams visited the outstations in Deirgoubel and Kefershema, as well as the Bedouin encampment near Beirut and the Chaldeans living in Haddet. Williams attests that, "We found all those whom we met in Lebanon kindhearted, affectionate and appreciative, and where they had enjoyed any opportunities we found them bright and energetic." He was not so warmly disposed to the local Maronite Christians and Muslims, about whom he remarks, "Unless you could visit this field you could not understand what a hold religions without God have upon the people." Williams commends Malick for her hard work, but expresses concern over the heavy load she was carrying, as "her income has been greatly reduced and the burden of the school, rent for missions, and provisions for native workers were a drain upon her finances, which it was difficult to meet." Williams closes by appealing for financial assistance to help Malick with "a means of transportation as there are no street cars, except in Beirut, and the expense of hiring drivers to take one about is very great."[30]

Williams and his wife then traveled to Jerusalem where they were joined by Noel Perkin, John Welch, and Hattie Hammond. At the end of her fortieth-year of ministry in Jerusalem, Brown had offered an appraisal of her ministry:

> I am so glad that down through the years as I served Him in Sunday school work, in visiting in city and villages, in prison work and in our chapel which the Lord so graciously gave us in answer to prayer, He has by His wonderful grace given me to see some souls yield to the power of His precious Word, and find peace and joy in Jesus, their Savior. I have seen Him touch a few in His mighty healing power and I have known a few to be baptized in His blessed Holy Spirit . . . I am so happy to be here and will be glad if He permits me to serve Him here till He comes.[31]

The AG delegation was not so optimistic. They published their report, "A Visit with our Missionaries in Palestine," in the *Pentecostal Evangel*, stating that the purpose of their visit was "to obtain a better understanding of the difficulties and problems that confront our missionary representatives in these lands."[32] The first morning after their

---

29. Williams, "A Visit to Lebanon," *Pentecostal Evangel* (February 27, 1937) 8.

30. Ibid., 9.

31. "Forty Years a Missionary," *The Pentecostal Evangel*, (April 6, 1935) 11.

32. "A Visit with our Missionaries in Palestine," in the *Pentecostal Evangel* (April 17, 1937) 8.

arrival the delegation was seated around the long table at Shemariah, the Missionary Home under the direction of "our aged, though still energetic sister, Elizabeth Brown," with whom they were duly impressed. "Miss Brown has passed her three score years and ten, yet each morning at seven o'clock she is promptly at the table for breakfast and continues her day of activity like the rest." Along with Brown, Serena Hodges and Ida Beck were also headquartered at Shemariah. The book room at Shemariah was by this time discontinued due to a shortage of funds. John Warton was serving as pastor of the assembly that met in the chapel attached to the Shemariah mission center. In another section of Jerusalem, Laura Radford had her mission station not far from the Garden Tomb. The non-AG missionaries working with Radford are mentioned but not named. The delegation commends Radford for her able work in preparing younger missionaries for their ministry. Anna Adams was at this time overseeing the outstation in Ramallah, seventeen miles from Jerusalem. The delegation described the assembly at Ramallah as "a hungry group of people who listen very attentively to the Word of the Lord as it is given forth from week to week."[33]

Guided by John Warton, the delegation visited a number of holy sites, of which they speak disparagingly, impugning the "discordant noises, evil smells, and heathenish shrines." From their perspective, in Jerusalem "there is religion in its various forms everywhere but little of the power." A number of examples are cited: "A Jew at the wailing wall stops in his prayers to carry on some business transaction with his friend. The Arab coming out of his place of prayer sets upon a fellow worshiper who has been found guilty of associating with the government as a spy and the man is brutally murdered. A funeral procession passes by from a Catholic Church in Bethlenem and the women are wailing but later we see the same ones laughing and talking together."[34] The cultural insensitivity of these observations is only exceeded by the religious intolerance that is exuded.

In their evaluation of the accomplishments of the mission, the officials presented a mixed report. While granting a "certain romantic interest" connected with Palestine, they stressed that "in actual realization it is perhaps one of the most difficult and discouraging countries to work in as far as the gospel ministry is concerned." Getting to the bottom line, they asked, "Do the people listen to the gospel? Very, very few. They have ears but they hear not; like Ephraim the people are joined to their idols." The officials are aware that Jerusalem has been tough sledding for the "consecrated men and women of many denominations and sects," and that for all the labor and prayers poured into Jerusalem, there is very little to show for it. They say the same is true of the Pentecostal mission: "There are over twenty missionaries and Christian workers from different Pentecostal groups in the city of Jerusalem, but though each one may have been able to reach a few yet like the seed that fell on stony ground the harvest has been comparatively small. The great need of the country is for a new move of the Holy Spirit, but one cannot help but wonder whether the time of visitation is temporarily

33. Ibid.
34. Ibid.

past and the new day of opportunity not yet fully come."[35] The AG officials bemoan the fact that unfortunately very few have as yet received the baptism with the Spirit. Nevertheless, they also offer a measure of affirmation. They commend Brown and Hodges for equipping two Arab women who were running an outstation in Tulkaren. They were impressed with how these young women, who are converted Arabs, had won the respect of the people of the community and a goodly number were coming to the meetings they conducted. They also commend Elizabeth Brown for "encouraging cases of conversion in her prison work." They underscore how striking it was that "a number who have been converted trace the time of their conversion to a special vision or revelation of Christ to their hearts rather than to some message given by a preacher of the gospel as is the case in our own land."[36]

Next the AG delegation went on to spend two weeks in Es Salt, which they describe as a town of 20,000 built around both sides of a hill. They report that Saul and Pearl Benjamin and Vera Swarztrauber were "working in very primitive conditions but doing much to win the confidence and respect of the people." Through the 200 students at the mission school, the parents are reached and "thus homes and hearts are opened to the truth." The officials note that "many of the children have been saved and some have had remarkable visions of Christ and of heaven." While in Es Salt the officials were lobbied by a delegation of the leading men of the town for provision of a church building, about which the officials demurred, saying that "there are hundreds of others in a similar position who are poor and need a church building so that we could only promise to pray with them that their problem might be solved." The officials claimed to notice a difference in the countenance of those who had accepted the Lord Jesus as their Savior, such as the earnest Christian wife who gave more consideration in her family than would have been the case with a non-Christian family. From Es Salt the officials went to Amman for a visit with the Whitmans, who were also laboring to reach the Arab people of Transjordan. They remark that "Mr. Whitman who has been on the field a number of years longer than his wife has acquired a beautiful grasp of the Arabic language which is such an asset in trying to win the people of that country."[37]

All in all, in the final analysis of the AG officials, the concluding evaluation of the Pentecostal mission was as follows: "We believe that although the results in the Palestine and Transjordan fields may not be as encouraging as in some other places, yet the command of our Lord stands and includes these people as some of those included in the term 'every creature' to whom we are constrained to give the gospel message."[38] This evaluation of the General Superintendent and the Missionary Secretary of the American AG was clearly a mixed review, raising doubts as to their support for investing dollars and personnel in a venture that produced meager returns in terms of the number of converts. In the reports of the missionaries themselves, one also finds a mixed review, consisting of great expectations tempered by onerous challenges and

35. Ibid., 8, 11.
36. Ibid., 11.
37. Ibid.
38. Ibid.

crushing disappointments. We will return to the evaluation of the mission in the final section of the next chapter.

Afterwards, Saul and Pearl Benjamin write, "We were greatly blessed and refreshed by their visit. One sister said to me that after they left Es Salt she felt that the whole town was empty. Needless to say that all here loved them and enjoyed their ministry." The Benjamins also report that their native evangelist had delivered a petition from a number families in Fhais who wanted to break away from the Roman Catholic Church. They asked the Benjamins to open a school among them, offering a house free in exchange for a teacher. This was a breath of fresh air, as some time before, when the Benjamins had held meetings in this same village, they were driven out by force. "We feel that we must not refuse them, but if we accept their invitation, still we have no teacher to send them." Hence, the appeal for support was made: "May we depend upon you to pray with us so that this difficulty may be solved and these people given an opportunity to hear the gospel and be saved? The Benjamins mentioned another difficulty. Es Salt was still recovering from a particularly harsh winter. Heavy rain, wind, snow, and cold had caused extensive damage to buildings, businesses, and gardens, all of which the Benjamins attributed to God's judgment."[39] If the winter weather had been harsh, the political climate was all the more difficult for the missionaries to endure.

HOLDING THE FORT

In spite of the positive spin that the missionaries put on their reports, they were straining to hold the fort under an unrelenting crossfire. We get an idea of how Pentecostals viewed the crossfire from Charles Peters, a short-term Pentecostal missionary, who filed a report of his observations of Jerusalem during April of 1937. He writes, "The past few have been great days in Jerusalem, the Moslems celebrating the feast of Nebi Musa and the Jews celebrating the Passover and the days of unleavened bread." Peters discusses the rival claims to the land made by Jews and Arabs. He asserts that, according to Genesis 17:8, God gave the land of Canaan to Abraham and his posterity as an *everlasting possession.* "To the Jew who loves the Torah, and to the Christian who believes the Bible to be Word of God, there can be no doubt about the title to that land, the *promised* land." But the Arabs, who have resided in the land for the past 1355 years, "have their own idea about the title, and have gone on a 'sit-down' strike in protest against immigration of Jews and the sale of Arab land to them." Recapitulating the Arab position, he says that they "contend that their historical connection with the land has been over as long a period as that of the Jews, and that they were promised their independence for their rebellion against the Turk, and for their aid in winning the Great War. They resent efforts to move them out at the will of rulers of other lands, or to so fill the land with Jews that Arabs would be in the minority." On the other hand,

---

39. Benjamin, "Greetings from Transjordan," *Pentecostal Evangel* (March 20, 1937) 9, 12.

the Jews, says Peters, gained the right to establish a National Home in Palestine, the right to go back to the land promised them.[40]

Peters gives an account of the deliberations of the English Royal Commission appointed to investigate the causes of the Arab Riots and hear the demands of both sides. He summarizes the major demands of the Jews and Arabs. The chief demand of the Jews was that "immigration be facilitated, that they be allowed to enter Palestine at a much faster rate." The Arabs made four definite demands:

1. That the project of the National Home be immediately discontinued.

2. That immigration of Jews be immediately and completely stopped.

3. That the sale of Arab land to Jews be prohibited by law.

4. That the British Mandate be at once terminated, and a treaty signed giving complete independence to Palestine as an Arab state.[41]

There was no doubt in Peters' mind as to which side he would take. But instead of saying so outright, he waxes eloquent with a pro-Zionist narrative plotted with a typical Pentecostal eschatological scenario:

> What an undying tale has been written and is still being written of two Semitic brothers Ishmael and Isaac, and of a land flowing with milk and honey, glorious because of the presence of God in the midst of His earthly people. This land later becoming a desolate, barren waste, a shameful scarecrow of its former self, through the sin of that people. It is now beginning again to pulsate with new life, springs bursting forth in the desert, the Plain of the Philistines filling up with orange groves, the Plain of Megiddo with dairy farms, the hills with vineyards, the cities and villages with new factories, homes, schools, hospitals, synagogues, the boulevards of Tel Aviv crowded with automobiles of American make, electric stop-and-go signals controlling the traffic, the Jordan harnessed to give light and power to much of Palestine, the great twelve hundred mile pipe line delivering the continuous stream of crude oil from Iraq to vessels in the new Haifa harbor, the Dead Sea giving up its wealth of potash and chemicals for shipment all over the world.

> Friends! We are living in a lawless age; in a chaotic, disordered, sin-sick world. But soon the Sun of Righteousness shall arise with healing in His wings, and we shall be dazzled by the brightness of His coming, and the blinded eyes of Israel shall be unveiled and they shall look on Him whom they pierced. And they shall be re-commissioned as God's witnesses in the earth. Soon the Lord Our Righteousness shall come with ten thousand of His saints to be King over all the earth, and Olivet shall quiver with joy at His blessed presence, and shall cleave asunder, half toward the north and half toward the south, and living waters shall flow out from Jerusalem. Israel shall be a blessing to all nations and the Gentiles shall minister to her. This includes even the flocks of Kedar, Ishmael's son.[42]

40. Peters, "Eretz Israel (The Land of Israel)," *Pentecostal Evangel* (April 24, 1937) 4–5.

41. Ibid., 5.

42. Ibid.

Peters' decidedly pro-Zionist views were representative of the perspective of the Pentecostal missionaries in Palestine. In casting their lot with the Zionists, the Pentecostal missionaries were in effect distancing themselves from the religious-ethnic group to whom most of their native pastors and converts belonged, Christian Arabs. To say that this posture contributed to the eventual failure of their mission would be an understatement.

Pressing Ahead Aggressively

The Pentecostal missionaries took advantage of the lull in the fighting to press ahead aggressively with their mission objectives. Saul Benjamin chartered a bus for a baptismal service at the Jordan River. Eleven were baptized, three boys and eight girls between the ages of fourteen and eighteen. In response to the invitation from the village of Fhais, the Benjamins returned and many homes were opened to them, affording opportunities for personal evangelism. They attributed the change of heart in Fhais to "the prayers of God's people in behalf of this place."[43] The school in Es Salt was also bearing fruit, as the Benjamins reported that in 1937 thirty children were saved.[44] During the summer of 1937 Vera Swarztrauber took up permanent residence with the Benjamins in Es Salt to give focused attention to the women's ministry. She immediately saw promising opportunities for effectual ministry among the women, girls and children. She also saw hindrances to the full use of her gifts in the prejudice of the native Christians against women leaders. This did not hinder her effectiveness in working with the women. She held a three day Bible school for young women and was gratified by the positive response. She writes, "The experience of these three days has also confirmed my conviction of the need for a Pentecostal Bible school in this country where our Christian young women and men may be trained in the Word."[45]

As of the end of 1937 a survey of AG missionary personnel in Palestine and Transjordania was published in the *Pentecostal Evangel*, showing that in Palestine eleven missionaries were working at four stations and nine outstations. In addition, the survey noted, "three native preachers and Bible women are working with our mission in Palestine and Transjordan." In Syria one missionary was serving at one station and six outstations. According to the survey, "The work in Shweifat comprises a gospel mission, a school of 75 students who are taught elementary subjects along with a knowledge of God's Word, and an orphanage of 15 boys and girls who are sheltered, clothed and fed under the kindly supervision of our missionary in charge."[46]

In the summer of 1938 political turmoil was brewing again. Ever since the previous summer, when the Royal Commission called for the partitioning of Palestine, debate had been raging over the partition plan. The *Pentecostal Evangel* weighed in on the debate, professing shock that Jerusalem was cut out of the proposed Jewish state.

43. Benjamin, "News from Transjordan," *Pentecostal Evangel* (July 31, 1937) 8.
44. "Es Salt, Transjordan," *Pentecostal Evangel* (August 28, 1937) 7.
45. Swarztrauber, "News From Transjordan," *Pentecostal Evangel* (October 9, 1937) 9.
46. "Palestine and Transjordan," & "Syria," *Pentecostal Evangel* (December 11, 1937) 2–3.

Citing Scripture, the editor complains, "Years ago God said to the prophet Zechariah, 'In that day will I make Jerusalem a burdensome stone for all people.' It will be a burdensome stone to all the nations until He comes whose right it is to reign, whose throne will be erected in Jerusalem."[47] The solution to the partition debate proffered in the *Pentecostal Evangel* was sadly deficient in coming to terms with the complex political and religious issues at stake in the Arab-Zionist conflict.

Once again the Arab revolt heated up and became deadly. Saul Benjamin had bad news, reporting in the summer of 1938 that the revolt showed no signs of abating in Transjordan, and the situation in Palestine was worse. He writes, "Palestine, especially seems to be a battlefield, trouble breaking forth sometimes in the north, sometimes in the south, and sometimes all over the land simultaneously, in guerilla warfare, killing not only the Jews but also those of the Arabs who are suspected to be party to the government." The British Government was doing all that it could to put an end to the "wave of crime which has already paralyzed the economic life of the country." So far, fortunately, "God is preserving His own through all this trouble, not one has been hurt or molested." However, the Benjamins did have a close call. When he and his family got a late start on a return trip from Amman, on the way they were stopped by the police because a short distance ahead a car had been stopped by rebels and the occupants robbed. Benjamin says that he and his wife then understood "why we had been detained in Amman, for had we left when we wanted to we might have been in the position of the other car."[48] These were frightening times for missionaries. It was understandable that Anna Adams and Pearl Benjamin departed with the children during the summer for a furlough in the United States, while Saul Benjamin remained on the field, planning to come home later.[49]

In October of 1938 Benjamin provides a vivid description of the political situation in Palestine and Transjordan. He reports that for nearly three years the region has been a continual battlefield and he has been living "in the midst of bloodshed and carnage, and the most ruining devastation one may wish to witness in these modern times." He continues, "The economic life of the country is paralyzed, and personal safety does not exist. One may walk out into the street and be taken for an Arab or a Jew and shot or stabbed. Though there may be a crowd of witnesses, no one will dare to lift his hand or voice in protestation, for his own life would be worth nothing after that."[50] And what is the source of the conflict? The Jews claimed the land by right of divine promise, while the Arabs claimed it by conquest, and neither would tolerate the rights of the other in any way. As Benjamin saw it, it was as if the age-long jealousies and enmity of the one people against the other—Ishmael despising Isaac—were coming to the forefront now. "The awful news of the last few days has been sickening, with a regular slaughtering of men and in many instances of women and children." This was more that Benjamin could bear. He now recognized that he had to return home on furlough "in order to

47. "Partitioning Palestine," *Pentecostal Evangel* (August 28, 1937) 7.
48. Benjamin, "News from Palestine and Transjordan," *Pentecostal Evangel* (June 11, 1938) 7.
49. "Two Home from Palestine," *Pentecostal Evangel* (July 16, 1938) 7.
50. Benjamin, "Sidelights of the Palestine Situation," *Pentecostal Evangel* (October 1, 1938) 7.

avoid serious danger to his health." And he was not the only missionary in need of a furlough. Serena Hodges would soon follow him home to the United States.[51]

Apparently Syria was a safer place for missionary work, yet Yumna Malick was feeling a financial pinch. She notified her readers that a native preacher among the Haurense, Milhem Shoucair, was in need of support. The editor of the *Pentecostal Evangel* interjects, "she has no support for him so has to give what she can from her own allowance. We believe this worker would be a good investment for some one to make for the kingdom of God."[52] John Warton had relocated in Syria. "For some time," writes Warton, "calls from the hungry hearts of Aleppo have come to us to visit them. Aleppo is in the northern part of Syria and has more than two hundred and fifty thousand population. There was no Pentecostal work there. Feeling it was the leading of the Lord, I accepted the call and went there." He encountered some difficulty in securing a place for meetings, but finally rented a large space for meetings. Although he was not allowed to advertise, Warton reports that "at times we had two or three hundred in the services. In a few days the interest increased and, praise God, we actually saw tears streaming from many eyes." Now regular services are going on led by a "very godly brother." Warton also reports an opening in Zahle among the Chaldeans. "Many hundreds of these poor people are as sheep without a shepherd, and are hungry to hear. Several times they came after me to visit them and preach to them. I shall never forget the first time I did so. They gathered long before the service, and how eagerly they listened. Many gladly responded to the call and accepted Christ as their personal Saviour." In addition, Warton tells about other works in Bagdad and among the Armenians and Assyrians in Beirut, averring that there are "many thousands waiting yet whom we are anxious to reach with the message of life."[53]

WORLD WAR II

During World War II, the economic squeeze of wartime conditions, the loss of contact with the home base, the hazards of maritime travel, and the disruption of mail service placed severe constraints on the Pentecostal missionaries in Palestine. The entry of Italy into the war in May of 1940 brought the war closer to Palestine. Aimed at disrupting British supply lines to Syria, the Italians bombed Haifa and Tel Aviv, causing a heavy death toll in the latter. These bombings motivated the British prime minister, Winston Churchill, to rethink his position on Palestine. Churchill was a longtime Zionist sympathizer. When he assumed power in 1940, Churchill was inclined to rescind the White Paper of 1939, which he viewed as an effectual repudiation of the Balfour Declaration. He also gave his approval to the training of Jewish commando units in sabotage, demolition, and guerilla warfare. However, given the threat posed by the Italians, Churchill changed his mind and conceded to the immigration quotas of the White Paper in the interest of appeasing the Arabs. This antagonized the Zionists,

---

51. Ibid.

52. "Syria," *Pentecostal Evangel* (August 13, 1938) 7.

53. Warton, "Opening a New Work in Syria," *Pentecostal Evangel* (August 5, 1939) 10.

who strongly sympathized with the Jews desperately fleeing the Holocaust and seeking refuge in Palestine.[54]

Courage of the Missionaries

In spite of difficult war conditions, Pentecostal missionaries showed their courage by deciding to return to the region. In 1939 Philip J. Shabaz and his wife returned to Iraq.[55] In 1940 other missionaries who were evacuated from Palestine for furloughs during the Arab revolts also returned. Vera Swarztrauber, now in Jerusalem, writes a note of appreciation for the *Pentecostal Evangel*, which she says had taken on a new value to the missionaries of late. "Several times I have read articles which have met a particular need rising just at that time. You will be happy to know that many of our old copies are distributed among the English soldiers. One has had the most glorious Baptism in the Spirit and devours every copy he can get."[56] By this time Serena Hodges and the family of Saul and Pearl Benjamin had safely returned to Palestine with thanks for the Lord's protection on their voyage through European waters.[57] Perkin acknowledges that there was some hesitancy about booking them to sail so soon after the outbreak of the war. But all went well, as seven Pentecostal missionaries on their way to the Congo were on the same boat. Hodges and the Benjamins gathered with them daily for prayer and fellowship, bolstering each other's sense of God's presence on this dangerous journey.[58] Serena Hodges sent a note of thanks "for the many whom I know were praying for our party during the days of travel in dangerous waters."[59]

Upon her return Hodges offered an assessment of the status of the mission in Jerusalem. She was delighted to find that "there were new faces in the congregation, and a real interest in Bible study—a fresh development since I went home on furlough." She perceived that Ida Beck and Vera Swarztrauber "have surely been used of the Lord this past year, and real decisions for the Lord have been made." Miss Brown was carrying on with her prison ministry, and now was assisted by Saul Benjamin, who was re-assigned to Jerusalem. She asks for "special prayer" for the women's meetings. It seems that some who had been saved were drifting away, a condition that could be reversed if the work of the Holy Spirit could be manifested among them. On a brighter note, Hodges says that "the Sunday School is a joy to see." Attendance is up over one hundred so that more teachers are needed. Finally, she observes that the work of the Ramallah outstation is going on as usual, but some of the children are of concern. "The real need is teaching along the line of walking in the Spirit."[60]

54. Bauer, *From Diplomacy to Resistance*, 110–24.
55. "Missionary Sailings," *Pentecostal Evangel* (October 21, 1939) 7.
56. Swarztrauber, "A Word from Jerusalem," *Pentecostal Evangel* (January 13, 1940) 5.
57. "News from Recent Sailings," *Pentecostal Evangel* (January 20, 1940) 15.
58. "Palestine," *Pentecostal Evangel* (February 10, 1940) 8.
59. "Serena Hodges Sends Greetings," *Pentecostal Evangel* (March 23, 1940) 8.
60. Ibid., 8–9.

Progress was reported in the Pentecostal church in Jerusalem, now under the leadership of Saul and Pearl Benjamin. Due to Saul Benjamin's emphasis on tithing, the church offerings more than doubled, bringing about what was perceived as a rising tide of spiritual blessing. As Benjamin impressed upon the congregation the meaning and importance of church membership, eleven new members were received and attendance steadily increased, "with new faces appearing at almost every service." The attendance hovered at about one hundred, and it was suggested that this number could be doubled or even tripled with the acquisition of a bus. It would appear that the children targeted by the Pentecostals were from Eastern Christian families, based on the comment that "many of the children fast on Sunday and attend the ritual of their own church, then come to our Sunday school before returning home to eat." Fasting was strictly enjoined upon Eastern Christians as a condition for participation in the Eucharist. Beyond Jerusalem, the work at Ramallah was in need of a native worker to preach there and in surrounding villages. Finally, it was stated that God was blessing the prison ministry that had been extensively developed by Elizabeth Brown.

In the summer of 1940, a good deal of alarm was stirred up over the precarious position of the missionaries in Palestine, given fears that World War II would spill over into Palestine as had been the case in the First World War. The *Pentecostal Evangel* shuddered at "the prize Palestine would be to some of the warring nations, yet no intimation has as yet come to us from our missionaries that they wish arrangements to be made for their withdrawal." The American consul had already recommended that John Warton and Philip Shabaz evacuate their respective posts in Syria and Iraq. The missionary secretary thought it "possible for these missionaries to go to Palestine in an emergency, and should it become necessary to evacuate our missionaries from Palestine they could leave in one company."[61] Concerns continued to be raised over the safety of the missionaries in the Middle East. At the end of the summer, the *Pentecostal Evangel* observed that, "The fields that are primarily affected at the present are Egypt, Palestine, Syria, and Iraq." Special provision was made to expedite the transfer of funds to the missionaries. Hence, Perkin writes, "All remittances to Egypt, Palestine, and Syria are now being made by cable, so that friends who are contributing for the support of missionaries in these fields will understand why it is they are not getting acknowledgments of their offerings from the missionaries."[62]

Death of A. Elizabeth Brown

With the turmoil of war once again swirling around the Pentecostal missionary community in Palestine, word came of the passing of an era. Elizabeth Brown died on August 4, 1940. She had served for fifty-two years as a missionary, forty-five of which were spent in Jerusalem. Brown's contributions to the Pentecostal mission in Palestine were inestimable. The *Pentecostal Evangel* credited her with a solitary distinction: "Her heart was in her work, and she had so won the respect and confidence of the govern-

61. "War and Missions," *Pentecostal Evangel* (July 20, 1940) 8.
62. "War and Missions," *Pentecostal Evangel* (August 31, 1940) 6.

mental authorities in Palestine that she had the only permit issued to anyone to visit all of the prisons in Palestine." She was a gifted evangelist who enjoyed great success in the conversion of Arabs to the Pentecostal message. The editor of the *Pentecostal Evangel* was confident that "there will be a host of souls in glory who will greet our beloved sister with thanksgiving for what she has meant to them through her faithful ministry of the Word." Brown was also a consummate fundraiser. When she asked for prayer that $10,000.00 be raised for the completion of the Shemariah mission station, the AG leadership would not extend a helping hand. Due to Brown's skill in prayerfully building a network of faithful supporters, consisting of individuals and churches, she raised the money and the building was completed, providing a home base for Pentecostal missionaries and a guesthouse for tourists.[63]

Now that Brown had passed away, the AG denominational officials seemed more concerned with the financial implications of her departure than the absence of her leadership. They wondered how they might sustain a continued inflow of contributions from Brown's financial contributors. Perkin saw the handwriting on the wall, observing, "A number of friends used to send money direct to Sister Brown for the carrying on of her work, and she made herself directly responsible for the supporting of a number of native workers. The cutting off of this support will be greatly felt on the field unless others can send in to take over the work which our Sister Brown has been carrying on these many years." The transition of leadership was not his concern. As he said, "there are other workers such as Brother and Sister Benjamin, Miss Hodges, Miss Swarztrauber, as well as our Sister Beck, who is now on furlough, who will take their share of responsibility; but there is about sixty dollars needed for the maintenance of workers who were supported through the gifts sent direct to Miss Brown."[64] This seems a crass addendum to a memorial tribute.

Perkin's insensitivity in memorializing the passing of Elizabeth Brown is regrettable. Her grief-stricken colleagues had lost a valiant senior missionary who was arguably irreplaceable. Just as missionaries were bracing themselves to carry on bravely, word came of the death of Veronica Warton in Syria, leaving her husband to care for their four children, ages 8, 11, 14, and 17.[65] Despite his loss, John Warton stayed at his post. With no indication of Warton's grief, the *Pentecostal Evangel* blithely reports, "Brother Warton, who for some time has been practically isolated due to the war, sends encouraging word that God is blessing in Syria and souls are being saved."[66] Given their personal losses, combined with news of coastal bombardment, this was surely a trying time for the missionaries. The *Pentecostal Evangel* announced that Haifa had been bombed twice during the summer with loss of life and predicted, "Eventually the nations will clash in "The Battle for Palestine."[67] Saul Benjamin writes,

63. "Promoted to Higher Service," *Pentecostal Evangel* (August 24, 1940) 8.

64. Ibid.

65. "With the Lord," *Pentecostal Evangel* (September 14, 1940) 8.

66. "From Lebanon, Syria" *Pentecostal Evangel* (September 28, 1940) 9.

67. "The Battle for Palestine," *Pentecostal Evangel* (September 14, 1940) 7.

You have undoubtedly heard long before this that Haifa was bombed twice—but that is as near as war has come to us . . . Conditions here are not easy, yet we feel it would be wrong for us to run and leave the work untended . . . In the opinion of the missionaries here, there is no reason for any of us to be panicky. Of course the prices of food are going up as is natural, but we are confident God has called us here and we shall be cared for. *We are staying in Palestine by our people and at our post.*[68]

Soon thereafter, it was reported, "The missionaries as a body have taken a definite stand that they will remain on the field as long as it is possible for them to do so."[69]

The year 1940 ended with a fairly positive affirmation of support from the Missionary Secretary. In an article entitled, "A Visit to the Holy Land," Perkin starts off by saying that "a kind of cloud overshadows the land as though God has temporarily turned His back upon it while the offer of salvation is made to others." But he acknowledges that God is still working in Palestine. "There are eight Council missionaries working in Palestine and a number of striking conversions have taken place both amongst the Arabs and the Jews." In particular, Perkin notes that since the outbreak of the war "greater interest in the gospel has been manifested and the attendance at meetings is better than ever before." There was no question about the potential for evangelism. Out of a total population of 1,683,320 in Palestine and Transjordan, there are 400,000 Jews, 91,000 Christians, and the rest are practically all Mohammedans. In this context, Perkin avers that "everything be done at the present to give out the message of salvation before further trouble comes to this section of the world." With the rumblings of war drawing near, Perkin muses, in tones of Christian Zionism, "The site of God's holy temple is now occupied by a Mohammedan mosque, while outside the religious element of Jewry weeps and prays for the restoration of Israel and God's glory to the holy city. Perhaps the time is not far distant when those prayers are to be answered, but until He comes again to reign in the city of David, we want to do our utmost to help human hearts to open to the King of Glory."[70]

Hope Springs Eternal

With hope springing eternal, in 1941 the *Pentecostal Evangel* was under the impression that the suffering in Palestine was breaking down the walls of estrangement between Jews and Arabs. It reported that the bombardment of Haifa and Tel Aviv did much to bring Arabs and Jews together. Jews were quick to help wounded Arabs, and contributed towards the relief of destitute Arab families; while hundreds of messages of sympathy were sent to the mayor of Tel Aviv by Arab leaders after the air raid on that all-Jewish city.[71] This report brought some relief from anxiety over the prospect that Palestine would again become an important front in a world war. Blending re-

68. Benjamin, "From Jerusalem, Palestine," *Pentecostal Evangel* (September 28, 1940) 9.

69. "Palestine," *Pentecostal Evangel* (November 2, 1940) 6.

70. Perkin, "A Visit to the Holy Land," *Pentecostal Evangel* (November 30, 1940) 13.

71. "Suffering in Palestine," *Pentecostal Evangel* (January 11, 1941) 13.

porting and theologizing, the *Pentecostal Evangel* suggests, "Many are wondering if it will become the scene of active warfare in this present war, and whether the valley of Armageddon will see the bloodiest part of the conflict."[72] There were good reasons for concern. It was reported that many people in Palestine were expecting that a terrible struggle was about to be witnessed. Jerusalem and the other cities of the Holy Land were blacked out at night. Air raid shelters had been constructed in Haifa, Tel Aviv, Jaffa, and other vulnerable cities. With its typical eschatological accent, the *Pentecostal Evangel* comments, "One day war *will* come to Palestine, whether it be before this war ends or later. The final battle of the age will be fought in the Plain of Esdraelon in Galilee, and the bloodshed will be terrible until until Christ and His saints appear in the clouds of glory to set up His holy earthly kingdom . . . May it not be that these very shelters that are being prepared in Palestine today are those into which men will run on that day of judgment seeking refuge from His anger, but seeking in vain?"[73] The present crisis was sufficiently troubling in itself without ruminations on the War of Armageddon.

Saul Benjamin had a more reassuring word for the readers of the *Pentecostal Evangel*, attesting that "God is among us, even though the terrifying news and awful voices of oppression are let loose on the world." He praises God for a Sunday when "God was present in power and blessing and the call was clearly given to open the gates and let Him come in. We feel we are on the verge of a real revival; pray for us."[74] For a time it seemed to the missionary executives in America that the "war clouds seem to have passed over our mission fields of the Near East" because "reports of 'all's well' are coming from the missionaries again." John Warton had returned to Beirut after having fled to Palestine, where he remained for several months. His oldest son, David, was away at Wheaton College, while the other children remained for the time being in Syria. Philip Shabaz in Persia reports, "The light of the Pentecostal truth is drawing upon many souls . . . We are having regular services in three places and the Lord is blessing." The missionaries in Palestine were saying "that they are all well and happy and feel that they are in the 'safest place in all the world.' A new interest in the gospel message seems to have taken hold of the people, and the meetings are being blessed of God." On a personal note, Saul and Pearl Benjamin announced the happy news of the arrival of a newborn boy, Jonathan Edwin, born August 28.[75]

Saul and Pearl Benjamin were clearly making significant strides in building up the infrastructure of the Jerusalem assembly. They succeeded in unifying the ministries of the various outstations by means of baptismal services and an annual convention held at the Shemariah mission station. The baptismal services provided an opportunity for members of the churches in outlying areas to come together for worship and fellowship. A bus was chartered to transport the participants to the Jordan River. At one such service on April 26, 1942, the baptismal candidates were from Jaffa, Jerusalem,

72. "Jerusalem in War Time," *Pentecostal Evangel* (February 8, 1941) 10.

73. "War in Palestine?" *Pentecostal Evangel* (February 22, 1941) 10.

74. Benjamin, "Jerusalem, Palestine," *Pentecostal Evangel* (June 21, 1941) 8.

75. "What's New in the Missions Department: Near East," *Pentecostal Evangel* (October 18, 1941) 8.

and Ramallah.[76] In 1942 Saul Benjamin writes, "Our choice to remain here has proved so definitely to have been the leading of the Lord that we are happy indeed that He has kept us from making any false move." His reason for saying so was that he had recently been party to seven conversions in two weeks. He explains that a young man he had met through his prison ministry had come by the mission looking for work. Subsequently, he and another young man were "saved" at a Monday evening informal service. They brought in others until in about two weeks seven were converted. "These coverts, not content alone to enjoy the experience, are anxious that their companions shall be saved. They are from a branch of the church which we have felt to be immune to the efforts of missionaries, but with God all things are possible." He concludes, "We are glad to report that in all the stations under our care God is working, both in this country and in Transjordan. While the difficulties are great, we are consistently looking away to Him whose Word cannot and will not fail."[77]

Conventions were a trusted technique in Pentecostal praxis. The fare usually consisted of sumptuous food, guest speakers, Bible study sessions, intense worship, and altar calls in which participants would be initiated into Pentecostal spirituality, i.e., conversion and the baptism of the Holy Spirit. The Benjamins organized the first annual convention, or as they termed it, "spiritual conference," in 1941. Saul Benjamin filed reports on these conventions, which were timed to coincide with the Feast of Pentecost. Benjamin reports that the second spiritual conference on May 23–25, 1942 included people from Es Salt, Jaffa, Ramallah, and north of Palestine. "The opening message by Habeeb Khoury, our colporteur, from the text Exodus 24:11, '. . . they saw God, and did eat and drink,' struck the keynote of the conference." Benjamin was pleased that the small Jerusalem assembly entertained forty out of town guests and fed about 100 people. The results were promising. One person was converted, two reclaimed their faith, and eight others presented themselves as candidates for water baptism. Benjamin was glowing: "It does rejoice our hearts to report continued conversions both here and in Ramallah. These converts, who are facing persecution from the Roman Catholic Church, need your prayers that they may stand true. All of us are well, including those across the river Jordan. We feel safe at present; as to the immediate future, it is in the hands of the One who we know will take care of us, come what may."[78]

The next two conventions were equally productive. The 1943 convention evoked a meaningful association in Saul Benjamin's mind. He writes, "The spiritual blessing attending the convention and the having 'all things common' for those few days is reminiscent of an occasion 1900 years ago. God grant that this convention may prove to be a portent of an even greater Pentecost than the first!" The keynote speaker was an Egyptian evangelist, Salib Boutros. His stirring addresses moved Benjamin to praise him as a Spirit-filled and Spirit-used man. Benjamin writes, "We believe he is in God's

---

76. Benjamin, "Palestine: 'Even in Troublous Times,'" *Pentecostal Evangel* (June 20, 1942) 8–9.

77. Ibid.

78. Benjamin, "Conference in Jerusalem," *Pentecostal Evangel* (July 25, 1942) 8.

order and in God's own time. His ministry bore, and is still bearing, precious fruit in our midst." Five people were baptized in the Holy Spirit. The 1943 convention was the largest of the four conventions organized by the Benjamins. It even went on the road, with the speakers itinerating in Jaffa, Es Salt and Amman, Irbid, and back to Jerusalem. "We thank God for what the convention and the evangelistic tour have meant to Palestine." An important outcome of the 1943 convention was the formulation of a plan for regular visitation of outlying churches "for the strengthening of the work." Another was a reaffirmation of the core value of "preaching Pentecost more clearly and consistently as this is undoubtedly the message for this hour."[79]

When something works, the human tendency is to replicate it. Such was the case with the 1944 convention. Salib Boutros was announced as the keynote speaker, but at a late hour he cancelled, leaving the Benjamins in the lurch. Replacements were hastily arranged and all went well. Benjamin asked two missionaries, Brother Kemp and Brother Watts, to fill in by leading the Bible classes on the topic of the personality, offices, gifts, and fruit of the Holy Spirit. The schedule called for intensive Bible studies in the daytimes and evangelistic services in the evenings with the native evangelists speaking. Benjamin writes, "The Holy Spirit was in charge of every service in a most blessed manner so that it was no effort to give out the Word of God. There were messages from different workers and an especially anointed one from an English brother in the Royal Air Force." Benjamin continues,

> It pleased the Lord to baptize five souls in the Holy Spirit. Three were baptized during the convention and two since. One of them is our teacher at Irbid who, though ordinarily timid, spoke for two and a half hours with new tongues. We have been meeting with constant opposition to our testimony, as have these who have been filled, but it is apparent that God has broken through the powers of darkness to give us these times of refreshing from His presence. May they continue to come![80]

Benjamin calculates that five were baptized and one hundred and fifty were fed, with attendees coming from Ramallah, Jaffa, Nazareth, Haifa, Beit Jala, Trans-Jordan, Irbid, Ajloun, Es Salt, and Jerusalem.[81]

The published reports of Saul Benjamin did not tell the whole story of the situation in Palestine. Evidently, he was constrained by security concerns from being completely forthright. Only later did he publicly divulge that "government spies" had infiltrated the meetings of the Pentecostal mission to see what was being done.[82] Another missing piece of information in the published reports was the debilitating effect that wartime conditions were having on the Benjamin family. Saul Benjamin had undoubtedly notified the mission officials of this in his private correspondence. Later, Saul and Pearl

79. Benjamin, "Speeding the Light in Palestine," *Pentecostal Evangel* (October 9, 1943) 9. Salib Boutros may be an incorrect name. Boutros Labib was a well known yet controversial Egyptian Pentecostal figure. See Conn, *Where the Saints Have Trod*, 266–68.

80. Benjamin, "Jerusalem Convention," *Pentecostal Evangel* (September 9, 1944) 10.

81. Ibid.

82. Benjamin, "Gold From Gilead," *Pentecostal Evangel* (November 9, 1946) 8.

Benjamin confided to J. Roswell Flower about the need of their family to "regain at least part of our health lost during those terrible days we spend in Palestine during the war."[83] So behind the veneer of positive reports in the *Pentecostal Evangel*, the true picture was that the difficult tenure of the Benjamins as AG missionaries in Palestine was winding down.

WORSENING CONDITIONS IN PALESTINE

As World War II dragged on, conditions had worsened in Palestine. The *Pentecostal Evangel* reported in June of 1944 that the strife between the Arabs and Jews in Palestine had not ended. It had merely been held down by the presence of Allied forces in the land. According to the New York *Times,* both Arabs and Jews were building up secret stores of arms, drilling their forces and perfecting their organizations in preparation for the day when the Allied forces would move on.[84] In 1941 the Mufti of Jerusalem, Haj Amin al-Husseini, met with Adolph Hitler, asking for an alliance against the Jews. While Hitler spurned Husseini's request for a declaration of support for the Arabs, he did state that,

> Germany stood for uncompromising war against the Jews. That naturally included active opposition to the Jewish national home in Palestine . . . Germany would furnish positive and practical aid to the Arabs involved in the same struggle . . . Germany's objective [is] . . . solely the destruction of the Jewish element residing in the Arab sphere . . . In that hour the Mufti would be the most authoritative spokesman for the Arab world. The Mufti thanked Hitler profusely.[85]

Worse yet, the Zionists turned against the British in April of 1942 after the *Struma*, a ship carrying Jewish refugees from Romania, was denied entry into Palestine and later sank in the Black Sea with only two survivors. As news about Nazi persecution of Jews in Europe reached Palestine, the Zionist militants of the Irgun and Stern Gang began to harass the British forces in an attempt to force the lifting of immigration restrictions. In November of 1944 Lehi extremists assassinated Lord Moyne, a British diplomat and close personal friend of Churchill, in Cairo. From this point on, Churchill renounced his Zionist sympathies and the British Government eschewed the idea of setting up a Jewish state in Palestine. By the end of the war, the British position in Palestine was increasingly untenable.[86]

83. Saul and Pearl Benjamin to the Rev. J. Roswell Flower, December 19, 1940, unpublished letter, Flower Research Center, Springfield, Missouri.

84. "Strife in Palestine," *Pentecostal Evangel* (June 3, 1944) 8.

85. Conversation of Adolph Hitler and the Grand Mufti of Jerusalem, November 28, 1941, Berlin, in Lacquer and Rubin, *The Israeli-Arab Reader*, 79–84.

86. Bauer, *From Diplomacy to Resistance*, 311–33.

Transition in Personnel

In this context of escalating tension, the reports of the missionaries indicate that a major transition in the Pentecostal missionary personnel in Palestine was underway. In 1945 the Benjamins returned to the United States to work with an Assyrian-American congregation in San Francisco. Eventually Saul Benjamin was employed by the U.S. Army Language School in Monterey, California as an Arabic teacher. After the departure of the Benjamin family, Laura Radford remained in Jerusalem until October 1947 when she went into retirement. In that same month, George and Christine Carmichael, appointed as missionaries of the General Council of the American AG, arrived in Palestine and took up residence at the Shemariah mission station in Jerusalem. Vera Swarztrauber and Ida Beck stayed at their posts, providing continuity. By this time, R. B. Rohold had passed away, and his wife, B. D. Rohold, continued the work of the Jewish Pentecostal mission in Haifa, assisted by Ruth Lawless. Another Jewish Pentecostal missionary, D. C. Joseph, was operating a mission in Jaffa. With this shift in personnel, the Pentecostal mission in Palestine continued to hold the fort.

In the next chapter, the historical narrative will bring the story of the Pentecostal mission in Palestine up to 2007. The major development during this period would be the establishment of a mission in the Hashemite Kingdom of Jordan (later the West Bank) by the Church of God (Cleveland, Tennessee).

7 | Retreat and Regrouping, 1946–2007

THIS CHAPTER WILL pick up the historical narrative of the Pentecostal mission in Palestine in 1946 on the eve of the partition crisis. The theme of this final period of the Pentecostal mission was retreat and regrouping. The War of 1948 prompted the retreat of the Assemblies of God (hereafter AG) missionaries from Jerusalem, as their Arab clients were caught up in the Palestinian Diaspora. In spite of an attempt to regroup the AG mission, it descended into a phase of decline, leading to its termination in 1977. However, all was not lost. As the AG mission was declining, a new mission started by Church of God (hereafter COG) was gathering momentum among the Arab Christians in the territory under Jordanian control. The progress of the COG mission work in Bethlehem, the Mount of Olives, and the village of Aboud will be described and the accomplishments of Margaret Gaines, the foremost leader of the COG mission in Jordan (later the West Bank) will be assessed. Recent developments in the AG and COG mission works will be briefly recounted as a postscript to the historical narrative. Then a summative assessment of the Pentecostal mission will presented as it was stated by Ida Beck, one of the missionaries who served in Palestine. Finally, this chapter will conclude with a causative explanation of the failure of the Pentecostal mission in Palestine.

CHANGING OF THE GUARD

The mission of the COG (Cleveland, Tennessee) in Palestine commenced in 1945 when J. H. Ingram came to Palestine and met with Hanna K. Suleiman and the forty Arab Pentecostals meeting in the Suleiman home. Suleiman later affiliated with the COG and was commissioned to serve as a missionary in Bethlehem. In 1946 D. B. Hatfield was commissioned by the COG to serve as its first American missionary in the Middle East. The Hatfield family sailed from New York on April 23, 1947, and arrived at Haifa, Palestine on May 8.[1] After years of distinguished service, Laura Radford left Palestine in October 1947 and went into retirement. In that same month, George and Christine Carmichael, appointed as missionaries of the General Council of the American AG, arrived in Palestine and took up residence at the Shemariah mission station in Jerusalem. Vera Swarztrauber and Ida Beck stayed at their posts, providing continuity. By this time, R. B. Rohold had passed away, and his wife, B. D. Rohold, continued the work of the Jewish Pentecostal mission in Haifa, assisted by Ruth Lawless.

---

1. Conn, *Where the Saints Have Trod*, 268.

Another Jewish Pentecostal missionary, Brother Joseph, was operating a mission in Jaffa. With this shift in personnel, the Pentecostal mission in Palestine continued to hold the fort.

Little is known about the Jewish Pentecostal missions in Palestine. In January of 1946 the *Pentecostal Evangel* provides a glimpse in an article by George Davis on the distribution of New Testaments in the Jewish colonies of Palestine. His source is an account of Ruth Lawless of the Rohold's Haifa mission. Lawless relates her experiences in evangelistic visitation among Zionist settlements. She and her fellow-workers would strategically arrive at their destination during the noon hour with a car laden with Hebrew, German, and English New Testaments, plus tracts in seventeen different languages. They would introduce themselves, saying, "We have come to visit you and bring you Bible literature to read if you are interested." According to Lawless, some had so little to read that anything was welcome. Others "quickly reveal to us lost souls hungry for God and His Word." On good days a large crowd might gather and the missionaries would ask, "Have you ever read the whole New Testament?" Lawless found that as soon as a few have accepted the proffered gift, then "others soon come, sometimes shyly, a little fearful of their fellows, to ask for the same 'little blue book' (the Prophecy New Testament). Sometimes they even come running to secure a copy." Lawless reports that "opportunities to preach the Word to an interested group are frequent." The author of the article surmises that Lawless' account was indicative of a trend. "From all sides come reports that the Jews are more open to the Word of God and the gospel message."[2]

Arrival of George Carmichael

George and Christine Carmichael arrived in Jerusalem as the partition crisis was fomenting. The conflict-torn land of Palestine must have presented a culture shock to the Carmichaels. George Carmichael had grown up on a ranch in western Nebraska. After his conversion, he was baptized in the Holy Spirit and immediately sensed that God was calling him to be a missionary. He states, "I believe that God puts a desire to evangelize in the heart of every new convert. The moment God puts His Spirit within us He puts His missionary program in our hearts."[3] Carmichael got with the program by evangelizing nearby ranchers. Equipped with a homemade briefcase full of tracts, he went "from ranch to ranch, walking over cow trails, and as I gave my testimony, God would come down in my heart in such blessing and joy. My friend, if you have lost the joy out of your heart, begin to testify and tell others about what Christ has done for you, and it won't be long until the old joy will come back and you will be shouting." Very soon Carmichael had worked up a thriving freelance ministry of evangelistic visitation and camp meetings. "I believe God wants us to give a word of testimony everywhere we go." After Carmichael sensed a call to go to Palestine, he promptly

2. Davis, "Giving New Testaments to Jewish People in Palestine," *Pentecostal Evangel* (January 19, 1946) 1, 12–14.

3. Carmichael, "Rebuilding Palestine," *Pentecostal Evangel* (February 19, 1949) 2.

responded, obtained credentials with the AG, and headed off to Palestine with his young wife.

On his way to Palestine, Carmichael stopped in New York City and went shopping for plumbing supplies. He happened upon a small Jewish store. When he mentioned that he was going to Palestine, the Jewish merchants heatedly argued among themselves whether a business like theirs could be financially viable in Eretz Israel "until they were ready to pack up and leave with me." Carmichael asked why they would want to go to Palestine and they said, "We don't know, but we want to go to Palestine." As Carmichael explains it, "God is putting a desire in the hearts of the Jews to return to Palestine. He cites a newspaper article describing Jewish refugees in Trieste, "They go down there with just a little bundle on their shoulders, maybe all the earthly possessions they have, and commit themselves to unseaworthy vessels to go to Palestine. They are driven by an irresistible force which one cannot explain." Carmichael insinuates that if the correspondent were a Bible student, he would know what that irresistible force is.[4]

When Carmichael and his wife arrived in Jerusalem in January of 1947, they took up residence at the Shemariah mission station. During their first night there they were awakened by the explosion of three bombs just a few blocks away, injuring a dozen people. Carmichael describes the scene:

> There is a tense atmosphere about the city. Tanks and armored cars are patrolling the streets, and sand-bag defenses are placed at all strategic points. On entering government offices, our pockets and purses are searched and we must show our identity cards. Several trucks loaded with soldiers have drawn up in front of our window and have formed a road block. The soldiers are mounting machine guns and stopping all traffic, while the passengers are subjected to search.[5]

Carmichael came to a sober realization that, "Americans are not any more popular here at present than the British!"[6] Despite the political turbulence in Jerusalem, however, Carmichael was "encouraged to find several spiritual young men attending the services, and I believe there is a possibility of developing several good workers from the group."[7] Unfortunately, Carmichael's hopes for these young men were never realized. Throughout 1947 conditions worsened to the point that it was hazardous to be on the streets at night and attendance at the meetings dwindled.

Arrival of D. B. Hatfield

In May of 1947 another missionary family arrived on the scene in Jerusalem. After D. B. Hatfield was commissioned by the COG, Cleveland, Tennessee to establish a mission in Palestine, he, his wife Myrtle, and their three young children boarded a ship

4. Carmichael, "What's Happening in Palestine," *Pentecostal Evangel* (August 28, 1948) 7.

5. Carmichael, "Greetings from Palestine!" *Pentecostal Evangel* (January 11, 1947) 8–9.

6. Ibid., 9.

7. Ibid.

for the "Promised Land." As they got their first glimpse of Palestine approaching the Haifa harbor, Hatfield says, "We began to feel a love rise within us for the country and its people."[8] Recognizing that he had brought his family to an unknown land, Hatfield states, "We were strangers in the Promised Land and first time missionaries in the Holy Land under assignment and appointment by the Church of God."[9] Before long the Hatfield family was rudely awakened to the dangers inherent in their assignment. On their first night in Jerusalem they lodged at the Eden Hotel and went out for an evening walk. A man on the street, recognizing them as naïve newcomers, asked them, "Do you see that balcony? Two British soldiers were shot and killed on that balcony last night by terrorists." Hatfield remarks that this was "enough to give us the shudders."[10] The family hunkered down in their hotel room, clamped down the shutters, and stayed out of the line of fire. The next day they promptly looked for a safer abode. Hatfield observes, "This was the condition that prevailed when we went there in 1947. This type of unrest has continued through the years, and even today it continues."[11]

The Hatfields had a contact in Jerusalem by the name of Hanna Suleiman. In 1945, while on one of his missionary tours, J. H. Ingram of the COG visited Jerusalem and was detained due to travel complications. He made good use of his time by attending a Pentecostal home fellowship led by Hanna and Nieme Suleiman, whom he acquainted with the COG. Suleiman had been baptized in the Spirit in 1929 and was well acquainted with A. Elizabeth Brown and Laura Radford.[12] Suleiman describes the meetings in his home: "When we gathered for prayer, the Spirit of God revealed Himself in real languages, with interpretations and visions of Christ and heaven, also giving wonderful prophecies. We know this was preparation by God, who was in the future to establish a real church for Himself in Palestine, as He did on the day of Pentecost in the first century of the Christian era."[13] Ingram must have been impressed because he invited the Suleimans to join the COG and work in Palestine. The Suleimans accepted and were approved as missionaries of the COG.

After the Hatfields found an apartment, they returned to the Eden Hotel and met Hanna and Nieme Suleiman and their two children, Jean and David, "It was wonderful to meet someone who knew about our purpose in coming to the Holy Land," especially because the Suleimans "had been of the Pentecostal faith for many years, so my message was not strange to them."[14] Later Suleiman became a licensed minister in the COG, holding services in his home. In the meantime, the Hatfield's settled into the American Colony Hotel and studied Arabic at the Newman School of Language. Unsure of whether they would settle in Palestine or Egypt, in September of 1947 the

8. Hatfield, *Triumphant—The Gates of Hell Cannot Have Me*, 235.

9. Ibid., 248.

10. Ibid., 267.

11. Ibid., 268.

12. Conn, *Where the Saints Have Trod*, 267.

13. Suleiman, "History of the Church of God in Palestine," *The Church of God Evangel* 43.29 (September 20, 1952) 6.

14. Ibid., 268, 276.

Hatfields obtained a seven day visa and made a reconnaissance trip to Egypt, only to be quarantined due to a cholera epidemic. With tensions mounting over the U.N. partition of Palestine, their return to Jerusalem was delayed. Then the war of 1948 broke out and they were stuck in Egypt for seventeen months.[15] For nineteen months the Hatfields and Suleimans lost contact.

Back in Jerusalem, the Carmichaels were caught in the firestorm of events leading up to the disaster of 1948. In August of 1947 George Carmichael notified the readers of the *Pentecostal Evangel*, "Since we last wrote you, we have been placed in the security zone." This meant that Shemariah was cordoned off and was no longer accessible to anyone who lacked a permanent pass to the zone. If effect, this shut down the church that had been meeting there. Carmichael explains, "When the British women and children were evacuated and security zones created, we were enclosed by miles of coiled barbed wire, and our ministry to civilians was curtailed." However, a door of opportunity was opened with the soldiers. At this time there were 120,000 British troops in Palestine. The Carmichaels recognized how to make the best of their situation. "We felt we should take advantage of the opportunity to minister to the hundreds of soldiers billeted all around us." During the rainy season they served tea and cakes in the evening, much to the soldiers' delight. Through this kindness the Carmichaels gained the trust of the soldiers and "they began coming to our services and visiting us in the mission house." Soon a revival of sorts broke out with twelve conversions. Carmichael states, "The war is over in many parts of the world, but Jerusalem continues to be an armed camp, and these soldiers, who are in constant danger from bombs and gunfire need a Savior. We are enjoying our ministry with these lads and desire to see many of them find Christ here, in the city where He died for their salvation. Pray that God will work mightily among them."[16]

Carmichael was a first-hand observer of events on the ground in Palestine in 1946–48. He was quick to point out that "the Jews are going back in unbelief. They have no hope in Christ, but they are religious, fantatically so—religious to the core, steeped in Zionism and Judaism." He recounts a conversation he had with a member of the Haganah. At the time this militant Zionist group was bombing buildings, destroying vehicles on the roads, and murdering British soldiers in cold blood. "I asked him if they were eventually going to bomb the Mosque of Omar, in order to get possession of the Temple area. He looked at me as if I were insane, and said, 'Man, that is holy ground. We wouldn't put a bomb in the Temple precinct.' Yet they felt no compunctions of conscience in destroying other property and taking human life."[17]

Since it was impossible to hold a convention at Shemariah, as was the practice in previous years, in 1947 Es Salt was selected as an alternative site. Carmichael reports that the church was filled service after service. "It was an inspiration to the missionaries," says Carmichael, "to see the Arab Christians rejoicing and praising God. Over

---

15. Ibid., 272–74, 278, 285.

16. Carmichael, "Palestine Holds Nations' Interest," *Pentecostal Evangel* (August 9, 1947) 8.

17. Ibid.

thirty came to the altar for salvation during the conference." Apparently the meetings would have continued for some time except that an outbreak of bubonic plague closed down the convention in Es Salt. Nevertheless, the revival continued in other locations. Carmichael reports that Habib, one of the native Pentecostal evangelists, held a week of meetings in El Hussein that attracted large crowds. "Several were saved. They have arranged for me to have a baptismal service there." In addition, Ayoub, a native evangelist from Irbid, was holding services in the Greek Orthodox Church near El Hussein and reported "splendid services with good attendance." Reinforcing the continuity with past success, Carmichael observes, "There is a real opportunity for reaping in Trans Jordan from the sowing of Saul Benjamin and others during the past years."[18]

As the Arabs and Zionists fought pitched battles against each other and the British forces, the upturn in violence imperiled the progress of the mission. Carmichael laments, "The comparative quiet that we have enjoyed in Palestine for the past several weeks is apparently a thing of the past." During a recent Sunday evening Carmichael says there was constant shooting, interspersed with explosions. "One never knows these days when he will be caught in a curfew and have to sit in the car for two hours or more, since everything is immobilized the moment the siren sounds."[19] Although Carmichael did not condone the terrorist methods of the militant Zionists, he was a Zionist sympathizer. He believed that "anyone with spiritual perception cannot help but see the mighty steppings of God in the world today. I believe the end of the age is upon us." For evidence he points to the re-gathering of the Jewish people in Palestine. He writes, "I have seen the Jews coming from different parts of the world—from China, Czechoslovakia, Austria, Italy, and the concentration camps of Germany. At Haifa I saw 28 boats lying there in the harbor. They had been captured by the British on the high seas, and had been brought to Haifa, and the Jewish refugees had been trans-shipped to Cyprus. God is bringing these Jews home."[20] Carmichael states, "The Jews are establishing the State of Israel." He recalls how he saw the Zionist forces put up the Jewish flag with its six-pointed Star of David on the day that Partition was announced:

> I watched as they ran the flag up over Jerusalem. Those Jews went almost wild. Jews with long white beards, wearing little scull caps, climbed upon two wheeled oil carts used for delivery of gas and kerosene. There were two and three of these old men astride one barrel, waving their flags and shouting. An old gray-haired Jew said, "I've been waiting since 1885 for this great event. It is time for the Messiah to come." And he was shouting this down King George Avenue, "It is time for the Messiah to come."[21]

Indeed, for a Pentecostal Zionist this was an exhilarating moment.

---

18. Carmichael, "The Es Salt Conference," *Pentecostal Evangel* (November 15, 1947) 8–9.
19. Ibid.
20. Carmichael, "What's Happening in Palestine," 7.
21. Ibid.

RETREAT OF MISSIONARIES IN THE WAR OF 1948

During their short tenure in Palestine, the Carmichaels were caught in the crossfire of the warring parties. George Carmichael writes, "We were in constant guerilla warfare. First it was between the English and the Jewish terrorists, and later it involved the Arabs also." By 1948 Carmichael found it difficult to obtain food, and had to settle for purchasing groceries for one day at a time. According to Carmichael, the native Christians, both Hebrew and Arabic, were being severely persecuted by the Muslim-dominated Arab nationalist movement. Most of the Arabic Christians fled to Transjordan as refugees and found it almost impossible to obtain employment. Even before they left Jerusalem, their homes were looted and they lost everything they had. Carmichael specifically states that the native Pentecostal community in Jerusalem was dispersed, "just as it says in Acts 8 that 'they that were scattered abroad went everywhere preaching the Word.'" In fact, several native Pentecostals are "now in Transjordan preaching the gospel, who never would have gone from Jerusalem had it not been for the persecution that has arisen through Partition." At this time the standing of Americans in Palestine was tenuous, to say the least. Carmichael surmises, "We had lost the good will of the Arabs by voting for Partition, and incurred the ill will of the Jews by refusing to enforce it." Hence, he came to the conclusion that "conditions were such that it was almost impossible for an American to remain any longer. Hence, he purchased an airline ticket, and made arrangements for transit to the airport in Lydda. On April 2, 1948, he retreated from the field of battle, scurrying from building to building to avoid sniper fire, hopped in a taxi, and by that evening was on a plane flying back to the United States.[22] Carmichael was one of the last Pentecostal missionaries to leave before open warfare broke out between the Zionist militants and the Arab nationalists.

COG MISSION IN THE WEST BANK

With the Hatfield family quarantined in Egypt, Hanna and Nieme Suleiman established a COG congregation in Bethlehem in 1948. During the war at least 500,000 people had been caught in the crossfire between the Zionists and the five Arab nations that attempted to thwart the newly established State of Israel. In the crush of the Palestinian Diaspora, many refugees resorted to living in tents, caves, and under trees out in the fields because there were no houses for them. The Suleiman family had fled from Jerusalem at the beginning of the war and had settled in Bethlehem. They soon began holding services in their home. Hatfield explained the situation in a report to his American readership: "We gathered people together and had services in Brother Suleiman's home. Many of the people who lived in Jerusalem before the trouble, live in Bethlehem now. There is a good opportunity to begin a work in Bethlehem, where at present there is no Pentecostal work but several Pentecostal people that need a place for worship."[23]

22. Ibid., 3.
23. Hatfield, "Palestine," *Church of God Evangel* (July 16, 1949) 5.

The political situation stabilized when jurisdiction over Bethlehem was transferred from the Egyptian army to the Hashemite Kingdom of Jordan. After relocating from Egypt to Cyprus in May of 1949, which provided a safe and convenient point of entry to Israel and Jordan, Hatfield came to Bethlehem and rented a building known as "the cave."[24] In this location, Hatfield says, the gospel was preached, the sick prayed for, sinners repented, and souls converted at an old-time altar. In spite of harsh religious opposition from Catholic, Orthodox, and Lutheran groups, the church grew with a Sunday School of 170 pupils directed by Jean Suleiman. The Suleimans were assisted by Isaac Simaan, an Egyptian of Coptic background, Martha Rosenstein, a German nurse, and Samuel Murad, a Jacobite.[25] Hatfield proudly states, "The Church of God was now an established work in Bethlehem and located on the street of the Prophet David, beside David's well in Bethlehem." By the summer of 1950 the COG church in Bethlehem had grown to 100 in weekly attendance.[26] Hatfield says, "Our church in Bethlehem was a soul saving station to many and a well of living water to several Moslem people of the Mohammedan faith." In his memoirs Hatfield tells of the conversion of two Muslim men. After Paul and David Moses were baptized by Hatfield in the Jordan River, they were threatened by their relatives and forced to flee for their lives.[27] Outreach stations were soon established in Beit Jala and Beit Sahur. All seemed to be going well when the Suleimans immigrated to America in the fall of 1950. Apparently the COG mission board brought the Suleiman family to Cleveland, Tennessee, so that the children, Jean and David, could attend Lee College and Hanna and Nieme could obtain U.S. citizenship and raise financial support by visiting churches and leading revivals.[28] The departure of the Suleiman family necessitated a transition of leadership. Suleiman writes, "Our Brother Isaac Simon, who once belonged to the Assemblies of God and is a native of Egypt, is now successfully carrying on the work there while we are in America. Lately we have another church opened in Jerusalem (old city), and people are getting hungry for this great message."[29] The pastor of the Church of God congregation in Jerusalem was Elijah Nusha, an Arab refugee.

Suleiman was hopeful that the "Lord will help us to open places in Syria and Lebanon, since these places fall in the immediate vicinities of Palestine (Jordan), Brother Hatfield is able to supervise the work from a near point, the Isle of Cyprus."[30] From his vantage point in Cyprus, Hatfield's view of the situation was dimmer. He identifies three formidable challenges, the first of which was the crushing poverty and unemployment in Jordan. He writes, "One cannot help choking as he beholds the piti-

24. Walker, "Missionaries Return to Middle East," *Church of God Evangel* (April 22, 1950) 13.

25. Conn, *Where the Saints Have Trod*, 271.

26. "Rev. D. B. Hatfield, Mrs. Hatfield, Darryl Lynn and Sheralyn," *Church of God Evangel* (July 22, 1950) 5.

27. Hatfield, "New Converts in Palestine Persecuted," *Church of God Evangel* (October 6, 1951) 10.

28. Suleiman, "My Experience on the Ship Coming to the United States," *Church of God Evangel* (December 2, 1950) 6.

29. Suleiman, "History of the Church of God in Palestine," 10.

30. Conn, *Where the Saints Have Trod*, 272–73.

ful sights."[31] The second was the lack of property. In a missive entitled, "Help Us Build the Church a Home," he writes, "There are many things that make it imperative for us to have our own church property in these parts. In the first place, where in the world is more deserving of the Church of God's best in buildings and general missionary efforts than on the soil where or Lord and His apostles once trod?"[32] Hatfield goes on to discuss more concrete reasons before making an appeal for donations. The third obstacle was the absence of indigenous leaders. Hatfield states that the work in Jordan was left almost without any native workers. He acknowledges that the membership was small in Bethlehem, as well as most of our other places in that country, because, as he puts it, "we have needed workers and were not able to get people we could depend on as leaders among the natives." This telling acknowledgement speaks to the evaluation of the Pentecostal mission to which we will conclude this chapter.[33]

The COG used a method that was proven to be effective in earlier Pentecostal missions in Palestine and elsewhere, the convention. A convention would usually feature a local evangelist as speaker and a baptismal service at the Jordan River. Protracted meetings over the space of a week allowed time for extended fellowship, reinforcement of the Pentecostal message, and opportunities for conferees to experience Pentecostal baptism in the Spirit. The first COG convention organized by Hatfield met on April 9–12, 1953, in Ramallah, located in what was then Jordanian territory. According to Hatfield, the convention was a grand success. Of the seven persons baptized in the Jordan, six were from Ramallah and one was from Beit Sahour. Hatfield writes, "The Lord blessed in a marvelous way, and we concluded the service with a healing line in which God manifested His healing presence."[34] The convention may have been the highlight of Hatfield's ministry among the Palestinians. As he increasingly focused his attention on the congregation he had planted in Cyprus, Hatfield's activities in Bethlehem were confined to infrequent visits. Soon it was apparent that new leadership was needed for the COG work in Jordan.

In 1953, George M. Kuttab (1922–2006), a native of Jerusalem and former pastor of the Nazarene Church in Zarka, Jordan, affiliated with the COG and assumed leadership of the congregations in Bethlehem, Beit Jala, and Beit Sahur.[35] In 1962 the COG purchased land on the Mount of Olives and a church was built, including a residential facility. Kuttab assumed primary leadership of the newly established COG church on the Mount of Olives, which until 1967 was located outside of Israel in the territory of the Hashemite Kingdom of Jordan. Kuttab was well suited for the Arab population in East Jerusalem. He proclaimed, "I am a Palestinian Christian." He was known as a patriot of the Palestinian cause who would often speak out against the injustices done

31. "The Rev. D. B. Hatfield Writes," *Church of God Evangel* (May 10, 1952) 9.

32. Hatfield, "Help Us To Build the Church a Home," *Church of God Evangel* (July 7, 1952) 12.

33. Hatfield, *TRIUMPHANT—The Gates of Hell Cannot Have Me*, 279–81; Hatfield, "From the Middle East Bible Lands," *Church of God Evangel* (April 21, 1951) 13.

34. Hatfield, "Annual Convention in the Jordan Kingdom (Old Palestine)," *Church of God Evangel* (October 31, 1953) 7.

35. Conn, *Where the Saints Have Trod*, 272–73;

to the Palestinians. He passed on his passion for Arab nationalism to his children and grandchildren, instilling in them an appreciation of Arab culture and language. Kuttab was committed to the value of education and often said, "Do whatever you want in life but first get an education." Kuttab established a day school that operated in the church facilities as an outreach ministry. However, his patriarchal leadership style and intemperate nature may have inhibited the growth of the congregation. According to his family, "Diplomacy was not his strong suit. He has no capacity for hypocrisy or even tact. He spoke his mind without hesitation, come what may."[36] Such remembrances may shed light on the strains in his relationship with the newly arrived American missionary, Margaret Gaines.

The Ministry of Margaret Gaines

In 1964 Margaret Gaines (1931–), a graduate of Lee College, arrived in Israel after serving ten years in Tunisia and two years in France as a COG missionary. The world missions board had decided that her "experience with Arabs in Tunisia and knowledge of Arabic would prove beneficial to the missionary endeavors in Jordan."[37] Gaines was assigned to work with George and Frocina Kuttab at the COG church on the Mount of Olives. Her assistance with the Christian day school was greatly anticipated. What was not anticipated was the difficulty Gaines would experience in adjusting to the Arab culture of Palestine, which was more traditional than Tunisia.

Gaines immediately faced cultural tensions, which she attributed to clashing norms of Arab and Western cultures. In her autobiography Gaines describes what precipitated an immediate conflict with Kuttab. The conflict started when Kuttab reacted angrily because Gaines had gone to the post office without asking for his permission. Without knowing it, Gaines had violated the local custom that wives and all women in an Arab household must explicitly obey the patriarch. She made matters worse by rebuking Kuttab in no uncertain terms: "I told him his customs and traditions would not be binding on me. I was not a member of his household and neither the church nor the government required that type of subjugation."[38] Although Gaines regretted her cultural blunder, the confrontation left scars on her relationship with Kuttab. A second event led to a further deterioration of that relationship. Gaines questioned the manner of disciplining children in the day school after observing that the teachers made liberal use of corporal punishment, which she interpreted as a venting of frustration on the students. Her attempt to correct what she perceived as "unmerciful beatings" backfired and led to the closing of the school, which greatly displeased Kuttab. As Gaines recalls, the Arab leaders of the church "slyly referred to me in their sermons by telling stories of how 'a queen who is allowed to rule for one day will destroy a kingdom.'"[39] Needless

---

36. "Celebrating the Life of George M. Kuttab," http://daoudkuttab.com/2006/george.htm.

37. Gaines, *Of Like Passions: Missionary to the Arabs*, 133.

38. Ibid., 141.

39. Ibid., 143.

to say, Gaines was off to a shaky start, yet she quickly overcame her initial *faux pas* and proved herself to be a tireless worker.

Early on in her ministry Gaines started two churches. The first was in the village of Aboud, thirty-three miles northwest of Jerusalem. According to tradition, Aboud was the birthplace of the Old Testament prophet Obadiah.[40] Aboud had been an important Christian site with a population of 40,000 in the fifth century. Since then its population decreased to 3,000, of which half were Christian and half were Muslim. An Anglican missionary, Miss Nicholson, had previously served in Aboud from 1898 to 1914 and founded a school. When Gaines arrived on the scene in 1964, Nicholson's students could still recite the psalms and sing the songs she taught them. Ibrahim Saleh, who had been a teacher in the school founded by Nicholson and lived until 1972, was instrumental in the establishment of a COG congregation in Aboud. For many years Zarefie Saleh, Ibrahim's daughter, had prayed daily for God to send a missionary to Aboud. When Gaines first met the Saleh family, she and Zarefie were immediately drawn to each other. Gaines accepted Zarefie's invitation to come and conduct services in the Saleh home and the next week regular services began, resulting in the founding of the COG church in Aboud. For sixteen months Gaines traveled to Aboud once a week to hold a children's meeting and an adult worship service. In September 1965 she rented a small apartment and lived in Aboud from Thursday through Saturday each week. Before long the congregation outgrew the Saleh house and Gaines had to rent a room to accommodate the church services. The second church planted by Gaines was in Amman, Jordan. At roughly the same time that she started itinerating to Aboud, Gaines rented an apartment in Amman and spent Friday to Sunday there.[41]

A major focus of Gaines' ministry in Jordan was child evangelism. The abundance of receptive children who were hungry for attention proved to be unmanageable. Gaines likened the mobs of children in the villages to a "seething cauldron." She describes the scene at Shepherd's Field near Bethlehem where twice a week she and Kuttab squeezed two hundred children of various ages into two rooms each with space for forty: "Crowding, standing, pushing, pinching, fussing, giggling, whispering, outright talking, reciting and singing at lung capacity volume: these words describe mildly Shepherd's Field evangelism class which, in varying proportions, illustrates the other villages." Gaines soon came to the conclusion that the COG mission in Jordan did not have "the capacity to handle all those who are willing to hear the gospel." With an onerous burden of responsibility weighing heavily upon her and Kuttab, Gaines implores her readers, "This will only be possible if there is a common burden. Will you share the yoke with us?"[42]

The perennial struggles of the COG mission were the lack of finances and personnel. Gaines had a knack of making connections that helped her to build up a network of supporters. For example, in 1965 she met Barbara Jensen, a Lutheran charismatic

40. Gaines, "Birth of a Church," *Church of God Evangel* (December 1, 1969) 7.
41. Gaines, *Of Like Passions*, 168–70.
42. Gaines, "The Seething Cauldron," *Church of God Evangel* (November 16, 1964) 9.

who was on a Holy Land tour. Gaines was exceptionally grateful when Jensen and her husband returned twice for prolonged work vacations. On one of these occasions they spent six weeks ministering to the villagers. The case of Olyda Overgaard, an Episcopalian charismatic and tour director from America, was similar. Seemingly out of the blue, Overgaard called Gaines just when the mission finances had run out, met up with Gaines in Bethlehem, and handed her an envelope with much needed cash. Gaines was not one to publicize her lack of resources in order to solicit help. She preferred to rely on prayer and wait upon God for provision. On one occasion, after Gaines joined with the Kuttabs for prayer, a revival broke out, producing a harvest of dedicated young men and women, whom they grouped for special training.[43] Along with Robert O'Bannon, the new COG overseer of the Middle East, Gaines organized the Middle East Theological Institute, which was a form of theological education by extension with a curriculum of worship, study, work, and recreation. The young men worked with O'Bannon on work projects like the digging of cisterns. The young ladies worked with Gaines—washing, shopping, cooking, and cleaning. Supervision of the school fell to Gaines in O'Bannon's absence.[44]

Political events placed a damper on the COG mission and exposed Gaines to many ordeals. In 1964 the Palestinian Liberation Organization was founded by the Arab League with the purpose of waging an armed struggle for the liberation of Palestine.[45] By July Jordan suspended its ties with the PLO, disavowing the PLO raids across Jordan into Israel, which nonetheless continued unabated. As a reprisal to these raids, on November 13, 1966, Israel launched a tank and aircraft attack on the Palestinian village of Sammu near Hebron, killing eighteen, wounding one-hundred, and demolishing one hundred and thirty houses, a school, a clinic, and a mosque. In retaliation, Gaines reports, the Muslim leaders called for a jihad and civil defense measures were immediately undertaken: "We painted our car lights blue and taped our windows. Fear mixed with frenzied nationalism dominated our emotions. Everyone knew what was inevitable. No one knew when or how it would erupt."[46]

In 1967 King Hussein of Jordan went to Egypt and pledged his loyalty to Egypt and the Arab nations in the event of an attack of Israel. This lulled the Palestinians into a false sense of security, causing them to suppose, "Now there will be no war. Israel would never attack the united Arab front. If she doesn't attack, neither shall the Arabs. So war now is unlikely."[47] Consequently, the Jordanians called off a seven-month state of alert. But Gaines was not convinced. On Sunday June 5, 1967, she prophesied, "Do not expect peace. This is the last time we shall worship in this sanctuary before it is hit by bombs. By next Sunday war will break out and disperse us. Some of you will not survive. Prepare to face the issue."[48] The next morning the war broke out, trapping

43. Gaines, *Of Like Passions*, 145.

44. Ibid., 145–47.

45. http://www.un.int/wcm/content/site/palestine/pid/12355.

46. Gaines, *Of Like Passions*, 148.

47. Ibid.

48. Ibid., 149.

Gaines and the Kuttab family, save George who was travelling in Europe, in the church on the Mount of Olives. Against the advice of the American Consul, Gaines decided to make a treacherous trip to Bethlehem and take refuge in the COG building. This was a propitious move because the next day Israeli bombardment hit the church from which Gaines and the Kuttab family had fled. Gaines recalls what she saw on the journey to Bethlehem: "All along the way the roads were full of refugees fleeing from the immediate battle zone of Jericho or even to the east bank of Jordan."[49] Ensconced in Bethlehem, the group with Gaines waited out the six days of the war, praying as they heard the roar of the Israeli aircraft, falling bombs, and explosions. George Kuttab's nephew, Mubarak Awad, known as Moby, used Gaines' car to rescue the wounded and transport them to the hospital. "Many died, God spared Moby . . . and my little ambulance received not a scratch."[50] When the fighting ceased, fearing a massacre floods of refugees were put to flight by messengers crying out, "Flee! You have only two hours in to evacuate the city. Flee for your lives!"[51] Gaines describes the resulting panic: "Thousands of terrified adults wearing expressions of utter despair passed under our balcony in silent half-trot. Carrying hastily wrapped bundles, they dragged weary, terror-stricken children whose short legs could scarcely keep up but whose quickened imagination drove them onward from the unknown devourer that pursued them. Had they only known the Lord!"[52] Once again the Palestinian Diaspora was in high gear.

Provocation on both sides had led to a war that neither side wanted or planned for. Surprisingly, in a mere six days Israel soundly defeated the armies of Egypt, Jordan, and Syria. In the process the Israelis occupied the West Bank, East Jerusalem, Gaza, the Sinai Peninsula, and the Golan Heights. Three weeks after the war was over, Gaines was permitted to return to the church on the Mount of Olives to make a damage assessment. Gaines describes the scene:

> Three bombs had hit the church. Two had opened wide holes in the stone walls. A third had ripped out the iron window frame, twisted it up like a corkscrew, and stabbed it right through the pulpit. The songbooks and Bibles were scattered all over the floor and buried under the debris of the splintered benches and the fallen plaster that been riddled by small arms fire. The apartment adjoining the church was also heavily damaged. It would have been most likely that anyone would have escaped death had they stayed there during the battle. Thank God I had been spared.[53]

When East Jerusalem came under the jurisdiction of Israel, Gaines was forced to go through the tedious process of waiting in lines to secure a new identity card, register the church property and her car in Israel, and obtain an Israeli driver's license. After obtaining a permit, Gaines traveled to Aboud, the village where she had

49. Ibid., 153

50. Ibid., 155.

51. Gaines, "Kept," *Church of God Evangel* (December 18, 1967) 4.

52. Gaines, *Of Life Passions*, 157.

53. Ibid., 158.

started a church in 1964. Fortunately, the war had scarcely touched the village. The residents were under a curfew, which allowed Gaines to visit them at night. However, her visit was cut short when an Israeli military commander accused Gaines of being a spy and interrogated her for two hours. She was ordered to appear before a higher official in Ramallah, who also interrogated and released her. "The whole episode was a trial to my overtaxed body and spirit, but it gave me unique opportunities to witness to my Savior and present His gospel to men of important status."[54] After another three months Gaines was able to get resettled on the Mount of Olives. As the Palestinians in the West Bank Arab adjusted to the occupation in 1968, Gaines sensed that her presence was not as crucial as when the war first ended. At the request of the COG Missions Board, on July 18, 1968 Gaines left for a furlough in America.[55]

While Gaines was on furlough, the Kuttab family moved to the United States in the winter of 1968. Kuttab's replacement was Milton Hay, overseer of the COG missions in the Middle East. During her furlough Gaines managed to scrape together enough money to launch a building project in Aboud, which was completed during the summer of 1969. The land for the building was donated by Abu Majid, the brother of Zarefie Saleh.[56] The building consisted of a stone edifice and an enclosed garden. Including furniture and an electric generator, the cost was $10,000, all of which was paid for before the dedication on September 13, 1969, which was remarkable given that the only means of livelihood for most of the congregation was their olive trees and small gardens. To the dismay of Gaines, Hay refused to be involved in the building program because it had not been authorized according to the standard operating procedures of the COG. About this, Gaines writes, "The most lonely experience I had ever known (even though I had no one to blame for it) was to have an overseer with whom I could not confer."[57] Stress and exhaustion took a toll on Gaines' body, leading to an illness for which she was hospitalized for three months in 1969.

The next years saw the expansion of the mission work in Aboud beyond what Gaines could have imagined. The people of the village had been begging Gaines to begin an elementary school for girls. This time Gaines worked through the system, conferring with Hay in the submission of a budget request to the COG Mission Board. The request was approved, to Gaines' surprise, and in February, 1970, planning for the school project kicked into high gear. An application was submitted to the director of education of the Ramallah District for a license to operate a school. Some said approval would take a long time, but the application was approved in six weeks. Gaines found a carpenter who could build the desks, benches, and chalkboards at a reasonable price. She then rented the lower level of a house and readied the facility for the 1970–71 school term. In the meantime, she designed a curriculum and prepared materials. Gaines assumed the role of head mistress, aided by a nifty book she procured in a bookstore in Jerusalem, entitled *What To Look For When Inspecting Schools*. This

54. Ibid., 159.

55. Ibid., 165.

56. Gaines, "Birth of a Church," *Church of God Evangel* (December 1, 1969) 8.

57. Gaines, *Of Like Passions*, 171.

book covered the wide array of issues in administrating a school, such as sanitary conditions, scheduling, attendance records, faculty meetings, supervision of teachers, lesson plans, and testing. During the summer she interviewed candidates and hired a faculty of four teachers. The Aboud Elementary School began according to schedule.[58]

With the school up and running, Milton Hay moved on, leaving Gaines in charge of directing the COG mission until a successor would arrive. After sixteen months, Gaines exclaims that it was a matter of "unspeakable comfort" when Walter and Elfreida Grenier from Germany arrived to join Gaines in the COG mission in Israel. With the school overcrowded, Gaines prayed for divine guidance in finding a larger facility: "Lord, we shall have outgrown our premises by this time next year. Are you going to work this problem out without me? Is there something I need to do?" The answer came back, "On the Shukba Rad there is a plot of land. Buy it and build a school."[59] That Gaines did, thanks to funds donated by Rev. C. B. Shaal and the Everett, Pennsylvania Church of God.[60] Gaines was determined to build a facility large enough to accommodate growth. She worked with an architect and signed a contract for the construction of a sixteen-room school building "as the Lord provides." A few weeks later, in February 1972, the COG overseer in Europe and the Middle East, J. Herbert Walker, visited the Holy Land. Gaines told him of the building project and asked him to preside over the groundbreaking ceremony. "How far are you along with your plans," he inquired. Gaines replied, "The contract is signed and the contractor is preparing to begin the building as soon as the rainy season is over." Walker asked, "What type of building are you planning, and what are the estimated costs? Gaines answered, "I'll show you the blueprint. The costs are estimated at $42,000." Taking a deep breath, Walker intoned, "Don't look back, Sister Margaret. When did you sign the contract?"[61] Looking over the contract, Gaines saw that it was signed exactly twenty-five years after she received her call to be a missionary. This she took as divine approval of the building project. Once again the indomitable Margaret Gaines was running out ahead of the normal procedures of the COG.

The school building was completed in March 1973, despite delays due to the devaluation of the Israeli currency, shortages of supplies and laborers, and a cost overrun increasing the debt to $100,000, which was paid in full five months before the dedication.[62] During April Gaines enlisted the students in helping with the move to the new building. On September 3, 1973, T. R. Morse, representing the Church of God World Missions Department, officiated at the dedication ceremony, which was attended by the mayor, town council, principal of the government school for boys, and representatives of the Greek Orthodox and Latin Catholic Churches.

One month later Israel came under attack on the highest holy day of the Jewish calendar. Gaines writes, "While the Israelis fasted on Yom Kippur, the Arabs attacked,

58. Ibid., 172–75.
59. Ibid., 179.
60. Gaines, "We Dedicate This School," *Church of God Evangel* (June 24, 1974) 23.
61. Ibid., 183.
62. Gaines, "We Dedicate This School," *Church of God Evangel* (June 24, 1974) 22.

initiating the war of October 1973. At that very time Gaines was undergoing an electrocardiogram at the Hadassah Hospital in Jerusalem after doctors had informed her that she was likely to have a heart attack. "Before I could continue with any treatment, the hospital was filled with wounded soldiers from the Yom Kippur war, and doctors were all mobilized."[63] A year later, in April 1974, due to the stress of an unrelenting workload, Gaines suffered the predicted heart attack as she was driving from Ramallah to Aboud. Fortunately, an able assistant, Arlene Miller, who had arrived in 1973, covered for Gaines during her recuperation.[64]

Gaines was back at her post for the 1974–75 school year, in spite of her diminished physical strength. An ominous development took place during this year, when "certain religious elements" in Aboud hatched a plot to have the school closed but to no avail. Gains writes, "The new Catholic priest, a pro-charismatic and beautifully cooperative Christian, stood firmly with us, making a united front of Christian solidarity which discouraged opposition."[65] For the next four years Gaines was absorbed in her duties as the school administrator, developing curriculum, performing class inspections, and supervising teachers. She was pleased to report that "the results, which I did not know how to evaluate myself, obtained the highest evaluation of numerous local and foreign educators who visited our school. The director of education told me frankly that or school ranked the highest in the West Bank. That is what the Lord wrought. May His name receive all the praise and glory!"[66] However, the strain of a heavy workload left Gains totally exhausted and in dire need of rest. In twenty-seven years of active mission service, she had taken a total of only seventeen months of furlough, most of which were spent in deputation. After the World Missions Board granted her a year's leave of absence, Gains left Israel in time to arrive home for Christmas 1978.

Gaines returned to Israel after a much needed sabbatical. For several years the mission benefited from a period of relative political stability in the West Bank. The installation of electricity in 1983 boosted the quality of life in Aboud. From this time on the villagers were able to enjoy of the conveniences of refrigerators, washing machines, televisions, and other household appliances. By this time most of the people were sleeping on beds and relaxing on sofas and armchairs. Work in Israel even at the minimum wage allowed families to enjoy a sense of prosperity and relief from hardship. The population grew as young married couples settled in Aboud. Small two-room houses sprung up and the streets were paved. The 1980s were, as Gaines puts it, "a time of real hope and contentment. Although it could not have been called an economic boom by any stretch of the connotation, the slight easing of dire poverty has birthed confidence in the future."[67]

In February 1983 Gaines turned the management of the school over to Arlene Miller and devoted herself full-time to church work. She applied herself to the task of

63. Gaines, *Of Like Passions*, 189.

64. Ibid., 188–90.

65. Ibid., 192.

66. Ibid., 194–95.

67. Ibid., 202.

leadership development, which was essential to the sustainability of the Palestinian church. Gaines organized a weekly Ladies Ministry with the intention of meeting the spiritual needs of women and offering a ministry to children. The ladies held bazaars in which they sold their embroidery, foods, and novelties. Gaines also worked with the women of Aboud to develop a number of children's ministries, such as the Blue Belles, the Joy Belles, the Young Ladies Ministries, and the Christian Service Brigade. Gaines raised up a number of promising women leaders through the Girls Club Counselor Enrichment Training Course. These leaders included Raika El Khoury, her nieces Mary and Hannie El Khoury, and Selwa Subhi, who later married Nihad Salman.[68] Gaines singles out Raika El Khoury for special commendation: "She has taught most of the ladies in the school at one time or another, so they greatly respect her wisdom and holiness. Through her teaching they learn how to pray, to trust God, to train their children, to love and honor their husbands, and to reflect Christ in their relationships with extended families and neighbors."[69] The progress made by Gaines in leadership development should be seen as one of her most important accomplishments.

In 1985 the school in Aboud was embroiled in an ominous controversy. The Israel Department of Education mandated that the school in Aboud offer instruction in Islam taught by an imam or other Muslim teacher. Gaines agreed with Miller that it would be inappropriate to teach the Muslim religion at a Christian school. Hence, in order to preserve the Christian emphasis in the school, the Muslim children were regretfully dismissed. This decreased the student body in half. The Muslim parents implored Gaines to keep their children, but she told them that the government had forced the issue and that was that.[70]

With political tensions escalating in the Palestinian territories, the First Intifada erupted in 1987. This uprising began with boys throwing rocks at Israeli tanks and then escalated into a massive strike. The Intifada was the cause of polarization in the West Bank, dividing the camp between those who favored and those who were opposed to the strike and demonstrations. It also disrupted the schools when students left class to demonstrate and throw stones. This in turn led the Israeli army to shut the schools at noon. In response to outbreaks of violence, the Israeli authorities closed Bir Zeit University, forcing students to study clandestinely, moving from one secret location to another. The effect was that it took Palestinian students four years to complete the equivalent of a two-year program. In Aboud resentment against the COG church and school intensified during the Intifada. Gaines and Miller, being Americans, were accused of holding pro-Israeli, anti-Arab sentiments. This was probably due to their refusal to participate in strikes and demonstrations, on the grounds that they were devoted to the tasks of educating children and Christian ministry. They reasoned that "children in elementary school were too young to understand the politics and that they

68. Ibid., 207.
69. Ibid.
70. Ibid., 205–6.

would serve themselves and their people better by staying in class and not striking or demonstrating."[71]

When the Gulf War erupted on January 16, 1991, the COG World Missions Department asked Margaret Gaines and Arlene Miller to evacuate. Miller did so right away, but Gaines was detained due to a delay in the processing of her exit visa. She remained in the West Bank under a curfew imposed because of the threat of scud attacks. For forty-two days no one was allowed to go outside. Schools, churches, and shops were closed. Gaines describes the precautions she took in case of a missile attack. She writes, "I had a gas mask, and a radio kept me informed of the scud attacks and when to enter or leave the sealed room."[72] The horror of scuds was not the only problem faced by the people of Aboud. They faced food shortages. Living under impoverished conditions, they did not possess the wherewithal to procure supplies of food. For years they had not been allowed to work in Israel and few jobs were available in the West Bank, resulting in the lack of money to buy food. Gaines played a crucial role in securing food for the people of Aboud. With the help of a generous grocer who supplied milk and flour at cost, and donations delivered by Paul Schmigdall, the overseer of COG missions in Palestine, Gaines was able to provide for the needs of the congregation. During breaks in the curfew, the Pentecostal people could be found in the church praising God for his mercy and provision.

Beset with a worsening heart condition in 1991–92, Gaines was relying more and more on the local leadership she had equipped to carry on the ministry of the church and school in Aboud. In 1992 Butros and Mary Mualem, who had been studying at the East Coast Bible College in Charlotte, North Carolina, returned to Aboud and assumed leadership of the church. Gaines writes, "It was an enormous pleasure to watch the national workers carry on so efficiently."[73] By 1993 Gaines decided that her full-time presence was no longer needed in Aboud and shifted her focus to the COG church on the Mount of Olives. She started a day school in connection with the church and went about planting a new church in the village of Jifna, between Jerusalem and Aboud. But these labors were too much for her heart. She suffered a fourth heart attack on February 13, 1996. Afterwards she permanently relocated to the Mount of Olives church in order to be closer to medical facilities, which were lacking in Aboud.

Gaines had one more building project to undertake. In 1997 the Israel Department of Education mandated that the kindergarten must move out of the elementary school building in Aboud. In consultation with Paul Lauster, the COG regional superintendent for the Mediterranean and Middle East, Gaines acquired an adjacent parcel of land and made plans for the construction of a church ministries facility to accommodate not only the kindergarten but also thirteen ministries of the church. When funds could not be secured according to the regular operating procedures, Gaines made a personal appeal to the Women in Action Rally at a meeting in Sevierville, Tennessee,

71. Ibid., 205.
72. Ibid., 208.
73. Ibid., 212.

the very place where she had received her call to the mission field, and the response was overwhelming, $60,000 in cash and pledges. The footings for the new building were laid in July, 1998. A team of volunteers from the U.S. went to Aboud in October 1998 and worked on the building. After the volunteer team left in November, the work continued with unpaid labor until December when the first floor was completed, allowing the church ministries to move in. The upper two floors were completed in time for the 1999–2000 school year, at a total cost of $200,000, part of which came from funds donated by Gaines. During her last trip to Aboud in 1999 Gaines inspected the fruit of her ministry in Aboud, the church, the parsonage, the original school building, and the new ministry building and prayed, "How did it all happen? From where did all of this come?" Gaines heard the still small voice of the Lord answer back, "You did it." "Now God," she answered, "anyone with common sense or uncommon sense would know that a 20-year-old Alabama girl who left America with only two years of college, little experience and no money could never have achieved such results. What do you mean?" Once again Gaines heard the voice say, "You did it. But trusting me enough to stay in my workshop, producing piece by tiny little piece of confusing and seemingly totally unrelated parts over many years, you did it for me. And I assembled it."[74]

In March 1999 Gaines retired and left the field.[75] She could take satisfaction in the fruit of her ministry. The school's enrollment had increased from 32 to 121 between 1993 and 1999. Gaines understood well that many people contributed to the success of her missionary career. The women to whom she had passed the leadership baton were performing brilliantly. Led by the head administrator Suhaila, the faculty included Raika El Khoury, Somaya Issa, Miriam El Khoury, Rima Azar, Iftihar Salem, Layla Hameed, Hannie El Khoury, Senneh Shaheen, and Mary Mualem. The Department of Education held the principal and the teachers in high regard. As Gaines recalls, "The Aboud Elementary School is rated as superior in all the Occupied West Bank."[76]

Recent Developments of the AG and COG Missions

The Pentecostal mission of the COG in the West Bank has proven to be more sustainable than the AG work. Whereas the original AG mission met its demise in 1977, the COG mission more or less successfully navigated the transition to indigenous Palestinian leadership. However, in relative degrees, both were hampered by the incongruence of Pentecostal Zionism in the Arab context.

The demise of the original AG mission in Palestine occurred after a period of steady decline. In 1958 the American AG denomination decided to phase out their American missionaries and transfer the *Shemariah* ("kept by Yahweh") mission station in Jerusalem to a congregation of Jewish followers of Jesus, under the auspices of the Rev. Zeer W. Kofsman, a Jewish Pentecostal missionary sponsored by the French

74. Ibid., 218.

75. The COG sent out a missionary couple to Aboud in 1999, but they returned home in 2001 due to a medical emergency. "Our Missionaries in the Holy Land," *Mission Line* 18.3 (Summer 2002) n.p.

76. Gaines, *Of Like Passions*, 213.

Assemblies of God. In 1960 the American AG ceased its work in Israel and in 1961 leased the mission station in Jerusalem to the Messianic Assembly of Israel, led by five elders, one of whom was Kofsman.[77] The other elders of the Messianic Assembly of Israel were Elyas Sarikas, Warren Graham, Jacob Goren, and Victor Smadja.[78] A small congregation was maintained for a few years but disintegrated due to doctrinal infighting. In 1970 the property was sold to an American Reformed Synagogue. A final attempt was made in 1974 to settle American AG missionaries in Israel but failed when Jim and Janie Hodges could not obtain visas. As a result, the original mission suffered its demise in 1977.[79]

In 1987 an attempt was made to regroup the AG mission with the establishment of "Present Situation and Future Vision," a sponsoring organization which started up a number of ministries, including schools in East Jerusalem and Haifa, and a bookstore in downtown West Jerusalem. The school in East Jerusalem started with forty students from kindergarten to eighth grade. As of 2007, the enrollment was 420 students, kindergarten to twelfth grade. The Galilee Bible School was established in 1992 in Haifa. More than fifty graduates have completed its biblical studies program. This school continues to offer extension classes and biblical training for pastors and lay people in various locations, from Shfar'Am to Ramle and Jerusalem. The Torch book store in Jerusalem was established in 1971. It is located next to the central post office and provides Christian literature, Bibles, and a Christian presence. The name of the bookstore is based on Isaiah 62:1: "For Zion's sake I will not keep silent, for Jerusalem's sake I will not remain quiet, till her righteousness shines out like the dawn, her salvation like a blazing torch" (NIV). Although the leaders of Present Situation-Future Vision attest to playing a hand in the growth of congregations from Ramle to Haifa to the Galilee villages, the jury is still out on the ultimate success of this attempt to re-establish the AG work in Israel on an indigenous footing.[80]

As noted above, directed by the indomitable Margaret Gaines from 1964 to 1999, the COG mission achieved a contextualized ministry among the Palestinian Arabs in the West Bank. Gaines fully identified with the Palestinian Arab situation in relation to Israel. When once asked by an interviewer, "Sister Gaines, if I understand correctly, you are a missionary to Israel," she deftly replied, "To be more exact, I think we have to say that I am a missionary in Israel . . . My address is Israel, but I am a missionary in a village on the occupied west bank of the Jordan."[81] In her autobiography she critiqued the Israeli settlement policy, specifically blaming Menachem Begin for not keeping

77. Osterbye, *The Church in Israel*, 48, 195–96.

78. Juster and Hocken, "The Jewish Messianic Movement," http://www.tjcii.org/userfiles/Image/messianic-jewish-movement-an introduction-Eng.pdf.

79. Perkins, "Israel and Missions," 21–29. Carmichael, "Israel," *Pentecostal Evangel* (April 30, 1961) 25–26; Kofsman, "After the Pentecostal Conference," *Pentecostal Evangel* (September 17, 1961) 13; Kofsman, "Call Her Not Mara," *Pentecostal Evangel* (April 18, 1965) 27; Kofsman, "The Resurrection of the Hebrew Language," *Pentecostal Evangel* (June 16, 1968) 10–11.

80. See "Assemblies of God," http://www.ucci.net/members1.xml.

81. Polen, "Margaret Gaines, Missionary in Israel," *Church of God Evangel* (November 28, 1977) 18.

his promise to freeze settlement construction after the Camp David Peace Accords in 1978. Nonetheless, Gains recognized that both sides were fault in escalating the violence that wreaked economic havoc on the economies of Israel and Palestine alike. Gaines sums up her critique by stating, "Unfortunately, Israel trusted in her military power and technology. She ignored the fact that the human spirit cannot be broken and that force breeds force."[82]

Gaines also succeeded in developing an indigenous Palestinian leadership, most notably in the village of Aboud. Nonetheless, while Gaines formed a strong bond with the people of Palestine by unshackling herself from Pentecostal Zionism, the same cannot be said of her host denomination, which has traditionally embraced a Christian Zionist stance. The COG presently maintains a permanent department known as "Ministry to Israel." Its statement of purpose, which can be found in Directories/ Divisions & Departments/ Ministry to Israel on the COG website, is typical of Christian Zionism: "Ministry to Israel is a channel of blessing through which Christians provide comfort to the Jewish People."[83] The COG maintains no such department for ministry to the Palestinian people, which, as we shall see below, is a sore point with two protégés of Margaret Gaines. Furthermore, a 2002 publication, *Mission Line*, which reports the current activities of COG missionaries, gives evidence of pro-Israel sympathies. One page contains entries on "Church of God Ministries in the Middle East" and "Our Missionaries in the Holy Land." While the overwhelming bulk of COG missions in the region are with Arab Christians, the former entry is illustrated by a picture of Orthodox Jews saying prayers in a location adjacent to a barbed wire fence. The latter entry, describing the ordeals of the American family that followed Margaret Gaines in Aboud, is illustrated by two photographs, one of which is the Dome of the Rock and the other is an Orthodox Jewish boy with sideburn curls and a traditional hat. The impression is falsely given that COG missions in the Middle East and the Holy Land are aimed at a Jewish target audience. Sensitivity is clearly lacking in regards to how this impression would be received by someone like Nihad Salman, a Pentecostal pastor in Palestine and protégé of Margaret Gaines who earned a MDiv degree in 1991 from the COG seminary in Cleveland, Tennessee.

During my 2002 sabbatical in Jerusalem, I had a conversation with Nihad and Salwa (nee Subhi) Salman in which they expressed their disappointment with the pro-Israel bias of the American COG. Nihad and Salwa credited Margaret Gaines not only for her ministry in Aboud, but also for introducing them to each other. After their marriage they became co-pastors of the Bethlehem COG church. However, they eventually tired of what they perceived as the intractable Zionist bias of the COG leaders and pastors whom they guided on tours of the Holy Land. Nihad and Salwa complained that, "The American missionaries in this region were busy within Israel, supporting ministry to Jews. They had forgotten about us." They were also bothered that Pentecostal tours would roll through Bethlehem to see the sights, and then go back to

---

82. Gaines, *Of Like Passions*, 204.

83. http://www.ministrytoisrael.com.

Israel to go to church and meet pastors. "It is as if we didn't exist." Eventually Nihad and Salwa left the COG and in September 1999 established Immanuel Evangelical Church, an independent church plant in Bethlehem, which has grown to more sixty families and 250 people. Immanuel Church has in turn planted two more churches in Ramleh and Haifa, and has opened two Christian book stores, one in Bethlehem and the other in Haifa. With the sponsorship of World Vision and the Church of the Brethren in Germany, Immanuel Evangelical Church has constructed an outreach center in Beit Jala with a vision for evangelization through compassion and caring for the community. It is noteworthy that the church planted by the Salmans flourished after their disengagement from the COG. The success of Immanuel Evangelical Church represents a gain for the Palestinian Christian presence in the Holy Land and a loss for COG. I would suggest that, as in the case of the AG, the sustainability of the COG mission in Palestine was compromised by the Zionist sympathies of its host denomination in America.

EVALUATION OF MISSION ACCOMPLISHMENTS

The Pentecostal mission in Palestine can be credited with many accomplishments over one hundred years. Those of signal importance would be the development of the Shemariah mission station by Elizabeth Brown, the opening of the work in Es Salt by Laura Radford and its growth due to leadership of Saul and Pearl Benjamin, the progress made by the Benjamins in building an infrastructure in the AG church in Jerusalem, and the success of Margaret Gaines in forging a contextualized COG mission in the West Bank. But most important of all were the people of Palestine whose lives were transformed by the living Christ. Of them Saul Benjamin writes,

> I have witnessed several revivals in Trans-Jordan, the first of which was so powerful that it attracted wide attention, not only from the civil population but also from the educational authorities of the government. Many students from the highest governmental school flocked to the meetings. They would come to the altar to pray and go away singing our revival songs. Government spies came to the services to see what was being done, and went away convinced that we were preaching a powerful gospel. Some confessed that they feared lest their continued attendance might make them Christians also.[84]

The Pentecostal missionaries in Palestine are to be commended for all that they did to build intercultural bridges spanning the gap between the worlds of Azusa and Jerusalem. Nevertheless, the missionaries themselves recognized the shortcomings of their mission in Palestine. We will now attend to a summative assessment offered by one of the Pentecostal missionaries who had served in Palestine. Although this assessment dates to 1943 and does not take into account the COG mission, it nevertheless presents a perceptive analysis of the strengths and weaknesses of the Pentecostal mission.

---

84. Benjamin, "Gold from Gilead," *Pentecostal Evangel* (November 9, 1946) 8–9.

Ida Beck's Assessment

The missionaries in Palestine knew full well that the future viability of their mission was in doubt. Below we will attend to the assessment of one of the missionaries. Ida Beck aired her appraisal of the problems and opportunities of the mission in Palestine in an address to the AG Missionary Conference in March of 1943. She was dismayed by the misconceptions held by many Christians concerning the mission in Palestine. "Missionary work in Palestine seems strange to them." A young girl once said to Beck, "Isn't it strange that we should have to send missionaries to Palestine, the land where Jesus lived and gave His life?" Beck observes that the typical American Pentecostal image of Palestine was "mingled with sentiment because of its inseparable connection with the life of our Lord and sacred history, or perhaps the interest lies in the fulfillment of prophecy in that land." It grated on Beck when someone would tell her that she was "very fortunate to have had a trip to the Holy Land." Beck saw such perceptions as "very regrettable" because they overlooked the "real need for missionary endeavor" in Palestine and the surrounding region. She wished that those at home would understand the realities of the Palestinian context. To begin, she explains that in Palestine three powers are locked in conflict, namely Islam, Judaism, and Christianity. Each regards Jerusalem as a sacred city. "It is as though these three great powers meet in opposition and those who have the souls of these people at heart feel and meet the conflict."[85]

Beck presents an overview of each of the Abrahamic faiths. She begins with Islam, which has the greatest number of followers in Palestine. In Beck's view, "these are bigoted and fanatical in devotion to their prophet and his teaching. They pray five times daily, and yet their lives are not changed. They lead very wicked lives and can do almost anything in the name of their religion. The common saying among Christian Arabs is, 'Trust a Mohammedan as far as you can see him.'" She acknowledges the "tremendous difficulties in getting the gospel to them." A Muslim who converts to Christianity is "in danger of losing his life at the hands of his own people." To make matters worse, Christians tend to question the sincerity of such converts, hindering their assimilation. Nevertheless, Beck insists that "we have seen some of them saved." She wonders if the results, which are admittedly small, are due to a failure on the part of the Christian Church, in real earnest seeking God for the salvation of these people.

Judaism presents the same problem as Islam in its "hatred toward anything that has to do with Christ, as it has since the time the Jews rejected Him." Furthermore, it is now "more difficult for a Jew in Palestine to accept Christ because each racial community is so distinctly separate from the other." As with Muslims, as soon as it is known that a Jew has become a Christian, "immediately he is ostracized from home and family and boycotted in business." Beck notes that recently Jews have been more responsive to the gospel than ever before. "There is a great demand for the Scripture, response to Bible classes, and some have professed their faith in Christ, openly and secretly. There is a springing forth of life."

---

85. Ida Beck, "Problems and Opportunities in Palestine," *Pentecostal Evangel* (July 3, 1943) 10.

Beck, as most Pentecostal missionaries, speaks disparagingly of Eastern Christianity. "The Christianity we find in Palestine is dead." By this she means that the Christians of Palestine are not "born-again believers, but merely adherents to one of the Catholic sects or a Protestant community. It is merely a system of forms and rituals and a superstitious belief." She is of the opinion that Eastern Christians have adopted a "Moslem fatalism" and have "settled into a dormant state accepting life as it comes." In spite of her negativity, Beck pragmatically states that "the greatest freedom for work is presented among these Christians." In other words, they are the most receptive of the indigenous religious communities of Palestine. They are also responsive, as Beck points out. "The majority of our converts are from this group. We have seen them thoroughly saved, filled with the Spirit, and living lives for God."[86]

In assessing the Pentecostal missionary personnel, Beck rates the staff as "splendid." The missionaries "went to the field with a purpose to fulfill the call of God upon their lives and have fitted into the needs and lives of the people very well. She commends her colleagues for having "a good working knowledge of Arabic language, which is so very essential—since most of work is with the Arabic peoples." Now Beck comes to the bottom line. There is no doubt that the Pentecostal missionaries are "giving of themselves wholeheartedly to the work." Yet, Beck must admit that "our numbers however are limited which prevents the expansion which we would like to see." Beck immediately rushes to the defense, pointing to the consecration and sense of duty that motivated the missionaries to disregard the advice of the American consul and bravely remain on the field when hostilities broke out in Europe and danger was threatening. Beck stresses that the missionaries were preoccupied by the very great need of "strengthening, encouraging, and building up the native Church, so that if the day came when the missionary must leave, they could carry on alone. As yet she hadn't become strong enough, nor had she efficient leadership to do this. Indeed, this was a premonition of what was to come in 1948.[87]

In discussing the problems and progress of the work, Beck put an onus upon the Arabic people, whom she says "know very little about discipline." She continues, "We have often commented that they are just children grown up. Neither have they learned the spirit of co-operation. Arab children exhibit volatility at play." For example, "if in play something doesn't suit one child he may become angry and pick up a stone and throw it at his friend. It is each man for himself." Beck attests, "We saw these characteristics during the recent years of trouble between the Arab and the Jew. Because of some broader-minded men among the Arabs wouldn't link themselves with the Arab cause in carrying out their brigand operations and rebellion—the Arabs killed them, thus doing away with men who really could have helped them as a people." Beck sees some progress in the maturing of a cooperative spirit among Arab converts. For instance, a group of leaders in the Jerusalem church organized a prayer group that held small group meetings in different sections of the city, inviting those who would not attend

86. Ibid.
87. Ibid., 10–11.

open services. The results were positive. One man was saved for whom the native workers had been praying for years and the next Sunday brought his family to church. Beck also says that progress had been made toward the "self-supporting church and we believe as they follow on to know Christ, they will be better enabled to bear the burden of the work."[88]

Beck delineates three immediate needs of the churches in Palestine. The first is the training of younger men as preachers, evangelists, and leaders. Beck assuredly states, "If these young men with their secular training could be given a good Biblical training and then be sent out into untouched villages in Palestine and Transjordan, I believe there would be real progress and growth in the church and another of our needs met, that of further evangelization." Yet, Beck realizes, for this to happen, "we must have the help of our native church to reach out and really evangelize as we should." The second immediate need is for a Bible School to train young workers who sense the call of God. "When the late Miss A. E. Brown built our mission house, she built with that aim in view, so we have facilities for taking care of students, but we have lacked in missionary personnel." Beck mentions a missionary, probably Laura Radford, who went to Palestine with this kind of work in mind, for which she is well qualified, but has been preoccupied with other more urgent tasks. The third immediate need was for additional missionary personnel. Beck specifies the kind of worker she had in mind. It should be someone who was qualified to open a Bible school that would serve "not only Palestine and Transjordan but also the other Arabic-speaking countries." There is a pressing need for someone of the caliber of Elizabeth Brown or Laura Radford, a "senior worker" who could "supervise the young trained workers who would be placed in new fields."

Beck concludes by offering a word to prospective missionaries. To begin, she stresses that pastoral experience is an excellent background for foreign work, as preparation both for dealing with church problems and also for working in harmony with others. Beck places a premium on learning the value of our General Council fellowship. She states, "If a prospective missionary cannot work in harmony and fellowship with his church and fellow pastors here at home, he will find it more difficult on the foreign field." Secondly, Beck emphasizes the importance of children's ministry, especially for the woman missionary, and underlines the usefulness of experience in running children's meetings, Sunday School, and Vacation Bible School. She says, "Young hearts are more tender and open to the truth and we have seen some very gratifying results among them." Here Beck is alluding to the strategy favored by many missions for gaining inroads into unresponsive populations through the education of children. Starting from the bottom up, so to speak, missionaries should train their young converts to assume roles as teachers and leaders. Beck goes on to say, "Also through the young we find opening wedges are made into homes and hearts of the older. Entry into Moslem homes has been gained in this way."[89]

88. Ibid.
89. Ibid., 11.

Finally, Beck closes, "The Lord has placed a tremendous responsibility upon us as His followers and we want by His help to be faithful to that trust. If Jesus tarries and this war comes to a close, we hope to see the work in Palestine and Transjordan go forward with an increased missionary staff and a trained native ministry anointed by God, for His glory."[90] To a great extent, this is exactly what Margaret Gaines achieved in the COG mission. However, as noted above, the COG failed to consolidate the achievements of Gaines in the areas of education and leadership development because it alienated two of its most promising leaders, Nihad and Salwa Salman. Why did this occur? A causative explanation may be found below.

Causative Explanations of Failure

Alas, Ida Beck's hopes for an increased missionary staff and a trained native Palestinian ministry did not materialize in the AG mission. The Pentecostal mission in Palestine never yielded appreciable numerical results in terms of conversions, the development of self-supporting congregations, and the training of national leaders. Therefore, one might justifiably conclude that the Pentecostal mission in Palestine was a failure. Other Pentecostal mission fields in Africa, Asia, and Latin America dramatically outstripped the mission in Palestine. One might ask why. A number of causative explanations will be entertained.

First of all, Palestine presented inherent cultural obstacles to missionary success. The religious enclaves of Jews and Muslims were largely impervious to Western missionaries. Second, for centuries Palestine had been a site of religious violence and horrific warfare. It was simply a dangerous place in which to live, much less to be a missionary. Third, the missionaries lacked the wholehearted support of denominational officialdom in the American AG, the largest Pentecostal denomination.[91] For example, consider the not so hidden message in this report of a missionary conference in the *Pentecostal Evangel*: "Noel Perkin, Missionary Secretary, on the last night of the session spoke concerning the need of giving the gospel to the Jews. He said many young people get a concern for the Jews and want to go to Palestine, but there are greater opportunities for laboring among the Jews in the United States, as it is really much easier.[92]" Fourth, the Zionist sympathies of the missionaries worked against contextual identification with the interests of their Arab clients. In the final analysis, of the above causative explanations, the fourth one was especially decisive.

The Zionist sympathies of the Pentecostals missionaries worked like a double-edged sword. On one hand, Pentecostal Zionism added special significance to the

90. Ibid.

91. According to Blumhofer, in 1937 the AG Missions Secretary Noel Perkin "advocated the placement of concentrations of workers where they were most likely to succeed in establishing self-governing, self-supporting, and—most importantly—self-propagating churches." Blumhofer, *The Assemblies of God: A Chapter in the Story of American Pentecostalism. Volume 1—To 1941*, 304. This development occurred in the same year in which Perkin and the AG officials visited the fields in Syria, Palestine, and Transjordan, and rendered a mixed review.

92. Perkin, "Work Among the Jews," *Pentecostal Evangel* (June 13, 1936) 5.

presence of the missionaries in Palestine. On the other hand, it hampered the formation of a contextualized mission among the Arab peoples who were receptive to the Pentecostal message. The bottom line was that the missionaries were more attuned to the Zionist sympathies of their support base in America than to the existential struggles of their Palestinian Arab target audience. The missionaries served a significant ideological function on behalf of the wider Pentecostal community. They were strategically situated to serve as brokers of Pentecostal Zionism. Their frequently published communiqués from the field provided the wider Pentecostal community with a running commentary on current events and political developments in Palestine. The Pentecostal missionaries in Palestine contributed to the diffusion of the sympathy of Pentecostals for Zionism. Two examples will suffice in support of this point.

In a message delivered in Chicago during World War I, Elizabeth Brown expressed her belief that God used the First World War to bring about this restoration. Her conviction was that "God has promised this land to Israel, but because of disobedience and sin He said they should be turned out of it during Gentile dominion . . . God, no doubt, has been letting the Western front rage in war, to keep the eyes of the world off the important thing He was doing right over there." She then asks, "Doesn't it look like the nation is going back? . . . Isn't this the restoration of the people to their land?"[93] An answer in the affirmative was implied.

Years later, Saul Benjamin provided a first-hand account on the situation in Transjordan. Although himself of Assyrian extraction, he was a Zionist sympathizer, as were most Pentecostals. He writes, "We have been passing through testing times. Politically in Palestine the Arabs are being stirred up against the fulfillment of God's promises to Israel with regard to their returning to the Promised Land . . . It would be very difficult to tell you on paper what has been accomplished by the Jews in the land since their return. We can without exaggeration say the desert is blossoming like the rose."[94]

To conclude, the missionaries successfully employed the rhetoric of Pentecostal Zionism in making a case for the unique eschatological significance of the mission in Palestine. Yet, as a result, they precluded themselves from forging a sustainable intercultural bridge to the context of their Arab clients. Nothing short of a critical awareness of the incommensurability of Pentecostal Zionism in the cultural context of Palestine would have increased the chances for success of the Pentecostal mission in Palestine.

With the historical narrative of the Pentecostal mission in Palestine concluded, we now proceed to two chapters that will examine the ideology of Pentecostal Zionism in depth and assess its legacy.

93. Brown, "A New Regime in the Holy Land," *The Latter Rain Evangel* (January 1919) 4.

94. Saul Benjamin to Assemblies of God Headquarters, March 16, 1937, unpublished letter, Flower Pentecostal Research Center, Springfield, Missouri.

8 | Pentecostal Zionism

F ROM THE EARLY days of their movement, Pentecostals strongly sympathized with Zionism.[1] This chapter lays the groundwork for an assessment of legacy of Pentecostal Zionism in the next chapter by looking into the phenomenon of Pentecostal Zionism in some depth. To begin, Pentecostal Zionism will be set in the context of Christian Zionism and the ideology of its chief evangelical advocate, William Blackstone, whose writings were published in the Pentecostal press. Then the views of notable Pentecostal proponents of Zionism will be described and the coverage of Zionism in the Pentecostal periodicals will be extensively documented. Finally, two examples of the contribution of the Pentecostal missionaries in Palestine to the diffusion of Pentecostal Zionism will be presented and evaluated.

CHRISTIAN ZIONISM IN AMERICA

Christian Zionism pre-dated the Zionist Congress of 1897 by a substantial margin.[2] While the response of the Jewish community to the Zionist Movement was mixed, with the Reformed congregations tending to be more positive than the Orthodox,[3] the response of the Christian community in America was mainly positive, particularly among evangelical Protestants.[4] According to Dwight Wilson, virtually all American premillennialists supported the Zionist Movement.[5] Pentecostals joined conservative evangelicals in jumping on the Christian Zionist bandwagon and expressing sympathy with the Jewish people. For example, *Trust* ran an article from *The New Palestine* by Pierre Van Paasen demanding, "It is time that the Jew was accorded justice." It was quite common for articles in Pentecostal periodicals to express outrage over the persecution of the Jewish people. Van Paasen continues, "Let us no longer regard the Jew as an alien, a parasite, a stranger, who must be tolerated as a necessary evil." Rather, he argues, the Jew is asking for justice in order to "dwell in peace from persecution

---

1. Gannon, "The Shifting Romance with Israel," 92–93, 121–35. The term "Zionism" is derived from the biblical word "Zion," which originally designated a stronghold in Jerusalem, first inhabited by Jews in the time of King David. Later the Old Testament prophets used "Zion" to refer to Jerusalem as a spiritual symbol. In its modern political sense, Zion refers to the Jewish homeland in Palestine, which in Hebrew is called *Eretz Yisrael*, the "Land of Israel."

2. See Tuchman, *Bible and Sword: England and Palestine from the Bronze Age to Balfour*, passim.

3. Glick, *The Triangular Connection: America, Israel, and American Jews*, 42–50.

4. Merkley, *Christian Attitudes Towards the State of Israel*, 6.

5. Wilson, *Armageddon Now!: The Premillenarian Response to Russia and Israel Since 1917*, 47.

on the banks of the Mediterranean and in the Valley of Esdraelon that he may yet give the world new light and live out his destiny as the champion of justice 'in whom all mankind will be blessed.' Let us not stand in his way, lest we be found fighting against his God."[6] Early Pentecostals probably identified with Zionism because of their acceptance of dispensationalism as the framework of their worldview. Pentecostals agreed with the dispensational premise that the Jews were God's apocalyptic time-piece. Hence, Pentecostals warmly resonated with Paul Rader's statement, published in the *Christian Evangel*, that "The key to the true philosophy of history is the Jew . . . The restoration of the Jew to his national rights and the going back of the Jew to his own land is just the setting that is required for the battle of Armageddon."[7] As with other evangelical dispensationalists, early Pentecostals also treated the War of Armageddon as a controlling motif of their eschatology. This fact will come to light in our examination of primary source evidence below.

William Blackstone

The leading figure among American premillennial Christian Zionists was William E. Blackstone (1841–1935). Blackstone was born in Adams, New York, the town in which the revivalist Charles Finney was converted. Blackstone was an insurance agent with an avid interest in biblical prophecy. Shortly after his marriage to Sarah L. Smith, her wealthy father died leaving a substantial estate with instructions that it be administered by William in support of evangelical and missionary causes. Eventually Blackstone left the insurance business and became a full time evangelist and writer. He served as a missionary in China, traveled widely, published his books and pamphlets, lectured often at prophecy conferences, and vigorously spoke out in favor of Zionism. According to historian Paul Merkley, he was "one of the most influential and admired religious figures of his generation."[8]

Among Christians, Blackstone was best known for his widely read *Jesus is Coming* (1878), but among Zionists he was recognized for a significant political contribution. He composed a memorial, a petition entitled "Palestine for the Jews," and had it signed by over four hundred notable Americans representing the fields of higher education, the law, the judiciary, politics, philanthropy, and religion.[9] He then sent it to President Benjamin Harrison on March 5, 1891, with a cover letter. In that letter he assured the President that "the signatures could be indefinitely multiplied."[10] He also clearly stated his belief, supported by biblical proof texts, that the opportunity for political action was providential. He writes,

---

6. Van Paasen, "Zionism and Christianity," *Trust* (January–February 1926) 19–20.

7. Rader, "Armageddon," *Christian Evangel* (May 18, 1918) 2–3.

8. Merkley, *Politics of Christian Zionism*, 60.

9. Glick, *The Triangular Connection*, 29–30.

10. Cited in Ibid., 30.

> Here seem to be many evidences to show that we have reached the period in the great roll of centuries, when the everlasting God of Abraham, Isaac and Jacob is lifting up His hand to the Gentiles (Isaiah 49:22) to bring His sons and daughters from far, that he may plant them again in their own land, Ezekiel 34, etc. Not for twenty-four centuries, since the days of Cyrus, King of Persia, has there been offered to any mortal such a privileged opportunity to further the purposes of God concerning His ancient people.[11]

For this Blackstone was memorialized by Zionists. Today at the Herzl Museum in Israel one can see the Bible that Blackstone gave to Herzl with selected passages highlighted. Supreme Court Justice Louis D. Brandeis wrote to Blackstone "that you are the Father of Zionism, as your work antedates Herzl."[12] In 1918 when Blackstone was honored at a Zionist conference, he had the occasion to address the delegates, and said, "I am and for thirty years have been an ardent advocate of Zionism. This is because I believe that true Zionism is founded upon the plan, purpose, and fiat of the everlasting and omnipotent God, as prophetically recorded in His Holy Word, the Bible."[13]

Because of Blackstone's pervasive influence on evangelical Protestants, including early Pentecostals, and his contribution to the spread of dispensational eschatology, we will closely examine what he says about Zionism. Israel figured largely in Blackstone's eschatology. He refers to Israel as "God's sun-dial," and states, "If we want to know our place in chronology, our position in the march of events, look at Israel."[14] He predicts, "Israel shall be restored to Palestine and no more be pulled put out of their land. Hundreds of prophecies affirm this dispensational truth . . . The title deed to Palestine is recorded, not in the Mohammedan Serai of Jerusalem nor the Serglio of Constantinople, but in hundreds of millions of Bibles now extant in more than three hundred languages of the earth."[15]

Blackstone cites Luke 21:24 as the hermeneutical key for his position. This verse states that "Jerusalem was to be trodden down until the times of the Gentiles be fulfilled." Blackstone argues that, in view of the "signs of nation life," namely that Israel "is actually returning to Palestine, then surely the end of this dispensation 'is nigh, even at the doors.'"[16] At this point Blackstone brings up the subject of Zionism, which he defines as "the present movement of the Jews to return to the land of their fathers. Zionism is a modern term expressing the national hopes and sentiments of the Jews."[17] Blackstone was troubled, as were other evangelicals, by the secular tenor of Zionism. He acknowledges that the leaders of the Zionist Movement, Theodore Herzl and Max Nordau, were agnostics. "The orthodox Jews who have enlisted under the Zionist banner, are animated by the most devout religious motives. But the agnostics aver that

11. Cited in Merkley, *Politics of Christian Zionism*, 68.

12. Ibid., 60.

13. Cited in ibid., 61.

14. Blackstone, *Jesus Is Coming*, 234.

15. Ibid., 235.

16. Ibid., 236.

17. Ibid.

this is not a religious movement at all. It is purely economic and nationalistic."[18] As a further justification, Blackstone celebrates what appeared to be the providential opportunity, afforded by the Zionist Movement, to free the Holy Land from the oppressive rule of the Ottoman Empire. Yet, he still struggles to comprehend how a secular Jewish state in Palestine could be the fulfillment of prophecy, especially in view of the fact that the leaders of the Zionist Movement were atheists. He writes, "In the midst of these disputes, the Zionists have seized the reigns and eschewing the help of Abraham's God they have accepted agnostics as leaders and are plunging madly into this scheme for the erection of a Godless state. But a Bible student will surely say, this godless national gathering of Israel is not the fulfillment of the glorious divine restoration, so glowingly described by the prophets. No, indeed!"[19] Nonetheless, Blackstone managed to resolve the sticking point by lifting up a countervailing prophecy, Zechariah 2:1–2, which calls on Israel to "gather yourselves together" as "a nation that has no longing" (for the Lord). Then he asks, "Could this prophecy be more literally fulfilled than by this present Zionist movement?"[20]

Blackstone grants the crass agnosticism of the Zionist movement. "One of the speakers at the first congress said of the Sultan, 'If His majesty will now receive us, we will accept Him as our Messiah." In addition, Herzl himself is reported to have said, "We must buy our way back to Palestine, salvation is to be by money." To Blackstone, these sentiments were distasteful but not insurmountable. To show that Zionism was a sign that the end of the dispensation was near, he pulls out the pre-millennial trump card, prophetic date calculation. He calculates that the first Zionist Congress assembled just 1,260 years after the capture of Jerusalem by the Muslims in 637. Citing Daniel 12:7, he surmises, "It is probable that 'the times of the Gentiles' are nearing their end, and that the nations are soon to plunge into the mighty whirl of events connected with Israel's godless gathering, 'Jacob's trouble' (Jer. 30:6, 7), that awful time of tribulation, like which there has been none in the past, nor shall be in the future."[21]

Taking comfort in his belief that Christians will not have to pass through the same fires of affliction, Blackstone is enthralled at the thought of the Second Coming of Christ. "Oh! Glorious Hope. No wonder the Spirit and the Bride say come. No wonder the Bridegroom saith, 'Surely I come quickly,' and shall not we all join with the enraptured apostle, 'Even so come, Lord Jesus'?"[22] Blackstone ends his book with a call for increased consecration of his readers to world evangelization: "O fellow servants, let us improve the wonderful opportunities of our day to make investments of eternity . . . Let us engage, with all our might, in this world-wide mission work. Let us give of our means, our prayers and our words of encouragement to those who go to preach

18. Ibid., 238.
19. Ibid., 240.
20. Ibid.
21. Ibid., 241.
22. Ibid.

in the by-ways and hedges and in distant lands (Rom. 10:15), and, if possible, let us go ourselves."[23]

Finally, Blackstone delivers the eschatological pay-off punch. "Then shall we hasten the day of God."[24] Now we can clearly see the significance of Blackstone's attitude toward Israel. His endorsement of Zionism is due not to the intrinsic goodness of the movement itself, but rather to its function of hastening the Second Coming of Christ. The same can certainly be said of the early Pentecostals, as we will see below.

There is evidence that Blackstone exercised a direct and discernible influence on the early Pentecostals. His writings were published in Pentecostal periodicals. In 1916 *The Weekly Evangel* published an article by Blackstone on "The Times of the Gentiles." In determining the duration of the "times of the Gentiles," Blackstone attempts to unlock the secrets of "Scripture time." He employs the typical numerical calculations of premillennial eschatology, finally determining that the terminal years of the times of the Gentiles could be 1916, 1927, or 1935. He postulates that the first terminal date would mark a significant beginning of the restoration of the land of Palestine to the Jews. Then he poses the question, "Does not this give great significance to the Zionist movement on the part of the Jews and to all that is now being said and done by Gentiles, to secure Palestine for the Jews, in the outcome of the present war?"[25] Of course, the answer he is looking for is a hearty, "Yes!" Anticipating that some of his readers may have been wary of date-setting, as they would have reason to be on the basis of Matthew 24:36, he resorts to a dispensationalist loophole: "Some may say, 'Ah! You are setting a date for the Lord's coming.' No, beloved! All these dates pertain to Israel the earthly people. The church, which is the "called out' (Acts 15:14) heavenly people, has no date for the coming of our Lord to receive it unto Himself. We are to be live constantly on the watch, and be found ready when He comes."[26] This distinction between the timetable for Israel's restoration and the Second Coming was characteristic of dispensationalism. To the extent that Pentecostals employed this distinction, they adopted the dispensational system from which it was derived. James Goff offers another example of Blackstone's influence on early Pentecostals. Albert E. Robinson, then an official in the Fire Baptized Holiness Church, recounted that, as a young man, he had been fearful of the subject of Christ's return. Through a visiting layman, he gained access to Blackstone's book and ultimately became convinced of a more hopeful view. "The result of that night's conversation was that I started on a study of the coming of the Lord in a way I had never known before, and the Bible became a new Book."[27]

23. Ibid., 241, 243.

24. Ibid., 243.

25. Blackstone, "The Times of the Gentiles," *The Weekly Evangel* (May 13, 1916) 7.

26. Ibid., 8.

27. Goff, "Closing Out the Church Age," 10.

PENTECOSTAL PROPONENTS OF ZIONISM

Like Blackstone, the early Pentecostals were Christian Zionists. The views of some of the notable Pentecostal proponents of Zionism will be outlined.

Charles Parham

Just as Charles F. Parham is credited with being the first to propose the doctrinal formula of speaking with tongues as the "Bible evidence" of the baptism of the Holy Spirit, he was also the groundbreaker in the construal of Pentecostal Zionism. Beginning in the late 1890s, Parham publicly embraced the fledgling Zionist movement and predicted that God would soon restore the Jewish homeland in Palestine. According to Edith Blumhofer, "Parham's lectures on Zionism sometimes proved vastly more popular than his stance on the gospel."[28] Charles Parham incorporated a talk on Zionism, entitled "Restoration of Religion's Birthplace to Its Rightful Heirs," into his repertoire. In this talk, he is reported to have said,

> It is not a proposition of restoring the Jews to Palestine, but to restore Palestine to the Jews. What we want to see is the Jews return to their native land. If they desire to remain in America in preference to returning to Palestine that is their privilege. Many Jews who live in America will remain here, but the Jews who live in Russia will go to Palestine as soon as they can after Palestine is restored to them. As soon as the Jews begin returning business in that country will increase, and the increase in business will demand an increase of those engaged in merchandising, and it will be a question of but a short period until Palestine becomes one of the greatest business centers of the world.[29]

According to Goff, Parham publicized Herzl's efforts to buy Palestinian land from the sultan of Turkey for ten million dollars and optimistically predicted that the dream of a Jewish homeland would soon be a reality. He portrayed the horrors of anti-Semitism in Russia and defended the Jewish people from the popular stereotypes often prejudicially placed on them.[30]

During his revival meetings in Galena, Parham acquired fifteen Palestinian costumes, which served as visual aids for his messages on the topic of the restoration of Palestine to the Jews as a fulfillment of biblical prophecy. The publicity flyer for these meetings, entitled "*Jerusalem*" in bold letters, announces, "Jerusalem—Her Costumes and Customs will be graphically portrayed and illustrated by Chas. F. Parham."[31] Parham purchased the Palestinian costumes from Tom Allen, a Civil War veteran who had lived in Palestine for ten years and needed the money to travel to California where he planned to retire in an Old Soldier's Home. For the price of a train ticket,

---

28. Blumhofer, *Restoring the Faith*, 53.

29. "Restoration of Palestine," *Joplin Globe*, n.d., 2, Parham Papers.

30. Goff, *Fields White Unto Harvest*, 101.

31. "Jerusalem," Parham Papers.

he sold the costumes to Parham.[32] Parham did everything he could to sensationalize the Jewish connection in his ministry, but in 1908 he stretched it too far. Hoping to restore his tarnished reputation, due to an allegation of sexual misconduct, he widely publicized a plan to travel to the Holy Land in search of the Ark of the Covenant.[33] He claimed to have discovered where the lost ark was located and promised that he would unearth it. W. R. Quinton notified the readers of *Word and Work* that "Bro. Parham expects to sail from N.Y. in early Sept. for the holy land."[34] However, his scheme came to naught. He was castigated by Pentecostal notables. Without naming Parham, the British Pentecostal leader, Alexander Boddy, writes,

> Having been asked whether I could recommend the people of a mission to give money to one who has sent out typed circular letters asking for support in a proposed trip to Palestine to search for the Ark, I must answer with a decided NO! I would recommend those interested to read the copy of Apostolic Faith of Houston Texas, May 1907. They will see the verdict of a gathering of Pentecostal leaders on the man who is now asking for this help. To search for the Ark, even if it was at all likely to be found, is a retrograde step. It is Christ alone whom we need.[35]

To Parham's embarrassment, his attempt to raise money was abortive. He got as far as New York, then returned empty handed, with the alibi that he had been mugged. Soon thereafter he was virtually shunned by the movement he had started.[36]

Albert Weaver

Weaver was a short-term missionary in Palestine. He writes of himself, "In 1906 it was the privilege of the writer to be present at the Jewish Zionist conference held in Basle [sic], Switzerland. Dr. Hertzl [sic], the founder of Zionism, had just passed away, and Dr. Max Nordau was appointed his successor."[37] Weaver remembers well the fractious debate over the British Government's offer of a tract of land in Uganda. Ultimately the faction in favor of Palestine won the day, largely out of respect for Herzl's dying request that his bones be carried back to Palestine when the Jewish people became a nation in their own land. Weaver leaves no question as to where he stood on the debate. He asserts, "One of the greatest indications of God's time for the return of the Jews to their land, is that Satan is doing his utmost through human agency to allure

---

32. Bills, "The Houston Connection: After Topeka and Before Azusa Street," 6.

33. See the flyer entitled "Notice!" in the Parham Papers, which says that Parham is "going to Palestine in search of the Ark of the Covenant in October 1908. The Masonic Lodge and other organizations have spent thousands of dollars in searching for this sacred treasure, but every effort has been in vain. Mr. Parham has every reason to believe he has at last discovered its whereabouts."

34. Quinton, "Texas Camp Meeting," *Word and Work* (June 1908) 184–85.

35. Boddy, "Digging for the Ark," *Confidence* 7 (October 15, 1908) 22.

36. "Notice About Parham," *Word and Witness* (October 20, 1912) 3.

37. Weaver, "Human or Divine: Which Shall It Be?" *Latter Rain Evangel* (December 1929) 18. Theodor Herzl died in 1904.

them to some other country."[38] Weaver thinks that if the Ottoman Sultan was to offer a grant of land in Mesopotamia to Jews, this would be a step in the right direction. "This being originally Abraham's Home Land, although not Palestine proper, it may be providential."[39] Writing several years later, Weaver attests, "Israel's return has been rapidly going on, and the writer has seen it with his own eyes. The following is a noted fact. As much as we all hate war, God uses it, nevertheless as a means to an end; and the late war did not cease until this territory which was promised to the Patriarchs was wrenched out of the hands of the Turks. Literal Israel then is seeking and returning to her long-promised possessions, as is quite noticeable."[40] However, much to the dismay of Pentecostals who shared Weaver's views, in 1930 the British Government put the brakes on Jewish immigration to Palestine.

Weaver was particularly enamored of the Zionist Movement because, as he saw it, it was opening the door "to give the Gospel to both Jew and Mohammedan, especially the former." Weaver was more positively disposed toward the Jews. He writes, "We are indebted to the Jews for the Gospel," and goes on to explain that, "From them we received our Bible, the writers of which were Jews. The first disciples and apostles were Jews, and also the early church was Jewish. Our Saviour was a Jew. Is it not a sacred duty to give unto them in return?"[41] Along with many other conservative evangelicals and Pentecostals, Weaver seemed to think that the Jewish people were receptive as never before to the Christian message. Of course most Jewish people would have probably disagreed. Nonetheless, Weaver is to be commended for his robust appreciation of the Jewish roots of Christianity.

David Wesley Myland

David Wesley Myland was perhaps the most theologically innovative of the Pentecostal proponents of Zionism. Myland was the originator of the "latter rain covenant," which was a creative theological synthesis designed as an apologetic for the Pentecostal Movement. In his lectures on "The Latter Rain Covenant" at the Stone Church in Chicago in 1910, Myland draws an analogy between the Pentecostal Movement and the Zionist Movement. He claims that as renewal is coming to the church through the latter rain of the Pentecostal Movement, so a complementary renewal is occurring in the land of Palestine. Referring to what he calls a "latter rain connection," Myland observes, "Spiritually the latter rain is coming to the church of God at the same time it is coming literally upon the land." For Myland the return of the Jews to Palestine was more than coincidental. He suggests, "Significant is it also that at this time Israel is turning back to her land."[42] Myland sees a convergence of portentous events that were

---

38. Weaver, "Palestine," *Word and Work* 31.9 (September 1909) 198.

39. Ibid.

40. Weaver, "Human or Divine: Which Shall It Be?" *Redemption Tidings* 6.10 (October 1930) 7.

41. Weaver, "Palestine," 198.

42. Myland, "The Fifth Latter Rain Lecture: The Fullness and Effects of Pentecost," *Latter Rain Evangel* (September 1909) 13.

especially meaningful in light of Pentecostal eschatology: "Now we begin to under-stand this great prophecy: 'I will pour out My Spirit'—literally on Israel, spiritually on God's church, dispensationally to bring in the consummation of the ages and open the millennium, the age of righteousness. To this great point we are converging, and we see enough now that ought to make anybody willing to go through a life of continual sacrifice to hasten that day."[43] Like Parham, Myland attributed great theological import to the Zionist Movement.

In these lectures Myland places significant emphasis on Zionism. He rejoices that "Palestine is again getting 'the days of heaven,' and so has this Convention; we have been getting a little of 'the days of heaven'; we have sought that, and God has been true to the spiritual aspect of the Latter Rain Covenant just as much as He is to the literal aspect."[44] By the literal aspect, Myland meant the Zionists who were "returning their attention to the land." Myland discusses the colonization fund established by Baron de Hirsch with a largesse of five million dollars. Like other Pentecostal Zionists, he makes much of the reported grant of the sultan of free land to Jews who would settle in Mesopotamia as citizens of the Ottoman Empire. In reality, this was a ploy of the sultan to prevent the Jews from returning to Palestine.[45] However, like scores of Pentecostal writers after him, Myland wove a web of eschatological intrigue around the notion that the Jews would settle in Mesopotamia and come into Palestine in due time. "They are going around in their own way, and by and by Mesopotamia will not be able to keep them any longer, and they will go into Palestine."[46] Myland supposes that Mesopotamia could easily support a population of 50 million. He thought plans were afoot among the Zionists to orchestrate a surge of Jewish settlers into Mesopotamia. He says,

> Now while we have been holding this Convention in Chicago, these very things have been transpiring. Those Jews have been working out the literal phase of the Latter Rain Covenant while we in this Convention have been working out the spiritual side, and when the literal and the spiritual come together, then is brought about a third phase, the dispensational aspect. That is why I traced this covenant historically, spiritually and dispensationally. We have literal Israel re-turning to their land at the same time that the literal latter rain is coming to its normal fall upon that land. This together with the spiritual latter rain falling upon God's spiritual Israel today, betokens in a remarkable way that the closing days of the Dispensation are upon us.[47]

Myland was convinced that what he saw was not perceivable to the Zionists. He observes, "You will notice the Jewish teachers that have sprung up, who are teaching

43. Ibid., 15.

44. Myland, "Literal and Spiritual Latter Rain Falling Simultaneously: God's Ancient People Are Returning to their Native Land," *Latter Rain Evangel* (October 1909) 19.

45. Friedman, "The System of Capitulations and its Effects on Turco–Jewish Relations in Palestine, 1856–1897," 285–86.

46. Myland, "Literal and Spiritual Latter Rain," 19.

47. Ibid.

about Palestine and the Zionist societies, that it is time to go back to Palestine. They do not know the meaning of it all, but it is according to the will of God, through the prophecies, and unwittingly they are doing it. God's sovereign arm is over every movement after all, keeping it from going to pieces; hence the stir at this time in all parts of the world over Palestine."[48] And indeed there was a stir among the early Pentecostals. Myland can be credited with stimulating Pentecostal reflection on the significance of the return of the Jews to Palestine. In his "Latter Rain Covenant," he brought together eschatological ideas on which most conservative evangelicals and Pentecostals agreed but then molded them in into a creative synthesis of Christian Zionism and Pentecostal restorationism.

George F. Taylor

Zionism was interpreted by Pentecostals as a sign that the second coming of Christ and the salvation of the Jews were near at hand. This view was shared by George F. Taylor, a leader of the Pentecostal Holiness Church. In his treatise on *The Second Coming*, Taylor mused that "the Great Tribulation causes some to turn to God, and to seek His salvation."[49] By the time of the Great Tribulation, "the Jews will have gathered back to Palestine in their unbelief" and then a spiritual breakthrough will occur. "At the second coming of Jesus, the Jews as a nation will accept Him as their Savior." Taylor's certainty rested upon his firm conviction that "God's covenant can never be broken. The seed of Abraham *must* possess the land of Canaan *forever*."[50] Taylor states the premise of Pentecostal Zionism, namely, that the Jewish people hold an eternal claim to a deed of title on the land of Israel by virtue of the Abrahamic covenant.

William H. Cossum

In the spring of 1910, W. H. Cossum presented a series of prophetical lectures at the Stone Church in Chicago in which he gave prime attention to the Zionist Movement. In one of these lectures he narrates the origins of the Zionist Movement, beginning with the Dreyfus affair, in which a Jewish officer in the French army was falsely convicted of treason and unjustly imprisoned. The Dreyfus affair convinced Theodor Herzl, an Austrian journalist covering the story in Paris, that the only answer to the problem of anti-Semitism was a Jewish state vouchsafed by international recognition.[51] Cossum sets forth the Basel Program of the First Zionist Congress of 1897, ensuing debates over the location of the Jewish state, the decision that the Jewish state must be in Palestine, and the development of Jewish agricultural colonies in Palestine. He also spins a tale about events in Mesopotamia that he thinks are laying the foundation for the emergence of the Anti-Christ. Clearly, the main motive for Cossum's interest in

48. "Latter Rain Covenant," 45.

49. Taylor, *The Second Coming of Jesus*, 64.

50. Ibid., 70, 192, 198.

51. See Herzl, *The Jewish State*.

Zionism is, as he puts it, "to show its setting in whole prophetic movement," that is, its bearing upon Pentecostal eschatology.

Cossum locates the Zionist movement in the context of a pre-millennial scenario, conceiving of it as a harbinger of the Great Tribulation. He agrees with Taylor, declaring, "The Jews are to be gathered back to their native land in *unbelief.* They will go through the awful tribulation prophesied by Daniel, by Jeremiah, and also by our Lord."[52] This bout of suffering will be far worse than the massacre of one million Jews during the Roman destruction of Jerusalem in 70 CE or the Spanish expulsion of 100,000 Jews in the fifteenth century. Despite their sufferings the Jewish people have proved themselves to be indestructible and now they are returning to Palestine. Cossum says, "Look at the black stream that is going toward Palestine, thousands of them, toward the plain of Esdraelon and the plain of Sharon, which is one vast garden. Palestine has eighteen or twenty flourishing colonies; all the fertile plains are held by Jewish agriculturists, and this is the race which for centuries has been scattered among the nations, and which they have been trying to wipe off the face of the earth."[53]

To ameliorate the tragic prospect that the return of Jewish people to Palestine leads inexorably to the Great Tribulation, Cossum avers, "These fires of tribulation are for purification" and will produce a "company that have been purified to meet Jesus when He returns to this earth."[54] Cossum adheres to the same basic scheme as Parham. A company of 144,000 Jews will convert to Christ, be gathered out of the firepot of the Tribulation, and serve as Spirit-filled evangelists who will usher in the salvation of all Israel. He sees the Pentecostal Movement as a portent of things to come in Palestine:

> The Spirit is being poured out over there, too, there will be a mighty spiritual movement; the miraculous will be manifested in Palestine while the Jews are being gathered. God will be at work among His people; the sick will be healed and miracles will be worked with the result that there will be an awful conflict, and as you read in Revelation you will find that the lines of demarcation between Antichrist's people and Christ's people will be more and more clean cut, and the 144,000 who meet Christ will come out of this awful conflict.[55]

With Christ's Second Coming, the Jewish nation will universally recognize Jesus as the genuine Messiah and redeemer of Israel. "Then Zionism will have reached its prophetic goal."[56]

52. Cossum, "Mountain Peaks of Prophesy and Sacred History: The Indestructible Jew," *Latter Rain Evangel* (April 1910) 4.

53. Ibid., 6.

54. Cossum, *Mountain Peaks of Prophecy and Sacred History*, 63–64.

55. Cossum, "Mountain Peaks of Prophecy and Sacred History: The Zionist Movement," *Latter Rain Evangel* 2.8 (May 1910) 9.

56. Cossum, *Mountain Peaks of Prophecy and Sacred History*, 66, 68.

J. Roswell Flower

J. Roswell Flower never tired of acclaiming the special place of the Jewish people in the redemptive plan of God. He was one of the founders of the General Council of the Assemblies of God in 1914 and was the chief architect of the 1927 revision to the fourteenth article of the AG "Statement of Faith," which forthrightly anticipated the "salvation of national Israel." Gannon makes the significant observation that, "No other twentieth century denomination had such a clause referencing 'national Israel' as integral to its basic system of faith."[57]

Susan Duncan

Susan A. Duncan of the Elim Institute in Rochester, New York was responsible for guiding the editorial opinion of *Trust* in a decidedly pro-Zionist direction. Her reports on current events clearly reveal her Zionist sympathies. Introducing a news bulletin on Hebrew University, Duncan writes, "The opening of the great University of Palestine is one of the most marked events since the capture of Jerusalem by Allenby in 1917 . . ."[58] Hyperbole gets the best of her as she exclaims, "How rapidly now all will head up, under the indomitable Jewish spirit now rising to the fore in Palestine! Amen, even so come Lord Jesus!"[59] To put it mildly, Duncan was enthusiastic about the restoration of the Jewish national home in Palestine. Using the biblical metaphor of the budding fig tree, she observes early in 1929, "The fig-tree (the Jew) as for some years been active and the buds have been swelling until now really leaves are to be seen, and it appears to our mind that for the past few months these leaves have taken on life and revealing fresh verdure as in spring-time."[60] It seemed to Duncan that "fresh enthusiasm" had been "kindled among all Jews in America" by a visit of Field Marshall Allenby to the United States. At a reception in honor of Allenby, Duncan reports that a presiding pastor complimented the "liberator of Palestine" by likening him to the Emperor of Rome. In the same article Duncan addresses the divisions within the Jews between Zionists and non-Zionists. She approvingly tells of a recent convention in New York that called for unity among Jews. She urges the church to "make way for the Jew, whose right it is to come into his own." Duncan, as Pentecostals generally, was bullish on the Zionist movement not because she saw in it any inherent value, but rather because of its instrumental function of corroborating the Pentecostal metanarrative. She was convinced that after the Jews returned to Palestine, then would come "the calling out of the Bride." In Duncan's mind, the return of the Jews to Palestine was a signal that the Holy Spirit would soon call out, seal, and ripen for harvest "that company who are to be caught away as the 'first-fruits' unto God and His throne."[61] In this company Duncan included herself and her fellow Pentecostals.

57. Gannon, "Shifting Romance with Israel," 136.

58. Duncan, "Prophecy Fulfilling," *Trust* 24.3–4 (May–June 1925) 19.

59. Ibid., 21.

60. Duncan, "Another Corner Turned or 'L'Union Sacree.'" *Trust* 27.11–12 (January–February 1929) 8.

61. Ibid., 8–10.

Myer Pearlman

Myer Pearlman, a converted Jew, was perhaps the most gifted of Pentecostal theologians. As he was beginning his career as a theological educator in the American AG, he published an article entitled "The Jewish Question from the Viewpoint of a Converted Jew." He begins by asserting that, of all people, Christians should be interested in the Jews. "So then," he writes, "Christians should be interested in the Jew and not only interested in the Jew but they should love the Jew."[62] He forthrightly states that one reason that the Jew has tended to oppose Christianity is because "those who have professed the name of Christ have been those who have cursed and hated and persecuted him." He traces the history of this persecution and then provides a sympathetic account of the career of Theodore Herzl and the Zionist Movement. He concludes with an affirmation of "the Bible solution to the Jewish problem," namely that the "Jews will be restored to Palestine by the Lord Himself and all the nations of the world will honor them and recognize them as a great nation."[63]

One year after the formation of the state of Israel in 1948, Pearlman's views on the Jewish question were published posthumously in an article entitled, "Those Strange People, the JEWS!" Pearlman argues that the Jewish people are between a rock and a hard place. He writes, "The Jew's present position is due the fact that he cannot escape the consequences of the Old Covenant, and he will not accept the blessings of the New." So, Pearlman asks, what can the followers of Jesus do to assist Israel along her path from reproach to glory? Pearlman emphatically states that the Christian Church must take the right attitude toward the Jews. This means that Christians must eschew anti-Semitism and acknowledge that the Jews still have a role to play as God's chosen people. "God is not through with them. Many Old and New Testament scriptures predict the restoration of Israel to kingdom privileges, and these prophecies are bound up with those relating to Christ's second coming. 'And so all Israel shall be saved.' Rom. 11:26."[64] Pearlman's outlook on the Jewish problem represents a clear repudiation of replacement theology.

William Nagel

William H. Nagel was an independent Pentecostal evangelist. In 1937 he wrote an article on the Zionist Movement, entitled "The Jew—What is Your Attitude?"[65] Nagel argues that the Christian attitude toward the Jew should be one of friendship, i.e., philosemitism. Nagel relates a conversation he once had over tea with a Jewish surgeon in Europe, who remarked, "In my experience with Christians I have found that the man who holds to the Scriptures is a friend of ours, and people who hate us do not really believe the Bible." For Nagel, friendship with Israel translated into support of Zionism.

---

62. Pearlman, "The Jewish Question from the Viewpoint of a Converted Jew," *Pentecostal Evangel* (June 4, 1927) 1.

63. Ibid., 8, 12.

64. Pearlman, "Those Strange People, the JEWS!" *Pentecostal Evangel* (August 20, 1949) 15.

65. Nagel, "The Jew—What Is Your Attitude?" *Pentecostal Evangel* (January 23, 1937) 2–3, 11–12.

He writes, "People ask me, 'Why are in you sympathy with the Zionist Movement, and why do you sympathize so much with the Jews?' I am in sympathy with the Zionist Movement because I believe the Spirit of God is using it as a means of fulfilling His Word in bringing the Jews back to Palestine." Pointing to biblical prophecies that were being fulfilled, Nagel puts the question in his title to the reader:

> I sympathize with the Jews because I believe the Church has failed to properly represent Christ to them. She has been the cruel instrument of oppression, persecution and death in the hands of unregenerate leaders, who have taught the Jewish people to hate the name of Jesus. I am in sympathy with the Jews because of the challenging question one of them asked me one day, "Did not your own teacher, Jesus, command you to love us?" And, furthermore, I am always obliged to befriend them as those startling words keep ringing in my ears, "And people who hate us do not really believe the Bible." My Christian friend, what is your attitude?[66]

One can verify how Pentecostals would have responded to Nagel's question by thumbing through Pentecostal periodicals, which is exactly what the next section of this chapter will do.

ZIONIST SYMPATHIES IN PENTECOSTAL PERIODICALS

A survey of early Pentecostal periodicals substantiates the claim of Ray Gannon that the early Pentecostal movement exhibited a deep and abiding sympathy with the Zionist Movement.[67] To begin, we will examine the Pentecostal commentary on the Zionist Movement.

Pentecostal Support for the Zionist Movement

The Pentecostal periodicals issued many favorable reports on the Zionist movement. The *Bridegroom's Messenger* took a pro-Zionist stance in 1910, printing a rejoinder to the Allgemeine Mission Conference's 1901 critique of the Zionist Movement, which claimed that "Zionism will not hasten the conversion of Jews, but rather delay it." Acknowledging that Zionism is not a religious movement, the author nonetheless observes, "At the same time the apostles of Zionism were busy drafting people for their ranks, the number of Jewish conversions increased everywhere."[68] In Austria, the number of Jewish conversions increased from one baptism for every 1,200 Jews a year in 1863–73, to one in every 430 Jews a year in 1880–89, and to one baptism for every 260 since 1903, the point being that the prospects for Jewish evangelism had improved since the emergence of the Zionist Movement. *Trust* was also warmly disposed to the Zionist Movement. In 1911 R. W. Cobb placed two striking developments side by side:

66. Ibid., 2–3, 11–12.

67. Gannon, "Shifting Romance with Israel," 4.

68. "The Jews: Would Zionism Hinder the Conversion of the Jews?" *Bridegroom's Messenger* 4.75 (December 1, 1910) 2.

"*Do you know* the Jews are returning to Palestine by the thousands in unbelief? . . . *Do you know* that the prophecy of Joel is beginning to be fulfilled, and that men, women and children of all nations are speaking in other languages under the power and outpouring of the Holy Spirit?"[69] With eschatological fervor, the author states that these signs were foretold to occur in the world before Jesus would come again. In the next issue, the editor of *Trust* introduces a speech by Dr. Max Nordau, a prominent Zionist leader, by commenting that "God is moving on behalf of Israel, and hastening the day when they shall bud and blossom, and enter upon their mission as Evangelizers of the world." In the speech Nordau urges Jews to organize and be united in "faith in the eternal Jewish future." On the same page an article by A. E. Thompson, a Christian and Missionary Alliance missionary in Palestine, paints a bright picture of promising developments in Palestine, proclaiming, "The progress of today is but the prophecy of tomorrow. It is dawn in Palestine. Some of us will see the sun rising . . . In every direction there are stirrings of new life."[70]

The pro-Zionist sentiments expressed above were not due to a temporary wave of enthusiasm. To the contrary, they represent a sustained and consistent point of view in Pentecostal periodicals throughout most of the twentieth century.[71] The *Bridegroom's Messenger* writes, "Many of the Lord's people have watched the progress of the Zionist movement with considerable interest, but a few of them, perhaps, are conscious of the far-reaching effects which have already resulted therefrom."[72] Max Moorhead, a Pentecostal missionary in India, was one who was watching with great interest. He writes,

> There is a movement called Zionism a secular, political movement amongst Jews; and this movement has representatives in many parts of the civilized world where we find the Jews have settled. These tens of thousands of wide awake, influential and patriotic Hebrews have for the past 20 years and more been sending their delegates to the annual Zionist Congress, which for many successive years has been held at Basle, Switzerland. The goal to which all Zionists are anxiously looking is the unification of scattered Israelites into a Jewish state; and their watch cry has ever been: 'Israel, awake! Return to Palestine.'[73]

Moorhead was enthusiastic about the Zionist Movement because it seemed to betoken a spiritual awakening among the Jews of eschatological significance. He says that in the distance he could hear the thunder of the "coming Tribulation storm and tempest." In 1916, at a convention in Newark, New Jersey, H. H. Cox spoke of the "stirring in Jewish circles," and exclaimed, "Oh, beloved, these are things that should

69. Cobb, "A Note of Warning," *Trust* 10.7 (September 1911) 8.

70. "In the Last Days 'Apostasy,'" and Thompson, "Present Day Palestine," *Trust* 10.8 (October 1911) 15.

71. Jones, "Palestine: A Great Sign of the Present Age," *The Elim Evangel and Foursquare Revivalist* (July 26, 1929) 201–3; Appelman, "God Over Palestine," *Pentecostal Evangel* (May 14, 1949) 6–7; Mayo, "Israel, God's Last Day Miracle," *Pentecostal Evangel* (December 17, 1950) 3–4, 12–14.

72. "Parable of the Fig Tree," *Bridegroom's Messenger* 5.107 (April 1, 1912) 4.

73. Moorhead, "Sign of the Fig Tree," *Bridegroom's Messenger* 5.119 (October 15, 1912) 4.

awaken us concerning the coming of the Lord Jesus. The Zionist Movement has more than a million dollars in their control, ready to build the temple in Jerusalem when Israel gets Palestine. More than that, the people of Israel in this country are saying, 'We are a nation and we want a country.'" Cox went on to quote from a newspaper clipping reporting that an upcoming "Congress of American Jews is to demand, at the conclusion of the war, the return of Palestine to its ancient owners. For the Jews are a nation, and they must have a land, and Palestine is theirs."[74] At this time the Balfour Declaration was only a year away and the Pentecostal press was hot on the trail of the events that pointed toward it.

Always in the know about developments in the Zionist Movement, *Trust* reported in October of 1917 that Israel Zangwill had returned to the Zionist fold and said "that it was almost certain that at the end of the war Palestine would fall into hands of the allied Powers. This historic event will give the Zionists the opportunity to realize their ideal, which is the establishment of a publicly secured, legally recognized home for the Jewish people in the Holy Land."[75] With perhaps an inkling of the Balfour Declaration, in the fall of 1917 Elizabeth Sisson, a prominent Pentecostal conference speaker, comments, "The Zionist movement has taken fresh impetus . . . Zionists are doing more than they know."[76] In early 1918, on the heels of the British capture of Jerusalem, the *Latter Rain Evangel* reported on a convention of Federated Zionist Societies in Chicago, which convened "to plan for an idealistic republic in the Holy Land . . . The fact that the British Army are now occupying Jerusalem and that Great Britain has declared herself favorable to the establishment of an independent Jewish State, lent great fervency to the assemblages."[77] One cannot escape the conclusion that the Pentecostal periodicals were strongly sympathetic to the Zionist Movement.[78]

S. B. Rohold was a Pentecostal Jewish missionary who served in Haifa, Palestine. In an address at the Stone Church in Chicago, he sized up the situation in Palestine. His assessment is realistic. He explains that anti-Semitism was the underlying factor that brought about three great events that had recently happened. The first is the Balfour Declaration; the second is the first Aliyah with its settlements, and the third is modern Zionism. But, Rohold is sad to report, the Jews of Palestine are not united, that is, except on the issue of the Stone which the builders rejected. All humor aside, Rohold solemnly insists, "I do not retract one iota of what I have said about the Jew going back to Palestine. I believe it, but there are many difficulties to face; there are 600,000 Arabs there. You cannot set them aside."[79] Rohold's last point was telling. Yet it was not what

74. Cox, "The Time Table in the Word of God: Stirrings in Jewish Circles and Heading up of Events," *Latter Rain Evangel* (May 1916) 2–3.

75. "Zangwill and Zionists," *Trust* 16.8 (October 1917) 11.

76. Cited in Sexton, "Is the Fig Tree Putting Forth Leaves?" *Pentecostal Holiness Advocate* (November 15, 1917) 6.

77. "This Year in Jerusalem," *Latter Rain Evangel* (January 1918) 13.

78. See "Off for Palestine," *The Church of God Evangel* 11.25 (June 19, 1920) 3.

79. Rohold, "Zionism: Past, Present and Future: Lack of Unity in Jewish Circles the Great Hindrance," *Latter Rain Evangel* (February 1918) 16.

most Christian Zionists, including Pentecostals, wanted to hear. However, the inability to come to grips with the Arab presence and an equal Arab right to self-determination was a serious chink in the armor of Pentecostal Zionism.

Nevertheless, Rohold's realistic assessment did not deflate the irrepressible optimism among Pentecostals concerning the Zionist Movement. E. L. Langston looked back at what had been accomplished in Palestine since the First Zionist Congress of years ago and cheered the results—the growth of the Jewish population in Jerusalem, the success of the agricultural colonies of Jews, and the revival of spoken Hebrew.[80] Reporting on the Zionist Convention in Baltimore, Edgar Scurrah quoted the Jewish Zionist leader, Loius Zipsky who proclaimed, "Thus, our historic claim to the right to establish the Jewish National Home in Palestine . . . is indubitably assured." It seemed to Scurrah that, "All these things are saying to us, 'Lift up your heads for your redemption draweth nigh.' Amen, even so come Lord Jesus, come Quickly!"[81]

As the years passed, Pentecostal Zionism did not lose its fervor. In 1928 the editor of *Trust* avers, "The 'Zionists' are playing an important part in the 'restoration' promised to the Hebrew race. Indescribable difficulties have been surmounted in their efforts to re-habilitate the land of Palestine." The editor calls for "earnest prayer that every design of Satan may be frustrated and that God's purpose for the Jew may be accomplished in so far as is necessary to prepare the way for the hour of their great and final deliverance through the appearing of our Lord and Saviour, their Messiah and King."[82] It appears that Pentecostals were most concerned with the eschatological upshot of the Zionist Movement, because it corroborated the Pentecostal metanarrative.

When rifts in Zionism disturbed the smooth implementation of the game plan of the Pentecostal metanarrative, the Pentecostal editors vented their irritation. For instance, in reporting on the flap between Chaim Weizmann and the Revisionists, led by Vladimir Jabotinsky, who favored a strategy of aggressive insurgency, the *Pentecostal Evangel* reports, "Today there is a remarkable lack of accord in the ranks of Zionism . . . They (the Revisionists) are not satisfied with Palestine merely becoming a home for Jews who want to return, but demand the establishment of a Jewish state." The editor then adds a brief comment: "It is quite clear from the prophecies of Haggai and Zechariah that God was more concerned with their spiritual condition than with their political prospects."[83] This kind of commentary, of which there is plenty in the *Pentecostal Evangel*, exemplifies the spirit of Pentecostal Zionism. It did not appreciate the complexity of Zionist politics, nor did it aspire to political action. Its ultimate concern was not with the Zionist project *per se*, but with its eschatological utility. This is seen in the coverage of the 1931 Zionist Congress in Basel. The *Pentecostal Evangel* reports that Weizmann was "deposed" and Nahum Sokolow elected the new president. It goes on to quote Samuel J. Rosensohn's explanation of why the Zionist movement is bound to succeed: "Jewish faith and Jewish longing to reconstitute their National

---

80. Langston, "The Chosen People and the Chosen Land," *Weekly Evangel* (March 23, 1918) 2–3.

81. Scurrah, "Zionist Convention in Baltimore," *Trust* 22.7 (September 1923) 13.

82. "Zionist Movement," *Trust* 27.7–8 (September–October 1928) 9.

83. "Rifts in Zionism," *Pentecostal Evangel* (August 1, 1931) 4.

Home in Palestine is as strong today as it has ever been, and will persist long after the forces antagonistic to the Zionist cause shall have ceased to exist." Again, a snippet of commentary follows: "We fear the sheep who are gathering together in Palestine—today there are some 160,000 there—without a shepherd, will be the sure prey of the wolves. But the Shepherd, He who was wounded in the house of His friends, is coming back. He is the only hope of the Jew, of the Gentile, and of the Church of God."[84] Such commentary, venturing a facile extrapolation from the Pentecostal metanarrative, fell far short of perceptive analysis. Clearly, for Pentecostals the value of Zionism was instrumental in so far as it legitimated the Pentecostal metanarrative.

The Pentecostal periodicals continued to express their support for Zionism and provided commentary on current events in Palestine. Before considering the contribution of the Pentecostal missionaries in Palestine to Pentecostal Zionism, we will survey the Pentecostal commentary on the Balfour Declaration, the Capture of Jerusalem, the Wailing Wall Riots, the Arab-Zionist conflict, and the establishment of the state of Israel in 1948.

Balfour Declaration

The Balfour Declaration was a boon to Pentecostal Zionism. In 1917, the *Weekly Evangel* reported that with British army drawing close to Jerusalem, the Foreign Secretary, Arthur Balfour, sent a letter to Lord Rothschild: "Mr. Balfour shows that the Government views with favor the establishment of Palestine as a national home for the Jewish people and will use its best endeavors to facilitate the achievement of its object."[85] Indicative of its bias, the *Christian Evangel* omits the clause in the Balfour Declaration assuring that the British Government would not infringe upon the rights of the land's other inhabitants, i.e., the Arabs. In her piece, "British Flag Waving Over the Towers of Jerusalem," Elizabeth Sexton rejoices, "But now that Jerusalem has passed into the hands of Christian powers, we have reason to expect that the great nations of the earth will recognize the right of the Jews to become a nation, with Palestine as their own country." Unlike the *Weekly Evangel*, Sexton cites the Balfour Declaration in full and comments, "It is an epoch for the Jews, and we shall soon see the wonderful regathering of God's ancient people back to their own land . . . The Mohammedan and the Turk no longer rule over the holy city . . . Jerusalem is to be trodden down no longer . . . But this does not mean that the Jew will have no more persecution or suffer hardships, or wars. Jacob's trouble will continue."[86] After citing a tract by Philip Sidersky on the Jewish flag, Sexton ominously predicts, "This same Jesus is soon coming back, and His holy feet shall again stand on the Mount of Olives. The Jews will be a nation then, and their own flag will be waving over the Holy City, and that is the

---

84. "Jewish Activities," *Pentecostal Evangel* (September 5, 1931) 5.

85. "Palestine for the Jews," *Weekly Evangel* (December 1, 1917) 4.

86. Sexton, "British Flag Waving Over the Towers of Jerusalem," *Pentecostal Holiness Advocate* (January 31, 1918) 2.

nation that will be born in a day. Hallelujah!"[87] Years later, *Trust* pays tribute to Lord Balfour on the occasion of his death, by remembering him as "a friend of the Jew" and crediting him for the achievements in Palestine since the Balfour Declaration.[88]

British Capture of Jerusalem

Falling on the heels of the Balfour Declaration, the British capture of Jerusalem stirred Pentecostals deeply as they reflected on what the fall of the Ottoman Empire portended for the future, both in terms of the Zionist project and in terms of the end times scenario. William Cossum, regarded in Pentecostal circles as an expert in the fulfillment of biblical prophecy, viewed the British advance in Palestine, linked with the Balfour Declaration, as events of ultimate eschatological import, stating, "But grander and more fascinating than all is the great summit doctrine, glistening, gleaming about all, the *Coming of the King*."[89] In extending a propitiously timed invitation for a Jewish conference under the auspices of the Chicago Hebrew Mission, scheduled for January, 1918, the *Latter Rain Evangel* gleefully observes, "Ere these notes reach the public it is quite possible that the British Army will have control of Palestine. The evacuation of the Holy Land by the Turk has been an event for which many prayers have ascended, both by Jew and Christian, and now that it is being accomplished the keenest interest is being manifested by everyone who is watching the march of events."[90]

The British Pentecostal, Arthur Frodsham, criticized prominent Jewish leaders and Protestant ministers for missing the full spiritual meaning of the British take-over of Jerusalem. Basing his perspective on the book of Daniel in the Hebrew Scriptures, he contends that the significance lies in the immediate prospect of the end of the Gentile treading-down of Jerusalem and the drawing near of redemption.[91] He could not resist the urge to prognosticate the date that Jesus once said was unknown even to him, speculating that, "This year therefore has some special claims to be considered as a *very principal starting point* of the times of the Gentiles, which measured from that period, run out in A.D. 1917. The latest date they could terminate in would be 1934." He does not stop there, but continues,

> Further, 1917 is remarkable in that it sees the British in possession of Jerusalem, and the assurance of the British cabinet to the Jews that they are prepared to hand over Palestine to the Jews. The United States Government agreed on December 12th to the British proposal . . . Daniel says of the time of the end, 'Many shall be purified, and made white and tried.' Thank God, today we see many are being made pure and white by the outpouring of the Latter Rain . . . Watch and pray

---

87. Ibid., 3.

88. "Lord Balfour Gone," *Trust* 29.3–4 (May–June 1930) 18–19.

89. Cossum, "Satan Overreaches Himself: Days of Fulfillment Drawing Nigh," *Latter Rain Evangel* (December 1917) 3.

90. *Latter Rain Evangel* (December 1917) 11.

91. Frodsham, "What It Means: The British in Jerusalem," *Weekly Evangel* (December 22, 1917) 3.

that ye may be accounted worthy to escape all these things and to stand before the Son of Man.[92]

Frodsham's reckless predictions were in keeping with the mood of exhilaration that was expressed by the *Weekly Evangel*: "There is a latent subconscious feeling in the masses that the taking of Palestine portends something marvelous to happen."[93]

Reporting on the opportunely timed Jewish Conference mentioned above, the *Latter Day Evangel* states that the participants at the Moody Tabernacle on January 22–25, 1918, were electrified by the recent happenings in Palestine, observing, "The news of the abdication of the Turk from Jerusalem had just flashed around the world and hearts of Jew and Gentile alike were rejoicing over the victory, which meant to the prophetic student, the ending of Gentile times; and the soon return of the Jews to their beloved land."[94] Hattie Duncan was equally thrilled, exclaiming, "I do not know that I have ever been so thrilled and my spirit so stirred as when I read of the capture of Jerusalem by the British on December 10th, 1917. Do you realize this is the most tremendous event that has occurred since the Jews rejected and crucified their Messiah-King? This is fulfillment of prophecy." She was of course referring to the prediction of Jesus in Luke 21:24 that "Jerusalem shall be trodden down of the Gentiles, until the times of the Gentiles be fulfilled." In view of the transfer of Jerusalem into British hands, Duncan thought that the "times of the Gentiles" were ending. She presses her readers, "O let it grip you. That is why God is saying, Separate. Everything is being shaken, nothing in you can abide in the day of testing but that which has been wrought in you by the Holy Spirit." She drew a distinctively Pentecostal application to the doctrine of the rapture:

> I am not going to ask you if you have your Pentecost, but I am going to ask you to ask yourself "Am I ready for translation?" God is still saying to the Church "you can escape," there is not one on the whole earth but God could so prepare and transform that they could be translated. Instead of that however there is only a little handful who will enter in. The great mass will go into that great day of 'Jacob's trouble' both among the Jews and the Church.[95]

Pentecostals were filled with delirium concerning the British capture of Jerusalem. In 1920, as Ira David reminisced over the famous prayer uttered by the British General Allenby, in anticipation of the British assault on Jerusalem which never took place due to the Ottoman retreat, he declares, "God heard that prayer . . . I feel like stopping and singing the doxology."[96] In 1929 the Rev. E. N. Richey was still adulating Allenby, writing, "General Allenby, in complete fulfillment of prophecy, delivered Jerusalem out of the hands of the bloody Turk and into the hands of the Jew." For Richey as many other

92. Frodsham, "1917" *Weekly Evangel* (December 22, 1917) 7.

93. "The Jews, the Gentiles, and the Church of God," *Weekly Evangel* (January 19, 1918) 6.

94. "The Jewish Conference," *Latter Rain Evangel* (February 1918) 12.

95. Duncan, "The Faithful Remnant," *Trust* 17.1 (March 1918) 4.

96. David, "Jesus Is Certainly coming Back Soon: Abundant Proof that the End is Near," *Latter Rain Evangel* (September 1920) 17.

Pentecostals, this event was a fulfillment of biblical prophecy, signaling that "we may expect any time the return of the Lord in glory."[97]

Wailing Wall Riots of 1929

The Pentecostal exhilaration over the Ottoman defeat in the First World War was more than matched by the anathema unleashed a decade later over the Wailing Wall Riots of 1929. The Pentecostal periodicals were aware of the rumblings in the volcano of Arab resentment leading up to the crisis. At the end of 1928 *Trust* alerted its readers that the mandatory authorities had barred the Jews from their "Wailing Place," rendering it "now silent for the first time in centuries." The author holds that "this enforced silence is strikingly significant," asking, "May we not take it to mean that God is about to answer the centuries old prayer of His ancient people that was chanted at the Wailing Wall 'to have mercy on Zion,' 'to speak to the heart of Jerusalem,' 'May beauty and majesty surround Jerusalem,' 'May the Kingdom soon return to Jerusalem,' 'Haste, haste, Redeemer of Zion'? Surely the time is due for the removal of the Church. Jesus is coming soon."[98] Such hopes that the rapture would accommodate a quick solution to an intractable controversy proved to be illusory.

In 1929 the situation worsened, exploding in August into a major Arab uprising, causing many deaths. The Pentecostal periodicals responded with foreboding. In a front-page story, the editor of the *Latter Rain Evangel* viewed the riots through the lens of the ancient antipathy of the sons of Abraham, Isaac and Ishmael, symbolizing the Jews and the Arabs. She writes, with a heavy pro-Zionist accent, "The sympathies of the world have been turned toward Palestine, where the Jew is seeking to establish a national home. For two weeks, beginning Aug. 17, Jerusalem was the scene of terror, due to massacres and riots instigated by the Grand Mufti, President of the Supreme Moslem Council of Jerusalem."[99] According to the analysis of Susan Duncan, "It is again the old story of Ishmael and Isaac or flesh against spirit, for though the Jews are returning to Palestine in unbelief, yet they are the true seed of Abraham to whom the land was promised, while the Arab is the seed of Ishmael who was cast out and is forever warring against God's purposes of victory for spirit over flesh."[100]

The avid British Zionist Lord Melchett was a favorite of the Pentecostal Zionists. Duncan quotes Melchett at length and then comments, "The hand of Satan is clearly in evidence and now is the time for the Church to pray for the peace of Jerusalem, even the hastening on the Messiah's coming reign, for until then there can be no permanent peace for Jerusalem or the inhabited earth."[101] The eyewitness reports of the Pentecostal missionaries in Palestine, one of which will be considered at the end of this chapter, reinforced the ideological bias and simplistic eschatological outlook of

97. Richey, "Is the Messiah at Hand?" *Full Gospel Advocate* (February 15, 1929) 7.

98. "Jews' Wailing Place," *Trust* (November–December 1928) 19.

99. "Isaac and Ishmael," *Latter Rain Evangel* (October 1929) 1.

100. Duncan, "The Sorrowing Jew," *Trust* (November–December 1929) 16–17.

101. Ibid., 19.

the sentiments expressed above. No attempt was made to look with perspicuity at the underlying causes of the crisis. The Pentecostal periodicals stood firm in their Zionist sympathies. In 1930 the *Latter Rain Evangel* printed excerpts of a speech by Lord Melchett with his response to Wailing Wall Riots:

> There is no power on earth great enough to stop the march of Israel back to Palestine . . . The great cause to which many of us have dedicated so much of our lives, and in which many of us are passionately interested, must go forward. To build up successfully and triumphantly a National Home in which we hope our people can live securely and happily . . . And if we hear the fury of the Arab masses, I would venture to say that the indignation and hostility of the fifteen million Jews of the world is a great deal more important than that of 600,000 Arabs in Palestine.[102]

In quoting Melchett, a tacit agreement was implied with his devaluing of the rights of the Arabs in Palestine. The implication is that Pentecostals disregarded the Arab side of the story. Worse than that, some writers, such as Frederick Childe, demonized the Arab perspective, writing, "Those Arab riots in Palestine in 1929 are a foreshadowing of the coming determined efforts of the antichrist, who according to the 83rd Psalm is going to attempt to cut Israel off from being a nation and having the land that belongs to them."[103]

In the 1930s Pentecostals incorporated the Wailing Wall Riots into a conspiratorial reading of current events. The periodicals collected snippets of news stories that confirmed Pentecostal biases. These collages were a regular feature of the Pentecostal periodicals. An example is "The Signs of the Times" section in *Trust*. In 1930 Robert McKilliam sets a number of news reports in an eschatological context, writing, "We are hastening into the year 1930, a year which must be more or less momentous, as in fact every year until the Second Advent of our Lord. Some things should demand our close and prayerful attention. Among them are First.—All movements concerning Palestine and the New. The following are clippings from various sources."[104] McKilliam proceeds to comment on a number of stories. Under "Mohammedans, Catholics, Samaritans and Jews seek Jesus," he relates the "touching sight" of a personal reminiscence at the Wailing Wall. On a piece about "Rome, the Vatican and 'El Duce,'" he stirs up fears over Mussolini's imperial designs. In "Movements in India," he comments on the unrest over British rule. Then he purports to observe the ripening of "the apostasy" predicted for the end times and states that the "harvest of the earth is about ready for God's judgment sickle." Finally, he draws an application under the subtitle, "The Daily Signs of His Coming," pressing his readers, "Has the Holy Ghost had His way with you, to draw your spirit so near your Lord that *you* hear the first stirrings which the Coming One has sent forth—like wireless telegraphy—and can *you* discern the

---

102. "The Budding Fig Tree," *Latter Rain Evangel* (February 1930) 21.

103. Childe, "Christ's Answer to the Challenge of Fascism and Communism," *Pentecostal Evangel* (October 31, 1931) 7.

104. McKilliam, "The Signs of the Times," *Trust* (March–April 1930) 17.

import? Every day seems to us to throw, over all present conditions and circumstances, a deepening hush. To God's own, earth's din being silenced that we may hear more readily the rallying cry of the descending Lord."[105] From the above, once again we see that there was a clear connection between the Zionist sympathies of Pentecostals and their eschatological outlook.

The same connection between Pentecostal Zionism and eschatology is plainly visible in the "Editor's Notebook" section in the *Pentecostal Evangel*. Pentecostals were deeply vexed over the British White Paper of 1930 and the chairman of the commission of inquiry who produced it, Lord Passfield. The editor of the *Pentecostal Evangel* condemns Passfield for "limiting Jewish immigration to Palestine and limiting Jewish purchase of land there" and predicts a political slap-down, stating that "in a few days the British Government will publish a document which will practically set at naught Lord Passfield's White Paper." He goes on to report that "Ramsay MacDonald, Great Britain's Premier, has expressed himself as fully sympathetic with Jewish ideals in Palestine . . . Referring to the opposition of the Arabs, Mr. Ramsay MacDonald says, 'Much of it is propaganda.' . . . It would appear that this anti-Semitic White Paper has been overruled by God, who knows how to control the hearts of rulers." The editor avers "that in the fulfilling of the dream of returning to Palestine, which Israel has cherished for eighteen hundred years, all Jewry is becoming a unit." Yet, at the same time he forecasts that "the last world war will focus itself in Palestine, and, at the critical moment, when all appears lost, the Messiah will gain a decisive victory according to prediction."[106] Later that year, the editor informs his readers that two members of the British cabinet, Lord Reading, Foreign Secretary, and Sir Herbert Samuel, Home Secretary, are Jews. With obvious delight he reports,

> Lord Passfield, whose policy of restricting Jewish immigration to Palestine and limiting of the purchase of land by Jews in Palestine has been such a blow to Jewry, has been removed from his position. We believe these changes will mean much in days to come in connection with the gathering together of Jewry in the land God promised them. Dear Brother Kerr used to say that the reason for the last war could be summed up in one word—Israel. God's promises to His own people will have to be fulfilled.[107]

The articles cited above clearly demonstrate that the *Pentecostal Evangel* threw its lot in with the Jewish Zionists and characterized their opponents as anti-Semitic. This appears to indicate a thorough identification with the Zionist cause.

Arab-Zionist Conflict

The editorial perspectives of the Pentecostal periodicals on the Arab-Zionist conflict in Palestine were notoriously lacking in fairness. In 1925 *Trust* printed a diatribe from

105. Ibid., 18–20.

106. The Editor's Notebook, "Good News for the Jews," *Pentecostal Evangel* (February 28, 1931) 4–5.

107. The Editor's Notebook, "With Perplexity," *Pentecostal Evangel* (September 12, 1931) 4.

"a friend of Israel" who demands, "The Jews *must not make a covenant or treaty with the Arabs* . . . The Jews *must not accept an Arab king*. Only a Jew chosen by God . . . The natural course is for the Children of Israel to make peace with the Children of Ishmael. But if this is attempted, God's wrath will come upon you."[108] Frederick Childe would have agreed. He emphatically states, "The Arab riots in Palestine in August, 1929, were undoubtedly the work of this insidious propaganda and surely show the depth of race hatred." Referring to the rivalry between the sons of Abraham, Ishmael and Isaac, Childe weighs the relative rights of the Arabs and Jews to the land of Palestine: "The Arabs are the descendants of Ishmael . . . You know that the Arabs claim the right to possess the land of Palestine based upon conquest made 700 years ago, but the Jews (Israel) have a divine right to that land of Canaan which was given to them 3500 years ago through old father Abraham."[109] Far from a paean to inter-religious understanding, the editor of the *Pentecostal Evangel* claims, "The Moslems of today are the 'most missionary' of all the false religionists. From their colleges in Egypt they are turning out hundreds of graduates, everyone to be a missionary of Mohammed." This is alarming because "their message is one of war and not peace. Any day every Moslem may be called to a 'holy war' against both Christian and Jew."[110] Pentecostals did not have a monopoly on Islamophobia, which was pervasive in the secular and religious media of America. Borrowing fuel for the fire from *The Presbyterian*, the editor of the *Pentecostal Evangel* quotes a few acerbic lines from E. E. Helms, who writes, "Ten million Moslems are packed in and around Palestine. Nearly three million are within cry and call. The Arab sees in the incoming of the Jew into Palestine his outgoing. Therefore, while the Jew is enthusiastic to make Palestine his national home, the Arab is as enthusiastic to make it his national cemetery."[111]

Perhaps the editors of the Pentecostal periodicals did not fully comprehend the inflammatory nature of their publications. To speak approvingly of the destruction of the Dome of the Rock, as the Pentecostal periodicals did on a number of occasions, was tantamount to a sacrilege of the highest order for Muslims. Writing in 1932, Henry Proctor states the thinking behind such attitudes toward the Dome of the Rock: "Its removal will be a great source of joy to the Jewish people, because they are looking forward to a glorious rebuilt Temple at Jerusalem, to which they believe the Messiah will come suddenly . . ."[112] The editors of the Pentecostal periodicals borrowed a hefty amount of Islamophobia from kindred periodicals. One such example is found in the "Editor's Notebook" in the January 30, 1932 issue of the *Pentecostal Evangel*, which borrows material from S. J. Williams in the *Jewish Missionary Magazine*, which is indicative of the bias against the Arabs in the Pentecostal periodicals. Williams writes, "At the

108. "A Warning to Israel," *Trust* 24.9–10 (November–December 1925) 23–24.

109. Childe, "Christ's Answer to the Challenge of Fascism and Communism," *Pentecostal Evangel* (October 31, 1931) 7.

110. "Will the Moslems Rise?" *Pentecostal Evangel* (December 5, 1931) 5.

111. "The Editor's Notebook," *Pentecostal Evangel* (January 30, 1932) 5.

112. Proctor, "The Times of the Gentiles," *The Elim Evangel and Foursquare Revivalist* 13.38 (September 16, 1932) 596.

time of the massacre two years ago only thirty British police were on duty. But now the force has been enlarged to 700 police and over 2,000 soldiers." Williams explains why the increased British force was necessary: "A strong undercurrent of political hatred and intrigue frequently bursts out into public speeches and newspaper warnings. Jamal Husseini, secretary of the former Arab National Delegation to London, before a large group of American ministers and Sunday School teachers in the Hotel Fast, Jerusalem, this summer, boldly affirmed that Palestine is due for more severe Arab-Jewish clashes than ever before." Williams quotes Hyman Jacobs, a Hebrew-Christian missionary in Jerusalem, who likens Palestine to "a house where two brothers claim ownership; each side shows the will of their father written in his favor, and each cries, 'All is mine.' The two documents are the Old Testament and the Koran the two brothers are modern Ishmael and Israel, and the fight is on. We shall not be surprised if these little sparks, falling on dry prairie land, may some day burn into a prairie fire which will bring ruin and desolation from Dan to Beersheba." According to M. F. Mogannam, secretary of the Arab executive, trained in an American university, the Arabs would never recognize either the British mandate over Palestine or the Zionist movement. "And," said he, "if it comes to giving up our lives, many of us are ready to do that." According to M. R. Akhtar, editor of the *Falestin*, a weekly newspaper published by a Christian Arab in Jaffa, "In this part of the East what I see for the future is a United States of Arab peoples." Williams also reports, "Maulana Ahawkat Ali, brother of the dead Indian Moslem chief, declared in Jerusalem in late August that if the British government did not accede to certain Arab demands, their co-religionists in Syria, Arabia, Iraq, Persia, India, Egypt, Tripoli, Tunis and all the way across North Africa to Morocco will unite to defend Moslem interests." The editor then comments, "How long will it be before the Moslem world, 'including Persia, Libya, and Egypt, will be joined by Russia and a sovietized Germany in the battle of Armageddon against the Zionists, backed probably by the European League of Nations'? And will not America also be in this conflict? Joel speaks of 'all nations' being here."[113] The specter of Armageddon as the solution to the Arab-Zionist conflict was widely disseminated in the Pentecostal periodicals.

The *Pentecostal Evangel* had its good moments. In an article entitled, "Isaac and Ishmael Reconciled," it reports,

> On the eve of the Jewish Feast of Pentecost, twenty Arab notables came out to greet the scrolls of the Law, which were ceremoniously, re-instated in the temporary synagogue, kissed the scrolls, begged the forgiveness of the God of Torah for Arabs having harmed Jews, and swore to safeguard Jewish residents in the future. "We have not suffered half the trials and tribulations we deserve for murdering your brethren," said one of the Arabs to Haim Bajayo, a rabbi who conducted the scrolls back to Hebron. The same Arab guarded Jewish worshippers on their festival visit to the Patriarch's cave at Machpelah, protecting them against possible molestation.[114]

113. "The Editor's Notebook," *Pentecostal Evangel* (January 30, 1932) 5.
114. "Isaac and Ishmael Reconciled," *Pentecostal Evangel* (January 7, 1933) 4.

For the most part, though, the *Pentecostal Evangel* inflamed the prejudices of its reading audience. In "Ishmael's Opposition," the editor tells of a new paper being published in Jerusalem, *The Arab,* which "seeks to inflame Arab nationalist sentiment by articles dealing with their glorious past." One of its articles describes and illustrates with a full-page portrait the battle of Hattin, in which Saladin crushed the Crusaders on July 4, 1187. The editor explains that the Arabs are inflamed with the thought of possessing Palestine, Syria, Iraq, and Trans-Jordania, with Feisal the king of Iraq, as their king. This is because the majority of the Arabs are fiercely opposed to the Jews, and also to Great Britain, which holds the mandate of Palestine. The editor then offers the customary trailer of commentary: "How true is the prophecy given four thousand years ago concerning Ishmael, 'He will be a wild man; his hand will be against every man, and every man's hand against him.'"[115] Such characterizations only served to solidify Pentecostal prejudices against the Arabs of Palestine.

In the final analysis, the solution to the Arab-Zionist crisis in Palestine proposed in the Pentecostal press was not realistic. Apparently approving of the views of Newman Watts, a London journalist, the *Pentecostal Evangel* ran his article on "The Problem in Palestine." Watts searches for the reasons for the discord between Jews and Arabs in Palestine. He finds that the most vital difference between the two sides is religious and is driven by "political and religious elements far removed from any definite participation in the life of Palestine." He concludes, "Above all, however, Jew and Arab will be reconciled when they see in the Lord Jesus Christ their hope and salvation. Christ and Christ alone is the uniting bond between these two irreconcilables."[116] In effect, Watts is suggesting that if Jews and Muslims would give up their religions and convert to Christianity, the problem of Palestine could be solved.

Formation of the State of Israel in 1948

Back in 1910 the *Bridegroom's Messenger* had predicted the establishment of the state of Israel. The editor writes, "The beginning of building up of Zion may be altogether in unbelief, but when God's ancient people become a nation, and are again established in the land of their fathers, he can cause that this 'Nation be born in a day.' The unexpected and unprecedented changes of the past year emboldens our faith in a miracle working God who has told us to watch."[117] And the Pentecostals did watch and wait eagerly for the establishment of the state of Israel. The *Pentecostal Evangel* approvingly quotes the Jewish biographer Emil Ludwig on the Jewish situation. He says that "only in the union of all Jews all over the world in a national unit capable of representing Jewry and sitting at Geneva along with the fifty-two nations—as the fifty-third nation, in fact—can any solution be reached. This must and will be done. When the Jews have thus united as a nation, then only can they stand up with respect as one among the nations of the world, along with other minorities and smaller nations." The editor

115. "Ishmael's Opposition," *Pentecostal Evangel* (March 11, 1922) 5.

116. Watts, "The Problem in Palestine," *Pentecostal Evangel* (December 27, 1947) 10.

117. Sexton, "Watch the Fig Tree," *Bridegroom's Messenger* 3.55 (February 1, 1910) 1.

comments, "The time is coming when Israel shall take her God-given place among the nations and exert her God-appointed influence. 'And the Lord shall make thee the head and not the tail.' Deut. 28:13."[118] As an ardent Zionist, the editor of the *Pentecostal Evangel* insists, "The only solution of the Jewish problem is for them to take their place among other nations and live a normal national life in a land of their own."[119]

When in May of 1948 the Zionists proclaimed the formation of the state of Israel, the Pentecostal periodicals rejoiced.[120] In an article simply entitled, "Israel," the editor of the *Pentecostal Holiness Advocate* cites Isaiah 66:8, "Shall a nation be born at once?" and says that 700 years before Christ the Prophet Isaiah was busy writing last week's headline. "Yet, with all our fore-warning, the formation of the new State of Israel slipped up on us catching the whole world and most of the church by surprise. We had been preaching for years that it was coming and then when it came, we gasped and asked, 'Can it be a fact?' Yes, it is a fact brought to pass just as God, through His prophet, foretold it twenty-six hundred years ago." According to the *Pentecostal Holiness Advocate*, the significance of the state of Israel was purely eschatological. "So this is it—the beginning of the end. It won't be long now. It can't be long. Perhaps before this comment ever sees daylight on the printed page, the *Great Event* will have taken place, the Lord will have come and caught His bride away in the Rapture." No matter if the Lord should tarry another week, one thing is sure, "now we are on the last lap of the journey home."[121]

After a week to think it over, the *Pentecostal Holiness Advocate* backed away from its initial optimism, taking a skeptical view of the spiritual significance of the new state of Israel. "Israel's government is of the earth, not of God. The earth is his mother, politically speaking. The United States jumped to recognize the birth; but God was not excited by it. He is not yet ready to claim the new nation as His own." The editor downplays the importance of the outcome of Israel's war against the Arabs, "for Israel's *big day* is yet to come." What is really important is the conversion of the Jews during the Great Tribulation after the catching away of the bride of Christ. Out of this travail, the Jews will recognize at long last that the "Stone, which was set at nought by the builders, has become the head stone of the corner."[122] By the end of September, 1948, G. H. Montgomery, editor of the *Pentecostal Holiness Advocate*, was even more skeptical. He writes, "The new State has its political entity, the recognition of the world's greatest nations—that is all." Montgomery alleges that the nation of Israel has "no compass, no chart, no pilot, no anchor of the soul." As the scattered Jews come straggling back to the homeland of their fathers, hoping to take up where they left off, they

118. "Israel's National Destiny," *Pentecostal Evangel* (February 3, 1934) 5.

119. "The First Jewish Ship," *Pentecostal Evangel* (February 17, 1934) 5.

120. Appelman, "God Over Palestine," *Pentecostal Evangel* (May 14, 1948) 6–7; "God's Future Plans for Israel," *Pentecostal Evangel* (May 29, 1948) 4–5, 14. Gartenhaus, "The New State of Israel," *Pentecostal Evangel* (July 31, 1948) 7; Zeildman, "The Commonwealth of Israel," *Pentecostal Evangel* (November 13, 1948) 3, 11.

121. "Israel . . . ," *Pentecostal Holiness Advocate* 32.4 (May 27, 1948) 1.

122. "Before She Travailed," *Pentecostal Holiness Advocate* 32.5 (June 3, 1948) 1.

find only dissension, discord, and terrorism to greet them. Like a jigsaw puzzle with a missing piece, Israel's faith is missing. Without faith in the Messiah, Israel's trouble will continue until one day the Antichrist appears and eventually Jesus will return and the "scales of the ages will fall from their eyes, and they will look upon Him whom their fathers pierced, and He will be their Redeemer and Messiah."[123] The author's point is that no matter what the nations of the world may do or say, Israel's future will unfold according to the plan outlined in the Pentecostal metanarrative.

MISSIONARY BROKERS OF PENTECOSTAL ZIONISM

The Pentecostal missionaries were not the originators of Pentecostal Zionism. Rather, they inherited their Zionist sympathies by virtue of their acceptance of the role of Palestine in the Pentecostal metanarrative. The Pentecostal metanarrative supplied the missionaries with a larger story, which gave coherence and meaning to current events. As with every metanarrative, the Pentecostal narrative served a certain interest. In regards to Pentecostal Zionism, that interest was the legitimization the Pentecostal movement, which was adjudicated by linking Pentecostalism and the restoration of the Jewish homeland in Palestine.

Hayden White argues that stories provide meaning by "emplotment," that is, by the way in which a sequence of events is fashioned into a story. A plot is seldom chosen consciously by the storyteller. In most cases narratives are cast in one of four stereotypical modes of emplotment, namely, *tragedy, comedy, satire,* and *romance.* White claims that "since no given set or sequence of real events is intrinsically tragic, comic, farcical, and so on, but can be constructed as such only by the imposition of the structure of a given story type on the events, it is the choice of the story type and its imposition upon the events that endow them with meaning." The upshot of White's notion of emplotment is that it raises the questions of (a) whether *meaning* is already present *in* or created by imposing a mode of emplotment *on* a certain pool of evidence; (b) whether the narrative refers to a reality outside itself or must be understood as an autonomous, nonreferential, purely subjective attempt to reshape a certain interpretive community's *understanding* of the past; and (c) whether the truth-claims of narrative discourses are different from the truth-claims of fictional literature. Postmodernists argue that the distinction between factual narratives and fictional narratives can no longer be upheld and that the truth claims of historical narratives cannot be more "true" than fiction, only "different." In light of the postmodernist historiographical theory of White, if taken to its logical conclusion, the Pentecostal metanarrative was a subjective representation of the Pentecostal worldview as opposed to an account of what actually did happen or might have happened but did not.[124] That is to say, it was not fact or fiction, but rather a representation of the Pentecostal reality.

---

123. G. H. Montgomery, "Israel Without God," *Pentecostal Holiness Advocate* 32.22 (September 30, 1948) 1.

124. Kofoed, *Test and History*, 12–14.

Generally speaking, the discourse of the missionaries in Palestine constitutes a representation of events on the ground in Palestine as seen through the lens of the Pentecostal perspective. More specifically, the contribution of the missionaries to Pentecostal Zionism was functional. The missionaries functioned as brokers of Pentecostal Zionism. A "broker" is one who arranges transactions, a dealer in second-hand goods. The missionaries were ideally situated to play the role of brokers because as eye-witnesses they observed and reported on the unfolding of events on the ground in Palestine. In their reports the missionaries kept the readers of the Pentecostal periodical abreast of the latest developments in the building of a Jewish national home. In one sense, the missionaries were similar to journalists purporting to report news on location with a modicum of impartiality. But in another sense, they were partisans whose commentary was colored by an ideological commitment to Pentecostal Zionism. The missionaries represented the events they reported so as to confirm the Pentecostal metanarrative. In so doing they only told half the story, the Zionist side, or, more precisely, the Pentecostal version of it.

Two examples of missionary reports with a Pentecostal Zionist slant will be presented, the first by S. B. Rohold and the second by Laura Radford.

S. B. Rohold

In 1929 S. B. Rohold, a Jewish Pentecostal missionary in Haifa, surveyed the present position of the Jews in Palestine.[125] He states, "What fanciful, imaginary and inventive stories are being told with great zest by orators, speakers on platform, pulpit and in the press, which the simple, the guileless, yes, also even the wise believe!" Rohold mentions the tales he has in mind. Some were saying that the Jews had completed plans for the rebuilding of the temple and were secretly making the necessary utensils. Others were saying that the Jews had laid up stores of ammunition, guns, tanks, and airplanes, waiting for the command to rise up and kill all the Muslims and Christians. "Such were the invented stories about tiny little Palestine, with the small Jewish population of 165,000."[126] An example of the kind of reckless "stories" Rohold spurns is an article in the *Full Gospel Advocate,* in which the author claims that a rabbi had happily exclaimed, "The Mosque of Omar will be torn down and a wonderful temple like Solomon's will be built there." He goes on to say, "A large group of Jerusalem Jews have petitioned the League of Nations for a portion of the old temple site to be awarded to the Jewish nation."[127] Such views were not limited to American Pentecostals. In the British Pentecostal periodical, the *Elim Evangel,* Charles Kingston passed on the rumor that repairs on the Dome of the Rock had been halted because the Muslims could not locate a deed of ownership of the land. From this Kingston reasons that "this may

---

125. Rohold, "The Present Position," *Trust* (May–June 1929) 7–11, 14–15.

126. Ibid., 7.

127. "Material for Solomon's Temple Now Ready," *Full Gospel Advocate* (January 10, 1930) 4. Interest among Pentecostals in the rebuilding of the temple intensified after the formation of the state of Israel in 1948. See Zeidman, "Rebuilding the Nation and Temple," *Pentecostal Evangel* (June 18, 1949) 5–6, 12–13.

mean that Jewish money will buy the Mosque, and either convert into the temple for worship of the God of their Fathers, or rebuild upon its ancient site a new Temple."[128] Rohold recognized that such stories were simply spurious rumors.

From his vantage point in Palestine, Rohold reports what he sees in Palestine, especially in regards to the spiritual condition of his fellow Jews. But his story is also a subjective representation that serves his interest as a Jewish Christian evangelist. When most Christians think of Palestine, their attention is immediately drawn to Jerusalem, but not so with Rohold. He acknowledges that Jerusalem is the nominal capital of Palestine, but regrets that its religious life is dominated by Christian groups who are warring over their holy places and Jews who are busy disputing meaningless Talmudic minutiae and denouncing one another. He says that the real action is in the countryside and takes his readers to the top of a mountain near Nazareth which commemorates the place from which the people of the synagogue wanted to cast off Jesus. He asks his readers to imagine what Jesus might have seen from this promontory.

> There is something more which our Lord saw with His wonderful eye that could behold the ages to come, He saw what we see now as the "Tents of Israel," the many Jewish colonies. Forty thousand Zionist *Chalutzim*, laboring with all the fibre of their being, reclaiming the land, "Thy land shall no more be desolate," rebuilding the national home. He also saw what we see now, that the swamps are removed, malaria eliminated, physical health restored, beautiful gardens, large fields of corn, orchards, fat cattle with pure milk, olives, and vines.

Rohold perceives that Jesus saw further, "that the spiritual awakening would come from those unselfish young men and young women, whom we venture still to call the 'returning remnant.' It is here (Isa. 11:11–12) that one can come and study at close quarters the new leadership in things spiritual."[129]

Rohold's rounds of evangelistic visitation took him to the Jewish agricultural colonies, where he found a remarkable openness to discuss the claims of Christ. Yet, Rohold is pained by what he has read of these colonists in the Pentecostal press, which accused them of being "irreligious, immoral, Bolshevists; their aim was to destroy Christianity (to destroy Christianity in Palestine is an anomaly). How entirely false were all these so-called predictions. Jewish missionaries are preaching freely in Palestine, even more freely than in Britain and America." The colonists have accomplished much, which, Rohold says, would take pages to tell. "But all this does not compensate and fill the longing hearts of the returning remnant. It is a spiritual longing. They have come to a close realization, a deep consciousness, that although they have succeeded in redeeming a part of the land, Israel as a people is not redeemed." Rohold was finding that the strictures of rabbis against mingling with missionaries like him had lost their force. "The annual outcry and warning against the Missions has lost its savor. There has been established 'a point of contact,' which no Rabbinical anathemas can possibly destroy.

128. Kingston, "The Jew in Relation to the Coming of the Lord," *The Elim Evangel and Foursquare Revivalist* 8.17 (September 1, 1927) 261.

129. Rohold, "The Present Position," *Trust* (May–June 1929) 7–11, 14–15.

We fully realize that there is a true 'softening of the heart.' To us it is one of the greatest signs, that inspires us with every possible hope."[130]

Rohold was a broker of Pentecostal Zionism. He accepted the belief of most Pentecostals that the return of the Jews to Palestine was divinely orchestrated. However, he rejected characterizations of the Jews of Palestine that in his mind were misrepresentations of what was actually happening. Rohold attempted to disabuse Pentecostals of misconceptions in their minds implanted by the oversimplifications of the complex reality of current events in the Holy Land.

Laura Radford

Laura Radford was also a broker of Pentecostal Zionism. Writing in the aftermath of the Wailing Wall Riots of 1929, Radford admits, "We ought not to have been surprised at the sudden outbreak of the Arab hordes on the 23rd of August." She says that for some days beforehand "the general talk had been that the Grand Mufti of Jerusalem was calling the Moslems of all the villages in Palestine to come into Jerusalem on that Friday to massacre all the Jews, yet no one believed that such an outrageous act could possibly be committed, and the Government and people were alike taken unawares." Radford credits most of the Muslims in Jerusalem and other cities for refusing to comply with the Mufti's call for an uprising, but "the ignorant village youths fell easy prey to the promise of the all the spoil they could gather, and in the days following, the possession of a Kodak, piano stool, silver sugar bowl, or some other such article, has been the cause of arrest of many men in the villages from which the rioters came." Radford personally attests to the horror of the "cruel sights of the day before and to take from our ears the echoes yet there of the cries of the men, women and children who were being beaten and cruelly tortured all over the land, as well as within a few yards of our house."[131]

Radford provides graphic details of the riots, observing that the success of the uprising in Jerusalem was,

> a signal for a general attack upon the Jews all over the land, and in many places entire families, including even the little children, were cut to pieces by the rioters with fiendish delight. A large number of rioters were mere youths who had been stirred to this mad frenzy by their religious and political leaders, leaders who stayed in places of security while these hordes of ignorant youths rush heedlessly into death itself; but as they fell they were hurriedly carried away so that no one can estimate how many were killed. The official report fixes the total deaths at 250, but many of us believe it was more than double that number.[132]

Radford was disappointed that most of the Arab papers took a defiant attitude against the Government, stipulating that there could be no peace until the Balfour

---

130. Ibid., 15.

131. Radford, "A Day of Terror in Jerusalem," *Latter Rain Evangel* (November 1929) 21.

132. Ibid.

Declaration was annulled. Unfortunately, as she saw it, many of the Palestinian Christians were drawn into the controversy "by the flattery and intrigue of the Arab (Moslem) leaders. The Christians are but a small part of the population of Palestine, and confess they are too weak to stand alone, but they are afraid to side with the Government against the Moslems."[133]

Radford mentions the upcoming Committee of Inquiry and wonders if it is up to the task of dealing with tensions rooted in the Crusades of centuries before. She writes, "And now the world powers are forced to consider how to control, if not to eliminate from Palestine, this power of 'systematized deviltry' that has suddenly burst forth with the same atrocities that accompanied all the Moslem invasions of the early centuries."[134] In a follow-up report, Radford describes the conditions in Jerusalem:

> Outside the city things are slowly swinging back to normalcy, but not so in Jerusalem. The anti-Jewish boycott continues, and fear and hatred have paralyzed every activity in the city; shoppers, whether Christian or Moslem, if seen going into a Jewish shop will be beaten or stoned. Jews are yet frequently stabbed and that without provocation. On Nov. 2nd, which is known as Balfour Day, all Arab shops were closed and most of the houses draped in black as another protest against the Balfour declaration. The atmosphere is so charged with hatred and spiritual darkness that it seems hard to breathe in Jerusalem, and so I ask you again to pray for the peace of Jerusalem, and that the door be kept open for us to minister Christ to perplexed and troubled hearts.[135]

It is evident that Radford made a game effort to avoid casting a blanket of aspersion on all Arabs. She empathizes with the dilemma of Arab Christians who went along with the boycott out of fear of the repercussions of appearing to be a collaborator with the British. Nevertheless, her true sympathies lay elsewhere. Understandably, the trauma of the riots had the effect of reinforcing her abhorrence of Islam and solidifying her Zionist sympathies.

Although both Rohold and Radford strived to dispel the blind spots and oversimplifications of Pentecostal Zionism, they nevertheless presented one-dimensional perspectives of the question of Palestine. As with other proponents of Christian Zionism, the Pentecostal missionaries in Palestine were slanted in favor of the Zionist project and out of touch with the infringements of the civil rights of the Arab majority. We now turn to an assessment of the legacy of Pentecostal Zionism.

133. Ibid., 21–22.

134. Ibid.

135. Radford, "News from the Mission Fields," *Latter Rain Evangel* (February 1930) 18.

T HE LEGACY OF the Pentecostal mission in Palestine is intertwined with the legacy of Pentecostal Zionism. This chapter will analyze the diffusion of Pentecostal Zionism in connection with the Pentecostal missionaries in Palestine, beginning with Derek Prince, who married a Pentecostal missionary in Palestine, Lydia Christensen. Prince played a leading role in the charismatic and the pro-Israel movements in the 1960s and 1970s. His views on philosemitism will be discussed and his theological influence will be traced in the writings of contemporary renewalist, i.e., Pentecostal and charismatic, authors. This is the bright side of the legacy of Pentecostal Zionism. The dark side consists of two repercussions of Pentecostal Zionism, namely, Islamophobia and a disregard for the human rights of Palestinian Arabs. Two exhibits of the dark side of the legacy of Pentecostal Zionism will be presented. The first exhibit consists of two pieces of evidence in the form of articles written by former Pentecostal missionaries in Palestine, Vera Swarztrauber and George Carmichael. The second exhibit is comprised of three articles on the Six Day War of 1967 published in the *Pentecostal Evangel*. These exhibits will be faulted for telling only the pro-Israel side of the story of Israeli-Arab conflict and neglecting the Arab side. To fill in the gap, the Palestinian Arab side of the story will be told. Finally, an assessment of the contribution of Pentecostal Zionism to peace in Israel/Palestine will be offered.

DIFFUSION OF PENTECOSTAL ZIONISM

The legacy of the Pentecostal mission in Palestine is not confined to classical Pentecostal circles. There was a direct historical connection between the Pentecostal missionaries in Palestine, the charismatic movement, and the pro-Israel movement. The one who forged this connection was Derek Prince (1915–2003).

Derek Prince

The ministerial career of Derek Prince spanned the Pentecostal and charismatic movements.[1] In the early 1940s Prince did doctoral studies at Cambridge in classical phi-

---

1. The Pentecostal movement began in 1901. Its trademark doctrine, known as "initial evidence," held that all Christians should seek a post-conversion religious experience called baptism of the Holy Spirit with the accompanying physical evidence of speaking in tongues. The charismatic movement

losophy, specializing in Plato. During World War II he enlisted with the Royal Army as a noncombatant. During his military training in Scarborough, England, he visited a small Elim Pentecostal church, and was converted and baptized in the Holy Spirit. Shortly afterward he was shipped out to North Africa. During a leave in Palestine, he was baptized in the Jordan River by Saul Benjamin, a Pentecostal missionary whom Prince had met in Jerusalem.[2] After the war Prince was assigned to a duty station in Palestine. In February, 1946 he married a Danish Pentecostal missionary, Lydia Christensen, who earlier had collaborated with "Laura Radcliffe" in her work with orphan children in Jerusalem.[3] After his marriage to Christensen, Prince moved to Ramallah and shared in her ministry to the Arab population and in parenting her eight adopted daughters, of whom six were Jewish, one was Arab, and one was English. Her home served as a mission outpost and hospitality station for lonely British soldiers, like Prince. Christensen ushered Prince into the circle of Pentecostal missionaries, from whom he imbibed an enthusiastic philosemitism.

As the tension mounted in Ramallah during the debate in the United Nations over the partition of Palestine, Prince and his family received death threats, compelling them to relocate to Jerusalem at the end of 1947. When in November, 1947 the UN decided to provide a place of refuge in Palestine for the Jewish populations displaced by World War II, Arab riots broke out in Jerusalem. After the British Mandate terminated in May, 1948 and full-scale warfare ensued between five Arab nations and the state of Israel, the Pentecostal missionaries fled their posts and the Prince family moved into the Pentecostal "Shemariah" mission station founded by the late A. Elizabeth Brown, where they remained during intense fighting until they too were evacuated in the summer of 1948.[4] The Prince family landed in London, where Prince planted a Pentecostal church. For eight years he served as a pastor of this congregation. In 1957 Derek and Lydia Prince went to Kenya, Africa as missionaries. In 1959 they adopted their ninth child, an African baby girl. Later the Princes relocated to Canada and then the United States, from which Derek launched an international teaching ministry. His influence on the global charismatic movement was quite significant. Prince was a central figure in the Shepherding Movement.[5] Eventually he returned to Jerusalem and with his second wife, Ruth, and they built a home, dedicated as a place of intercession, fellowship, and the promotion of "understanding and reconciliation between Jews and Christians."[6] For the last twenty years of his life, Derek Prince divided his time

---

began in 1960. While gravitating toward the Pentecostal experience of Spirit baptism and speaking in tongues, the charismatic movement differed from classical Pentecostalism in that its adherents eschewed the doctrine of initial evidence and remained in their mainline denominations rather than join Pentecostal denominations. Pentecostals and charismatics both claim that the New Testament gifts of the Spirit are operative today. Barrett and Johnson, "Global Statistics," 290–91.

2. Mansfield, *Derek Prince: A Biography*, 98.

3. A pseudonym for Laura Radford. See Prince, *Appointment in Jerusalem*, 101.

4. Perkins, "Israel and Missions," 18.

5. Moore, "Shepherding Movement," *NIDPCM*, 1060–2062.

6. "Derek Prince: The Man and his Ministry," 13.

between Fort Lauderdale, Florida, and Israel until his death on September 24, 2003 in Jerusalem.[7]

Prince's *The Last Word on the Middle East* (1982) was inspired by a formative spiritual experience he had in Palestine in 1946.[8] One evening, as Prince was standing on a hill overlooking Jerusalem from a point straddling Mount Scopus and the Mount of Olives, looking out over the old city of Jerusalem and the temple mount, he came to the conclusion that God was about to restore a Jewish state in Palestine. As he meditated upon passages of the Hebrew prophets Zechariah and Ezekiel, the conviction settled upon him that the global destiny of the world would hinge on the nation of Israel. Prince explains the title of his book: "The central theme of biblical prophecy, as it is being unfolded in our time, revolves around the land and the people of Israel. God is carrying out His predetermined plan to regather the Jewish people from their worldwide dispersion and restore them to their ancient homeland. The best way to comprehend this plan is the let God's Word speak for itself. In the Bible, God Himself has already spoken *the last word on the Middle East*."[9] The main points of *The Last Word on the Middle East* will be exposited because Prince's argument is relevant to the legacy of the Pentecostal mission in Palestine, the first aspect of which is philosemitism.

Prince writes, "Over the past two years I had witnessed part of the process of the healing of these two breaks—between that of the people of Israel and their land. Did the logic of history indicate that this would be prelude to the healing of the second break—that between the people of Israel and the Christian Church?"[10] Prince's answer was in the affirmative. While resuming his doctoral research at Hebrew University in 1946–48, Prince studied the post-biblical history of the Jewish people and Christian anti-Semitism, from which he concluded that, "Throughout the long centuries of their dispersion, the worst sufferings of the Jewish people were inflicted upon them by Christians. Christian anti-Semitism was based on and nourished by a combination of theology and popular legend."[11] He lamented that the charge of deicide leveled against the Jewish people by Christians led to the wholesale massacre of Jewish communities, one example of which occurred in the twelfth century when the Crusaders burned to death a congregation of Jewish people in a Jerusalem synagogue.[12] Prince's chilling assessment was that the Jewish people were the innocent victims of false Christian theology. Prince emphatically rejected replacement theology, which holds that the church has superseded Israel, arguing that God "still regards Israel as His people" and has never wavered in his "commitment to restore them both to their land and

---

7. For autobiographical information, see Derek Prince, *Jubilee 1995 Celebration: 50th Year in Ministry*, 1–23. For biographical information on Derek Prince, see Linda Howard, "A New Beginning"; and Mansfield, *Derek Prince: A Biography*.

8. Prince, *The Last Word on the Middle East*, 13–25.

9. Ibid., 54.

10. Ibid., 21.

11. Ibid., 27.

12. Ibid., 109.

His favor."[13] He laid the main responsibility for the violence done against the Jewish people, including the Holocaust, at the door of the Christian church. "We could sum up the outworking of the historical processes involved by saying that the Nazis merely reaped a harvest that the Church had sown."[14]

Prince predicted a spiritual renewal among the Jewish people on the basis of his observation of "a significant change in the general attitude of the Jewish people toward the work of the Holy Spirit and toward the Person of Jesus . . . It is now happening before our eyes! The Jewish people are once again ready to receive and respond to God's Holy Spirit."[15] He contended that is was now incumbent upon the church to play its part. He asks, "How shall we respond?" First of all, Prince urged Christians to accept their responsibility for the crimes of anti-Semitism, including culpability for the Holocaust. Further, he asserted that Christians can make amends by "becoming co-workers with God in blessing Israel and all nations. Specifically, this would entail praising God for the restoration of Israel, proclaiming the good news of the re-gathering of the Jewish people in their homeland, praying for the peace of Jerusalem, and comforting Israel in view of the centuries of suffering endured by the Jewish people. The challenge set before the Christian church, Prince avers, is to seize the opportunity for the special ministry of preparing the hearts of Israel for the second coming of Jesus. "God is calling Bible-believing Christians worldwide to take part in this end-time ministry of preparing the hearts of Israel for their Messiah."[16] The point I want to make is that Prince was espousing the main tenets of what was to become the evangelical Christian pro-Israel movement.

Derek Prince's international teaching ministry expanded widely in the 1970s. According to his biographer, Stephen Mansfield, "His chief theme in his latter years was love for Israel." According to Mansfield, Prince held replacement theology in disdain because of its role in causing anti-Semitism. Prince feared that Western Christians had not grasped the theological significance of the formation of the state of Israel. If they had, he believed that they would have renounced replacement theology, and in so doing, their admiration and support of Israel would have been more resolute. Furthermore, Mansfield writes, "The truth is that Derek understood the whole of his life in terms of Israel . . . Asked on his deathbed what his last commission from God had been, he said hoarsely, 'To pray for the peace of Jerusalem.'"[17] During his life Prince had many opportunities to proclaim his pro-Israel views. He says of himself,

> In recent years it has been my privilege to make this proclamation in the United States and in various countries around the world—some within the continent of Europe, and others that were formerly part of the British Empire. Among the former are Germany, Switzerland and Sweden. Among the latter are England, Northern Ireland, Australia, New Zealand, Jamaica and South Africa. In each of

13. Ibid., 81.
14. Ibid., 110.
15. Ibid., 83.
16. Ibid., 125.
17. Mansfield, *Derek Prince*, 270–71.

these places I have directed people's attention to this specific verse in Jeremiah 31:10, and then I have said to them: "Today this Scripture is being fulfilled in your ears."[18]

In the very places mentioned by Prince the Christian pro-Israel movement has thrived among charismatics. Prince is recognized by renewalist participants in this movement as a guiding thinker. Malcolm Hedding, the current executive director of the International Christian Embassy in Jerusalem and an ordained Pentecostal pastor from South Africa, quotes Prince at the beginning of his *Understanding Israel.*[19] Now we will turn our attention to the next step in the historical development of philosemitism in the Renewal movement, the Christian pro-Israel movement, through which Prince's ideas on the church and Israel were disseminated.

Pro-Israel Movement

Beginning in the 1970s, numerous Christian pro-Israel organizations were formed in Israel, the United States, and elsewhere. Perhaps the most influential of these groups in Israel itself is the International Christian Embassy of Jerusalem. Because of its charismatic leanings and its sponsorship of an annual event drawing thousands of its supporters to Jerusalem from across the globe, many of whom are affiliated with Pentecostal and charismatic churches, we will focus on the Embassy. Its story tells us a great deal about the legacy of philosemitism that is cherished in the Pentecostal-charismatic renewal movement.

The Embassy is an offshoot of the Almond Tree Branch, a small group of evangelicals and charismatics that met weekly in Jerusalem during the mid-1970s for prayer, singing, Bible study, and discussion. This group came up with the idea of organizing a major gathering of Christian supporters of Israel to celebrate the Feast of Tabernacles, based on the Old Testament injunction in Zechariah 14:16 for Gentiles to gather in Jerusalem for this festival.[20] Until this time there was no notable Christian celebration of Succoth. The first celebration was held in 1979 as a weeklong assembly comprised of speeches, sermons, seminars, a biblical meal at the Dead Sea, and a "love for Israel" march through the streets of Jerusalem. The Embassy came into existence the next year.

When in 1980 the Israeli Knesset proclaimed Jerusalem as the capital of Israel, most of the embassies and consulates in Jerusalem relocated to Tel Aviv in protest. The Almond Tree Branch group came out in support of Israel by announcing the creation of an International Christian Embassy Jerusalem (hereafter ICEJ). Johann Luckhoff was designated as the administrative director of the Embassy and Jan van der Hoeven assumed the position of ICEJ spokesman. The Embassy's logo, two olive branches

18. Prince, *Last Word on the Middle East,* 117.

19. Hedding, *Understanding Israel,* 19, 20, 23.

20. "Then the survivors from all the nations that have attacked Jerusalem will go up year after year to worship the King, the LORD Almighty, and to celebrate the Feast of Tabernacles." Zechariah 14:16 (NIV).

spread over a globe with Jerusalem at its center, is indicative of its self-proclaimed mission. Based on Zechariah 14:16, it was said to symbolize "the great day when Zechariah's prophecy will be fulfilled, and all nations will come up to Jerusalem to keep the Feast of Tabernacles during Messiah's reign on earth."[21] At a time when the Israeli government was besieged with worldwide criticism in the media, it welcomed the support of the ICEJ and helped in securing a suitable building in Jerusalem, which, as it turned out, was the former residence of the illustrious Jewish theologian, Martin Buber. Besides sponsoring the annual Feast of Tabernacles event, which draws about 5,000–7,000 attendees per year, the ICEJ has raises funds for Jewish immigration and carries out benevolence programs for new Jewish immigrants. The ICEJ maintains branches in many countries.[22]

The message of the ICEJ is philosemitism. Its overarching goals are to proclaim the message of Christian Zionism to the international Christian community and to convince Christians of their responsibility to comfort and support the state of Israel.[23] Its critics depict the Embassy leaders as the darlings of the Likud party leadership and a stumbling block to peace, claiming, "The ICEJ has been a divisive rather than a reconciling factor in the Middle East, particularly between the Arab and Jew in the 'holy' land. ICEJ's literature and presentations by its leaders convey hostility toward Islam and the Arab governments."[24] Among the Embassy's critics are Israelis with an aversion to Christian missionary activity among Jewish people. They fear that the Embassy may harbor a hidden missionary agenda. As a result, the stickiest issue in the relation of the ICEJ and Israelis is its attitude toward Messianic Judaism, which is made up of Jewish followers of Jesus who are ardent evangelists. This is a vexing dilemma because the Embassy and the messianic movement in Israel are natural allies, given their shared affinity to the renewal movement.

Messianic Judaism

Peter Hocken includes the rise of Messianic Judaism as one of the major surprises marking the growth of the Pentecostal-charismatic movement of the twentieth-century.[25] The connection Hocken makes between Messianic Judaism and the charismatic movement sheds light on the historical development of the legacy of the Pentecostal mission in Palestine. Despite the best efforts of Pentecostals and others, prior to the

21. Ariel, *Philosemites or Antisemites?* 21.

22. According to the ICEJ website, branches are located in Austria, Australia, Barbados, Brazil, Canada, Colombia, Congo, Costa Rica, Croatia, the Czech Republic, Denmark, El Salvador, Estonia, Fiji, Finland, France, Germany, Guatemala, Honduras, Hungary, Iceland, Ireland, India, Latvia, Malaysia, Mexico, Nepal, Netherlands, New Zealand, Nigeria, Norway, Philippines, Portugal, Russia, Slovakia, the Solomon Islands, South Africa, South Pacific Islands, Sri Lanka, Sweden, Switzerland, Tanzania, the United Kingdom, Uruguay, the United States, and Zimbabwe. See http://www.icej.org/index.html.

23. Wagner, *Anxious for Armageddon*, 105–7.

24. Ibid., 105.

25. Hocken, *The Glory and the Shame: Reflections on the 20th-Century Outpouring of the Spirit*, 19–20.

1970s the results of Jewish evangelism were somewhat miniscule. There had always been a small number of Jews who acknowledged Jesus as Messiah. In the past, so-called "Hebrew Christians" abandoned their Jewish way of life and were absorbed into Gentile Christian culture. Beginning in the 1970s, however, the number of Jewish followers of Jesus increased as Jewish evangelism took a new twist. Culturally relevant outreach methods were pioneered by organizations such as Jews for Jesus and Chosen People Ministries. The name change of the Hebrew Christian Alliance of America to the Messianic Jewish Alliance of America signaled a resurgence of the Jewish roots of the Christian faith. The Messianic Jewish movement spawned congregations that observed the Jewish calendar and feasts, utilized Hebrew terminology, and adhered to a "messianic theology" based on the premise that Jewish followers of Jesus are still Jewish. When a Jewish person accepts Yeshua as Messiah, this does not involve a rejection of Judaism but rather its fulfillment. Messianic Jews therefore referred to themselves as "completed Jews." As one might imagine, this assertion proved to be controversial.

Returning to the legacy of the Pentecostal mission in Palestine, it is significant that Hocken identifies the charismatic movement as a significant factor in the growth of Messianic Judaism. He claims that "Messianic Judaism is predominately charismatic."[26] Hocken's claim is substantiated by the findings of an important study of the messianic movement in Israel. An extensive survey sponsored by the Caspari Center for Biblical and Jewish Studies in Jerusalem, conducted by Kai Kjaer-Hansen and Bodil F. Skjott in 1999, found that there were eighty-one Israeli Messianic Jewish congregations and house groups in Israel and Palestine. Approximately 6,000 people belong to these congregations, of whom about half are Jewish adults.[27] Although it is not widely known, many of the Israeli messianic fellowships are charismatic in character, that is, speaking in tongues, prophesying, and healing prayer are regular occurrences. A good portion of the Russian messianic congregations are Pentecostal. They differentiate themselves as either the "quiet Russians," who prefer a traditional worship style, or "noisy Russians," who use a more expressive, Western-influenced charismatic style.[28] Other charismatic congregations have been influenced by the Toronto blessing, which has caused division in Israel, as elsewhere.[29] Hocken offers an explanation of the charismatic element in Messianic Judaism: "In the wisdom of God it required the massive energy of this outpouring of the Spirit to make possible the creative interaction of Jewish forms of worship with the confession of Jesus as the Messiah."[30] Be that as it may, the fact remains that the messianic movement has played a pivotal role in the diffusion of the legacy of Pentecostal Zionism and its attendant philosemitism. As Hocken says, Messianic Judaism has faced the Christian community with crucial questions: What happened to the Jewish church of the origins? Can the Jewish roots of

26. Ibid., 38.

27. Kjaer-Hansen and Skjott, *Facts and Myths about Messianic Congregations in Israel*, 57–67.

28. Ibid., 51.

29. Ibid., 19.

30. Hocken, *The Glory and the Shame*, 38.

the church be restored? Further, Messianic Judaism has given rise to a body of popular literature that assesses the problems of replacement theology and anti-Semitism from a renewalist perspective.

To summarize, it has been shown that the legacy of Pentecostal Zionism consists of philosemitism, an attitude of affirmation and support of the Jewish people. Pentecostal Zionism was prevalent among the Pentecostal missionaries in Palestine and was passed on to Derek Prince and transmitted by him to the charismatic renewal movement. Prince's theology was a mix of charismatic spirituality, philosemitism, and support for the state of Israel. In some respects, Prince paved the way for the emergence of the Christian pro-Israel movement. Finally, we have seen that messianic Jewish movement in Israel has a strong charismatic element and we have touched on its theological implications. Now we will assess the evidence for the transmission of Pentecostal Zionism in popular renewalist writings.

POPULAR RENEWALIST LITERATURE

The Pentecostal mission in Palestine has bequeathed an attitude of philosemitism to the contemporary Pentecostal-charismatic renewal movement. In the past Pentecostals and charismatics have been among those who have supported and admired the state of Israel. Current writers in the Pentecostal-charismatic renewal movement are carrying on the legacy of Pentecostal Zionism. I will survey six major theological themes in the popular literature on Israel and the Church.

Pentecostal Affinity for Zionism

Current renewalist authors have endorsed the longstanding affinity of Pentecostals for Zionism. In doing so, they have carried forward the legacy of Pentecostal Zionism. David Allen Lewis devoted a portion of a chapter in his 1994 book to the Pentecostal Revival. He writes, "When the Pentecostal revival started around 1901 there was an immediate affinity for the scattered Jewish people and a realization that Israel, as a nation, would live again in her ancient homeland."[31] Lewis does not mention Charles Parham's Zionism but he identifies Parham's daughter-in-law Pauline Parham as an ardent Christian Zionist, as well as her daughter, Bobbi Hromas, former director of the American Christian Trust. Lewis also cites evidence from Pentecostal periodicals of Pentecostal support for the restoration of the Jewish homeland in Palestine. He explains the significance of Article 14 of the Statement of Fundamental Truths of the Assemblies of God, which affirms that the millennial reign of Christ "will bring the salvation of national Israel."[32]

Another renewalist author, Don Finto, points to the parallels he observes between spiritual awakenings and events in Israel. In his *Your People Shall Be My People*, Finto writes, "Seventy percent of those who have come to faith since the birth of Zionism, or

31. Lewis, *Can Israel Survive in a Hostile World?* 181.
32. Ibid., 186.

over 50 percent of those who have ever come to faith, have come since the founding of the State of Israel in 1948."[33] He notes that the birth of modern Pentecostalism and the birth of Zionism both happened around the turn of the nineteenth century. The Latter Rain Revival, the great healing ministry that swept through the world fifty years ago, occurred simultaneously with the birth of the state of Israel in 1948. Finto points out that the Six Day War, in which Israel took possession of Jerusalem, occurred in the same year as the beginning of the Jesus Movement, through which so many Jewish young people began to believe that Jesus/Yeshua is the Messiah of Israel.[34] What is the meaning of these coincidences? According to Finto, the explanation lies in a divine confluence between the return of Jewish people to their homeland and global spiritual renewal.

Christian Responsibility for the Holocaust

The second theme is an acknowledgement of Christian responsibility for the Holocaust. Finto calls upon Christians to "confess personally and on behalf of the Church for centuries of persecution of Jewish people."[35] Lewis acknowledges that Christianity was the prime cause of anti-Semitism for the past 1,800 years.[36] Don Schwarz, the author of *Identity Crisis: Israel and the Church*, cites extensive anti-Semitic Christian pronouncements from the patristic period. He then states, "Many of the atrocities Hitler used against the Jews were handed down from the church leaders and the Christian councils. Some of these include making the Jews wear a certain piece of clothing to identify them as Jewish for the purpose of different types of persecution, moving them into slums or ghettos, and other assorted physical abuses."[37] The renewalist writers recognize that the well of Christian witness to the Jewish people has been poisoned by a history of Christian anti-Semitism. In Lewis' estimation, "Many Christians have relinquished their right and authority to witness to Jews. They know little about the Holocaust, about the Inquisition, the Crusades, the expulsions, the forced conversions, the dark side of Church history. Little is known of the fact that the visible Church has been largely responsible for the anti-Semitism of the past 1,700 years."[38]

Don Finto has put his views into action through the Toward Jerusalem Council II. Its goal is "to repair and heal the breach between Jewish and Gentile believers in Yeshua, dating from the first centuries of the Church, and to do so primarily through humility, prayer, and repentance."[39] He tells the story of traveling with a Jewish and Christian group to Spain. He and his group observed the chains with which Jewish people had been tortured and killed five centuries earlier, still hanging from the walls

33. Finto, *Your People Shall Be My People*, 43.

34. Ibid., 44.

35. Ibid., 19.

36. Lewis, *Can Israel Survive in a Hostile World?* 38.

37. Schwarz, *Identity Crisis: Israel and the Church*, 93.

38. Lewis, *Can Israel Survive in a Hostile World?* 24.

39. Finto, *Your People Shall Be My People,* 104.

of the monastery in San Juan del los Reyes. Stunned, the group found its way to a park and huddled together. As a Jewish mother began to throw dust on her head, Finto sat beside her, following her lead. Jews and Gentiles held each other. After a season of silence, someone recited the traditional Jewish prayer for the dead, honoring the Jewish men, women, and children who had been tormented and murdered by past generations of "Christians."[40] One perceives an attitude of repentance in Finto's treatment of the Holocaust. Lewis' prayer is also indicative of this attitude:

> Almighty God, we confess our sins and the sins of the Church. As the ancient prophets of Israel confessed the sins of their nation—sins of which they had no personal guilt—so we confess the sins of our Church and our nation. We have not pleased You when we have participated in slander against the Jewish people. Forgive us for remaining silent when we should have spoken out against evil hatred of Your people, Israel. Forgive us for being intimidated in the face anti-Semitism . . . Amen.[41]

Denunciation of Anti-Semitism

The third theme is denunciation of anti-Semitism. Finto asserts that "anti-Semitism is still the longest-held and deepest hatred in human history."[42] In his teaching letter, "The Root of Anti-Semitism," Derek Prince examines the cause of anti-Semitism. He recalls a conversation he had in 1946 with Professor Dr. Ben Zion Segal of Hebrew University. According to Prince, Segal believed that the problem of anti-Semitism was basically sociological. The Jews were an alien minority with a distinctive culture of their own, out of harmony with the culture of the Gentile nations that harbored them. Once the Jews got a state of their own—which happened two years later—this would resolve the basic cause of Anti-Semitism. To this Prince replied,

"If you are correct that the basic cause of Anti-Semitism is sociological, then the establishment of a Jewish state should go a long way toward resolving the problem. But if—as I believe—the basic cause is spiritual, the establishment of a Jewish state will not resolve the problem, but will intensify it with one obvious focus: the newly established Jewish state." As Prince averred, the formation of the Jewish state did not resolve the problem of anti-Semitism. Hence, he continues, "Looking back now over nearly 50 years, I have to say—regretfully—that I believe history has proven me right. The establishment of the State of Israel has merely provided a more 'politically correct' name 'Anti-Zionism' in place of 'Anti-Semitism.' If anything, the virulence has increased."[43] Lewis agrees that anti-Semitism now appears in the guise of anti-Zionism. He argues that his colleagues at the National Christian Leadership Conference for Israel, Roman Catholic Edward Flannery, United Methodist Franklin Littell, and Isaac Rottenberg

40. Ibid., 86–87.

41. Lewis, *Can Israel Survive in a Hostile World?* 45.

42. Finto, *Your People Shall Be My People,* 65.

43. Prince, "The Root of Anti-Semitism," http://www.christianactionforIsrael.org/antiholo/dprince.html.

of the Reformed Church, have documented the anti-Semitic bias of the National and World Council of Churches.[44] Finto poses the obvious question, "Why now the continuation of anti-Semitism on all fronts?" His answer is that Satan is responsible for provoking hatred for the Jews because the promises of God will not be realized if Satan is successful in destroying Israel. Furthermore, the prophecies of Christ's return will not be fulfilled if Israel ceases to exist or even if the Jewish people lose their identity.[45] The British charismatic David Pawson places the onus on the church in his *When Jesus Returns*. He argues that Christians have set the pace for anti-Semitism by committing two gross theological errors. The first is the accusation the Jews killed Jesus. The whole nation of Israel was not involved in the crucifixion. The second is the claim that the church replaced Israel. He finds no biblical warrant for the assertion that God's covenant promises have been totally transferred from Israel to the church.[46] Finto suggests an appropriate response. He states, "Past generations of leaders have dishonored and even killed this special people whom God has marked for blessing. We are the descendents, both physically and spiritually, of those generations . . . From us as well, the Lord expects humility, acknowledgement of sin and appropriate action before the curse can be removed."[47]

Repudiation of Replacement Theology

The fourth theme is a repudiation of replacement theology. The popular renewalist writers concur that the view that the church has superseded or replaced Israel has played a major role in fomenting anti-Semitism. Finto observes that when generations of Christian theologians accepted the "replacement theory" as normative doctrine, they forgot the clear teachings of Jeremiah and Paul. The results continue to be deleterious. "In our own century, the idea that the Church has replaced Israel has so permeated our thinking that even recently published Bibles often contain marginal notes and chapter headings that continue to support this ancient error that results in hatred of Jews."[48] Schwarz, a charismatic messianic Jew, responds confrontationally:

> There are those who believe that the church has replaced Israel. Many would say that we in the church are now the descendants of the promise and that the Jewish people are not. In their estimation it is because of the Jewish disobedience to the law, or the rejection of Jesus that they are no longer in this covenant. If the Abrahamic covenant is based on obedience, we had all better get ready for a hot eternity! The Jews have not been excluded from this covenant. If the Lord

44. Lewis, *Can Israel Survive in a Hostile World?* 40; Rottenberg, *The Turbulent Triangle: Christians-Jews-Israel*, 54–58.

45. Finto, *Your People Shall Be My People*, 70–71.

46. Pawson, *When Jesus Returns*, 39.

47. Finto, *Your People Shall Be My People*, 103.

48. Ibid., 91.

doesn't keep His covenant with them, what makes you think that He will keep it with you?[49]

Prince takes a more reasoned approach. Referring to a study he did of the use of the term "Israel" in the New Testament, he writes, "I have discovered seventy-nine instances in the New Testament where the words Israel or Israelite occur. After examining them all, I conclude that the apostles never used Israel as a synonym for the church. Nor does the phrase *the new Israel* occur anywhere in the New Testament. Preachers who use that phrase should take care to define their use of it. They should also state that it is not found in the Bible."[50] Hedding refers to replacement theology as the *finished theology* and laments that it "has made anti-Semitism easier and more acceptable in the church. This, in turn, has contributed greatly to the appalling suffering that God's ancient people have had to endure through history. The awful periods of the Crusaders, the Spanish Inquisition and the pogroms of Russia are but a few examples of anti-Semitism perpetrated by the church."[51] In the same vein, Lewis makes the connection between replacement theology and the Holocaust:

> The Church pre-Nazi Germany was preaching the twin doctrines of Christian anti-Semitism. They are the *doctrine of replacement* and *the doctrine of contempt.* The theology of replacement contends that the Church has replaced Israel and that God no longer has any purpose for Israel. Contempt declares that the Jews crucified Jesus and therefore they are under a curse and whatever happens, including the Holocaust, is their just dessert . . . Thus in a Christian nation, out of a perverted Christianity came the Holocaust, costing the lives of six million Jews and also 50 million other casualties, lives lost as a direct result of the Second World War.[52]

As a result of the complicity of the church in the Holocaust, Christian witness to the Jews has been compromised. Finto avers, "We do not have the right to take words spoken to Israel and appropriate them to the Church until we have recognized their intended meaning to the people originally addressed." The promises only belong to the Gentile church because it was grafted in to Israel. "We do not replace the originally intended recipients . . . We come alongside Israel in receiving the promises, but we do not *replace* her!"[53]

Recovery of Jewish Roots of Christianity

The fifth theme is a call for the recovery of the Jewish roots of the Christian faith. The imprint of Messianic Judaism is clearly evident in the popular renewalist literature on Israel. For instance, Don Finto states that due to the messianic movement, he is

49. Schwarz, *Identity Crisis,* 36.
50. Prince, *Prophetic Destinies,* 15.
51. Hedding, *Understanding Israel,* 51.
52. Lewis, *Can Israel Survive in a Hostile World?* 39.
53. Finto, *Your People Shall Be My People,* 28.

passionate about seeing that his Jewish brothers and sisters express their faith within a Jewish framework and he yearns for the Gentile church to appreciate its own Jewish foundation stones.[54] The thesis of Don Schwarz's *Identity Crisis* is that the church has lost its Jewish roots, in which its true identity is grounded. He supports his thesis with biblical texts. From Ephesians 2:12–13, he surmises that Gentiles who come to Jesus Christ are included in the commonwealth of Israel and thereby receive the benefits of citizenship. He writes, "The only way to forgiveness of sin and a relationship with the God of Israel is by entering into the New Covenant, which fulfills the Abrahamic covenant, both of which God made with Israel."[55] On the basis of the image of the wild Gentile branches grafted onto the Jewish olive tree in Romans 11:16–24, he argues that "ancient Jewish faith holds up our modern belief system in Jesus."[56] The blessings of salvation come to the church through the Jews, to whom all followers of Christ are spiritually related. But in most churches the Jewish heritage of Christian faith is not taught.[57]

The renewalist authors offer explanations for the neglect of the Jewish roots of the Christian faith. Finto observes that from the time of the Council of Nicaea, the Jewish calendar, through which the Christian celebration of Easter could be coordinated with Passover, was replaced by the Latin calendar which etymologically associates the celebration of Easter with *Eostre*, the Teutonic goddess of spring.[58] To counteract the distancing of the church from its Jewish roots, Pawson wryly asserts, "Jesus was and is Jewish." However, "many Christians seem to have forgotten that their Saviour is a Jew and 'salvation is from the Jews' (John 4:22). The church seems to have pulled up its Jewish roots, for example, moving Easter, Whitsuntide, and Christmas away from the dates for Passover, Pentecost, and Tabernacles."[59] Schwarz reminds his readers that the first church was in Jerusalem. Citing Revelation 22:16, he writes, "Jesus not only came the first time as a Jew, but He will return as one in all His glory! . . . There judging the nations will be the glorified Jewish Messiah! He will be as Jewish as the beard of Moses, and I wouldn't want to be one who doesn't like the Jews on that day!"[60] Finto adds that the first followers of Jesus were "Sabbath-keeping, son-circumcising, Torah-observing, feast-celebrating Jews who now celebrate Jesus as the one who brought meaning to it all. None of these practices ceased when they believed in Yeshua."[61] He also states that although the apostle Paul held that salvation is alone through the finished work of Messiah Yeshua, he still observed the Jewish law and recognized the authority of the Jewish prophets. However, he laments, "The Church has become so Gentile in its prac-

---

54. Ibid., 19.

55. Schwarz, *Identity Crisis*, 48.

56. Ibid., 50.

57. Ibid., 55–56.

58. Finto, *Your People Shall Be My People*, 89.

59. Pawson, *When Jesus Returns*, 39.

60. Schwarz, *Identity Crisis*, 47.

61. Finto, *Your People Shall Be My People*, 77.

tice of faith that those of us who would reclaim a biblical Jewish expression are often considered a little strange—a small price to pay for the rediscovery of Jewish roots."[62]

Reaffirmation of Philosemitism

The sixth theme is a reaffirmation of philosemitism. Lewis states his view bluntly: "Christians should be Zionists. It is time to stop pushing this issue aside. Too much is at stake."[63] Actually, this is the view of all of the renewalist authors under consideration, as it was of countless Pentecostals before them. Malcolm Hedding, executive director of the International Christian Embassy in Jerusalem, expresses the prevailing rationale for the support of Israel in the popular renewalist literature. Hedding begins by countering the common conception that the basis of Christian Zionism is a belief in the fulfillment of Old Testament prophecy. He writes, "Christian support for Israel, or Biblical Zionism, is not based on the prophetic portions of the Word of God. This might sound strange to some of you who have for years had Israel presented to you as a type of eschatology or in a prophetic context." He goes on to locate the foundation of the Christian pro-Israel argument in covenantal theology. "Our support for Israel is based on something far deeper, and that is the promises of the Word of God or the great covenants of history that God made with the people of Israel. The prophetic portions of God's Word reinforce these great promises and validate them. But, the basis of Christian support for Israel is not the prophetic passages; it is indeed the great covenants that God made with this nation."[64] Hedding's line of argument proceeds as follows. He sees Israel as the conduit or delivery vehicle of world redemption. God chose Israel because he loved her. Through her the Messiah would come, fulfilling the Abrahamic covenant, which promised that God would bless the nations through Israel. This promise is unconditional and it is fulfilled in Jesus the Messiah. This is the basis of Christian support for Israel. The drama of world redemption is played out on the stage of human history with Israel at the focal point.[65] Hedding believes that the Word of God teaches there is a coming day when Israel will return in unbelief to the land of her forefathers. Her physical return will be followed by a spiritual recovery. Now the Jewish people have returned. The events which are unfolding in the Middle East will culminate in the return of Christ, at which time all demonic influence over the world will come to an end. Many think that the Middle East conflict is a secular political conflict. It is not. It has everything to do with the final purpose of God for the redemption of the world.[66]

Finto addresses the practical issues involved in supporting the state of Israel, laying out the following suggestions: Ask the Lord to cleanse our hearts of every vestige of anti-Semitism. Become aware that the world's news media is prejudiced against God's

62. Ibid., 80, 84.

63. Lewis, *Can Israel Survive in a Hostile World?* 25.

64. Hedding, *The Basis of Christian Support for Israel*, 5.

65. Ibid., 13–15.

66. Ibid., 45–47.

work and God's people. Seek ways to affirm Jewish people, to love them and bless them—whether or not they ever accept Jesus as Messiah. Prepare for future crises. Encourage and assist Jewish people to return to their ancestral inheritance. Bless the Jewish people financially. And establish prayer support groups to share in the ministry of those who are on the front lines of the battles.[67]

To summarize, the popular renewalist writers discussed above have carried forward the legacy of Pentecostal Zionism in these respects: They acknowledge Christian responsibility for the Holocaust, denounce anti-Semitism, repudiate replacement theology, call for a recovery of the Jewish roots of Christian faith, and reaffirm a philosemitic attitude toward Israel. The above theological themes, which constitute the legacy of Pentecostal Zionism, were diffused in a continuous stream of discourse from classical Pentecostalism to the contemporary charismatic movement. Now we turn to an analysis of the implications of the legacy of Pentecostal Zionism.

THE REPERCUSSIONS OF PENTECOSTAL ZIONISM

If Pentecostals and charismatics can be credited with promoting love for the Jewish people, the opposite is true of their attitude toward Muslims. Subsequent to 1948, a negative outlook on Islam was perpetuated in the Pentecostal periodicals. Pentecostal Zionism was accompanied by Pentecostal Islamophobia.

Pentecostal Islamophobia

An example of Pentecostal Islamophobia is found in an article authored in 1950 by Vera Swarztrauber, a veteran Pentecostal missionary in Palestine. It is entitled the "Challenge of Islam." This article is a manuscript from an address that Swarztrauber presented at the Central Bible Institute in Springfield, Missouri on April 6, 1950. Swarztrauber begins by recalling her first impression of the call of the *muezzin*, announcing the daily times of Muslim prayer: "I was sitting in my room studying Arabic one day an all at once I heard a wild, eerie cry. It wavered up and down in a weird, minor sort of way, chilling me. It sounded like the cry of a lost soul."[68] Soon the intonations of the *muezzin* receded into the background of Swarztrauber's consciousness and were replaced by many encounters with Muslims who responded to the Christian message. She recollects occasions when the faces of Muslims would "light up under the preaching of the Word, as the Holy Spirit began to work in them." However, after Muslim converts publicly confessed their faith in Jesus, they faced terrible persecution. "One night a crowd of screaming Moslem women came to our mission hall. Laura Radford, who was in charge, called the police station four or five times to get the police to come to end the disturbance." Finally, Radford arranged to send the young convert to Nazareth. "The women were screaming around the mission house when he got in the car for the trip. They tried to get in the car, too, but the chauffeur pushed them

---

67. Finto, *Your People Shall Be My People*, 177–84.

68. Swarztrauber, "Challenge of Islam," *Pentecostal Evangel* (November 26, 1950) 9.

out, got the car in motion, and took a circuitous route to Nazareth." All these efforts were to no avail, because the man's family found him, drugged him, brought him back to Jerusalem, and swiftly arranged a marriage to a Muslim girl. Swarztrauber relates another story of a Muslim family who decided as a group to convert to Christianity, then suddenly disappeared. After a few days the police found them in an empty cistern under the temple mount where they had been left to die. "They were rescued but they never came back to church." Swarztrauber avers, "I could go on and tell you story after story of Moslems who have believed and in whose life Christ has worked until persecution came. If not persecution, they are tricked into sin, maybe into smoking one cigarette. Back they go into the Islam mire."[69]

Next Swarztrauber explores the power of Islam. She poses a pressing question: "What is the reason for their strength?" In an attempt to discern the "hold of the false prophet of Arabia upon his followers," she asserts that the best explanation is "that the religion is one of Satan's masterpieces, his challenge to the Cross. Moslems deny the divinity of Christ. They deny His crucifixion. They say that He was caught up to heaven and that Barabbas took His place." The creed of Islam "says that there is no god but God and then they add that Mohammed is the prophet of God." Vexed that "all one has to do to become a Moslem is to confess that creed before a witness," she says that "the religion offers everything and declares nothing in the way of self-control and self-restraint. It is a veritable mystery of iniquity. It lays claim to spiritual infallibility." Her critique notwithstanding, Swarztrauber acknowledges the expansive swath of the globe under the sway of Islam, taking in North Africa, Egypt, Palestine, Syria, Asia Minor, the Balkan states, Iraq, Persia, Russian Turkestan, Central Asia, Afghanistan, North India, Western China, Indonesia, the Malay peninsula, and Java. She is relieved to report that Islam is broken up as a political force, yet dismayed that it remains strong as a religious force and is growing rapidly. Swarztrauber laments, "There is something that grips these people. It is indefinable. It is intangible. But it is terribly real."[70]

Swarztrauber then turns her attention to the problem of Muslim missions, observing that "the bulk of the untouched mission territories is Moslem. The great Moslem wall has stood for centuries." Therein is the challenge of Islam. "The sands of the time of the Gentiles are running out. The Jews are no longer in a Jerusalem that is being trodden down of the Gentiles. They are there in their own right and it means that our time is short. The great wall of Islam stands, flinging its defiant challenge in the face of the Cross." Having scrutinized the challenge of Islam, Swarztrauber confronts her audience with a query: "Does it mean anything to you?" Swarztrauber is obviously stymied by the challenge of Islam. She complains that everywhere she goes she finds "an appalling lack of understanding about the Islam situation. There is also great indifference and little prayer." She tells of a woman she met in Madison, Wisconsin, who confided that as she was praying for the Muslims, "in the Spirit she came up against that wall of Islam. She had felt the cruelty, the pride, and the defiance of the Cross

69. Ibid.
70. Ibid., 9–10.

of Christ." Swarztrauber recognizes that it will take an "extraordinary something" to break down the wall of Islam. "It is going to take dynamite to blast the wall. I do not know how the Lord is going to undertake, but I am convinced that He wants to do so." She closes her talk on a Pentecostal note. "On the day of Pentecost the last ones mentioned on the list who heard the speaking in other tongues, magnifying the name of the Lord, were Cretes and Arabian. Perhaps in this end of the dispensation we can lay hold on that also. There is hope that God will move on these people."[71]

Bias against Palestinian Arabs

Pentecostals not only espoused Islamophobia, but they were also prejudiced against the Palestinian Arabs. In the last chapter, we presented evidence of a bias against Palestinian Arabs in the coverage of the Arab-Israeli conflict in the Pentecostal periodicals. That this bias is part of the legacy of the Pentecostal mission in Palestine is demonstrated in an address presented by George Carmichael, a recent missionary to Palestine, to the students of the Central Bible Institute in early 1949.

George Carmichael, "Rebuilding Palestine"

Carmichael's address represents an unbalanced pro-Zionist interpretation of the War of 1948. Carmichael's ideology is typical of Pentecostal Zionist discourse. He legitimates his point of view by asserting that biblical prophecies are being fulfilled by the Zionists in Palestine. He cites Amos 9:14–15, "And I will plant them upon their land, and they shall no more be pulled up out of their land which I have given them, saith the Lord God." Carmichael then claims, "This scripture is literally being fulfilled today, and they are building the waste places." Much like other Pentecostal Zionists before him, Carmichael celebrates the accomplishments of the Jewish colonists in Palestine,

> They have gone into the malarial swamps on the plain of Esdraelon where it slopes into the valley of the Jordan, and by their industry have literally made it blossom as the rose. They have purchased land down by the Dead Sea that is comparable to the Bad Lands of South Dakota. The Jews are taking the water from the old spring that Elisha made sweet by pouring the salt into it, and they are running that water down across the brackish ground, washing the salt and sulphur out, and they have planted banana groves that bear luscious bananas— banana groves there on the plains of Jericho that used to be brackish and barren and useless even for grazing! They have developed cement plants and are taking potash and minerals from the Dead Sea.

As if to justify the legitimacy of the Jewish state, Carmichael predicts, "Given a free hand, now that they have their State of Israel, I believe that the prophecy of Isaiah 35:1, 'And the desert shall rejoice, and blossom as the rose,' will have its fulfillment."[72]

71. Ibid., 10.
72. Carmichael, "Rebuilding Palestine," *Pentecostal Evangel* (February 19, 1949) 6.

Carmichael leaves no doubt as to his bias. He claims that the Zionist victory was a divine miracle. He shares recollections of the dangerous times he experienced at the Shemariah mission station in Jerusalem, explaining, "During the severe fighting we were caught in the crossfire and we would have to lie down on the floor to get out of the line of fire." He says that not far away 2,500 Jews were surrounded by the Arabs in the Old City. In a somber tone, he recalls, "I read after I left Palestine that there were only 150 Jews out of this group that surrendered to the Arabs. The rest were killed or died of starvation." The Jews were attacked by five Arab armies converging on Jerusalem. "If God did not work a miracle they would be destroyed. They were surrounded by armies which were armed with the latest implements of war, and the Jews had nothing with which to fight except some arms smuggled in by the Zionist terrorists." It appeared there was not a hope in the world for the survival of the Jews in Palestine. Carmichael imagines, "I believe if a sacred history were written of this occasion the writer would say that there were five armies converging on Jerusalem, and they were ready to destroy the Jewish inhabitants, but God sent a spirit of jealousy among them which made them suspicious one of another." Carmichael attributes the defeat of the Arab armies to a lack of coordination, alleging that the Egyptians and Syrians held back from helping the Jordanians because they feared that King Abdullah would seize more territory than they. This delay afforded the Jews time to get supplies, which enabled them to defeat the Arabs. "In fact, the Jews are taking all Palestine, and I believe that before the trouble is over they will have Trans-Jordan too. God said He was going to bring the Jews back to Palestine and we have seen them coming." For Carmichael the Zionist victory is a sign that "the coming of Jesus is near at hand."[73]

Pentecostal Accounts of the Six Day War of 1967

The pro-Zionist perspective exemplified by Carmichael was a continuation of the discourse carried on by the Pentecostal missionaries in Palestine and the Pentecostal periodicals from 1908 to 1948. And it showed no signs of abating after 1948. In response to the so called Six Day War of 1967, the *Pentecostal Evangel* published three articles that demonstrate the ongoing currency of Pentecostal Zionism. The first of these articles, "Two Million Signs of the Times" by Pentecostal evangelist Harry J. Steil, was published on July 30, 1967. The theme of this article is drawn from a favorite text of Pentecostal Zionists, Jesus' brief parable of the fig tree in Luke 21:29–31: "Look at the fig tree and all the trees. When they sprout leaves, you can see for yourselves and know that summer is near. Even so, when you see these things happening, you will know that the kingdom of God is near." Steil organizes his thoughts around the image of four shoots of the fig tree, speaking euphemistically of Israel. First, the "numerical shoot" of the fig tree is the resilient growth of the worldwide Jewish population in spite of its decimation by the "Hitlerian slaughter." Before the extermination of six million Jews in the Holocaust the total Jewish population of the world was 16 million; in 1967 it was over 13 million. "This constitutes a very healthy 'shoot' on the fig tree."

73. Ibid., 7.

Second, the "territorial shoot" is the liberation of Palestine from the "bloody Turk" and the establishment of a national home for the Jews of the world. Steil states, "There are today in Palestine over two million Jews. Here are two million signs of the times. Quite a healthy shoot!" Third, the "political shoot" is symbolized by Israel's national flag displaying the Star of David, which is "the ensign of a nation that has come back from the dead to take its place at the council tables of the world. 'Behold the fig tree and all the trees'—having equal status, equal rights, equal voice among them. A very healthy shoot." Fourth, the "financial shoot" is the return on billions of dollars invested in the nation of Israel. Even though many statesmen said that Israel could not survive, the "financial shoot" has "sprung up out of the stump of the fig tree" and "is amazingly sturdy!" Steil then asks, "But how does all this talk about Israel concern us? We are not Jews." His answer is taken from the script of the discourse of Pentecostal Zionism. "No, but our Saviour was a Jew. He was born as a Jew, He died as a Jew, and He will return to earth as the Messiah of the Jews to deliver them from all their troubles. And when He returns, He will reign over all the earth as King of Kings and Lord of Lords." Steil gets to the bottom line, the nearness of the second coming of Christ, concluding, "Therefore, when we see this 'shooting forth' from the fig tree, we should be warned that His return is very near (Read Luke 21)."[74]

Ralph Riggs (1895–1971), a General Superintendent of the American Assemblies of God, authored an article entitled, "Who Is the Rightful Owner of Palestine?" To his credit, Riggs mentions that during the War of 1948 "700,000 Arabs fled from Palestine." His reason for doing so is not to empathize with the Arabs but rather to assert that the Jewish people, rather than the Arab refugees, are the rightful owners of Palestine. He bases his argument on the biblical covenant with Abraham, "a sevenfold covenant that God would give Palestine to the Jews forever." Against this backdrop, Riggs offers a pro-Zionist narrative of the War of 1948 and subsequent Arab-Israeli skirmishes. He writes, "Intense hatred smoldered through the following years, and in October 1956 war broke out again. Once more the Jews were victorious. In 100 hours they swept across the Sinai desert to the Suez Canal." Like Carmichael, Riggs strives to justify Israeli military victories on the basis of biblical prophecy. He states, "When God gave the promise to Abraham that the seed of Isaac would inherit Palestine, He also said that He would prosper the seed of Ishmael, his other son, and make of him 12 princes or nations (Genesis 17:20; and 25:16)." Riggs argues that this prophecy was fulfilled on June 5, 1967, when "exactly 12 Ishmaelite nations were at war with Israel! Count them: Morocco, Algeria, Tunisia, Libya, Egypt, Yemen, Kuwait, Saudi Arabia, Jordan, Syria, Lebanon, and Iraq. This time only 84 hours sufficed for Israel to conquer the Arab nations who outnumbered them 20 to 1." From this Riggs concludes, "This surely looks like a confirmation that God has given Palestine to the Jews."[75]

The third article was authored by Albert Hoy, who throws down the Christian Zionist gauntlet. He states, "Whether we accept Israel's success as an act of God or not,

74. Steil, "Two Million Signs of the Time," *Pentecostal Evangel* (July 30, 1967) 2–4.
75. Riggs, "Who Is the Rightful Owner of Palestine?" *Pentecostal Evangel* (July 30, 1967) 7.

there can be no contradiction of the Biblical assurance that the Lord's national people are foreordained to defeat any plan to expel them from the land of the their fathers." Hoy looks back to biblical prophecy, arguing that Jeremiah and Ezekiel predicted that toward the end of the times of the Gentiles, Israel would dwell securely in her own land. "Since she attained statehood on May 15, 1948, after 25 ominous centuries in the role of a world wanderer, she has been attacked again and again by her Arab neighbors. Always, however, she had not only repelled these attacks, but has strengthened her territorial position." According to Hoy, two facts are painstakingly clear. "Israel is in Palestine to stay, and the truth of the Bible is as applicable today as ever it was." Hoy insists that Israel's present position bears testimony to the steady unfolding of the divine revelation and he argues that a survey of the biblical prophecies of the return of Israel to her own land shows that "there is no mention whatever of a dual tenure of Jerusalem by Jews and Arabs." Hoy recognizes that although Jerusalem was occupied by the Israelis at the time of the cease-fire, the territorial claims of the victors were yet to be resolved. "The outcome will be awaited with profound interest by Christians everywhere. If the Israelis retain possession of the city, the veracity of the Bible can be further urged upon those who doubt it." Like Carmichael some twenty years earlier, and hosts of other Christian Zionist authors, Hoy sees further evidences of the confirmation of prophecy in "Israel's amazing ventures in soil fertilization and agricultural experimentation. He closes with the typical ruminations on the story line of premillennial eschatology. Jesus had stated in the plainest terms that when Israel regained complete jurisdiction over the city of Jerusalem, the times of the Gentiles would come to their conclusion and the time of his second coming would be near. Hoy is certain that the 1967 war was a sign that "these are the days in which believers are to look for the coming of the Lord."[76]

Each of the above articles is representative of the historic Pentecostal affinity to Zionism. This affinity can indeed be credited for promoting philosemitism. However, it must also be credited with a glaring disregard of the Arab point of view. The Pentecostal periodicals only told half of the story in regards to the Wars of 1948 and 1967. While celebrating the triumph the Jewish state, the Arab side of the story was virtually neglected. It is strange, in view of the fact that the Pentecostal mission in Palestine attracted most of its converts from the Arab Christian population, how little attention was paid to the impact of the war on the Arab Christians, Pentecostal and otherwise. Bits of information seep out, such as Hatfield's aside that most of the Arab Christians of Jerusalem were forced to flee when 500,000 Arabs were made homeless by the war. By 1967 Riggs had brought the number of Palestinian refugees up to 700,000. Nevertheless, these pieces of information are not elaborated upon in articles published in Pentecostal periodicals in 1948 and afterward. It is appalling that nothing more is made of the suffering endured by Arab Pentecostal community in Jerusalem. Any expression of sympathy and concern for the Arab Pentecostals in the Palestinian Diaspora is non-existent in the articles published in the *Pentecostal Evangel*. The prob-

76. Hoy, "Israel's Answer to the Critics," *Pentecostal Evangel* (July 30, 1967) 8–9.

able explanation for this oversight is a bias against Arabs. This is arguably a blind spot of Pentecostals. Like other Christian Zionists, Pentecostal Zionists disregarded the rights of the Arabs of Palestine. But more than that, they rendered their former Arab clients as non-persons by neglecting to account for their whereabouts and to inquire into their well being. To redress the deficit of compassion, which at the least was a sin of omission, the Arab side of the story will now be told.

TELLING THE ARAB SIDE OF THE STORY

To Pentecostals, as to Israelis, the War of 1948 marks the birth of the State of Israel, but to Palestinians it is known as "the Catastrophe."

The Arab Catastrophe of 1948

As the British Mandate was winding down in 1947, the United Nations produced a partition plan that would divide Palestine into a Jewish state, comprised of eastern Galilee, the upper Jordan Valley, the Negev and the coastal plain, and an Arab state in the rest of the land. Skirmishes flared up immediately after the passage of the U.N. resolution on November 29, 1947. Palestinian Arabs were incensed that the partition gave the Zionists 54 percent of the land, even though they owned only 7 percent. As Elias Chacour explains, the partition "gave the Zionists almost all of the fertile land, including the huge, main citrus groves that accounted for most of our people's export income . . . There was three times more cultivated land in this one area than the incoming, European settlers had cultivated in all of Palestine in the previous thirty years."[77] Large scale violence started in Jerusalem on December 2, 1947, when, according to Karen Armstrong, "an Arab mob streamed through the Jaffa Gate and looted the Jewish commercial center on Ben Yehuda Street. Irgun, the Zionist militia, retaliated by attacking the Arab suburbs of Katamon and Sheikh Jarrah. By March, 1948, 70 Jews and 230 Arabs had been killed in the fighting around Jerusalem."[78] At that moment the combined armies of five Arab League states—Egypt, Jordan, Syria, Iraq and Lebanon—launched a military intervention against the Jewish forces in order to prevent the loss of Palestine to the Zionist entity. On May 14, 1948, the day before the expiration of the British Mandate, David Ben-Gurion called a press conference and proclaimed the formation of the state of Israel. Already, the Zionist armed forces, known as the Haganah, were undertaking the massive project of removing Palestinians from the land designated for the Jewish state. The Arab armies were eventually outmaneuvered and soundly defeated, due to Western intervention. In July of 1948, according to the truce arranged by the United Nations, Palestine was split right through the middle of Jerusalem, with West Jerusalem going to Israel and East Jerusalem to the Hashemite Kingdom of Jordan.

---

77. Chacour, *Blood Brothers*, 46.

78. Armstrong, *Jerusalem: One City, Three Faiths*, 386.

The stark reality is that in 1948–49 the Israelis evicted 750,000 Palestinians from their homes, reduced them to refugees, and expropriated their villages, businesses and farms. The refugees either fled or were deported to the West Bank, Gaza and neighboring Arab nations, mainly Lebanon, Syria and Jordan. By the end of 1949, there were 1,000,000 Palestinians registered for relief with the United Nations Relief and Works Agency (UNRWA).[79]

After the War of 1948 the Palestinians were a dispossessed people. Only those in the Gaza enjoyed some semblance of political freedom. The West Bank was annexed by Jordan. The Gaza Strip was under Egyptian control. A significant number of the Palestinian refugees in the West Bank emigrated to the Gulf States and the West, but most remained and lived an impoverished existence in refugee camps. About 120,000 Palestinian Arabs remained in Israel. They eventually gained citizenship but were denied equal protection under the law, as well as the right to return to their homes or fair compensation for their losses. Israel fought two more major wars with neighboring Arabic states, in 1967 and 1973, resulting in the acquisition of more territory in the Golan Heights, the West Bank, the Gaza Strip, and the Sinai Peninsula, and in the creation of 300,000 more Palestinian refugees. At present the world population of Palestinians is about 4 million. About 800,000 of them are Arab citizens of Israel, 1 million live in the West Bank and Gaza under Israeli military occupation, another 1 million or so live in Jordan, approximately 450,000 live in Lebanon, and the rest live in the Gulf States, Europe, and North and South America.[80]

Stages in Palestinian National Consciousness

Naim Ateek points out that Palestinians have gone through a three-stage process in establishing their national consciousness.[81] The first stage was *shock* (1948–55). The Palestinians were stunned when Arab intervention failed and the international community gave overwhelming support to the provision of a homeland for the survivors of the Holocaust. Martial law was instituted on October 21, 1948, prohibiting Palestinians from traveling without a permit approved by the military governor of the district. The Jewish towns that had been Palestinian were completely off limits. In addition, Israel denied Palestinians legal protection by continuing the Emergency Defense Regulations of the British Mandate, allowing the Israeli military to enter Palestinian houses without a search warrant, to demolish them, and to expel Palestinians from their homes and deport them. In 1950 the Israelis enacted the Absentee Property Law, under which the army could confiscate any land that was abandoned or untended, thus facilitating the expropriation of the land of the 750,000 Palestinians who had been forced from their property. During this period 900,000 Jews immigrated to Israel, and most of them were settled on the land and in the houses of the dispossessed Palestinians.[82]

79. Ruether and Ruether, *The Wrath of Jonah*, 103.
80. Said, *The Question of Palestine*, 115.
81. Ateek, *Justice and Only Justice*, 33.
82. Ibid., 33–36.

The second stage of *resignation* (1956–67) was characterized by realistic adjustment to the unresolved conflict. Every Palestinian was issued an identity card which classified him or her as an "Arab." The term "Palestinian" was assiduously avoided. In 1969 Golda Meir, the Israeli Prime Minister, declared, "It was not as though there was a Palestinian people in Palestine . . . and we came and threw them out and took their country away from them. They did not exist." Any attempt to organize the Palestinian community was immediately repressed. News of the Palestinian catastrophe did not register on the scale of world opinion. Outside of the Arab world, the international community viewed the Palestinian problem as that of the refugees, not fully comprehending the injustices done to the Palestinians.[83]

The third and current stage of *awakening* (1967–) emerged in the aftermath of the Six Day War of 1967. The crushing defeat of the Arab armies demonstrated to the Palestinians that they could expect no deliverance from the Arab nations. This accelerated the development of organized Palestinian resistance. The Palestinian Liberation Organization (hereafter PLO), founded in 1964 by the Arab League, now came to represent the Palestinian national consciousness. The original purpose of the PLO was the destruction of Israel through armed struggle. Later, the PLO pragmatically accepted the fact that the state of Israel was there to stay and shifted its focus to the establishment of a Palestinian state on the West Bank and Gaza through international diplomacy. A minority, known as Rejectionists, refused to comply with this shift and stayed the course of terrorism. In 1974 the PLO was recognized by the Arab countries as the sole representative of the Palestinian Arabs. In the same year the PLO was granted observer status at the United Nations and was officially recognized by a majority of countries. It maintained diplomatic missions in all U.N. agencies and in ninety countries.[84] Ateek stresses, "Many people have come to see the PLO as merely a terrorist organization. But for almost all Palestinians the PLO is their national liberation movement."[85] The PLO established a network of cultural, educational and social welfare services. Its dominant military wing is called Fateh. The PLO is governed by the Palestinian National Council, and its president was for many years Chairman Yasir Arafat (1929–2004). The PLO has acted as the official voice of Palestinians wherever they may be, in Israel, the Occupied Territories, the Arab States or the West.[86]

Since the early 1970s there has been an awakened activism among the Palestinians, energized by a vigorous protest literature and inflamed by waves of guerilla warfare and two Intifadas, or "uprisings," during which the Palestinian population united in massive civil disobedience and defiance of Israel. Although the uprisings have been marred by egregious incidents of violence, they are the result of a process of conscientization, or as Ateek puts it, "Palestinianization,"[87] which was signaled by the appearance of a revisionist history, telling to story of the "Catastrophe" from a Palestinian point

83. Ibid., 36–38.

84. Said and Hitchens, *Blaming the Victims*, 33.

85. Ateek, *Justice and Only Justice*, 39.

86. Ibid., 38–44.

87. Ibid., 43.

of view. This revisionist history started with the publication of Sabri Jiryis's pioneering *The Arabs in Israel* (1976), and was followed with Elia Zurayk's *The Palestinians in Israel: A Study in Internal Colonialism* (1979).[88] For Palestinians, these publications represented their interpretation of their own history, narrating how they were driven from their own land and continue to live in apartheid-like conditions in Israel and the Occupied Territories.

Palestinian scholars would surely agree with what Miroslav Volf says in *Exclusion and Embrace* (1996) concerning the importance of remembering one's history of suffering. He writes, "What we have come to know we must remember, and what we remember we must tell. 'For as often as you eat this bread and drink the cup you proclaim the Lord's death until he comes' (1 Corinthians 11: 26). Just as the memory of Christ's death for our sins must be proclaimed, so also the memory of human suffering, caused and experienced, must be made public."[89]

PENTECOSTAL CONTRIBUTION TO PEACE IN ISRAEL/PALESTINE

In telling the Arab side of the story, I have highlighted some of the defining moments of recent Palestinian history. As we move now to an assessment of the Pentecostal contribution to peace in Israel/Palestine, the obvious will be stated. The conflict between the Israelis and the Palestinians centers on the possession of and sovereignty over the land of Israel/Palestine. The crux of the conflict is that two peoples are vying for one land. However, there is more to it. Israelis and Palestinians are stuck in a cultural impasse, in which each side has a vision of the other that excludes the other and leads to intractable differences in points of view. Both view their right to the land as inviolate and hence non-negotiable. As Miroslav Volf might say, the Israelis and Palestinians have viewed each other in *excluding* terms. Their "nonrecognition" and "misrecognition" of each other has inflicted harm, acted as a form of oppression, and imprisoned each side in a false, distorted and reduced mode of being.[90] On one side, the Palestinians view the Israelis as imperialistic, racist, Western colonizers and oppressors who have expropriated their ancestral land by force and aim at their expulsion or, if necessary, their extermination. On the other side, the Israelis view the Palestinians as barbaric, shiftless, subversive, and murderous terrorists whose claim to their ancestral land is superseded by the biblical entitlement of the land to the Jews.[91] Given the history of atrocities and recriminations on both sides, each point of view is understandable and may to a limited extent bear some ethical merit. However, it is a matter of life and death for the Israelis and Palestinians to make peace and learn to coexist. As Rosemary and Herman Ruether aptly point out, "Although neither was there as a national community before the twentieth century, both are there now. And for either party to try to

88. Said and Hitchens, *Blaming the Victims,* 3.

89. Volf, *Exclusion and Embrace,* 235.

90. Ibid., 19.

91. Said, *The Question of Palestine,* 8, 81–82, 90–92.

deny that the other exists as a national community is an exercise in futility."[92] Herein resides the urgent importance of hearing both sides of the story.

In excluding the Palestinian Arab side of the story Pentecostal Zionists were excluding the personhood of the Palestinian other. Telling the truth about history sometimes entails speaking a word of prophetic witness that exposes injustice in the light of critical analysis. The legacy of Pentecostal Zionism has a dark side. By espousing a bias against Palestinian Arabs and Muslims, the discourse of Pentecostal Zionism contributed to the forces working against peace in Israel/Palestine. It is perhaps an overstatement to say that Pentecostal Zionists directly undermined the peaceful coexistence of the Arabs and Jews of the Holy Land. Surely though, it is fair to say that the ideology of Pentecostal Zionism functioned as an accessory to injustice and conflict in Israel/Palestine. The evidence presented above supports the contention that the Pentecostal Zionist reading of biblical prophecy fell short of the ethical imperative of justice. I would suggest that the reason for this shortcoming was theological.

The cause of the Pentecostal contribution to injustice and conflict in the Holy Land can be located in the dispensational eschatology of early Pentecostalism. A number of early Pentecostals uncritically accepted the dispensational system formulated by John Nelson Darby and popularized by Cyrus I. Scofield.[93] The editors of several Pentecostal periodicals promoted the Scofield Reference Bible, even after it became apparent that the interpretive stance of its study notes was opposed to the distinctive Pentecostal emphasis on Spirit baptism with the accompaniment of speaking in tongues. To be fair, it should be granted that dispensationalism provided early Pentecostals with a philosophy of history with which to support the claim that their movement signified the final chapter in human history prior to the second coming of Christ.[94] Faced with denunciation and ridicule, early Pentecostals may have viewed dispensationalism as providing a tactical polemical advantage. Nonetheless, there are two reasons why this tactic was a wrong turn.

The first reason is that dispensationalism is theologically inconsistent with the core affirmations of Pentecostal theology. The inconsistency centers on the claim of Pentecostals that their movement constituted the fulfillment of the prophecy of the "latter rain" in Joel 2:23, 28, from which the Pentecost of Acts 2 is seen as the early rain and the Pentecostal Revival as the latter rain. In opposition to this claim, Darby and Scofield's dispensationalism was anchored to the assumption that the supernatural gifts of the Holy Spirit did not continue after the apostolic age. According to Darby, a great parenthesis occurred in church history in the early second century, marking the termination of the gifts of the Spirit bestowed on the Day of Pentecost. Since dispensationalists believed that God himself had ceased those supernatural gifts, most of them

---

92. Ruether and Ruether, *Wrath of Jonah*, xxi.

93. Bass, *Backgrounds to Dispensationalism*, 55; Prosser, *Dispensationalist Eschatology and Its Influence on American and Religious Movements*, 255–58.

94. Althouse, *Spirit of the Last Days*, 17–19, 41–44; Archer, *A Pentecostal Hermeneutic for the Twenty-First Century*, 52–57; Sheppard, "Pentecostals and the Hermeneutics of Dispensationalism," 9; Wacker, "Playing for Keeps: The Primitivist Impulse in Early Pentecostalism," 205–6.

regarded their purported reappearance in the twentieth century as a matter of human delusion at best, and Satanic counterfeit at worst. Hence, there was an inherent inconsistency between the basic tenets of dispensationalism and Pentecostal theology.[95]

There is a second reason for regarding the Pentecostal appropriation of dispensationalism as objectionable. To return to the argument of this book, Pentecostal periodicals disseminated an image of Israel/Palestine slanted by a pro-Zionist ideological agenda. They understood certain select biblical passages to predict a fixed sequence of historical events that would culminate during the last days in the city of Jerusalem with the Jewish people converting to Jesus as their Messiah. This eschatological scenario colored Pentecostals' interpretations of current events transpiring in Palestine in the first part of the twentieth century. By and large, Pentecostals believed that the immigration of Jewish people to Palestine was a sign of the imminence of the second coming of Christ, indicating that very soon a chain reaction would be activated leading to the War of Armageddon and the establishment of Christ's Millennial Kingdom in Palestine This popular theme of Pentecostal eschatology received prominent coverage in Pentecostal publications.[96]

It is evident that Pentecostals have left a legacy that is an impediment to peace in Israel/Palestine. By privileging the role of the Jews in their eschatological scenario, Pentecostals blocked from their field of vision the rights of other peoples, Arab Muslims and Christians, who made up the overwhelming majority of the population of Palestine.[97] As a result, the Pentecostal view of the Holy Land amounted to a representation made in the image of dispensational Christian Zionism. In contrast, a different picture emerges as one looks at the Holy Land through the lens of social justice and sees Israel/Palestine as the shared homeland of the children of Abraham, all of whom have equal rights.

In attending to what the Spirit may be saying in regards to the Pentecostal contribution to the peace in the Holy Land, we have concluded that in privileging the Zionist project and dismissing the rights of Arabs in Israel/Palestine, Pentecostals acted as accessories to injustice and conflict. These shortcomings have been laid at the doorstep of the dispensational element in early Pentecostal eschatology. In order to move beyond the shortcomings of Pentecostal Zionism, the author has told the Arab side of the story. In coming to terms with the legacy of Pentecostal Zionism, further steps could be taken if Pentecostal theologians were to engage in ecumenical dialogue with

95. Dayton, *Theological Roots of Pentecostalism*, 145; Macchia, "Pentecostal Theology," 1138; Solivan, *The Spirit, Pathos and Liberation*, 33–35, 44–45.

96. Boddy, "Seven Signs of His Coming," *Confidence* (December 1910) 291–93; Jamieson, "The Second Coming of Christ," *Weekly Evangel* (February 26, 1916) 6–7; Pocock, "Present-Day Signs of the End," *Trust* (January–February 1926) 16, 20; Stuernagel, "Signs of the Approaching End of the Age," *Latter Rain Evangel* (May 1927) 4–8; King, "Signs of the Coming of Our Lord," *Trust* (October 1915) 12–20; Booth-Clibborn, "The Goal of Prophetic Scripture," *Trust* (December 1918) 11–14; Frodsham, "The Return of the Lord: The Signs of the Times," *Pentecostal Evangel* (February 18, 1922) 6–7; Parker, "Christ is Coming Soon! An Outstanding Sign," *The Elim Evangel and Foursquare Revivalist* 9.19 (December 1, 1928) 313–15.

97. Said Aburish, *The Forgotten Faithful: The Christians of the Holy Land*, 3.

indigenous Christians in Israel/Palestine, which might include a discussion of issues raised in this chapter. In the process of that dialogue, Pentecostal theologians could have an opportunity to contribute to the forces working for peace in Israel/Palestine.

To conclude, the legacy of the Pentecostal mission in Palestine is a mixed bag. On the one hand, the missionaries made a significant contribution to the historic Pentecostal affinity to the Jewish People. They left a legacy of philosemitism that was passed down from Derek Prince to the charismatic movement, the pro-Israel movement, and still abides in the writings of popular renewalist authors. These authors have acknowledged Christian responsibility for the Holocaust, denounced anti-Semitism, repudiated replacement theology, issued a call for a recovery of the Jewish roots of Christian faith, and reaffirmed a philosemitic attitude toward Israel. On the other hand, the legacy of the Pentecostal mission in Palestine has a dark side. The Pentecostal missionaries have left a double-edged negative legacy by promoting Islamophobia and excluding the Arab side of the story. Pentecostal missionaries and other authors have caricatured Islam as a devil-inspired faith bent on world conquest, the sexual degradation of women, and conversion by the sword. This view dismisses the positive attributes of Islam as an Abrahamic faith and neglects its cultural contributions. In favoring the Zionist project and asserting the legitimacy of the state of Israel on the basis of biblical prophecy, Pentecostals disregarded the Arab right of self determination and nationhood. In telling the story of the Arab-Israeli conflict, Pentecostals have flatly turned their backs on the very Arab Christians who had turned to Pentecostalism. In so doing, they have contributed to the forces working against peace in Israel/Palestine.

10 | Conclusion

THE STORY OF the Pentecostal mission in Palestine is now told. It is a saga of valiant missionaries who were filled with the missionary Spirit and headed off to the legendary land of Palestine to carry out what they sincerely believed was a divine calling. Over a period of several decades, between 1908 and 2007, the Pentecostal missionaries established a presence in Jerusalem, from which they expanded their circle of influence to satellite outposts in Syria, Transjordan, and Persia. The major players in the company of Pentecostal missionaries in Palestine included Lucy Leatherman, A. Elizabeth Brown, Charles Leonard, Archibald Forder, Paul Joyner, Florence Bush, Yumna Malick, Laura Radford, Vida Baer, Pearl Lovesy, Saul Benjamin, Roy Whitman, John Warton, Serena Hodges, Ida Beck, Vera Swarztrauber, George Carmichael, Hanna Suleiman, B. D. Hatfield, George M. Kuttab, and Margaret Gaines. For the most part, these missionaries served without prior language acquisition, a financial plan, higher education, a guarantee of personal safety, and a studied knowledge of the history, culture, and politics of Palestine. They were unabashedly ignorant of what lay before them as they embarked for the Holy Land. But this did not matter to them because they were sure that God had called them to Palestine.

The story of the Pentecostal mission in Palestine has provided us with a window through which not only to bring to light a virtually unknown episode in the history of the global Pentecostal missionary movement but also to catch revealing glimpses of the Pentecostal worldview, as espoused in the discourse of Pentecostal Zionism. Pentecostals constructed their Zionist discourse by co-opting conservative evangelical dispensational pre-millennialism and modifying it to serve their own interests. Early Pentecostals highlighted the biblical metaphor of the latter rain, connecting biblical prophecies and contemporary rainfall patterns in Palestine, representing both as pre-figurations which legitimated the Pentecostal revival. They interpreted the rainfall statistics, obtained from the American Colony in Jerusalem, as a sign of the imminence of the second coming of Christ and sure proof that their movement would occupy center stage in the triumph of Christ's millennial kingdom which would be headquartered in the land of Palestine. The story of the Pentecostal mission in Palestine penetrates to the heart and soul of the early Pentecostal worldview.

SUMMATION OF FINDINGS

Pentecostal Zionism was and to some extent still is a constituent part of the worldview of Pentecostalism. The thesis that has been argued in this book is that the Pentecostal missionaries in Palestine functioned as brokers of Pentecostal Zionism. Although they failed in their objective of converting Jews and Muslims, and resorted to proselytizing Arab Christians, these missionaries can be credited with advocating philo-semitism and promoting the restoration of a Jewish national home in Palestine. However, in jumping on the Christian Zionist bandwagon, they disregarded the civil rights of the Arabs, espoused cultural antipathy toward Muslims, and left a legacy that continues to militate against peace in Israel/Palestine today. On the basis of these findings, one might conclude that the Pentecostal mission in Palestine was a failure. Yet, this judgment should be qualified. The early Pentecostal missionaries in Palestine can be credited with a number of accomplishments. As brokers of Pentecostal Zionism, they kept Pentecostals abreast of current events in the Holy Land. They galvanized Pentecostal views of the Zionist project and Arab resistance in Palestine as signs of the imminence of the second coming of Christ. They functioned as key figures in the construction of the discourse of Pentecostal Zionism. They also made a significant theological contribution in tilting Pentecostals away from replacement theology.

An overview of the major findings in each chapter will now be presented. In chapter 1, the Introduction, the methodology of this book was explained. Following Edward Said, my methodology entailed a reading the primary texts against the grain in the interest of detecting evidence of an imbedded ideology. The ideology scrutinized in this book is Pentecostal Zionism. The author has unearthed plentiful primary source exhibits of the ideology of Pentecostal Zionism.

In chapters 2 and 3, the very different worlds of Azusa and Jerusalem were explored and depicted as they were at the outset of the Pentecostal mission in Palestine in 1906. Chapter 2 constructed a portrayal of the Azusa Street Revival, appraised the formative influences of Charles Parham and William Seymour, and presented eyewitness accounts of the pneumatic manifestations displayed at Azusa. The global missionary movement unleashed by Azusa was described as it was viewed by participant-observers. The place of Palestine in the missionary vision of early Pentecostalism was analyzed and the trek of the Spirit-filled missionaries who headed out from Azusa to Jerusalem was traced. In chapter 3, a portrayal of the political, cultural, religious, and historical aspects of Jerusalem as it was in the period of late Ottoman Palestine was produced. Then the question was entertained of as to whether the entrance of the Azusa missionaries into and the world of Jerusalem could be considered an intercultural connection. A negative verdict was reached due to the effect of Pentecostal eschatology in clouding the Pentecostals' vision of Palestine as it was at the turn of the twentieth century. Image and reality parted company in Pentecostal eschatology for two reasons. First, what Pentecostals predicted did not happen. Second, Pentecostals were prejudiced in favor of Zionism. By elevating the role of the Jews in their eschatological scenario, Pentecostals blocked from their field of vision the rights of the Arab

Muslims and Christians who made up the overwhelming majority of the population of Palestine.

Chapters 4, 5, 6, and 7 narrated the history of the Pentecostal mission in Palestine from 1906 to 2007. The story of the Pentecostal mission in Palestine was reconstructed largely from the reports of the missionaries themselves. Chapter 4 focused on the formative contributions of the pioneer missionaries, Lucy Leatherman, Charles Leonard, and A. Elizabeth Brown. Chapter 5 highlighted the strategic leadership of A. Elizabeth Brown, the development of a mission station mission in Jerusalem, and the expansion of outstations in Syria, Transjordan, and Persia. Chapter 6 chronicled the story of the mission caught in the crossfire of the Arab-Zionist conflict and World War II, which hindered the mission in the accomplishment of its objectives. Chapter 7 described the changing of the guard after World War II, the disruption of the mission during the Wars of 1948 and 1967, and the shift toward a contextual mission in the West Bank due to the leadership of Margaret Gaines. In these narrative chapters the author extracted and examined the ideology of Pentecostal Zionism that is imbedded in the discourse of the missionaries and the Pentecostal periodicals. The narrative chapters were capped with a summative assessment of the achievements of the Pentecostal mission in Palestine. Finally, causative explanations for its failure to make and retain converts were offered.

Chapters 8 and 9 shifted from historical narrative to a post-colonial assessment of Pentecostal Zionism. Chapter 8 demonstrated the influence of William Blackstone, the leading advocate of Christian Zionism in America, on the early Pentecostals. This chapter proved that the proponents of Pentecostal Zionism and the Pentecostal press espoused a pro-Zionist bias which tended to neglect the civil rights of the Arab population of Palestine. In Chapter 9 we found that the legacy of the Pentecostal mission in Palestine is a mixed bag. On the one hand, the missionaries made a significant contribution to the historic Pentecostal affinity to the Jewish people. They left a legacy of philosemitism that was passed down from Derek Prince to the charismatic movement, the pro-Israel movement, Messianic Judaism, and the writings of popular renewalist authors who have made some important theological strides. They have acknowledged Christian responsibility for the Holocaust, denounced anti-Semitism, repudiated replacement theology, issued a call for a recovery of the Jewish roots of Christian faith, and reaffirmed a philosemitic attitude toward Israel. On the other hand, the legacy of the Pentecostal mission in Palestine has a dark side. The Pentecostal missionaries espoused Islamophobia by caricaturing Islam as a devil-inspired faith bent on world conquest, the sexual degradation of women, and conversion by the sword. This caricature dismisses the positive attributes of Islam as an Abrahamic faith and neglects its cultural contributions. Furthermore, in favoring the Zionist project and asserting the legitimacy of the state of Israel on the basis of biblical prophecy, Pentecostals disregarded the Arab right of self determination and nationhood. In telling the story of the Arab-Israeli conflict Pentecostals have flatly excluded the Arab side of the story. In so doing, they have contributed to the forces working against peace in Israel/Palestine.

MISSIOLOGICAL IMPLICATIONS

At critical junctures in the historical narrative, the author argued on the basis of primary source evidence that the missionaries functioned as brokers of Pentecostal Zionism. In one sense, the missionaries were similar to journalists purporting to report news on location with a modicum of impartiality. But in another sense, they were partisans whose commentary was colored by an ideological commitment to Pentecostal Zionism. The missionaries represented the events they reported so as to confirm the ideology of Pentecostal Zionism. In so doing they only told half the story, the Zionist side. One would think that Arab clients of the Pentecostal mission in Palestine would have been nonplussed by the Zionist leanings of the missionaries. Such leanings would have been likely to stir a sense of dissonance among Arab clients and perhaps sabotage the development of a healthy indigenous local church leadership, which was a telling flaw of the Pentecostal mission in Palestine.

A number of missiological implications can be educed from the historical narrative, using Edward Said's method of intercultural analysis. The Pentecostal views of the Other in Palestine—Jews, Arab Christians, and Muslims—were dualistic and oppositional. Even though the missionaries attested to philosemitism, they spoke in disparaging terms of Jewish religious practices in Palestine. They accused Eastern Christians of practicing idolatry and alleged that Islam was inspired by Satan. The missionaries' perceptions of the cultures of Palestine were ethnocentric and derogatory. Their use of "heathen" terminology was pejorative, insulting, demeaning, and perhaps indicative of cultural imperialism. The Pentecostal missionaries regarded their religion as superior not only to Judaism and Islam, but also to Eastern Christianity, which they characterized as a form of Christianity without Christ. In striving to evangelize Jews and Muslims and to proselytize Arab Christians, Pentecostals construed their work among these peoples in terms of conquest, warfare, and triumph, giving the impression that the missionaries were pitted against those whom they were attempting to convert. Furthermore, Pentecostal textual attitudes reinforced the notion of a clash of civilizations between the descendents of Isaac and Ishmael. The Pentecostal hermeneutic employed the Bible as an ideological textbook for the purpose of legitimating the Pentecostal Zionism and its attendant Islamophobia. The conclusion is inescapable that the Pentecostal missionaries held unfavorable attitudes toward the Jews, Arab Christians, and Muslims of Palestine. These attitudes certainly influenced the ability of the Pentecostal missionaries to build intercultural bridges.

It is an axiom of missiology that missionaries are to identify as much as possible with those to whom they are sent, not only acquiring linguistic fluency but also immersing themselves in the host culture and observing its customs, mores, habits, and traditions. Normally, a missionary will also absorb the host culture's attitudes toward neighboring peoples. By means of enculturation, missionaries build intercultural bridges of communication and witness. When enculturation is accomplished, the outcome is ideally the transmission and acceptance of the contextualized Christian message.[1] The question that now comes to the fore is to what extent the Pentecostal missionaries succeeded in contextualizing the Pentecostal message in the host cultures of Palestine.

It is significant that the Pentecostal missionary with the most favorable attitude toward Arabs and Muslims was the one who totally immersed himself in Arab culture, Archibald Forder. Margaret Gaines also succeeded in fully identifying with her Arab clients and developing indigenous leadership. However, Forder and Gaines were not representative of the rest of the Pentecostal missionaries. By and large, the Pentecostal missionaries held unfavorable attitudes toward the Jews, Arab Christians, and Muslims of Palestine. These attitudes certainly influenced the ability of the Pentecostal missionaries to build intercultural bridges. In the judgment of the author, the most significant shortfall of the Pentecostal mission in Palestine was its failure to create a sustainable and contextualized Christian community. In spite of their stated desire to nurture their converts in a protective and supportive community, the Pentecostal missionaries neither developed a significant following nor trained a stable corps of indigenous leaders.

With the exception of Forder and Gaines, the Pentecostal missionaries lived apart from the "native" Christians and were not in intimate touch with them. As a result, the cultural gap between the missionaries and their converts was not bridged. To close this gap, the essential requirement was a contextualized Christian environment in which converts could be cared for, supported, and trained for participation in the mission. The criticism that Western missionaries forced people to break from the prevailing culture without providing a viable alternative applies to the Pentecostal mission in Palestine. T. E. Backman writes in the *Moslem World* in 1939, "Conversion has too often been regarded as completed when a person formally breaks with his non-Christian background. But actually, as far as livelihood and sanctification are concerned, this is only the beginning. There must be a community of believers into which the convert may be brought. In that moment the need for fellowship is far beyond what the stay-at-home Christian can really imagine."[2] The Pentecostal missionaries did not fully comprehend what they were asking of their converts, nor did they provide the support system that was required for the necessary aftercare of their converts. Conversion in Palestine entailed a severe social dislocation, often a break in family, economic, and communal ties. To compensate, a new community which provided for its members holistically should have been developed. This is something that the Pentecostal missionaries did not accomplish.

In order to achieve effective intercultural communication in Palestine, the Pentecostal missionaries might have profited from a more studied understanding of the relationship between Christianity and Islam. Accounting for more than half the world's population between them, both Christianity and Islam are missionary religions with mutually exclusive claims to finality, universality, and truth; both believe themselves to be true to a degree the other is not. This inherent conflict of interests is

1. My discussion of enculturation borrows from Pikkert, "Protestant Missionaries to the Middle East: Ambassadors of Christ or Culture."

2. Bachmann, "Mission Frontier in Palestine," *The Moslem World* 29.3 (1939) 283.

compounded by a long history which has often been fraught with conflict and antagonism.[3] It is an open question whether the Muslims of Palestine rejected the message of the Pentecostal missionaries for theological reasons or because of a cultural impasse. The legal constraints against the evangelization of Muslims in Ottoman Palestine were not as strict as one might suppose. Public preaching was prohibited but that did not prevent private conversations, educational and medical efforts, the establishment of clubs and societies, and the distribution and sale of Scriptures. Even within Palestine under the British Mandate (1922–48), most missions did not favor the direct approach to evangelization. Instead, after extensive experience they were content to disseminate the Christian message through schools, medical clinics, and charity. To a large extent, the Pentecostals eschewed these indirect tactics. All of the missions made converts. Muslims were somewhat receptive to the Christian message. The breakdown came in retaining converts. When a Muslim converted to Christianity, he or she was frequently met with grass roots intimidation, threats, physical harassment, and even death. Direct evangelization was much more likely to evoke violent responses from the Muslim community. This is what diverted many missions from a confrontational approach to evangelizing the Muslims of Palestine. However, in the final analysis none of the Christian missions in Palestine succeeded in retaining a large number of converts from Islam.

Perhaps the most significant factor in the failure of the Pentecostal mission to retain its converts was its preferential option for Zionism. In Palestine the major wedge of political conflict was not between Christianity and Islam, but rather between the Zionist and Arab national movements. The Pentecostal missionaries sided with the Zionists, and they also expressed especially negative attitudes toward Islam and Muslims. Muslims would have had ample reasons for being wary of the Pentecostal missionaries. So might the Pentecostal mission's Arab Christian proselytes, as the Pentecostals held negative views of Arabs and Arabic culture. Ultimately, the explanation for the failure of the Pentecostal missionaries to make and hold a sizeable number of converts resides in the intercultural attitudes documented in this book.

Hence, the final conclusion of this book can be stated as follows: We have evaluated the Pentecostal dalliance with Zionism and concluded that it has led to a disregard for the civil rights of Arabs in Israel/Palestine. We have examined the intercultural attitudes of the Pentecostal missionaries and educed missiological implications which shed light on the failure of the Pentecostals to contextualize the Christian message in Palestine. And we have looked the legacy of Pentecostal Zionism square in the face and reached the sad conclusion that it has contributed to the forces working against peace in Israel/Palestine today. If Pentecostal Zionism is not viewed with favor today by Palestinian Christians, it is for good reason. Nevertheless, it was a formative influence in shaping the world view of early Pentecostalism and defining its legacy for future generations.

3. Zebiri, *Christians and Muslims Face to Face*, 5, 175.

CONTRIBUTION TO THE STUDY OF PENTECOSTALISM

The Arab-Zionist conflict in Israel/Palestine is a missing issue in the study of Pentecostalism, known to some as renewal studies.[4] While the mass media offer daily reports and commentary and the academy accumulates a wealth of specialized scholarly monographs on the question of Israel/Palestine, the scholars, academic societies, and peer-reviewed journals engaged in renewal studies have largely neglected this topic.[5] Pentecostal and charismatic biblical scholars have given close attention to the prodigious pneumatic manifestations marking the birth of the church in Jerusalem two thousand years ago.[6] However, historians of the Pentecostal and charismatic tradition have not given similar attention to more recent developments in Jerusalem. In fact, scholarly reflection on the realities of Israel/Palestine from a renewalist perspective is virtually nonexistent. Much less, no scholar of renewal studies has published an article or book on the history of the Pentecostal mission in Palestine. The topic of this book is an untouched field of published research.[7] It is hoped that this historical narrative will break new ground in addressing the question of Israel/Palestine from a renewal perspective.

This book constitutes an original contribution to the study of Pentecostalism in three respects. First, it has narrated the untold story of the Pentecostal mission in Palestine from 1906 to 2007. Second, it has documented the historic Pentecostal affinity for Zionism, as seen through the eyes of the Pentecostal missionaries in Palestine as well as the Pentecostal periodicals. Third, it has evaluated the legacy of Pentecostal Zionism, offering a suggestion as to how renewal theologians might atone for the injustices of the past and make a contribution to the forces working toward peace in Israel/Palestine.

---

4. Renewal studies can be defined as academic research and writing on Pentecostal and charismatic renewal movements.

5. Only three scholars have dealt with the question of Israel/Palestine from a renewal perspective. See Raymond L. Gannon, "The Shifting Romance with Israel: American Pentecostal Ideology of Zionism and the Jewish State"; Peter Hocken, *The Glory and the Shame*, 133–66; Hocken, *The Spirit of Unity*, 14–20; and Calvin L. Smith, *Pentecostal Power*.

6. See the bibliography on "New Testament Pneumatology, 1983–1993" in Mark W. G. Stibbe, "The Theology of Renewal and the Renewal of Theology."

7. Allan Anderson gives a brief synopsis of the Pentecostal mission in Palestine in his recently published study of the global Pentecostal missionary movement, *Spreading Fires*, 152–53.

Bibliography

PRIMARY SOURCES

Periodicals

Apostolic Faith (Kansas)

Parham, Charles F. "Jennie Glassey." *Apostolic Faith* 1.1 (May 3, 1899) 5.
———. "Redemption." *Apostolic Faith* 3.2 (February 1914) 5.

Apostolic Faith (Los Angeles, California)

"The Gift of Languages." *Apostolic Faith* 1.1 (September 1906) 1.
"A Message Concerning His Coming." *Apostolic Faith* 1.2 (October 1906) 3.
"Missionaries to Jerusalem." *Apostolic Faith* 1.1 (September 1906) 4.
"Pentecostal Experience." *Apostolic Faith* 1.3 (November 1906) 4.
"The Pentecostal Baptism Restored." *Apostolic Faith* 1.2 (October 1906) 1.
"Pentecost Has Come." *Apostolic Faith* 1.4 (December 1906) 1.
"Signs of His Coming." *Apostolic Faith* 1.6 (March 1907) 5.
"Testimonies of Outgoing Missionaries." *Apostolic Faith* 1.2 (October 1906) 1.
Barratt, T. B. "Baptized in New York." *Apostolic Faith* 1.4 (December 1906) 3.
Leatherman, Lucy. "Jerusalem." *Apostolic Faith* 2.13 (May 1908) 1.
———. "Pentecostal Experience." *Apostolic Faith* 1.3 (November 1906) 4.
McIntosh, T. J. "Missionaries in Palestine." 2.13 *Apostolic Faith* (May 1908) 4.
Mead, S. J. "New-Tongued Missionaries for Africa." *Apostolic Faith* 1.3 (November 906) 3.

Australian Evangel

Gee, Donald. "The Romance of Pentecostal Missions." *Australian Evangel* 3.1 (July 1928) 10.

Bridegroom's Messenger

"Brother J. H. King Writes." *Bridegroom's Messenger* 5.102 (January 15, 1912) 1.
"Elizabeth Brown Letter." *Bridegroom's Messenger* 5.107 (April 1, 1912) 2.
"From Brother T. J. McIntosh." *Bridegroom's Messenger* 2.38 (May 15, 1909) 2.
"From Bro. T. J. McIntosh." *Bridegroom's Messenger* 4.92 (August 15, 1911) 2.
"From Our Missionaries in Jerusalem." *Bridegroom's Messenger* 4.84 (April 15, 1911) 4.
"From Sister A. E. Brown, Jerusalem." *Bridegroom's Messenger* 4.91 (August 1, 1911) 3.
"From Sister Leatherman." *Bridegroom's Messenger* 5.111 (June 1, 1912) 3.
"Letter from Lucy Leatherman." *Bridegroom's Messenger* 1.16 (June 15, 1908) 1.
"Letter from Sister Leatherman." *Bridegroom's Messenger* 5.118 (September 15, 1912) 4.

Bibliography

"Letter from Sister Lucy Leatherman." *Bridegroom's Messenger* 6.122 (December 1, 1912) 1.

"The Jews: Would Zionism Hinder the Conversion of the Jews?" *Bridegroom's Messenger* 4.75 (December 1, 1910) 2.

"Parable of the Fig Tree." *Bridegroom's Messenger* 5.107 (April 1, 1912) 4.

Brown, Abbie Morrow. "A Visit to Hebron." *Bridegroom's Messenger* 5.96 (October 15, 1911) 4.

Brown, Anna Elizabeth. "Jerusalem, Palestine." *Bridegroom's Messenger* 5.107 (April 1, 1912) 2.

———. "Requesting Prayer for Palestine." *Bridegroom's Messenger* 2.41 (July 1, 1909) 1.

———. "Two Missionaries for Jerusalem." *Bridegroom's Messenger* 4.73 (November 1, 1910) 2.

Hanna, Ghali. "Pentecost in Egypt." *Bridegroom's Messenger* 2.32 (February 15, 1909) 1.

Leatherman, Lucy. "From Egypt." *Bridegroom's Messenger* 2.30 (January 19, 1909) 3.

———. "An Egyptian Missionary Receives His Baptism." *Bridegroom's Messenger* 2.23 (October 1, 1908) 1.

———. "From Assiout." *Bridegroom's Messenger* 2.29 (January 1, 1909) 1.

———. "From Sister Lucy Leatherman." *Bridegroom's Messenger* 3.48 (October 15, 1909) 2.

———. "From Sister Leatherman." *Bridegroom's Messenger* 3.50 (November 15, 1909) 1.

———. "From Sister Lucy Leatherman." *Bridegroom's Messenger* 3.51 (December 1, 1909) 4.

———. "Sound of Abundance of Rain." *Bridegroom's Messenger* 2.25 (November 1, 1908) 1.

Moorhead, Max. "Sign of the Fig Tree." *Bridegroom's Messenger* 5.119 (October 15, 1912) 4.

Sexton, Elizabeth. "Going with a Message." *Bridegroom's Messenger* 4.76 (December 15, 1910) 1.

———. "Increasing Missionary Activity." *Bridegroom's Messenger* 3.69 (September 1, 1910) 1.

———. "Pentecost in Jerusalem, Palestine." *Bridegroom's Messenger* 1.16 (June 15, 1908) 1.

———. "Pentecost in Jerusalem." *Bridegroom's Messenger* 1.17 (July 1, 1908) 1.

———. "Watch the Fig Tree." *Bridegroom's Messenger* 3.55 (February 1, 1910) 1.

Christian Evangel

"Charles S. Leonard, Egypt." *Christian Evangel* (December 26, 1914) 4.

"Jerusalem." *Christian Evangel* (October 31, 1914) 1.

"Jerusalem, Palestine." *Christian Evangel* (October 10, 1914) 4.

"The Land of Palestine." *Christian Evangel* (December 25, 1920) 13.

"Miss A. E. Brown writes from Jerusalem Palestine." *Christian Evangel* (September 20, 1919) 10.

"Missionaries Back From Jerusalem." *Christian Evangel* (March 3, 1917) 3.

"Sister A. E. Brown writes from Jerusalem." *Christian Evangel* (August 9, 1919) 10.

Bell, E. N. "The League of Nations." *Christian Evangel* (March 8, 1919) 2.

———. "War Paralyzed Us, Missionaries Write." *Christian Evangel* (October 10, 914) 4.

Blackstone, William. "The Times of the Gentiles." *The Weekly Evangel* (May 13, 1916) 7.

Boothby, Alberta. "An Interesting Letter from Egypt." *Weekly Evangel* (February 19, 1916) 12.

Brown, Anna Elizabeth. "Back to Jerusalem." *Christian Evangel* (February 22, 1919) 13.

———. "Behold, He Cometh." *Christian Evangel* (April 19, 1919) 3.

———. "Jerusalem, Palestine." *Christian Evangel* (June 28, 1919) 11.

———. "Port Said, Egypt." *Christian Evangel* (May 17, 1919) 2.

Bush, Florence. "Egypt." *Christian Evangel* (January 9, 1915) 4; (April 24, 1915) 4; (May 22, 1915), 4.

———. "Tidings from Jerusalem." *Christian Evangel* (September 12, 1914) 4.

———. "Trouble in Palestine." *Christian Evangel* (November 7, 1914) 1.

Flower, J. R. "The Kings of the East." *Christian Evangel* (November 7, 1914) 1.

Moll, Frank. "The Work in Africa and Egypt." *Christian Evangel* (November 14, 1914) 1.

Post, A. H. & Wife. "Missionaries Leave Egypt." *Christian Evangel* (December 26, 1914) 4.

Rader, Paul. "Armageddon." *Christian Evangel* (May 18, 1918) 2–3.

Smithson, Mary. "Jerusalem, Palestine." *Christian Evangel* (July 11, 1914) 4.

The Evening Light and Church of God Evangel

"Off for Palestine." *Church of God Evangel* 11.25 (June 19, 1920) 3.

"Rev. D. B. Hatfield, Mrs. Hatfield, Darryl Lynn and Sheralyn." *Church of God Evangel* (July 22, 1950) 5.

"The Rev. D. B. Hatfield Writes." *Church of God Evangel* (May 10, 1952) 9.

Joyner, Paul. "News From Jerusalem." *The Evening Light and Church of God Evangel* (March 18, 1922) 4.

———. "News from Jerusalem." *The Evening Light and Church of God Evangel* 12.51 (December 24, 1921) 4.

Cook, Robert F. "God's Prophetic Timepiece." *Church of God Evangel* (October 28, 1957) 4–5, 13.

Gaines, Margaret. "Birth of a Church." *Church of God Evangel* (December 1, 1969) 7.

———. "Kept." *Church of God Evangel* (December 18, 1967) 4.

———. "The Seething Cauldron." *Church of God Evangel* (November 16, 1964) 9.

———. "We Dedicate This School." *Church of God Evangel* (June 24, 1974) 23.

Hatfield, D. B. "Annual Convention in the Jordan Kingdom (Old Palestine)." *Church of God Evangel* (October 31, 1953) 7.

———. "From the Middle East Bible Lands." *Church of God Evangel* (April 21, 1951) 13.

———. "Help Us To Build the Church a Home." *Church of God Evangel* (July 7, 1952) 12.

———. "New Converts in Palestine Persecuted." *Church of God Evangel* (October 6, 1951) 10.

———. "Palestine." *Church of God Evangel* (July 16, 1949) 5.

Polen, O. W. "Margaret Gaines, Missionary in Israel." *Church of God Evangel* (November 28, 1977) 18.

Sidersky, Philip. "Leaksville, N.C." *The Evening Light and Church of God Evangel* 1.19 (December 1, 1910) 6.

Suleiman, Hanna. "History of the Church of God in Palestine." *The Church of God Evangel* 43.29 (September 20, 1952) 6–10.

———. "My Experience on the Ship Coming to the United States." *Church of God Evangel* (December 2, 1950) 6.

Walker, J. H. "Missionaries Return to Middle East." *Church of God Evangel* (April 22, 1950) 13.

Confidence

"German Conference." *Confidence* 2.1 (January 1909) 8.

"Latest News from our Jerusalem Missionary." *Confidence* 3.7 (July 1910) 172.

"News from Mrs. Lucy Leatherman." *Confidence* 5.7 (July 1912) 184.

"Off To Jerusalem." *Confidence* 3.4 (April 1910) 89.

"Pentecostal Items." *Confidence* 5.1 (January 1912) 18.

"The Pentecostal Movement." *Confidence* 2.6 (June 1909) 8–11.

"Sister Gerber." *Confidence* 8.11 (November 1915) 213.

"Sunderland International Pentecostal Congress." *Confidence* 2.6 (June 1909) 127–28.

"Syria-Safety of Brother A. Forder." *Confidence* 4.1 (January 1911) 15.

"The War." *Confidence* 8.1 (January 1913) 3–6.

"The War." *Confidence* 8.2 (February 1915) 27–29.

Barratt, T. B. "In Syria." *Confidence* 7 (October 15, 1908) 20–21.

Boddy, Alexander. "At Los Angeles, California." *Confidence* 5.10 (October 1912) 232–34.

———. "Digging for the Ark." *Confidence* 7 (October 15, 1908) 22.

———. "In Southern California: A Meeting at the Azusa Street Mission, Los Angeles." *Confidence* 5.11 (November 1912) 244–45.

———. "Jerusalem." *Confidence* 1.5 (August 15, 1908) 15.

———. "The Return of the Jews to the Holy Land." *Confidence* 13.3 (October–December, 1920) 51–55.

———. "Seven Signs of His Coming." *Confidence* (December 1910) 291–93.

Boddy, Jane. "Testimony of a Vicar's Daughter." *Confidence* (May 1908) 6–7.

Brown, Anna Elizabeth. "From Jerusalem." *Confidence* 5.2 (January–February, 1912) 18.

———. "Jerusalem: Distributing the Gospels." *Confidence* 6.2 (February 1913) 39–40.

———. "Jerusalem." *Confidence* 8.5 (May 1915) 91.

———. "Jerusalem in War-Time." *Confidence* 8.12 (December 1915) 227.

Hanna, Gahli. "Egypt." *Confidence* 2.1 (January 1909) 22.

Joseph, D. C. "Flight from the Holy Land: A Jewish Missionary Escapes from Haifa." *Confidence* 8.5 (May 1915) 94–95.

Leatherman, Lucy. "Jerusalem." *Confidence* 5.3 (March 1912) 59.

Malick, Yumna. "Syria: A Letter to Pastor Barratt." *Confidence* 1.9 (December 15, 1908) 17–18.

Post, A. H. "Egypt." *Confidence* 3.7 (July 1910) 165.

Bibliography

Elim Evangel and Foursquare Revivalist

Johnson, Andrew. "The Pentecostal Work in Sweden: Sacrifice and Hardship for the Gospel's Sake," *The Elim Evangel and Foursquare Revivalist* 6.5 (March 2, 1925) 49–50; 6.6 (March 16, 1925) 65.

Jones, J. 3. "Further Facts About Palestine" *The Elim Evangel and Foursquare Revivalist* 10.22 (September 29, 1929) 339–41.

———. "Palestine: A Great Sign of the Present Age." *The Elim Evangel and Foursquare Revivalist* (July 26, 1929) 201–3.

Kingston, Charles. "The Jew in Relation to the Coming of the Lord." *The Elim Evangel and Foursquare Revivalist* 8.17 (September 1, 1927) 261.

Kratz, Ronald R. "A Place Called Armageddon." *The Elim Evangel and Foursquare Revivalist* 12.2 (January 9, 1931) 30.

Parker, Percy G. "Christ is Coming Soon! An Outstanding Sign." *The Elim Evangel and Foursquare Revivalist* 9.19 (December 1, 1928) 313–15.

Proctor, Henry. "The Times of the Gentiles." *The Elim Evangel and Foursquare Revivalist* 13.38 (September 16, 1932) 596.

Radford, Laura. "Transjordania and the Borders of Arabia." *The Elim Evangel and Foursquare Revivalist* 11.33 (September 18, 1931) 604.

Rohold, R. H. "Concise Comments and Interesting Items." *The Elim Evangel and Foursquare Revivalist* 11.12 (March 21, 1930) 181.

Full Gospel Advocate

"Material for Solomon's Temple Now Ready." *Full Gospel Advocate* (January 10, 1930) 4.

Richey, Raymond. "Is the Messiah at Hand?" *Full Gospel Advocate* (February 15, 1929) 7.

Latter Rain Evangel

"The Budding Fig Tree." *Latter Rain Evangel* (February 1930) 21.

"Deepening Shadows on Palestinian Syria." *Latter Rain Evangel* (December 1925) 13.

"The Earthquake That Shook Palestine: When Tribes Begged for the Gospel." *Latter Rain Evangel* (September 1927) 10–11.

"Glory out of Shame." *Latter Rain Evangel* (August 1923) 13–14.

"House Problem." *Latter Rain Evangel* (April 1921) 14.

"Isaac and Ishmael." *Latter Rain Evangel* (October 1929) 1.

"The Jewish Conference." *Latter Rain Evangel* (February 1918) 12.

"Miss Laura Radford." *Latter Rain Evangel* (August 1924) 14.

"Miss Laura Radford Writing from EsSalt." *Latter Rain Evangel* (March 1928) 16.

"Miss Malick, Shweifat, Lebanon." *Latter Rain Evangel* (February 1925) 23.

"Miss Vera Swartztrauber." *Latter Rain Evangel* (March 1929) 15.

"News from the Mission Fields." *Latter Rain Evangel* (February 1930) 18.

"Not Through with the War." *Latter Rain Evangel* (August 1919) 23.

"Outgoing Missionaries." *Latter Rain Evangel* (October 1923) 10.

"Palestine and the Jew." *Latter Rain Evangel* (February 1921) 22–23.

"Rites Marking Holy Edict." *Latter Rain Evangel* (January 1915) 13–14.

"This Year in Jerusalem." *Latter Rain Evangel* (January 1918) 13.

"Turkey's Women Unveiled." *Latter Rain Evangel* (December 1924) 20–21.

"Yiddish Evangelist." *Latter Rain Evangel* (November 1908) 14.

Boddy, Alexander. "Pentecost in Sunderland." *Latter Rain Evangel* (February 1909) 9–10.

Brown, Anna Elizabeth. "A New Regime Among the Moslems." *Latter Rain Evangel* (January 1919): 4.

———. "Recent Conditions in Jerusalem." *Latter Rain Evangel* (April 1918) 5.

———. "Safe Return from Jerusalem of a Veteran Missionary: Ninety Days Thro' the War Zone Amid Peril and Hardship." *Latter Day Evangel* (October 1917) 20–24.

Bush, Florence. "God's Guidance and Blessing in Difficult Fields." *Latter Rain Evangel* (December 1915) 9–11.

Cossum, William. "Mountain Peaks of Prophesy and Sacred History: The Indestructible Jew." *Latter Rain Evangel* (April 1910) 4.

———. "Mountain Peaks of Prophecy and Sacred History: The Zionist Movement." *Latter Rain Evangel* 2.8 (May 1910) 6–9.

———. "Satan Overreaches Himself: Days of Fulfillment Drawing Nigh." *Latter Rain Evangel* (December 1917) 3.

Cox, H. H. "The Time Table in the Word of God: Stirrings in Jewish Circles and Heading Up of Events." *Latter Rain Evangel* (May 1916) 2–3.

David, Ira. "Jesus Is Certainly coming Back Soon: Abundant Proof that the End is Near." *Latter Rain Evangel* (September 1920) 17.

Forder, Archibald. "Hunting Arabs at Sinai." *Latter Rain Evangel* (January 1913) 13–14.

———. "And Ishmael Will Be a Wild Man." *Latter Rain Evangel* 1.11 (August 1909) 2–7.

———. "Some Facts About Modern Jerusalem." *Latter Rain Evangel* 3.3 (December 1910) 8–9.

———. "The Re-peopling of Moab." *Latter Rain Evangel* 3.6 (March 1911) 7–8.

Jago, E. O. "A Great Crisis! The Mohammedan's Slogan, a Call to the Church to Awake." *Latter Rain Evangel* (October 1913) 2–7.

Radford, Laura. "Trans Jordan and the Borders of Arabia." *Latter Rain Evangel* (June 1928) 10.

Kerr, Mrs. D. W. "A World Wide Appeal." *Latter Rain Evangel* (November 1922) 22–23.

Malick, Yumna. "The Gospel in Syria." *Latter Rain Evangel* (September 1923) 22–24.

———. "Results of Gospel Preached in Syria." *Latter Rain Evangel* (April 1930) 17.

Myland, D. Wesley. "The Fifth Latter Rain Lecture: The Fullness and Effects of Pentecost." *Latter Rain Evangel* 1.12 (September 1909) 13–19.

———. "The Latter Rain Covenant: Deuteronomy 11:10–21." *Latter Rain Evangel* 1.9 (May 1909) 15–21.

———. "Literal and Spiritual Latter Rain Falling Simultaneously: God's Ancient People Are Returning to their Native Land." *Latter Rain Evangel* 2.1 (October 1909) 17–23.

Piper, William Hammar. "Sermon, Jan. 17, 1909." *Latter Rain Evangel* 1.6 (March 1909) 7.

Radford, Laura. "A Day of Terror in Jerusalem." *Latter Rain Evangel* (November 1929) 21.

———. "A Sheikh Becomes a Christian." *Latter Rain Evangel* (January 1926) 15.

———. "A Forty Days Revival." *Latter Rain Evangel* (July 1929) 19.

———. "News from the Mission Fields." *Latter Rain Evangel* (February 1930) 18.

Rohold, S. B. "Zionism: Past, Present and Future: Lack of Unity in Jewish Circles the Great Hindrance." *Latter Rain Evangel* (February 1918) 16.

Stuernagel, A. E. "Signs of the Approaching End of the Age," *Latter Rain Evangel* (May 1927) 4–8.

Weaver, Albert. "Human or Divine: Which Shall It Be?" *Latter Rain Evangel* (December 1929) 18.

The Pentecost

Leatherman, Lucy. "Apostolic Revival in Egypt." *The Pentecost* 1.5 (January–February, 1909) 5.

———. "Coming Home." *The Pentecost* 1.10 (September 15, 1909) 4.

———. "A Missionary Trip Through Syria and Palestine." *The Pentecost* 1.4 (December 1908) 5.

The Pentecostal Evangel

"Advancing Backwards." *Pentecostal Evangel* (January 10, 1920) 4.

"Back to the Land." *Pentecostal Evangel* (January 18, 1936) 10.

"The Battle for Palestine." *Pentecostal Evangel* (September 14, 1940) 7.

"Brother John G. Wharton Arrives in Persia." *Pentecostal Evangel* (November 22, 1924) 10.

"The Budding Fig Tree." *Pentecostal Evangel* (October 1, 1921) 4.

"The Budding Fig Tree." *Pentecostal Evangel* (April 15, 1922) 1, 7.

"Elizabeth Brown." *The Pentecostal Evangel* (May 29, 1920) 13; (February 18, 1922) 6–7.

"Epistle from Jerusalem." *Pentecostal Evangel* (November 12, 1921) 12.

"Es Salt, Transjordan." *Pentecostal Evangel* (August 28, 1937) 7.

"Exodus of Jews from Germany." *Pentecostal Evangel* (March 11, 1933) 5.

"Ezekiel's Prediction of Impending Judgment." *Pentecostal Evangel* (May 13, 1922) 1, 9.

"The First Jewish Ship." *Pentecostal Evangel* (February 17, 1934) 5.

Bibliography

"The Fourth Missionary Conference." *Pentecostal Evangel* (October 18, 1919) 1, 4.

"From Lebanon, Syria." *Pentecostal Evangel* (September 28, 1940) 9.

"God's Future Plans for Israel." *Pentecostal Evangel* (May 29, 1948) 4–5, 14.

"Good News for the Jews." *Pentecostal Evangel* (February 28, 1931) 4–5.

"Good News from Trans-Jordan." *Pentecostal Evangel* (October 3, 1936) 6.

"Here and There." *Pentecostal Evangel* (August 16, 1924) 6–7; (January 3, 1925) 6.

"Isaac and Ishmael Reconciled." *Pentecostal Evangel* (January 7, 1933) 4.

"Ishmael's Opposition." *Pentecostal Evangel* (March 11, 1922) 5.

"Israel's National Destiny." *Pentecostal Evangel* (February 3, 1934) 5.

"Jerusalem, Palestine." *Pentecostal Evangel* (January 6, 1934) 10.

"Jerusalem in War Time." *Pentecostal Evangel* (February 8, 1941) 10.

"Jewish Activities." *Pentecostal Evangel* (September 5, 1931) 5.

"Keep Your Eye on Palestine." *Pentecostal Evangel* (November 25, 1922) 4.

"The Land of Palestine." *Pentecostal Evangel* (December 25, 1920) 13.

"Mass Movement to Palestine." *Pentecostal Evangel* (February 1, 1936) 11.

"Miss A. Eliz. Brown." *Pentecostal Evangel* (April 1, 1922) 13; (July 23, 1921) 13.

"Miss A. Elizabeth Brown." *Pentecostal Evangel* (September 30, 1922) 13; (January 20, 1923) 13; (September 8, 1923) 12.

"Missionaries for Jerusalem." *Pentecostal Evangel* (September 4, 1920) 12.

"The Missionaries in Jerusalem." *Pentecostal Evangel* (October 18, 1924) 10.

"Missionary News." *Pentecostal Evangel* (January 4, 1936) 4.

"Missionary Sailings." *Pentecostal Evangel* (October 21, 1939) 7.

"Need of Cards in Palestine." *Pentecostal Evangel* (January 26, 1935) 11.

"New Converts in Syria." *Pentecostal Evangel* (January 26, 1935) 11.

"News from Recent Sailings." *Pentecostal Evangel* (January 20, 1940) 15.

"News Items." *Pentecostal Evangel* (February 22, 1936) 6.

"New Workers for Palestine." *Pentecostal Evangel* (January 4, 1936) 4.

"Palestine." *Pentecostal Evangel* (February 10, 1940) 8; (November 2, 1940) 6.

"The Peace of Jerusalem." *Pentecostal Evangel* (April 13, 1935) 6.

"Palestine and Transjordan," & "Syria." *Pentecostal Evangel* (December 11, 1937) 2–3.

"Partitioning Palestine." *Pentecostal Evangel* (August 28, 1937) 7.

"Promoted to Higher Service." *Pentecostal Evangel* (August 24, 1940) 8.

"Prophecy Fulfilling in Jerusalem." *Pentecostal Evangel* (November 3, 1923) 9.

"Rain in Palestine." *Pentecostal Evangel* (April 16, 1932) 3.

"A Request for Prayer." *Pentecostal Evangel* (February 14, 1931) 10.

"Rifts in Zionism." *Pentecostal Evangel* (August 1, 1931) 4.

"Serena Hodges Sends Greetings." *Pentecostal Evangel* (March 23, 1940) 8.

"Strife in Palestine." *Pentecostal Evangel* (June 3, 1944) 8.

"Suffering in Palestine." *Pentecostal Evangel* (January 11, 1941) 13.

"Syria." *Pentecostal Evangel* (August 13, 1938) 7.

"Two Home from Palestine." *Pentecostal Evangel* (July 16, 1938) 7.

"Uprising in Palestine." *Pentecostal Evangel* (August 29, 1936) 9.

"A Visit with our Missionaries in Palestine." *Pentecostal Evangel* (April 17, 1937) 8, 11.

"Visiting the Bedouins." *Pentecostal Evangel* (September 5, 1936) 7.

"War and Missions." *Pentecostal Evangel* (July 20, 1940) 8; (August 31, 1940) 6.

"War in Palestine?" *Pentecostal Evangel* (February 22, 1941) 10.

"Wedding in Jerusalem." *Pentecostal Evangel* (January 14, 1933) 11.

"What's New in the Missions Department: Near East." *Pentecostal Evangel* (October 18, 1941) 8.

"Who's the Landlord of Palestine?" *Pentecostal Evangel* (February 4, 1933) 5.

"Will the Moslems Rise?" *Pentecostal Evangel* (December 5, 1931) 5.

"With the Lord." *Pentecostal Evangel* (September 14, 1940) 8.

"With Perplexity." *Pentecostal Evangel* (September 12, 1931) 4.

Adams, Anna. "Jerusalem, Palestine." *Pentecostal Evangel* (March 30, 1935) 11.

———. "Jerusalem, Palestine." *Pentecostal Evangel* (May 25, 1935) 11.

———. "Palestine." *Pentecostal Evangel* (June 6, 1936) 9.

Appelman, Hyman. "God Over Palestine." *Pentecostal Evangel* (May 14, 1949) 6–7.

Baer, Vıda. "Bible Evangelistic Mission Jerusalem." *Pentecostal Evangel* (October 25, 1924) 10.

———. "Evangelizing in Bible Lands." *Pentecostal Evangel* (September 13, 1924) 7.

———. "A Letter from Palestine." *Pentecostal Evangel* (March 15, 1924) 7.

———. "The Work in Jerusalem." *Pentecostal Evangel* (August 9, 1924) 10.

Beck, Ida. "Problems and Opportunities in Palestine." *Pentecostal Evangel* (July 3, 1943) 10–11.

Benjamin, Saul. "Blessings in Transjordan." *Pentecostal Evangel* (August 31, 1935) 9.

———. "Conference in Jerusalem." *Pentecostal Evangel* (July 25, 1942) 8.

———. "From Jerusalem, Palestine." *Pentecostal Evangel* (September 28, 1940) 9.

———. "Gold From Gilead." *Pentecostal Evangel* (November 9, 1946) 8.

———. "Greetings from Transjordan." *Pentecostal Evangel* (March 20, 1937) 9, 12.

———. "Jerusalem Convention." *Pentecostal Evangel* (September 9, 1944) 10.

———. "Jerusalem, Palestine." *Pentecostal Evangel* (June 21, 1941) 8.

———. "News from Palestine and Transjordan." *Pentecostal Evangel* (June 11, 1938) 7.

———. "News from Transjordan." *Pentecostal Evangel* (July 31, 1937) 8.

———. "Officials Inquire About Gospel." *Pentecostal Evangel* (June 20, 1936) 8.

———. "Palestine: 'Even in Troublous Times.'" *Pentecostal Evangel* (June 20, 1942) 8–9.

———. "Pray for the Peace of Jerusalem." *Pentecostal Evangel* (July 11, 1936) 7.

———. "Salt, Trans Jordan." *Pentecostal Evangel* (March 4, 1933) 10.

———. "Sidelights of the Palestine Situation." *Pentecostal Evangel* (October 1, 1938) 7.

———. "Speeding the Light in Palestine." *Pentecostal Evangel* (October 9, 1943) 9.

Brown, Anna Elizabeth. "Forty Years as a Missionary." *Pentecostal Evangel* (April 6, 1935) 11.

———. "Good News From Jerusalem." *Pentecostal Evangel* (January 26, 1924) 10–11.

———. "A Haven Found in Jerusalem." *Pentecostal Evangel* (January 22, 1921) 13.

———. "Helping to the Build the Bible School." *Pentecostal Evangel* (November 17, 1923) 8.

———. "Jerusalem." *Pentecostal Evangel* (June 29, 1935) 9.

———. "Jerusalem, Palestine." *Pentecostal Evangel* (March 30, 1935) 11.

———. "Jerusalem, Palestine." *Pentecostal Evangel* (April 16, 1921) 13.

———. "A Lighthouse in Jerusalem." *Pentecostal Evangel* (May 27, 1922) 12.

———. "News From Palestine." *Pentecostal Evangel* (October 19, 1929) 10.

———. "Our Work in Jerusalem." *Pentecostal Evangel* (March 29, 1924) 9.

———. "A Plea for the Work in Jerusalem." *Pentecostal Evangel* (March 29, 1924) 9.

———. "A Prisoner Taken Captive." *Pentecostal Evangel* (August 5, 1922) 12.

———. "Progress in Jerusalem." *Pentecostal Evangel* (October 4, 1924) 8.

———. "Special Services in Jerusalem." *Pentecostal Evangel* (October 15, 1921) 12.

———. "A Vacation in Syria." *Pentecostal Evangel* (October 28, 1922) 12.

———. "A Word from Jerusalem." *Pentecostal Evangel* (October 17, 1936) 11.

Carmichael, Christine. "Israel." *Pentecostal Evangel* (April 30, 1961) 25–26

Carmichael, George. "The Es Salt Conference." *Pentecostal Evangel* (November 15, 1947) 8–9.

———. "Greetings from Palestine!" *Pentecostal Evangel* (January 11, 1947) 8–9.

———. "Palestine Holds Nations' Interest." *Pentecostal Evangel* (August 9, 1947) 8.

———. "Rebuilding Palestine." *Pentecostal Evangel* (February 19, 1949) 2.

———. "What's Happening in Palestine." *Pentecostal Evangel* (August 28, 1948) 7.

Childe, Frederick. "Christ's Answer to the Challenge of Fascism and Communism." *Pentecostal Evangel* (October 31, 1931) 7.

Davis, George. "Giving New Testaments to Jewish People in Palestine." *Pentecostal Evangel* (January 19, 1946) 1, 12–14.

Frey, Mae. "Things as They Are in Society Today: Conditions That Call for Prayer and Our Utmost Endeavor." *Pentecostal Evangel* (May 24, 1924) 2–3.

Frodsham, Arthur. "The Return of the Lord: The Signs of the Times." *Pentecostal Evangel* (February 18, 1922) 6–7.

Gartenhaus, Jacob. "The New State of Israel." *Pentecostal Evangel* (July 31, 1948) 7.

Hodges, Serena. "Back in Jerusalem." *Pentecostal Evangel* (May 2, 1931) 11.

————. "Suggestions for Christmas Giving." *Pentecostal Evangel* (October 24, 1936) 18.

Hoy, Albert. "Israel's Answer to the Critics." *Pentecostal Evangel* (July 30, 1967) 8–9.

Kamber, S. J. "Persia." *Pentecostal Evangel* (February 9, 1935) 11, 14.

Kofsman, Z. W. "After the Pentecostal Conference." *Pentecostal Evangel* (September 17, 1961) 13.

————. "Call Her Not Mara." *Pentecostal Evangel* (April 18, 1965) 27.

————. "The Resurrection of the Hebrew Language." *Pentecostal Evangel* (June 16, 1968) 10–11.

Langston, E. L. "Signs of the Times." *Pentecostal Evangel* (March 3, 1923) 2–3, 8.

Lovesy, Pearl. "A Word from the Land of Palestine." *Pentecostal Evangel* (January 7, 1933) 11.

Malick, Yumna. "Among the Bedouins." *Pentecostal Evangel* (January 9, 1932) 13.

————. "Blessings in Far–Away Syria." *Pentecostal Evangel* (March 21, 1936) 9.

————. "Lebanon, Beyrout, Syria." *Pentecostal Evangel* (April 16, 1921) 13.

————. "Missionary Activities in Syria." *Pentecostal Evangel* (May 12, 1934) 10.

————. "Missionary Notes—Syria." *Pentecostal Evangel* (March 28, 1936) 7.

————. "The New Year in Syria." *Pentecostal Evangel* (March 18, 1922) 20.

————. "Pentecost in Syria." *Pentecostal Evangel* (October 4, 1924) 10.

————. "Syria." *Pentecostal Evangel* (March 9, 1935) 11.

————. "Work in Syria." *Pentecostal Evangel* (July 28, 1923) 12.

Mayo, Mae F. "Israel, God's Last Day Miracle." *Pentecostal Evangel* (December 17, 1950) 3–4, 12–14.

Moorhead, Max W. "The Perils of Bolshevism at Home and Abroad." *Pentecostal Evangel* (February 7, 1920) 2–3.

Nagel, William. "The Jew—What Is Your Attitude?" *Pentecostal Evangel* (January 23, 1937) 2–3, 11–12.

————. "Palestine—Why the Disturbances?" *Pentecostal Evangel* (September 5, 1936) 8–9, 13.

Panton, D. W. "Israel's Peril." *Pentecostal Evangel* (August 7, 1920) 2–3.

Pearlman, Myer. "The Jewish Question from the Viewpoint of a Converted Jew." *Pentecostal Evangel* (June 4, 1927) 1, 8–10.

————. "Those Strange People, the JEWS!" *Pentecostal Evangel* (August 20, 1949) 15.

Perkin, Noel. "Call to Advance." *Pentecostal Evangel* (January 24, 1965) 9.

————. "A Visit to the Holy Land." *Pentecostal Evangel* (November 30, 1940) 13.

————. "Work Among the Jews." *Pentecostal Evangel* (June 13, 1936) 5.

Peters, Charles. "Eretz Israel (The Land of Israel)." *Pentecostal Evangel* (April 24, 1937) 4–5.

Pike, John M. "The Wheat and the Tares." *Pentecostal Evangel* (November 27, 1920) 7.

Radford, Laura. "Days of Blessing in Palestine." *Pentecostal Evangel* (April 27, 1935) 10–11.

————. "Days of Terror in Palestine: Jerusalem the Scene of Bloody Massacre.

————. "Easter in Jerusalem." *Pentecostal Evangel* (March 26, 1932) 7.

————. "Hebron and Safed Filled with Indescribable Atrocities." *Pentecostal Evangel* (October 26, 1929) 15.

————. "Help Needed in Palestine." *Pentecostal Evangel* (December 13, 1924) 10.

————. "In a Dry and Thirsty Land." *Pentecostal Evangel* (February 16, 1924) 4.

————. "A Request from Palestine." *Pentecostal Evangel* (March 16, 1935) 5.

————. "Scripture Sales in Palestine." *Pentecostal Evangel* (February 22, 1936) 6.

————. "Victory." *Pentecostal Evangel* (August 2, 1930) 11.

Riggs, Ralph. "Who Is the Rightful Owner of Palestine?" *Pentecostal Evangel* (July 30, 1967) 7.

Shabaz, Philip. "Arrived in Persia." *Pentecostal Evangel* (June 20, 1931) 11.

————. "Our Persian Workers." *Pentecostal Evangel* (November 23, 1935) 5.

————. "Spirit Falls on Children in Persia." *Pentecostal Evangel* (June 15, 1935) 9.

Steil, Harry J. "The Trend Toward Armageddon." *Pentecostal Evangel* (July 18, 1936) 2.

————. "Two Million Signs of the Time." *Pentecostal Evangel* (July 30, 1967) 2–4.

Swarztrauber, Vera, "An Afternoon in a Palestine Village." *Pentecostal Evangel* (May 30, 1931) 7.

————. "News From Transjordan." *Pentecostal Evangel* (October 9, 1937) 9.

————. "A Word from Jerusalem." *Pentecostal Evangel* (January 13, 1940) 5.

Warton, John. "God's Ways with the Jews." *Pentecostal Evangel* (December 12, 1936) 7.

————. "Opening a New Work in Syria." *Pentecostal Evangel* (August 5, 1939) 10.

————. "Persia's Open Door." *Pentecostal Evangel* (January 12, 1924) 6–7.

————. "Survey of the Far East." *Pentecostal Evangel* (April 25, 1936) 6.

Watson, A. Stacy. "The Time of Jacob's Trouble: Copy of a Letter to a Jewish Rabbi." *Pentecostal Evangel* (September 30, 1922) 3.

Watts, Newman. "The Problem in Palestine." *Pentecostal Evangel* (December 27, 1947) 10.

Whitman, Roy. "Fulfilled Prophecy in Bible Lands." *Pentecostal Evangel* (February 16, 1935) 8.

Williams, E. S. "A Visit to Lebanon." *Pentecostal Evangel* (February 27, 1937) 8–9.

Zeildman, Morris. "The Commonwealth of Israel." *Pentecostal Evangel* (November 13, 1948) 3, 11.

———. "Rebuilding the Nation and Temple." *Pentecostal Evangel* (June 18, 1949) 5–6, 12–13.

The Pentecostal Holiness Advocate

"Before She Travailed." *Pentecostal Holiness Advocate* 32.5 (June 3, 1948) 1.

"Israel . . ." *Pentecostal Holiness Advocate* 32.4 (May 27, 1948) 1.

"Latest News from Jerusalem." *Pentecostal Holiness Advocate* 2.18 (August 29, 1918) 12.

"Unrest in Palestine." *Pentecostal Holiness Advocate* 43.22 (December 12, 1929) 7, 10.

Montgomery, G. H. "Israel Without God," *Pentecostal Holiness Advocate* 32.22 (September 30, 1948) 1.

Sexton, Elizabeth. "British Flag Waving Over the Towers of Jerusalem." *Pentecostal Holiness Advocate* (January 31, 1918) 2.

———. "Is the Fig Tree Putting Forth Leaves?" *Pentecostal Holiness Advocate* (November 15, 1917) 6.

Taylor, George F. "I Saw It in Palestine: Wailing Wall." *Pentecostal Holiness Advocate* 13.27 (October 31, 1929) 9–10.

Redemption Tidings

"Assemblies of God Missionary Policy." *Redemption Tidings* 2.2 (February 1926) 9.

"Missionary Briefs." *Redemption Tidings* 3.3 (March 1927) 10.

"Modern Missionary Methods Examined: The Present Crisis in China." *Redemption Tidings* 2.8 (August 1926) 9.

Radford, Laura. "Revival in Trans-Jordania: Spiritual 'Latter Rain' Falling." *Redemption Tidings* 6.8 (August 1930) 15.

Weaver, Albert. "Human or Divine: Which Shall It Be?" *Redemption Tidings* 6.10 (October 1930) 7.

Samson's Foxes

Tomlinson, A. J. "Jerusalem." *Samson's Foxes* 2.1 (January 1902) 2.

Trust

"Girdling the World." *Trust* (July–August 1909) 16.

"In the Last Days 'Apostasy.'" *Trust* 10.8 (October 1911) 15.

"Jews' Wailing Place." *Trust* (November–December 1928) 19.

"Letters from Students: From Miss Yuma G. Malick." *Trust* 17.2 (April 1918) 2, 10.

"Lord Balfour Gone." *Trust* 29.3–4 (May–June 1930) 18–19.

"A Warning to Israel." *Trust* 24.9–10 (November–December 1925) 23–24.

"Zangwill and Zionists." *Trust* 16.8 (October 1917) 11.

"Zionist Movement." *Trust* 27.7–8 (September–October 1928) 9.

Booth-Clibborn, Arthur S. "The Goal of Prophetic Scripture." *Trust* (December 1918) 11–14.

Brown, Anna Elizabeth. "From Jerusalem." *Trust* 11.4–5 (June–July 1912) 26.

———. "Jeruslalem." *Trust* 14.4–5 (June–July 1915) 27–28.

Bush, Florence and Mother, "Tanta, Egypt." *Trust* 14.3 (May 1915) 19.

Cobb, R. W. "A Note of Warning." *Trust* 10.7 (September 1911) 8.

Duncan, Susan. "Another Corner Turned or 'L'Union Sacree.'" *Trust* 27. 11–12 (January–February 1929) 8.

———. "The Faithful Remnant." *Trust* 17.1 (March 1918) 4.

———. "Prophecy Fulfilling." *Trust* 24. 3–4 (May–June 1925) 19.

———. "The Sorrowing Jew." *Trust* (November–December 1929) 16–17.

King, H. Pierson. "Signs of the Coming of Our Lord." *Trust* (October 1915) 12–20.

L., W.W. "The End at Hand." *Trust* 7.12 (February 1909) 17–18.

Malick, Yumna. "Sweifat–Lebanon–Syria." *Trust* (March 1925) 22–23.

Bibliography

―――. "Sweifat–Lebanon, Syria." *Trust* (September–October 1927) 21.

―――. "Syria," *Trust* 21.12 (February 1923) 14–15; (January–February 1932) 22–23.

McKilliam, Robert. "The Signs of the Times." *Trust* (March–April 1930) 17.

Pocock, William. "Present–Day Signs of the End." *Trust* (January–February 1926) 16, 20

Rohold, S. B. "Baptisms at Haifa." *Trust* 22.3 (May 1923) 12.

―――. "The Present Position." *Trust* (May–June 1929) 7–11, 14–15.

Scurrah, Edgar. "Zionist Convention in Baltimore." *Trust* 22.7 (September 1923) 13.

Thompson, A. E. "Present Day Palestine." *Trust* 10.8 (October 1911) 15.

Van Paasen, Pierre. "Zionism and Christianity." *Trust* (January–February 1926) 19–20.

Weekly Evangel

"Arrives in Egypt, Paul M. Joyner." *Weekly Evangel* (January 1, 1916) 13.

"Dr. Florence Murcutt." *Weekly Evangel* (October 21, 1916) 13.

"The Jews, the Gentiles, and the Church of God." *Weekly Evangel* (January 19, 1918) 6.

"Miss A. E. Brown." *Weekly Evangel* (January 15, 1918) 10.

"Palestine for the Jews." *Weekly Evangel* (December 1, 1917) 4.

Brown, Anna Elizabeth. "Back from Jerusalem." *Weekly Evangel* (October 6, 1917) 12.

―――. "Returning to Jerusalem." *Weekly Evangel* (March 9, 1918) 11.

Frodsham, Arthur. "1917." *Weekly Evangel* (December 22, 1917) 7.

―――. "What It Means: The British in Jerusalem." *Weekly Evangel* December 22, 1917) 3.

Jamieson, S. A. "The Second Coming of Christ." *Weekly Evangel* (February 26, 1916) 6–7.

Langston, E. L. "The Chosen People and the Chosen Land." *Weekly Evangel* (March 23, 1918) 2–3.

Lawrence, B. F. "The Pentecostal or 'Latter Rain' Outpouring in Los Angeles." *Weekly Evangel* (March 11, 1916) 4–5, 8.

Murcutt, Dr. Florence. "Gospel Seed Sowing in Palestine." *Weekly Evangel* (November 11, 1916) 4–5, 9.

Word and Witness

"Charles S. Leonard-Egypt." *Word and Witness* (April 20, 1914) 4.

"From Florence Bush." *Word and Witness* (November 20, 1913) 3.

"Missionaries Evacuated." *Word and Witness* (June 1916) 6.

"Miss Robertson-Egypt." *Word and Witness* (April 20, 1914) 4.

"Nazareth." *Word and Witness* (August 1915) 1.

"Notice About Parham." *Word and Witness* (October 20, 1912) 3.

Smith, Sarah. "Jerusalem, Palestine." *Word and Witness* (August 20, 1913) 1.

Word and Work

"Death of Brother Camp." *Word and Work* 32.7 (July 1910) 219.

"Extracts from Exchanges." *Word and Work* 29.9 (September 1907) 247.

"Missionaries in Danger." *Word and Work* 36.11 (November 1914) 341.

"Missionary To Jerusalem." *Word and Work* 30.10 (October 1908) 306; 30.11 (November 1908) 337.

"Pentecostal Work in Boston." *Word and Work* (May 1907) 147–48.

"Reports from the Field." *Word and Work* 34.5 (May 1912) 123.

Bartleman, Frank. "The Pentecostal Work." *Word and Work* 30.1 (January 1908) 19–20.

―――. "Work Abroad." *Word and Work* 32.9 (September 1910) 284–85.

Brown, Abbie Morrow. "Back To Jerusalem." *Word and Work* 33.2 (February 1911) 55.

―――. "Coming Home." *Word and Work* 34.3 (March 1912) 91.

―――. "God's Best." *Word and Work* 33.2 (February 1911) 40–41.

―――. "Letter from Jerusalem." *Word and Work* 33.4 (April 1911) 125.

―――. "Personal." *Word and Work* 31.10 (October 1909) 227.

―――. "A Plea for Jerusalem." *Word and Work* 33.4 (April 1911) 124.

Brown, Anna Elizabeth. "Never Was a Time." *Word and Work* 43.14 (October 8, 1921) 4.

Gerber, Maria A. "Orphanage in Turkey." *Word and Work* 37.11 (November 1915) 314.

Grace, C. M. "Jerusalem, Palestine," *Word and Work* 45.10 (October 1923) 14.

Joyner, Paul. "Jerusalem, Palestine." *Word and Work* 43.11 (August 27, 1921) 3.

Leatherman, Lucy. "Back From Jerusalem." *Word and Work* 36.11 (November 1914) 342.

———. "Letter From Egypt." *Word and Work* 35.11 (November 1913) 350.

———. "Letter From Jerusalem." *Word and Work* 30.11 (November 1908) 347.

———. "Returned from S. America." *Word and Work,* 43.6 (June 4, 1921) 9.

Leonard, Charles. "Cairo, Egypt." *Word and Work* 35.11 (November 1913) 346–47.

———. "From Egypt to Jerusalem." *Word and Work* 36.4 (April 1914) 122.

———. "From Jerusalem." *Word and Work* 31.11 (November 1909) 265.

———. "Jerusalem." *Word and Work* 32.8 (August 1910) 251.

———. "Jerusalem, Palestine." *Word and Work* 32.5 (May 1910) 149; 32.7 (July 1910) 218; 32.10 (October 1910) 311.

———. "Letter from Egypt, Dated 11–22–14." *Word and Work* 37.1 (January 1915) 6–27.

———. "Letter From England." *Word and Work* 31.6 (June 1909) 124.

———. "Letter From Jerusalem." *Word and Work* 33.3 (March 1911) 90.

———. "News from Jerusalem." *Word and Work* 36.10 (October 1914) 314–15.

———. "News From Palestine." *Word and Work* 31.12 (December 1909) 301.

———. "Some Impressions About Jerusalem and Palestine." *Word and Work* 32.1 (January 1910) 28.

———. "Suffering in Jerusalem." *Word and Work* 37.11 (November 1915) 311.

Lydia, Sister. "Jerusalem." *Word and Work* 30.10 (October 1908) 311.

Otis, Addie M. "Jesus Is Coming." *Word and Work* 30.6 (June 1908) 176.

Quinton, W. R. "Texas Camp Meeting." *Word and Work* (June 1908) 184–85.

Weaver, Albert. "Experiences Around Jericho." *Word and Work* 33.3 (March 1911) 87.

———. "Extracts from Letters." *Word and Work* 32.10 (October 1910) 342.

———. "Extracts from Letters." *Word and Work* 32.12 (December 1910) 378.

———. "Jerusalem, Palestine." *Word and Work* 46.4 (April 1924) 10.

———. "Letter From C. S. Leonard." *Word and Work* 32.3 (March 1910) 88.

———. "Letters from Palestine." *Word and Work* 33.1 (January 1911) 23.

———. "News from Palestine." *Word and Work* 31.12 (December 1909) 301.

———. "Palestine." *Word and Work* 31.9 (September 1909) 198.

———. "Regions Beyond." *Word and Work* 32.9 (September 1910) 281.

———. "Sunderland, England." *Word and Work* 31.6 (June 1909) 124.

———. "The World Gone Mad." *Word and Work* 33.6 (June 1911) 167.

Whitnall, D. E. "Pentecostal Experience." *Word and Work* 30.10 (October 1908) 303.

Archival Collections

Assemblies of God Publications: Pre-WWII. Flower Pentecostal Heritage Center, Springfield, MO. Digital Collection.

Smalley, William. "Alliance Missions in Palestine, Arab Lands, and Israel, 1890–1970." Unpublished manuscript, Christian and Missionary Alliance Archives, Colorado Springs, CO.

William E. Blackstone Papers, Billy Graham Center Archives, Wheaton, IL.

Healing Evangelists, 1881–1957. Flower Pentecostal Heritage Center, Springfield, MO. Digital Collection.

Parham Papers. Apostolic Faith Church, Baxter Springs, Kansas. Microfilm. Regent University Library, Virginia Beach, VA.

Anthologies of Source Documents

Klieman, Aaron S., editor. *Cultivating an Awareness: America and the Holy Land.* New York: Garland, 1990.

Autobiographies, Memoirs, Sermons, and Speeches

Bartleman, Frank. "Around the World By Faith: With Six Weeks in the Holy Land." In *Witness To Pentecost: The Life of Frank Bartleman*, 28–60. New York: Garland, 1985.

———. *How Pentecost Came to Los Angeles—How It Was in the Beginning.* c. 1925. Republished as *Azusa Street*, edited by Vinson Synan. Plainfield, NJ: Logos International, 1980.

———. *Witness to Pentecost: The Life of Frank Bartleman.* Reprint. Edited by Donald Dayton. New York: Garland, 1985.

Cossum, W. H. *Mountain Peaks of Prophecy and Sacred History.* Chicago: Evangel, 1910.

Cross, James A., editor. *Treasury of Pentecostal Classics: Writings from the First Century of the Church of God.* Cleveland, TN: Pathway, 1985.

Forder, Archibald. *With the Arabs in Tent and Town: An Account of Missionary Work, Life and Experiences in Moab and Edom and the First Missionary Journey into Arabia from the North.* London: Marshall Brothers, 1902.

Gaines, Margaret. *Of Like Passions: Missionary to the Arabs.* Cleveland, TN: Pathway Press, 2000.

Hatfield, D. B. *Triumphany—The Gates of Hell Cannot Have Me!* Longwood, FL: Xulo, 2003.

Joseph, D. C. *The Gospel to Israel (Late Haifa Mt. Carmel Mission) A Narrative of a Year's Dealings of God with D.C. Joseph.* London: n.p., 1916.

King, Joseph H. *Yet Speaketh: Memoirs of the Late Bishop Joseph H. King.* Franklin Springs, GA: Pentecostal Holiness Church, 1949.

Myland, David W. *The Latter Rain Covenant and Pentecostal Power.* c. 1910. Reprint. Edited by Donald Dayton. *Three Early Pentecostal Tracts.* New York: Garland Press, 1985.

Parham, Charles F. *The Sermons of Charles F. Parham.* c. 1911. Reprint. Edited by Donald Dayton. New York: Garland, 1985.

Parham, Robert L., editor. *Selected Sermons of the Late Charles F. Parham and Sarah E. Parham: Co-Founders of the Original Apostolic Faith Movement.* Baxter Springs, KS: Apostolic Faith Bible College, 1941.

Parham, Sarah E. *The Life of Charles F. Parham.* Baxter Springs, KS: Apostolic Faith Bible College, 1930.

Prince, Lydia and Derek. *Appointment in Jerusalem.* Charlotte, NC: Derek Prince Ministries-International, 1975.

Missionary Reports

"Missionary Secretary's Report, 1925," Combined Minutes of the General Council of the Assemblies of God in the United States of America and Foreign Lands, 1914–1925, 47.

Souvenir of the Twentieth Commencement of the Missionary Institute, May 1ˢᵗ, 1902. Christian and Missionary Alliance National Archives, Colorado Springs, CO.

"What Hath God Wrought? 1907 to 1908, Eleventh Annual Report. The Christian and Missionary Alliance, Adopted as the Annual Meeting of the Society, May 27, 1908, Nyack, NY. Christian and Missionary Alliance National Archives, Colorado Springs, CO.

"Crowned Year" 1908–1909, Twelfth Annual Report. The Christian and Missionary Alliance, Adopted at the Annual Meeting of the Society, May 25, 1909, Nyack, NY. Christian and Missionary Alliance National Archives, Colorado Springs, CO.

The Annual Report of the Christian and Missionary Alliance. Adopted at the Annual Meeting of the Society, May 24, 1910, Nyack, NY. Christian and Missionary Alliance National Archives, Colorado Springs, CO.

Zwemer, Samuel. "A New Census of the Moslem World." *Journal of the American Oriental Society* 44 (1924) 29–37.

Zwemer, Samuel, E. M. Wherry, and James L. Barton. *The Mohammedan World of Today: Being Papers Read at the First Missionary Conference on behalf of the Mohammedan World Held at Cairo, April 4th–9th, 1906.* New York: Revell, 1906.

General Works

Blackstone, William E. *Jesus Is Coming*. Chicago: Revell, 1908.

Eddy, S. "The Christian Approach in the Near East." *The International Review of Missions* 10 special edition (1921) 264–65.

Eddy, W. K. "Islam in Syria and Palestine." In *The Mohammedan World of Today*, 59–78. New York: Revell, 1906.

Frodsham, Stanley H. *With Signs Following: The Story of the Pentecostal Revival in the Twentieth Century*. Springfield, MO: Gospel, 1946.

Gairdner, William Temple. "The Missionary Significance of the Last Ten Years in Muslim Lands." *The International Review of Missions* 12 (1923) 3–58.

———. *The Reproach of Islam*. London: Young People's Missionary Movement, 1909.

———. "Values in Christianity." *The Moslem World* 18 (1928) 336–55.

———. "The Vital Forces of Christianity and Islam." *The International Review of Missions* 1 (January 1912) 44–61.

Graham, Stephen. *With the Russian Pilgrims in Jerusalem*. London: Macmillan, 1913.

Herzl, Theodor. *The Jewish State*. New York: American Zionist Emergency Council, 1896.

Hess, Moses. *Rome and Jerusalem: A Study in Jewish Nationalism*. New York: Bloch, 1918.

King, Joseph H. *From Passover To Pentecost*. Franklin Springs, GA: Advocate, 1976.

Lawrence, Bennet F. *The Apostolic Faith Restored*. c. 1916. Reprint. Edited by Donald Dayton. *Three Early Pentecostal Tracts*. New York: Garland, 1985.

Paton, W., and M. M. Underhill. "A Survey for the Year 1936." *The International Review of Missions* 26 (1937) 3–105.

———. "A Survey—Near East and Egypt." *The International Review of Missions* 17 (1928) 46–56.

Pinsker, Leo. *Auto-Emancipation*. Translated by D. S. Blondeim. New York: Federation of American Zionists, 1916.

Simpson, Albert B. *The Coming One*. New York: Christian Alliance Publishing, 1912.

Smith, Hannah Whitall. *The Christian's Secret of a Happy Life*. New York: Revell, 1888.

———. *The Unselfishness of God*. Princeton, NJ: Littlebrook, 1987.

Smith, Robert Pearsall, and Hannah Whitall Smith. *Walking in the Light*. Grand Rapids: Francis Asbury, 1986.

Taylor, George F. *The Second Coming of Jesus*. Falcon, NC: n.p., 1916.

———. *The Spirit and the Bride*. c. 1908. Reprint. Edited by Donald Dayton. *Three Early Pentecostal Tracts*. New York: Garland Press, 1885, c. 1908.

Thompson, A. E. *A Century of Jewish Missions*. New York: Revell, 1902.

Tucker, H. C. "The International Missionary Council at Jerusalem." *The Methodist Quarterly Review* 77 (October 1928) 576–86.

Zwemer, Samuel M. *The Disintegration of Islam*. New York: Revell, 1916.

SECONDARY SOURCES

Abdel-Malek, Anwar. "Orientalism in Crisis." *Diogenes* 44 (1959) 103–40.

Abu-Amr, Ziad. *Islamic Fundamentalism in the West Bank and Gaza: MuslimBrotherhood and Islamic Jihad*. Bloomington, IN: Indiana University Press, 1994.

Aburish, Said. *The Forgotten Faithful: The Christians of the Holy Land*. London: Quartet, 1993.

Adams, J. McKee. *The Heart of the Levant, Palestine-Syria: A Survey of Ancient Countries in the Interest of Modern Missions*. Richmond, VA: Foreign Mission Board, Southern Baptist Convention, 1937.

Addison, James Thayer. *The Christian Approach to the Moslem: A Historical Study*. New York: AMS, 1966.

Adler, Joseph. *Restoring the Jews to their Homeland: Nineteen Centuries in the Quest for Zion*. Northvale, NJ: Aronson, 1997.

Akhtar, Rajnaara. "The Impact of Zionism of Jewish, Christian, and Muslim Relations." *Al-Aqsa* 6.2 (Spring 2004) 11–12.

Alexander, Estrelda. *The Women of Azusa Street*. Cleveland, TN: Pilgrim, 2005.

Althouse, Peter. *Spirit of the Last Days: Pentecostal Eschatology in Conversation with Jürgen Moltmann.* London: T. & T. Clark, 2003.

Anderson, Allan. *An Introduction to Pentecostalism: Global Charismatic Christianity.* Cambridge: Cambridge University Press, 2004.

———. "Signs and Blunders: Pentecostal Mission Issues at 'Home and Abroad' in the Twentieth Century." *Journal of Asian Mission* 2.2 (September 2000) 193–210.

———. *Spreading Fires: The Missionary Nature of Early Pentecostalism.* Maryknoll, NY: Orbis, 2007.

Anderson, Allan, and Edmond Tang, editors. *Asian and Pentecostal: The Charismatic Face of Christianity in Asia.* Bagio City, Philippines: Regnum, 2005.

Anderson, Gerald H. "American Protestants in Pursuit of Mission: 1896–1986." *International Bulleting of Missionary Research* 12.3 (July 1988) 98–118.

———. *The Biography of Christian Missions.* London: Simon and Schuster Macmillan, 1998.

———. "World Christianity by the Numbers: A Review of the *World Christian Encyclopedia,* Second Edition," *International Bulletin of Missionary Research* 26.3 (July 2002) 128–30.

Anderson, Irvine H. *Biblical Interpretation and Middle East Policy: The Promised Land, America, and Israel, 1917–2002.* Gainesville, FL: University Press of Florida, 2005.

Anderson, Robert M. *Vision of the Disinherited: The Making of American Pentecostalism.* Oxford: Oxford University Press, 1979.

Antonius, George. *The Arab Awakening: The Story of the Arab National Movement.* New York: Putnam's Sons, 1946.

Appleby, Joyce O., et al. *Telling the Truth about History.* New York: Norton, 1994.

Appleby, R. Scott. *Spokesmen for the Despised: Fundamentalist Leaders of the Middle East.* Chicago: University of Chicago Press, 1997.

Archer, Kenneth J. "Early Pentecostal Biblical Interpretation," *Journal of Pentecostal Theology,* 18 (April 2001) 32–70.

———. *A Pentecostal Hermeneutic for the Twenty-First Century: Spirit, Scripture and Community.* London: T. & T. Clark, 2004.

Ariel, Yaakov. "An American Initiative for a Jewish State: William Blackstone and the Petition of 1891." *Studies in Zionism* 10.2 (1989) 125–37.

———. *Evangelizing the Chosen People: Missions to the Jews in America, 1880–2000.* Chapel Hill, NC: The University of North Carolina Press, 2000.

———. *On Behalf of Israel: American Fundamentalist Attitudes Toward Jews, Judaism and Zionism, 1865–1945.* Brooklyn, NY: Carlson, 1991.

———. *Philosemites or Antisemites? Evangelical Christian Attitudes toward Jews, Judaism, and the State of Israel.* Jerusalem: Hebrew University, 2002.

———. "An Unexpected Alliance: Christian Zionism and its Historical Significance." *Modern Judaism* 26.1 (2006) 74–100.

Armstrong, Karen. *Jerusalem: One City, Three Faiths.* New York: Ballantine, 1997.

Artzi, Pinhas, editor. *Bar-Ilan Studies in History: Ancient Near Eastern History.* Ramat-Gan, Israel: Bar-Ilan University Press, 1978.

———. *Bar-Ilan Studies in History II: Confrontation and Coexistence.* Ramat-Gan, Israel: Bar-Ilan University, 1984.

Aruri, Naseer, and Muhammad A. Shuraydi, editors. *Revising Culture: Reinventing Peace.* New York: Olive Branch, 2001.

Asad, Muhammad, trans. and commentary. *The Message of the Qur'an.* Bristol, UK: The Book Foundation, 2003.

Ateek, Naim S. *Justice and Only Justice: A Palestinian Theology of Liberation.* Maryknoll, NY: Orbis, 1989.

Ateek, Naim S., and Marc H. Ellis. *Faith and the Intifada: Palestinian Voices.* Maryknoll, NY: Orbis, 1992.

Auman, Moshe. *Conflict and Connection: The Jewish-Christian-Israel Triangle.* Jerusalem: Gefen, 2003.

Awa, Adel, et al., editors. *Arabic and Islamic Garland: Historical, Educational and Literary Papers Presented to Abdul-Latif Tibawi by Colleagues, Friends and Students.* London: The Islamic Cultural Centre, 1977.

Bachmann, T. E. "Mission Frontier in Palestine." *The Moslem World* 29.3 (1939) 275–84.

Badr, Habid, editor. *Christianity: A History in the Middle East*. Beirut, Lebanon: Middle East Council of Christian Churches, 2005.

Bain-Selbo, Eric. "Understanding the Other: The Challenge of Post-Colonial Theory to the Comparative Study of Religion." *Religious Studies and Theology* 18.1 (June 1999) 60–108.

Bar-On, Dan, and Saliba Sarsar. "Bridging the Unbridgeable: The Holocaust and al-Nakba." *Palestine-Israel Journal of Politics, Economics and Culture* 11.1 (2004) 63–70.

Barrett, David B. "The Twentieth-Century Pentecostal/Charismatic Renewal in the Holy Spirit, with Its Goal of World Evangelization," *International Bulletin of Missionary Research* 12.3 (1988) 119–29.

Barrett, David B., and Todd Johnson. "Global Statitstics." In *The New International Dictionary of Pentecostal and Charismatic Movements*, 284–302. Grand Rapids: Zondervan, 2002.

Barrett, David B., et al. *World Christian Encyclopedia*. Vol. 1. Oxford: Oxford University Press, 2001.

Bartal, Israel. "'Old Yishuv' and 'New Yishuv' Image and Reality." In *The Jerusalem Cathedra: Studies in the History, Archaeology, Geography and Ethnography of the Land of Israel*, I, 215–231. Jerusalem: Yad Izhak Ben-Zvi Institute, 1981.

Bar-Yosef, Eitan. "Christian Zionism and Victorian Culture." *Israel Studies* 8.2 (2003) 18–44.

Bass, Clarence. *Backgrounds To Dispensationalism: Its Historical Genesis and Ecclesiastical Implications*. Grand Rapids, Eerdmans, 1960.

Bat Ye'or, "Jews and Christians Under Islam: Dhimmitude and Marcionism." *Commentaire* (Spring 2002) 11–12.

Barzilay-Yegar, Devorah. "Crisis as Turning Point: Chaim Weizmann in World War I." *Studies in Zionism* 6.2 (Autumn 1982) 241–54.

Bauer, Yehuda. *From Diplomacy to Resistance: A History of Jewish Palestine, 1939–1945*. New York: Atheneum, 1970.

Bays, Daniel. "The Protestant Missionary Establishment and the Pentecostal Movement." In *Pentecostal Currents in American Protestantism*, 50–67. Urbana, IL: University of Illinois Press, 1999.

Beaver, R. Pierce. *Envoys of Peace: The Peace Witness in the Christian World Mission*. Grand Rapids: Eerdmans, 1964.

Ben-Arieh, Yehoshua. "The Growth of Jerusalem in the Nineteenth Century." *Annals of the Association of Geographers* 65 (1975) 252–69.

———. *Jerusalem in the 19th Century: The Old City*. Jerusalem: Yad Izhak Ben Zvi Institute, 1984.

Ben-Arieh, Yehoshua, and Moshe Davis, editors. *Jerusalem in the Mind of the Western World, 1800–1948*. Westport, CT: Praeger, 1997.

Bills, V. Alex. "The Houston Connection: After Topeka and Before Azusa Street." Unpublished paper, Society for Pentecostal Studies, March 16–18, 2000, Kirkland, Washington.

Bittlinger, Arnold. *The Church is Charismatic: The World Council of Churches and the Charismatic Renewal*. Geneva: World Council of Churches, 1981.

Blumhofer, Edith L. *The Assemblies of God: A Chapter in the Story of American Pentecostalism. Volume 1—To 1941*. Springfield, MO: Gospel, 1989.

———. "Pentecost in My Soul." *Assemblies of God Heritage* 9.1 (Spring 1989) 13–14.

———. *Restoring the Faith: The Assemblies of God, Pentecostalism, and American Culture*. Urbana, IL: University of Illinois Press, 1993.

Blumhofer, Edith L., Russell Spittler, and Grant Wacker, editors. *Pentecostal Currents in American Protestantism*. Urbana, IL: University of Illinois Press, 1999.

Booth, Marilyn. "'She Herself was the Ultimate Rule': Arabic Biographies of Missionary Teachers and Pupils." *Islam and Christian-Muslim Relations* 13.4 (2002) 427–48.

Bosch, David J. *Transforming Mission: Paradigm Shifts in Theology of Mission*. Maryknoll, NY: Orbis, 1991.

Braybrooke, Marcus. *Christian–Jewish Dialogue: The Next Steps*. London: SCM, 2000.

Brockway, Allan, et al., editors. *The Theology of the Churches and the Jewish People, Statements by the World Council of Churches and Its Member Churches*. Geneva: World Council of Churches, 1988.

Bundy, David. "Bibliography and Historiography of Pentecostalism Outside North America." In *The New International Dictionary of Pentecostal and Charismatic Movements*, edited by S. M. Burgess and E. M. van der Mass, 405–17. Grand Rapids: Zondervan, 2002.

Burge, Gary M. *Who Are God's People in the Middle East? What Christians Are Not Being Told about Israel and the Palestinians*. Grand Rapids: Zondervan, 1993.

Burgess, Stanley M. *The Holy Spirit: Ancient Christian Traditions*. Peabody, MA: Hendrickson, 1984.

———. *The Holy Spirit: Eastern Christian Traditions*. Peabody, MA: Hendrickson, 1989.

———. *The Holy Spirit: Medieval Roman Catholic and Reformation Traditions: Sixth–Sixteenth Centuries*. Peabody, MA: Hendrickson, 1997.

———. "Pentecostalism in India: An Overview." *Asian Journal of Pentecostal Studies* 4.1 (January 2001) 85–98.

Burgess, Stanley M., and Edward Van Der Maas, editors. *The New International Dictionary of Pentecostal and Charismatic Movements*. Grand Rapids: Zondervan, 2002.

Burgess, Stanley M., Gary B. McGee, and Patrick Alexander, editors. *Dictionary of Pentecostal and Charismatic Movements*. Grand Rapids: Zondervan, 1988.

Caplan, Neil. "Zionist Visions of Palestine, 1917–1936." *The Muslim World* 84.1–2 (January–April 1994) 19–35.

Carmel, Alex. "The Activities of the European Powers in Palestine, 1799–1914." *Asian and African Studies* 19 (1985) 43–91.

———. "The German Settlers in Palestine and their Relations with the Local Arab Population and Jewish Community, 1868–1918." International Seminar on the History of Palestine and its Jewish Settlement during the Ottoman Period. Institute of Asian and African Studies, Hebrew University of Jerusalem, 1970.

———. "A Note on the Christian Contribution to Palestine's Development in the 19th Century." In *Palestine in the Late Ottoman Period: Political, Social and Economic Transformation*, 302–7. Jerusalem: Yad Izhak Ben-Zvi, 1986.

Cerillo, Augustus. "Interpretive Approaches to the History of American Pentecostal Origins." *Pneuma* 19 (1997) 29–52.

Chacour, Elias. *Blood Brothers*. Grand Rapids: Chosen, 1984.

———. *We Belong to the Land: The Story of a Palestinian Israeli Who Lives for Peace and Reconciliation*. San Francisco: HarperSan Francisco, 1990.

Chapman, Colin. "Israel and Palestine: Where is God in the Conflict?" *Encounters Mission E-zine*, 5 (April 2005) 1–15. Online: http://www.redcliffe.org/uploads/ documents/israel_palestine1_05.pdf.

Charlesworth, James H. *Jews and Christians: Exploring the Past, Present, and Future*. New York: Crossroad, 1990.

Cleveland, William L. *A History of the Modern Middle East*. Boulder, CO: University of Colorado, 1994.

Cohen, Israel. *The Zionist Movement*. New York: Zionist Organization of America, 1946.

Cohn-Sherbok, Dan. *The Politics of Apocalypse: The History and Influence of Christian Zionism*. Oxford: One World, 2006.

———, editor. *The Future of Jewish-Christian Dialogue*. Lewiston, NY: Mellen, 1999.

Colbi, Saul P. *A History of the Christian Presence in the Holy Land*. Lanham, MD: University Press of America, 1988.

Conn, Charles W. *Like a Mighty Army: A History of the Church of God*. Cleveland, TN: Pathway, 1977.

———. *Pillars of Pentecost*. Cleveland, TN: Pathway, 1956.

———. *Where the Saints Have Trod: A History of Church of God Missions*. Cleveland, TN: Pathway, 1959.

Cox, Harvey. *Fire From Heaven: The Rise of Pentecostal Spirituality and the Reshaping of Religion in the Twenty-first Century*. Reading, MA: Addison-Wesley, 1995.

Creech, Joe. "Visions of Glory: The Place of the Azusa Street Revival in Pentecostal History." *Church History* 65.3 (September 1996) 405–25.

Crombie, Kelvin. *For the Love of Zion: Christian Witness and the Restoration of Israel*. London: Hodder & Stoughton, 1991.

Curtis, Richard K. *They Called Him Mister Moody*. Grand Rapids: Eerdmans, 1962.

Davidson, Lawrence. *America's Palestine: Popular and Official Perceptions from Balfour to Israel's Statehood*. Gainesville, FL: University Press of Florida, 2001.

Davis, Moshe, editor. *With Eyes Toward Zion*. Vol. 1. New York: Praeger, 1977.

———. *With Eyes Toward Zion*. Vol. 2. New York: Praeger, 1986.

———. *With Eyes Toward Zion*. Vol. 3. New York: Arno Press, 1991.

Dayton, Donald W. *Theological Roots of Pentecostalism*. Peabody, MA: Hendrickson, 1987.

Dempster, Murray W., Byron D. Klaus, and Douglas Peterson. eds. *The Globalization of Pentecostalism: A Religion Made To Travel.* Oxford: Regnum, 1999.

Dieter, Melvin Easterday. *The Holiness Revival of the Nineteenth Century.* Metuchen, NJ: Scarecrow, 1980.

Diprose, Ronald E. *Israel and the Church: The Origins and Effect of Replacement Theology.* Rome: Instituto Biblico Evangelico Italiano, 2000.

———. *Israel in the Development of Christian Thought.* Rome: Instituto Biblico Evangelico Italiano, 2000.

Doron, Joachim. "Classic Zionism and Modern Anti-Semitism: Parallels and Influences (1883–1914)." *Studies in Zionism* 8 (1983) 169–204.

Doukhan, Jacques B. *Israel and the Church: Two Voices for the Same God.* Peabody, MA: Hendrickson, 2002.

Downer, Alexander. "Extremist Islam Hold Little Appeal." *Middle East Quarterly* 12.4 (Fall 2005) 63–68.

Drory, Joseph. "Jerusalem during the Mamluk Period (1250–1517)." In *The Jerusalem Cathedra: Studies in the History, Archaeology, Geography and Ethnography of the Land of Israel,* I, 190–92 13. Jerusalem: Yad Izhak Ben-Zvi Institute, 1981.

Durch, Ryan. "Beyond Cultural Imperialism: Cultural Theory, Christian Missions, and Global Modernity." *History and Theory* 41 (October 2002) 301–25.

El-Awaisi, Abd Al-Fattah Muhammad. *The Muslim Brothers and the Palestine Question, 1928–1947.* London: Tauris Academic Studies, 1998.

Epstein, Lawrence J. *Zion's Call: Christian Contributions to the Origins and Development of Israel.* Lantham, MD: University Press of America, 1984.

Esber, Rosemarie M. "Rewriting the History of 1948: The Birth of the Palestinian Refugee Question Revisited." *Holy Land Studies* 4.1 (May 2005) 55–72.

Eshkoli Wagman, H. "'Destruction Becomes Creation': The Theological Reaction of National Religious Zionism in Palestine to the Holocaust." *Holocaust and Genocide Studies* 17.3 (Winter 2003) 430–58.

Ettinger, Shmuel and Israel Bartal. "The First Aliyah: Ideological Roots and Practical Accomplishments." In *The Jerusalem Cathedra: Studies in the History, Archaeology, Geography and Ethnography of the Land of Israel,* II, 197–227. Jerusalem: Yad Izhak Ben-Zvi Institute, 1982.

Fackre, Gabriel. *Ecumenical Faith in Evangelical Perspective.* Grand Rapids: Eerdmans, 1993.

Fahmy, Nabil. "The Changing Paradigm of the Middle East: Its Elements and Challenges." *Mediterranean Quarterly* 15.2 (May 2004) 6–16.

Falk, Gerhard. *The Restoration of Israel: Christian Zionism in Religion, Literature, and Politics.* New York: Lang, 2006.

Farques, Philippe. "The Arab Christians of the Middle East." In *Christian Communities in the Arab Middle East,* 48–66. Oxford: Clarendon, 1998.

Fasheh, Munir. "Reclaiming Our Identify and Redfining Ourselves." In *Faith and the Intifada: Palestinian Christian Voices,* 61–70. Maryknoll, NY: Orbis, 1992.

Faupel, D. William. *The Everlasting Gospel: The Significance of Eschatology in the Development of Pentecostal Thought.* Sheffield, UK: Sheffield Academic, 1996.

Finto, Don. *Your People Shall Be My People: How Israel, the Jews and the Christian Church Will Come Together in the Last Days.* Ventura, CA: Regal, 2001.

Flannery, Edward H. *The Anguish of the Jews: Twenty-three Centuries of Anti-Semitism.* New York: Macmillan, 1965.

Fleischmann, Ellen L. "The Impact of American Protestant Missions in Lebanon and the Construction of Female Identity, c. 1860–1950." *Islam and Christian-Muslim Relations* 13.4 (2002) 411–26.

———. "'Our Moslem Sisters': Women of Greater Syria in the Eyes of American Protestant Missionary Women." *Islam and Christian Relations* 9.3 (October 1998) 307–24.

Flokstra III, Gerald J. "Sources for the Initial Evidence Discussion: A Bibliographic Essay." *Asian Journal of Pentecostal Theology* 2.2 (1999) 243–59.

Flower, J. Roswell. "Publishing the Pentecostal Message," *Assemblies of God Heritage* 2.3 (Fall 1982) 1–8; 2.4 (Winter 1982–83) 6–7.

Foster, Frank Hugh. *The Modern Movement in American Theology: Sketches in the History of American Protestant Thought from the Civil War to the World War.* Freeport, NY: Books for Libraries, 1939.

Freas, Erik. "Muslim Women in the Missionary World." *The Muslim World* 88.2 (April 1998) 141–64.

Fredriksen, Paula, and Adele Reinhartz, editors. *Jesus, Judaism, and Christian Anti-Judaism.* Louisville: Westminster John Knox, 2002.

Friedman, Isaiah. "The System of Capitulations and its Effects on Turco-Jewish Relations in Palestine, 1856–1897." In *Palestine in the Late Ottoman Period: Political, Social and Economic Transformation,* 280–93. Jerusalem: Yad Izhak Ben Zvi, 1986.

Frodsham, Stanley F. *With Signs Following: The Story of the Pentecostal Revival in the Twentieth Century.* Springfield, MO: Gospel, 1946.

Gadamer, Hans-Georg. *Truth and Method.* London: Continuum, 1975.

Gannon, Raymond L. "The Shifting Romance with Israel: American Pentecostal Ideology of Zionism and the Jewish State." PhD diss., Hebrew University, Jerusalem, Israel, 2003.

Gat, Moshe. "Britain and Israel Before and After the Six Day War, June 1967: From Support to Hostility." *Contemporary British History* 18.1 (Spring 2004) 54–77.

Gaudeul, Jean-Marie. *Encounters and Clashes: Islam and Christianity in History.* 2 vols. Rome: Pontifical Institute for Arabic and Islamic Studies, 2000.

Gilbar, Gad G., editor. *Ottoman Palestine 1800–1914: Studies in Economic and Social History.* Leiden: Brill, 1990.

Gitre, Edward J. "The 1904–05 Welsh Revival: Modernization, Technologies, and Techniques of the Self." *Church History* 73.4 (December 2004) 792–827.

Glick, Edward B. *The Triangular Connection: America, Israel, and American Jews.* London: George Allen and Unwin, 1982.

Goddard, Hugh. "Christian-Muslim Relations: A Look Backwards and a Look Forwards." *Islam and Christian-Muslim Relations* 11.2 (2000) 195–212.

Goff, James R., Jr. "Charles F. Parham and His Role in the Development of the Pentecostal Movement: A Reevaluation." *Kansas History* 7.3 (Autumn 1984) 226–37.

———. "Closing Out the Church Age: Pentecostals Face the Twenty-First Century." *Pneuma* 14.1 (Spring 1992) 7–21.

———. *Fields White Unto Harvest: Charles F. Parham and the Missionary Origins of Pentecostalism.* Fayetteville, AR: The University of Arkansas Press, 1988.

———. "Millenarian Thought among Early Pentecostals, 1898–1908. Unpublished paper, Fayetteville, AR, March 1984.

Goitein, Shlomo. "Jerusalem in the Arab Period (638–1099)." In *The Jerusalem Cathedra: Studies in the History, Archaeology, Geography of the Land of Israel,* II, 168–96. Jerusalem: Yad Izhak Ben-Zvi Institute, 1982.

Goldhill, Simon. *Jerusalem: City of Longing.* Cambridge, MA: Belknap, 2008.

Grafton, David D. "The Use of Scripture in the Current Israeli-Palestinian Conflict." *Word and World* 24.1 (2004) 29–39.

Greenberg, Ela. "Educating Muslim Girls in Mandatory Jerusalem." *International Journal of Middle Eastern Studies* 36.1 (2004) 1–19.

Greenspoon, Leonard J., and Ronald A. Simkins, editors. *"A Land Flowing with Milk and Honey": Visions of Israel from Biblical to Modern Times.* Omaha, NE: Creighton University Press, 2001.

Groden, Michael, and Martin Kreiswirth, editors. *The Johns Hopkins Guide to Literary Theory and Criticism.* Baltimore: Johns Hopkins University Press, 1994.

Grose, Peter. *Israel in the Mind of America.* New York: Schocken, 1984.

Hadawi, Sami. *Bitter Harvest.* Delmar, NY: Caravan, 1979.

Haddad, Yvonne Yazbeck. "Islamic Depictions of Christianity in the Twentieth Century: The Pluralism Debate and the Depiction of the Other." *Islam and Christian-Muslim Relations* 7.1 (1996) 75–93.

Haija, Rammy M. "The Armageddon Lobby: Dispensationalist Christian Zionism and the Shaping of US Policy Toward Israel-Palestine." *Holy Land Studies* 5.1 (2006) 75–95.

Hart, William D. *Edward Said and the Religious Effects of Culture.* Cambridge: Cambridge University Press, 2000.

Hartzfeld, David F., and Charles Nienkirchen, editors. *The Birth of a Vision.* Beaverlodge, AB, Canada: Buena, 1986.

Hawley, John C., editor. *Christian Encounters with the Other.* Washington Square, NY: New York University Press, 1998.

Heck, Paul L. "Orientalism and Post–Modernism: A Note on Studying Islam with Muslims." *Islamochristiana* 26 (2000) 95–106.

Hedding, Malcolm. *The Basis of Christian Support for Israel.* Jerusalem, Israel: International Christian Embassy, 2004.

———. *Understanding Israel.* Oklahoma City: Zion's Gate International, 1990.

Hermann, Tamar. "The Bi-National Idea in Israel/Palestine: Past and Present." *Nations and Nationalism* 11 (2005) 381–401.

Hocken, Peter. *The Glory and the Shame: Reflections on the 20th Century Outpouring of the Holy Spirit.* Surrey, UK: Eagle, 1994.

———. *Streams of Renewal: The Origins and Early Development of the Charismatic Movement in Great Britain.* Exeter, UK: Paternoster, 1986.

———. *The Spirit of Unity: How Renewal is Breaking Down Barriers between Evangelicals and Roman Catholics.* Cambridge: Grove, 2001.

Hodges, Serena M., editor. *Look on the Fields: A Missionary Survey.* Springfield, MO: Gospel, 1956.

Hollenweger, Walter. *The Pentecostals.* Minneapolis, MN: Augsburg, 1972.

Holtrop, Pieter N., and Hugh McLeod, editors. *Missions and Missionaries.* Woodbridge, UK: Boydell, 2000.

Holtzmann, Livnat, and Eliezer Schlossberg. "Fundamentals of the Modern Muslim–Jewish Polemic." *Israel Affairs* 12 (2006) 13–28.

Howard, Linda. "A New Beginning." *Charisma* (April 1984) 38–43.

Hughes, Richard T., editor. *The American Quest for the Primitive Church.* Chicago, IL: University of Illinois Press, 1988.

Hunt, Stephen, editor. *Christian Millenarianism: From the Early Church to Waco.* Bloomington, IN: Indiana University Press, 2001.

———. "Deprivation and Western Pentecostalism Revisited: The Case of 'Classical Pentecostalism.'" *PentecoStudies* 1.1 (2002) 1–27.

———. "Deprivation and Western Pentecostalism Revisited: Neo-Pentecostalism." *PentecoStudies* 1.2 (2002) 1–29.

Huntington, Samuel. *The Clash of Civilizations and the Remaking of the World Order.* New York: Simon & Schuster, 1996.

Hwa Yung. "Endued with Power: The Pentecostal-Charismatic Renewal and the Asian Churches in the Twenty–First Century." *Asian Journal of Pentecostal Studies* 6 (2003) 66–72.

Ibn Warraq. *Defending the West: A Critique of Edward Said's Orientalism.* Amherst, NY: Prometheus, 2007.

Iggers, George. *Historiography in the Twentieth Century.* Hanover, NH: Wesleyan University Press, 1997.

Irvin, Dale T. "Pentecostal Historiography and Global Christianity: Rethinking the Question of Origins." *Pneuma* 27.1 (Spring 2005) 35–50.

Irvine, Lee I, editor. *The Jerusalem Cathedra: Studies in the History, Archaeology, Geography and Ethnography of the Land of Israel.* Jerusalem: Yad Izhak Ben-Zvi Institute, 1981.

Irwin, Robert. *Dangerous Knowledge: Orientalism and Its Discontents.* New York: Overlook, 2006.

Jabbour, Nabeel T. "Islamic Fundamentalism: Implications for Missions." *International Journal of Frontier Missions* 11.2 (1994) 81–86.

Jeppesen, Knud. "Justice with Mercy: About a Contemporary Palestinian Theology." *HTS Theological Studies (Hervormde Teologiese Studies)* 64.1 (2008) 195–206.

Jacobsen, Douglas. *Thinking in the Spirit: Theologies of the Early Pentecostal Movement.* Bloomington, IN: Indiana University Press, 2003.

Jenkins, Keith. *On 'What Is History?': From Carr to Elton to Rory and White.* London: Routledge, 1995.

Jongeneel, Jan A. B. *Philosophy, Science, and Theology of Mission in the 19th and 20th Centuries: A Missiological Encyclopedia. Part I: The Philosophy and Science of Mission.* New York: Lang, 1995.

Juster, Daniel, and Peter Hocken. "The Messianic Jewish Movement: An Introduction." Ventura, CA: Toward Jerusalem Council II, 2004. http://www.tjcii.org/userfiles/Image/messianic-jewish-movement-an-inttroduction-Eng.pdf.

Kabha, Mustafa. "The Palestinian Press and the General Strike, April–October 1936: *Filastin* as a Case Study." *Middle Eastern Studies* 39.3 (July 2003) 169–89.

Kanafani, Ghassan. *The 1936–1939 Revolt of Palestine.* New York: Committee for a Democratic Palestine, 1972.

Kaniel, Yehoshua. "The Terms 'Old Yishuv' and 'New Yishuv': Problems of Definition." In *The Jerusalem Cathedra: Studies in the History, Archaeology, Geography and Ethnography of the Land of Israel, I,* edited by Lee Levine, 232–45. Jerusalem: Yad Izhak Ben-Zvi Institute, 1981.

Kark, Ruth. "The Impact of Early Missionary Enterprises on the Landscape and Identity Formation of Palestine, 1820–1914." *Islam and Christian-Muslim Relations* 15.2 (2004) 209–35.

Karsh, Efraim. "The Long Trail of Islamic Anti-Semitism." *Israel Affairs* 12.1 (2006) 1–12.

Karkkainen, Veli-Matti. "Pentecostal Theology of Mission in the Making." *Journal of Beliefs and Values* 25.2 (2004) 167–76.

Kay, William K. *Inside Story: A History of British Assemblies of God.* Mattersey, UK: Mattersey Hall, 1990.

———. "Three Generations On: The Methodology of Pentecostal History." *European Pentecostal Theological Bulletin* 11.1–2 (1992) 58–69.

Kay, William K., and Anne E. Dyer, editors. *Pentecostal and Charismatic Studies.* London: SCM, 2004.

Kennedy, Valerie. *Edward Said: A Critical Introduction.* Cambridge: Polity, 2000.

Kerr, Malcolm. Édward Said, *Orientalism. International Journal of Middle Eastern Studies* 12 (1980) 544–47.

Kjaer-Hansen, Kai, and Bodil F. Skjott. *Facts and Myths about the Messianic Congregations in Israel.* Jerusalem: United Christian Council in Israel, 1999.

Klieman, Aaron S. *Foundations of British Policy in the Arab World: The Cairo Conference of 1921.* Baltimore: Johns Hopkins Press, 1970.

Kofoed, Jens. *Text and History: Historiography and the Study of the Biblical Text.* Winona Lake, IN: Eisenbrauns, 2005.

Kolatt, Israel. "Organization of the Jewish Population of Palestine and the Development of Political Consciousness before World War I." International Seminar on the History of Palestine and Jewish Settlement during the Ottoman Period. Institute of Asian and African Studies. Hebrew University, Jerusalem, 1970.

Kornberg, Jacques. "Theodore Herzl: A Reevaluation." *The Journal of Modern History* 52.2 (1980) 226–52.

Kramer, Martin. *Ivory Towers on Sand: The Failure of Middle Eastern Studies in America.* Washington, DC: The Washington Institute for Near East Policy, 2001.

Kressel, Neil J. "Antisemitism, Social Science, and the Muslim and Arab World." *Judaism* 52.3–4 (2003) 225–45.

Küng, Hans. *Judaism: The Religious Situation of our Time.* London: SCM, 1992.

Kushner, David, editor. *Palestine in the Late Ottoman Period: Political, Social and Economic Transformation.* Jerusalem: Yad Izhak Ben Zvi, 1986.

Lacqueur, Walter, and Barry Rubin, editors. *The Israeli-Arab Reader: A Documentary History of the Middle East Conflict.* New York: Penguin Putnam, 2008.

Laroui, Abdallah. *The Crisis of the Arab Intellectual: Traditionalism or Historicism?* Translated by D. Cammell. Berkeley: University of California Press, 1976.

Levine, Lee I., editor. *The Jerusalem Cathedra: Studies in the History, Archaeology, Geography and Ethnography of the Land of Israel.* Jerusalem: Yad Izhak Ben-Zvi Institute, 1982.

Lewis, Bernard. *Islam and the West.* New York: Oxford University Press, 1993.

Lewis, David Allen. *Can Israel Survive in a Hostile World?* Green Forest, AZ: New Leaf, 1993.

Lingenfelder, Christian J. "The Elephant in the Room: Religious Extremism in the Israeli-Palestinian Conflict." Master's Thesis, Naval Postgraduate School, Monterey, CA, 2006.

Littell, Franklin H. *The Crucifixion of Jesus: The Failure of Christians To Understand the Jewish Experience.* Macon, GA: Mercer University Press, 1975.

Little, Donald P. "Three Arab Critiques of Orientalism." *The Moslem World* 69.2 (1979) 110–31.

Lord, Andrew. *Spirit–Shaped Mission: A Holistic Charismatic Missiology.* Milton Keynes, UK: Paternoster, 2001.

Lowe, Lisa. *Critical Terrains: French and British Orientalisms.* Ithaca, NY: Cornell University Press, 1991.

Lowe, Malcolm. *Orthodox Christians and Jews on Continuity and Renewal: The Third Academic Meeting between Orthodoxy and Judaism. Including a History and Bibliography of Dialogue between Orthodox Christians and Jews.* Jerusalem: Ecumenical Theological Research Fraternity, 1994.

Lyotard, Jean-Francois. *The Postmodern Condition: A Report on Knowledge*. Minneapolis, MN: University of Minnesota Press, 1984.

Macchia, Frank. "Pentecostal Theology." In *The New International Dictionary of Pentecostal and Charismatic Movements*, 1120–41. Grand Rapids: Zondervan, 2002.

Macpherson, Duncan. "Prophetic Preaching, Liberation Theology, and the Holy Land." *Holy Land Studies* 3.2 (2004) 233–44.

Makdisi, Ussama. "'Anti-Americanism' in the Arab World: An Interpretation of a Brief History." *The Journal of American History* 89.2 (2002) 538–58.

———. "Reclaiming the Land of the Bible: Missionaries, Secularism, and Evangelical Modernity." *The American Historical Review* 102.3 (1997) 680–713.

Mansfield, Stephen. *Derek Prince: A Biography*. Lake Mary, FL: Charisma House, 2005.

Manuel, Frank E. *The Realities of American-Palestine Relations*. Washington, DC: Public Affairs, 1949.

Marsden, George M. *Fundamentalism and American Culture: The Shaping of Twentieth-Century Evangelicalism: 1870–1925*. Oxford: Oxford University Press, 1980.

Marten, Michael. "Anglican and Presbyterian Presence and Theology in the Holy Land." *International Journal for the Study of the Christian Church* 5.2 (July 2005) 182–99.

———. *Attempting To Bring the Gospel Home: Scottish Missions in Palestine, 1839–1917*. London: Taurus Academic Studies, 2006.

———. "Imperialism and Evangelization: Scottish Missionary Methods in Late 19th and Early 20th Century Palestine." *Holy Land Studies* 5.2 (2006) 155–86.

Martin, David. *Tongues of Fire: The Explosion of Protestantism in Latin America*. Oxford: Blackwell, 1990.

Martin, Larry. *The Life and Ministry of William J. Seymour: A History of the Azusa Street Revival*. Joplin, MO: Christian Life, 1999.

Masalha, Nur. *The Bible and Zionism: Invented Traditions, Archaeology and Post-Colonialism in Israel-Palestine*. London: Zed, 2007.

McClung, L. Grant, Jr., editor. *Azusa Street and Beyond: Pentecostal Missions and Church Growth in the Twentieth Century*. South Plainfield, NJ: Bridge, 1986.

McGee, Gary B. "The Azusa Street Revival and Twentieth-Century Missions." *International Bulletin of Missionary Research* 12.2 (1988) 58–61.

———. "Early Pentecostal Missionaries: They Went Everywhere Preaching the Gospel." *Assemblies of God Heritage*. 3.2 (1983) 6–7.

———, editor. *Initial Evidence: Historical and Biblical Perspectives on the Pentecostal Doctrine of Spirit Baptism*. Peabody, MA: Hendrickson, 1991.

———. "Miracles and Mission Revisited." *International Bulletin of Missionary Research* 25.4 (2001) 146–56.

———. "Overseas (North American Pentecostal) Missions." In *The New International Dictionary Pentecostal and Charismatic Movements*, 896–97. Grand Rapids: Zondervan, 1988.

———. *"This Gospel . . . Shall Be Preached": A History of Assemblies of God Foreign Missions to 1959*. Springfield, MO: Gospel, 1986.

McTague, John T. *British Policy in Palestine, 1917–1922*. Lanham, MD: University Press of America, 1983.

Merkley, Paul C. *Christian Attitudes Towards the State of Israel*. Montreal: McGill-Queen's University Press, 2001.

———. *The Politics of Christian Zionism, 1891–1948*. Portland, OR: Cass, 1998.

Milton-Edwards, Beverly. "Political Islam and the Palestinian-Israeli Conflict." *Israel Affairs* 12.1 (2006) 65–85.

Mitchell, Richard P. *The Society of the Muslim Brothers*. Oxford: Oxford University Press, 1969.

Mitri, Tarek. "Christians in the Arab East: An Interpretation of Contemporary History." In *Christianity: A History in the Middle East*, edited by Habib Badr, 853. Beirut: Middle East Council of Churches, 2005.

———. "Who Are the Christians of the Arab World?" *International Review of Mission* 89.352 (2000) 12–27.

Moore, S. David. "Shepherding Movement." In *The New International Dictionary of Pentecostal and Charismatic Movements*, edited by S. M. Burgess and E. van der Maas, 1060–6 2. Grand Rapids: Zondervan, 2002.

Moorhead, James H. *American Apocalypse: Yankee Protestants and the Civil War, 1860–1869.* New Haven: Yale University Press, 1978.

Morris, Benny. "Falsifying the Record: A Fresh Look at Zionist Documentation of 1948." *Journal of Palestine Studies* 24.3 (1995) 44–62.

Muhammad, Khalil. "Zionism, the Qur'an, and the Hadith." *Judaism* 54.1–2 (2005) 79–93.

Murray, Iain H. *The Puritan Hope: A Study in Revival and the Interpretation of Prophecy.* Edinburgh: Banner of Truth, 1971.

Murre-van den Berg, Heleen, editor. *New Faith in Ancient Lands: Western Missions in the Middle East in the Nineteenth and Early Twentieth Centuries.* Leiden: Brill, 2006.

Nafi, Basheer M. *Arabism, Islamism and the Palestinian Question, 1908–1941: A Political History.* Reading: Ithaca, 1998.

———. "Palestine at the End of the Ottoman Era: Age of Political Breakup." *The Muslim World* 84.2–3 (1994) 317–33.

Neill, Stephen. *A History of Christian Missions.* Middlesex, UK: Penguin, 1964.

Nienkirchen, Charles W. *A. B. Simpson and the Pentecostal Movement: A Study in Continuity, Crisis, and Change.* Peabody, MA: Hendrickson, 1992.

Noel, Napoleon. *The History of the Brethren.* Denver: Knapp, 1936.

Okkenhaug, Inger Marie. *The Quality of Heroic Living, of High Endeavor and Adventure: Anglican Missions, Women and Education in Palestine, 1888–1948.* Leiden: Brill, 2002.

Olson, Carl. "Politics, Power, Discourse and Representation: A Critical Look at Said and Some of His Children." *Method and Theory in the Study of Religion* 17 (2005) 317–36.

O'Mahony, Anthony, editor. *Palestinian Christians: Religion, Politics and Society in the Holy Land.* London: Melisende, 1999.

Osterbye, Per. *The Church in Israel: A Report on the Work and Position of the Christian Churches in Israel, with Special Reference to the Protestant Churches and Communities.* Lund, Sweden: Gleerup, 1970.

Ould-Mey, Mohameden. "The Non-Jewish Origin of Zionism." *The Arab World Geographer* 5.1 (2002) 34–52.

Pacini, Andea, editor. *Christian Communities in the Arab Middle East: The Challenge of the Future.* Oxford: Clarendon, 1998.

Padwick, Constance E. *Temple Gairdner of Cairo.* London: SPCK, 1929.

Pappe, Ilan. *A History of Modern Palestine: One Land, Two Peoples.* Cambridge: Cambridge University Press, 2004.

———. "The One-State Solution in Historical Perspective." *Race Traitor* 16 (2005) 49–60.

———. "Zionist Historiography, Old and New: Review Article." *Holy Land Studies* 4.2 (2005) 91–95.

Pawson, J. David. *When Jesus Returns.* London: Hodder & Stoughton, 1995.

Perkins, Raymond C. "Israel and Missions." Unpublished paper, Assemblies of God Graduate School, Springfield, Missouri, August 1977. Updated September 1996.

Perry, Yaron. *British Mission to the Jews in Nineteenth-Century Palestine.* London: Cass, 2003.

Pikkert, Pieter. "Protestant Missionaries to the Middle East: Ambassadors of Christ or Culture." ThD diss., University of South Africa, 2006.

Poewe, Karla, editor. *Charismatic Christianity as a Global Culture.* Columbia: University of South Carolina Press, 1994.

Polowetzky, Michael. *Jerusalem Recovered: Victorian Intellectuals and the Birth of Modern Zionism.* Westport, CT: Praeger, 1995.

Porath, Y. *The Emergence of the Palestine-Arab National Movement, 1918–1929.* London: Cass, 1974.

———. *The Palestinian Arab National Movement: From Riots to Rebellion.* London: Cass, 1977.

Porter, Stanley E., Michael A Hayes, and David Tombs. *Faith in the Millennium.* Sheffield, UK: Sheffield Academic, 2001.

Pragai, Michael J. *Faith and Fulfilment: Christians and the Return to the Promised Land.* London: Valentine and Mitchell, 1985.

Prince, Derek. *From Jordan to Pentecost.* Fort Lauderdale, FL: Derek Prince, n.d.

———. *The Last Word on the Middle East.* Grand Rapids: Chosen, 1982.

———. *Prophetic Destinies.* Orlando, FL: Creation House, 1992.

———. "The Root of Anti–Semistism." A Derek Prince Teaching Letter, No. 7. http://www.cdn-friends-icej.ca/antiholo/dprince.html.

———. *Three Messages for Israel*. Fort Lauderdale, FL: Derek Prince, 1969.

Prior, Michael. "The State of Israel and Jerusalem in the Jewish–Christian Dialogue: A Monologue in Two Voices." *Holy Land Studies* 3.2 (2004) 145–70.

———. *Zionism and the State of Israel: A moral inquiry*. London: Routledge, 1999.

Prosser, Peter E. *Dispensational Eschatology and Its Influence on American and British Movements*. Lewiston, NY: Mellen, 1999.

Racevskis, Karlis. "Edward Said and Michel Foucault: Affinities and Dissonances," *Research in African Literatures* 36.3 (2005) 83–97.

Raebeck, A. "Learned Hatred: The Socialization of Israeli and Palestinian Children." *World Outlook* 30 (2004) 51–66.

Raheb, Mitri. *Bethlehem Besieged: Stories of Hope in Times of Trouble*. Minneapolis: Fortress, 2004.

———. *I Am a Palestinian Christian*. Minneapolis: Fortress, 1995.

Raheb, Mitri, and Fred Strickert. *Bethlehem 2000: Past and Present*. Heidelberg: Palmyra, 1998.

Rausch, David. A. *Zionism within Early American Fundamentalism, 1878–1918: A Convergence of Two Traditions*. New York: Mellen, 1979.

Richter, J. *A History of Protestant Missions*. New York: AMS, 1910.

Robeck, Cecil M. *The Azusa Street Mission and Revival: The Birth of the Global Pentecostal Movement*. Nashville: Thomas Nelson, 2006.

Robeck, Cecil M., editor. *Charismatic Experiences in History*. Peabody, MA: Hendrickson, 1985.

Ross, Dorothy. "Grand Narrative in American Historical Writing: From Romance to Uncertainty." *The American Historical Review* 100.3 (1995) 651–77.

Rottenberg, Isaac C. *The Turbulent Triangle: Christians–Jews–Israel: A Personal–Historical Account*. Hawley, PA: Red Mountain Associates, 1989.

Rubinstein, William D., and Hilary L. Rubinstein. *Philosemitism: Admiration and Support in the English-Speaking World for Jews, 1840–1939*. London: Macmillan, 1999.

Ruether, Rosemary. *Faith and Fratricide: The Theological Roots of Anti-Semitism*. Eugene, OR: Wipf and Stock, 1995.

Ruether, Rosemary, and Herman J. Ruether. *The Wrath of Jonah: The Crisis of Religious Nationalism in the Israeli-Palestinian Conflict*. Minneapolis: Fortress, 2002.

Russell, Letty M. "God, Gold, Glory and Gender: A Postcolonial View of Mission." *International Review of Mission* 93.368 (2004) 39–49.

Saddington, James A. "Prophecy and Politics: A History of Christian Zionism in the Anglo-American Experience, 1800–1948." PhD diss., Bowling Green State University, 1996.

Said, Edward W. "Arabs, Islam, and the Dogmas of the West." *The New York Times Book Review*, October 31, 1976, 4.

———. *Covering Islam: How the Media and the Experts Determine How We See the Rest of the World*. New York: Vintage, 1981.

———. *Culture and Imperialism*. New York: Vintage, 1993.

———. *Orientalism*. New York: Vintage, 1978.

———. *Out of Place: A Memoir*. New York: Vintage, 1999.

———. *Power, Politics and Culture: Interviews with Edward W. Said*. Edited with an Introduction by Gauri Viswanathan. London: Bloomsbury, 2001.

———. *The Question of Palestine*. New York: 2nd ed. Vintage, 2002.

———. *Representations of the Intellectual: The 1993 Reith Lectures*. New York: Vintage, 1994.

Said, Edward W., and Christopher Hitchens. *Blaming the Victims: Spurious Scholarship and the Palestinian Question*. London: Verso, 1988.

Salih, Mushin M. "The Muslim Brothers' Group in Jerusalem in 1946: Documentary Highlights." [Arabic]. *Majallat al-Dirasat al-Filastiniyya* 58 (2004) 67–83.

Salomon, William J. "A Dialog of Faith: Reflections on Middle East Conflict From Jewish, Muslim, and Christian Perspectives." *Journal of Beliefs and Values* 26.1 (2005) 65–75.

Samir, Khalil Samir. "The Christian Communities, Active Members of Arab Society throughout History." In *Christian Communities in the Arab Middle East: The Challenge of the Future*, 60–91. Oxford: Clarendon, 1998.

Sandeen, Ernest R. *The Roots of Fundamentalism: British and American Millenarianism, 1800–1930* Chicago: The University of Chicago Press, 1970.

Saperstein, Marc. *Moments of Crisis in Jewish-Christian Relations*. Philadelphia: Trinity, 1989.

Schmidgall, P. "American Holiness Churches in the Holy Land, 1890–1990: Mission to the Jews, Arabs and Armenians." PhD diss., Hebrew University of Jerusalem, 1996.

Scholch, Alexander. "An Ottoman Bismark from Jerusalem: Yusuf Diya al-Khalidi (1842–1906)." *Jerusalem Quarterly* 24 (2005) 33–38.

Schwarz, Don. *Identity Crisis: Israel and the Church*. Enumclaw, WA: WinePress, 2004.

Scudder, L. R. *The Arabian Mission's Story: In Search of Abraham's Other Son*. Grand Rapids: Eerdmans, 1998.

Sebastian, Mrinalini. "Mission Without History? Some Ideas for Decolonizing Mission." *International Review of Missions* 93.368 (2004) 75–96.

Sela, Avraham. "The 'Wailing Wall' Riots (1929) as a Watershed in the Palestinian Conflict. *The Muslim World* 84.1–2 (1994) 60–94.

Shamir, Israel. "Russians in the Holy Land." *Race Traitor* 16 (2005) 117–25.

Sharkey, Heather J. "Arabic Antimissionary Treatises: Muslim Responses to Christian Evangelism in the Modern Middle East." *International Bulletin of Missionary Research* 28.3 (2004) 98–104.

———. "Empire and Muslim Conversion: Historical Reflections on Christian Missions in Egypt." *Islam and Christian-Muslim Relations* 16.1 (2005) 43–60.

Shaull, Richard, and Waldo Cesar. *Pentecostalism and the Future of the Christian Churches*. Grand Rapids: Eerdmans, 2000.

Shavit, Yaakov. "Fire and Water: Ze'ev Jabotinsky and the Revisionist Movement." *Studies in Zionism* 4 (1981) 215–36.

Shenk, Wilbert. "The 'Great Century' Reconsidered." *Missiology* 12.2 (1984) 138–42.

Shepherd, Naomi. *The Zealous Intruders: The Western Rediscovery of Palestine*. San Francisco: Harper & Row, 1987.

Sheppard, Gerald T. "Pentecostals and the Hermeneutics of Dispensationalism: The Anatomy of an Uneasy Relationship." *Pneuma* 6.2 (1984) 5–33.

Shohat, Ella. "The 'Postcolonial' in Translation: Reading Said in Hebrew." *Journal of Palestine Studies* 33.3 (2004) 55–75.

Shumsky, Dimitry. "Post-Zionist Orientalism? Orientalist Discourse and Islamaphobia among the Russian-speaking Intelligensia in Israel." *Social Identities* 10.1 (2004) 83–100.

Sizer, Stephen. *Christian Zionism: Road-Map to Armageddon?* Leicester, UK: InterVarsity, 2004.

———. "The Political Agenda of Christian Zionism." *Al-Aqsa* 6.2 (2004) 15–22.

Smith, Calvin L. *Pentecostal Power: Expressions, Impact, and Faith of Latin American Pentecostalism*. Leiden: Brill, 2011.

Smith, Jane I. "Christian and Missionary Views of Islam in the Nineteenth and Twentieth Centuries." *Islam and Christian-Muslim Relations* 9.3 (1998) 357–73.

Solivan, Samuel. *The Spirit, Pathos and Liberation: Toward an Hispanic Pentecostal Theology*. Sheffield, UK: Sheffield Academic, 1998.

"Spirit and Power: A 10-Country Survey of Pentecostals." Washington, DC: The Pew Forum on Religion and Public Life, 2006. http://www.pewforum.org/Christian/Evangelical-Protestant-Churches/Spirit-and-Power.aspx.

Spittler, Russell P. "Implicit Values in Pentecostal Missions." *Missiology* 16.4 (1988) 409–24.

Sprinkler, Michael, editor. *Edward Said: A Critical Reader*. Oxford and Cambridge: Blackwell, 1992.

Stanley, Brian. *The Bible and the Flag: Protestant Missions and British Imperialism in the Nineteenth and Twentieth Centuries*. Leicester, UK: Apollos, 1990.

———. "Conversion to Christianity: The Colonization of the Mind?" *International Review of Mission* 92.366 (2003) 315–31.

Stein, Kenneth W. "A Historiographic Review of Literature on the Origins of the Arab-Israeli Conflict. *The American Historical Review* 96.5 (1991) 1450–65.

Stibbe, Mark W. G. "The Theology of Renewal and the Renewal of Theology." *Journal of Pentecostal Theology* 3 (1993) 71–90.

Strachan, Gordon. *The Pentecostal Theology of Edward Irving*. Peabody, MA: Hendrickson, 1973.

Swanson, Herb. "Said's Orientalism and the Study of Christian Missions." *International Bulletin of Missionary Research* 28.3 (2004) 107–12.

Synan, Vinson. *The Century of the Holy Spirit: 100 Years of Pentecostal and Charismatic Renewal, 1901–2001*. Nashville: Thomas Nelson, 2001.

———. *The Holiness-Pentecostal Tradition: Charismatic Movements in the Twentieth Century*. 2nd ed. Grand Rapids: Eerdmans, 1997.

Taji-Farouki, Suha, and Basheer M. Nafi. Editors, editors. *Islamic Thought in the Twentieth Century*. London: I. B. Tauris, 2004.

Tamcke, Martin, and Michael Marten, editors. *Christian Witness between Continuity and New Beginnings: Modern Historical Missions in the Middle East*. Berlin: Lit, 2006.

Tanenbaum, Marc H., Marvin R. Wilson, and A. James Rudin, editors. *Evangelicals and Jews in Conversation on Scripture, Theology, and History*. Grand Rapids: Baker, 1978.

Teitelbaum, Joshua. "The Muslim Brotherhood and the 'Struggle for Syria,' 1947–1958: Between Accommodation and Ideology." *Middle Eastern Studies* 40.3 (2004) 134–58.

Tibawi, Abdul-Latif. *Arab Education in Mandatory Palestine*. London: Luzac, 1956.

———. *British Interests in Palestine, 1800–1901*. Oxford: Oxford University Press, 1961.

———. "English-Speaking Orientalists: A Critique of Their Approach to Islam and Arab Nationalism." *The Moslem World* 53.1 (1963) 185–204.

———. "English-Speaking Orientalists: A Critique of Their Approach to Islam and Arab Nationalism. (Second Part) " *The Moslem World* 53.10 (1963) 298–313.

———. *Islamic Education—Its Traditions and Modernization into Arab National Systems*. London: Luzac, 1972.

———. *The Islamic Pious Foundations in Jerusalem: Origins, History and Usurpation by Israel*. London: Islamic Cultural Center, 1978.

———. *Jerusalem: Its Place in Islam and Arab History*. Beirut: Institute for Palestine Studies, 1969.

———. *A Modern History of Syria: Including Lebanon and Palestine*. London: Macmillan, 1969.

———. "On the Orientalists Again." *The Muslim World* 70.1 (1980) 56–61.

Tomson, Peter J., and Doris Lambers-Petry. *The Image of Judaeo-Christians in Ancient Jewish and Christian Literature*. Tübingen: Mohr Siebeck, 2003.

Townshend, Charles. "The Defense of Palestine: Insurrection and Public Security, 1936–1939." *The English Historical Review* 103.409 (1988) 917–49.

Thomas, David, editor. and trans. *Early Muslim Polemic against Christianity: Abu 'Isa al-Warraq's "Against the Incarnation."* Cambridge: Cambridge University Press, 2002.

Tracy, Olive. *The Nations and the Isles: A Study of Missionary Work of the Church of the Nazarene in the Nations—Israel, Jordan, Syria, Lebanon, Italy—and the Isles—the Cape Verde Islands*. Kansas City, MO: Nazarene, 1958.

Tuchman, Barbara W. *Bible and Sword: England and Palestine from the Bronze Age to Balfour*. New York: Ballantine, 1956.

Urofsky, Melvin I. *American Zionism: From Herzl to the Holocaust*. Lincoln, NE: University of Nebraska Press, 1975.

Vander Werff, L. L. *Christian Mission to Muslims: The Record. Anglican and Reformed Approaches in India and the Near East*. South Pasadena: William Carey Library, 1977.

Vital, David. "The History of the Zionists and the History of the Jews." *Studies in Zionism* 6.2 (1982) 159–70.

Vogel, Lester I. *To See a Promised Land: Americans and the Holy Land in the Nineteenth Century*. University Park, PA: Pennsylvania State University Press, 1993.

Volf, Miroslav. *Exclusion and Embrace: A Theological Exploration of Identity, Otherness, and Reconciliation*. Nashville: Abingdon, 1966.

———. "The Social Meaning of Reconciliation." *Interpretation* 54.2 (2000) 158–72.

Wacker, Grant. "Are the Golden Oldies Still Worth Playing? Reflections on History Writing Among Early Pentecostals," *Pneuma* 8 (1986) 81–100.

———. *Heaven Below: Early Pentecostals and American Culture*. Cambridge: Harvard University Press, 2001.

———. "The Holy Spirit and the Spirit of the Age in American Protestantism, 1880–1910." *Church History* 72.1 (1985) 45–62.

———. "Playing for Keeps: The Primitivist Impulse in Early Pentecostalism." In *The American Quest for the Primitive Church*, 196–219. Urbana, IL: University of Illinois Press, 1985.

Wagner, Clarence H., Jr. *Lessons from the Land of the Bible*. Jerusalem: Bridges for Peace, 1998.

Wagner, Donald E. *Anxious for Armageddon: A Call to Partnership for Middle Eastern and Western Christians*. Scottdale, PA: Herald, 1995.

Walia, Shelley. *Edward Said and the Writing of History*. Cambridge: Icon Books, 2001.

Walls, Andrew F. *The Cross-Cultural Process in Christian History: Studies in the Transmission and Appropriation of Faith*. Maryknoll, NY: Orbis, 2002.

Wasserman, Jeffrey S. *Messianic Jewish Congregations: Who Sold This Business to the Gentiles?* Lanham, MD: University Press of America, 2000.

Watson, Francis. *Text, Church and World: Biblical Interpretation in Theological Perspective*. Edinburgh: T. & T. Clark, 1994.

Weber, Timothy P. *Living in the Shadow of the Second Coming: American Premillennialism, 1875–1925*. Oxford: Oxford University Press, 1979.

———. *On the Road to Armageddon: How Evangelicals Became Israel's Best Friend*. Grand Rapids: Baker Academic, 2004.

Weiss, Yisroel D. "Judaism and Zionism: Two Conflicting World Views." *Al-Aqsa* 6.2 (2004) 9–10.

Werblowsky, R. H. Zwi. "The Meaning of Jerusalem to Jews, Christians, and Muslims." In *Jerusalem in the Mind of the Western World, 1800–1949*, edited by M. Davis, 7–21. Westport, CT: Praeger, 1997.

Wetherell, David. "The Use and Misuse of Religious Language: Zionism and the Palestinians." *Holy Land Studies* 4.1 (2005) 73–86.

White, Hayden V. *Metahistory: The Historical Imagination in Nineteenth-Century Europe*. Baltimore: Johns Hopkins Press, 1973.

Wilkinson, Paul Richard. *For Zion's Sake: Christian Zionism and the Role of John Nelson Darby*. Milton Keynes, UK: Paternoster, 2007.

Wilson, Marvin R. *Our Father Abraham: Jewish Roots of the Christian Faith*. Grand Rapids: Eerdmans, 1989.

Wilson, Dwight. *Armageddon Now!: The Premillenarian Response to Russia and Israel Since 1917*. Grand Rapids: Baker, 1977.

Windschuttle, Windschuttle. "Edward Said's 'Orientalism Revisited.'" *The New Criterion* 17.5 (1999). Online: http://www.newcriterion.com/archive/17/jan99/ said.htm#back1.

Wood, James E. *Jewish-Christian Relations in Today's World*. Waco, TX: Baylor University Press, 1971.

Woods, Daniel. "Failure and Success in the Ministry of T.J. McIntosh, First Pentecostal Missionary to China." *Cyberjournal for Pentecostal-Charismatic Research* 12 (2003). http://www.pctii.org/cyberj/ cyberj12/woods.html.

Wright, Fred. *Father, Forgive Us: A Christian Response to the Church's Heritage of Jewish Persecution*. London: Monarch, 2002.

Young, Robert J. C. *Postcolonialism: An Historical Introduction*. Malden, MA: Blackwell, 2001.

———. *White Mythologies: Writing History and the West*. London: Routledge, 1990.

Yusuf 'Ali, 'Abdullah. *The Meaning of The Holy Qur'an*. Beltsville, MD: Amana, 2001.

Zebiri, Kate. *Christians and Muslims Face to Face*. Oxford: Oneworld, 1997.

Zweig, Ronald W. "British Plans for the Evacuation of Palestine in 1941–1942." *Studies in Zionism* 8.2 (1983) 292–303.

Zwemer, Samuel M. "The Allah of Islam and the God of Jesus Christ." *Theology Today* 3.1 (1946) 64–77.

Name and Subject Index